1996

TRANSFORMATIONS
OF CONSCIOUSNESS

TRANSFORMATIONS OF CONSCIOUSNESS

Conventional and Contemplative Perspectives on Development

Ken Wilber, Jack Engler, and Daniel P. Brown

WITH CHAPTERS BY

John Chirban, Mark Epstein, and Jonathan Lieff

FOREWORD BY

Mardi J. Horowitz, M.D.

Shambhala

Boston & London

1986

Shambhala Publications, Inc.
Horticultural Hall
300 Massachusetts Avenue
Boston, Massachusetts 02115

Shambhala Publications, Inc.
Random Century House
20 Vauxhall Bridge Road
London SW1V 2SA

9 8 7 6 5

Printed in the United States of America
Distributed in the United States by Random House,
Inc., in Canada by Random House of Canada Ltd., and
in the United Kingdom by the Random Century
Group.

LIBRARY OF CONGRESS CATALOGING IN PUBLICATION DATA

Wilber, Ken
    Transformations of Consciousness.
    Bibliography: p.
    Includes index.
    1. Developmental Psychology. 2. Consciousness.
I. Engler, Jack.   II. Brown, Daniel P., 1948–
III. Title.
BF713.W55   1985   153   85-2486
ISBN 0-87773-309-0 (pbk.)
        0-87773-371-6
        0-394-74202-8 (Random House: pbk)
        0-394-55537-6 (Random House)

CONTENTS

FOREWORD

Eastern philosophies have long focused on the uses of disciplined experiences as exercises of consciousness for self-development. Beginning as an unusual branch of medical psychiatry rather than academic psychology, psychoanalysis for the mere past century has also concerned itself with exercises of consciousness to enhance self-development from pathological states. From time to time, a study across boundaries between psychoanalysis and the meditative-contemplative philosophies of life paths has been attempted. Now is the time for a more extended dialogue across domains.

The Eastern philosophies, exported to the West, have been divested of many religious trappings that led to conservative traditionalism. Psychoanalysis has expanded to cover many streams of psychodynamic observation and theory formation. Moreoever, developmental psychology and developmental theories of psychopathology have been advanced. The stages and phases of the human life cycle are now under re-examination for real, evolutionary possibilities. The massive use and abuse of hallucinogens and other mind-altering drugs and the widespread availability of not only psychotherapy but quickie therapies functioned, for all their harms, as a social liberation. Serious scholarship may now flow into the channels opened.

The various possible pathways for individual development are the central themes in this domain. No one can do everything in a transient life, and the options require as much clarification as possible. In selecting a psychotherapy form for a patient, the clinician has to weigh the current condition and related problem, the stage of character development of the client, and the values and goals of the patient as well, and these three in relation to the chances and potentials for change along different pathways. Similarly, the individual or mentor guiding a subject toward personal growth has to weigh the current stage, the existing self-organization, and the values of that person in relation to skill-enhancing procedures.

I do not mean to downplay the seriousness of this effort by use of the word "skill." There are mental skills that profoundly affect the individual and thus profoundly affect human society. There are mental skills that allow the growth of self-organization so that different earlier views are contained in a more complex, higher-order, unifying symbol structure. These meaning structures of self-organization then permit new ways of understanding the world. Perceptions are more subtly and coherently organized, and existing memories, agendas, and motives are also reconstructed by these templates or schemata.

Schemata are inner working models that contain information abstracted out of and generalized from earlier experiences. Mental development means elaborating existing schemata into new forms as well as nesting schemata into useful hierarchies. Memories are reworked in this process, and different plans for self-expression and gratification, or avoidance of threat, are formed. Time, whether in psychotherapy or meditation, is required for such personal reformulations. Procedures that are enabling for one type of person may, however, be impeding for another type of person. That is why a serious, scholarly period of dialogue—involving many books and other works—is needed at this time.

The mind seldom rests. Modern life presents information at an extraordinary rate. Many capsules of unfinished business would be ready to burst open for rethinking if a moment's respite were to occur. Repressive brooding, anxious worry, embarrassed rehearsals of anticipated performances are common. Yet the topic, mode, and manner of ongoing conscious thought can be affected by will and intention. Suggestions can be made to "free-associate," "focus on breathing," "report dreams," "switch to visual images," "tune up background mood," or "listen to far-off sounds," as well as to select or let go of certain topics. One can learn from such exercises and can in a given mental state accomplish some aspects of self-reschematization that cannot be accomplished in other states of mind.

At some point in mental development, meditation becomes possible—exactly when has not been determined. Meditation frees the alert mind from external demands and also from the internal themes of unfinished business that pressure for planning and problem-solving. Like dreams, this special form of contemplative consciousness may allow a reworking of mental schemata and enduring attitudes in a unique way. Such changes in schemata may allow new conscious experiences, which then feed back to other changes. Persons may be at various stages in this process, and a variety of techniques may work or not work, help or harm at any phase. This book examines this issue.

As the reader approaches this book on the meditative disciplines and various dynamic psychology theories, he or she should be aware of some key issues. The theory assembled by crossing these domains is new, in flux, and not generally validated. The scientific efforts, as in the Rorschach studies of advanced meditators, are in fledgling, pilot stages. This is a "first book," not a final theory presentation, the beginning of this era's voyage insofar as it incorporates the "transpersonal" view of the disciplined use of contemplation.

Contemplative development is, in a way, a generation of new self structures. There are at least two cartographies of stages of contemplative development in this book in these chapters by Brown and Wilber. These theorists have much in common, yet there is an interesting difference. Both authors concern themselves with issues of 1) how the mind processes information, and 2) how the mind schematizes the position of self with regard to this information. Brown emphasizes the former, in stages of the regulation of how information is transformed and organized. Wilber emphasizes the latter, using what in psychoanalysis is now called the object-relations approach to representations of self and others. The Brown cartography emphasizes how information flows and is affected by self views; the Wilber cartography emphasizes the degree of separation of self from nonself, the degree of self boundary and being beyond self boundary in inner view.

These efforts of classification theory relate to important issues of what disciplines or techniques of either meditation or psychotherapy are "good" for what kind of person. That is, they are theories used to address the question of which segment of a population is ready for what level of practice. While those issues of useful practices are not solved by this book, the issue is clearly joined. This issue is part of a modern dialogue on the role of individuality and the social nature of self-development.

There does seem to be concordance about views about the early stages of self-development. The undeveloped self forms both in relationship to others and out of deep structural givens about self. Not only is a sense of "I-ness" developed, but a sense of "we-ness" or relatedness is developed as well. Either track can have pathological variants. These relationships are at first ones of dependency. Relationship schemata then develop in which the self is connected but more autonomous from the presses of others or the conventions of the immediate social group.

Then what happens? Must the well-developed person go off into more solitary practices in order to develop further? If so, how and when would he or she return to social connection? Here we return to the question of values. Shedding the view of life as painful and the release from the cycle of reincarnation as a desirable goal, a modern Western approach to self-development is one of life-enhancement for one and all. The physical exploration of the globe must now be supplemented by an evolution of mind. Mindedness is not necessarily contained in a specific individual, since ideas and ways of experiencing are "transpersonal." The goal of self-development is not necessarily escape from mortality or a fantasy of immortality.

The developed person can be a more effective leader, creative contributor, empathetic caretaker. Neither the tragic views nor the narcissistic views of the individual need pertain to the quest initiated in this book.

Mardi Horowitz, M.D.
Professor of Psychiatry
University of California, San Francisco

PREFACE

This book consists of various, closely related attempts to articulate a "full-spectrum" model of human growth and development, a model that includes the stages of development typically investigated by conventional psychology and psychiatry, as well as the stages of development apparently evidenced in the world's great meditative and contemplative traditions. All of the authors of this volume share the belief that a more comprehensive and integrated view of human development can be achieved if both of these major traditions, conventional and contemplative, can be brought together in a mutually enriching fashion.

This book owes its existence to two individuals in particular: Miles Vich and Seymour Boorstein. Miles Vich is the editor of the *Journal of Transpersonal Psychology*. All but two of the following chapters first appeared in *JTP*, and were thus brought to fruition under his guidance and expert editorship. He also agreed to edit the two chapters that did not originally appear in *JTP*. Thus, not only did Miles help edit every chapter in this book, he was of invaluable assistance in assembling the book as a whole. The authors wish to express their gratitude for his generous help and support.

For those readers who are not yet aware of the *Journal of Transpersonal Psychology*, the authors would like to point out that this journal is generally regarded as the preeminent publication in the field of psychology which attempts to bridge conventional and contemplative disciplines. It has a wide following among psychologists, psychiatrists, philosophers, theologians, and laypersons interested in the fascinating interface between psychology and spirituality, and between clinical and contemplative perspectives. Psychodynamic, behavioral, and humanistic approaches are all well-represented within its pages, along with the contemplative and meditative approaches of the world's great spiritual traditions. The authors personally believe that this journal is unique, and deserves the widest possible readership. We have presented the following chapters in exactly the same format as they originally appeared in *JTP*, in part to give the reader a sense of the *Journal* itself. Readers who would like more information about *JTP*, or would like to correspond with any of the authors about points raised in this volume, are invited to write to the *Journal of Transpersonal Psychology*, 345 California Avenue, Suite No. 1, Palo Alto, CA 94306.

If Miles helped bring this book to completion, the idea for the book itself began in a conversation with Dr. Seymour Boorstein. Seymour is one of a growing number of psychiatrists who are using both psychodynamic and meditative approaches in a therapeutic setting without blurring the differences between them. He had collected several dozen case histories on this approach to treatment that were so interesting and provocative that they were to form a central part of this book. Ironically, and very regrettably, as the book itself began to take shape, it became apparent that it was to be a book on clinical theory rather than clinical practice, and that case histories and their discussion should await a separate volume. Were it not for Seymour, however, this book would never have been conceived. Like Miles, he has been one of the patrons and mentors who have spurred and supported the development of this field in a quiet but major way, personally as well as professionally. The authors would therefore like to dedicate this volume to Miles Vich and Seymour Boorstein.

Ken Wilber
Jack Engler
Daniel P. Brown

ABOUT THE AUTHORS

DANIEL P. BROWN, Ph.D., is director of psychology training and clinical services and director of behavioral medicine at Cambridge Hospital/Harvard Medical School. His areas of interest include psychotherapy and supervision of psychotherapy with psychotics, ethnopsychiatry, and translation of meditation texts from Tibetan and Sanskrit.

JOHN T. CHIRBAN, Ph.D., is a clinical psychologist and theologian; Chairman of the Department of Human Development and Director of the Office of Counseling and Guidance at Hellenic College and Holy Cross School of Theology; and Associate in Human Development at Harvard University. Dr. Chirban also maintains a private practice in psychotherapy in Cambridge, Mass.

JACK ENGLER, Ph.D., is Clinical Director of the Schiff Psychiatric Day Treatment Center of Cambridge Hospital and a supervising psychologist on the faculty of Harvard Medical School. He did his graduate work at the universities of Munich, Oxford, and Chicago, and his clinical training at The Menninger Foundation, McLean Hospital, and the Yale Psychiatric Institute. He studied Theravadin Buddhist psychology and vipassana meditation for several years in India, where he was a Fulbright Fellow at the Post-Graduate Institute of Buddhist Studies in Nalanda. He also studied meditation with the head of this lineage in Burma, the Venerable Mahasi Sayadaw. He is on the Board of Directors of the Insight Meditation Center in Barre, Mass., the principal center for the practice of vipassana in the West. Dr. Engler is also a Field Editor for the *Journal of Transpersonal Psychology*. He has taught at several universities and has given numerous papers, workshops, and courses around the country on Eastern and Western psychotherapies and models of psychological development. His first introduction to the contemplative traditions was as a student of Thomas Merton at the Trappist Monastery of Gethsemane. He now lives in Newton with his wife and is looking forward to starting a family.

MARK D. EPSTEIN, M.D., a graduate of Harvard College and Harvard Medical School, is a psychiatrist with a practice in psychotherapy in New York City, and is currently on the psychiatric staff of New York Hospital–Cornell Medical Center, Westchester Division, and an Instructor in Clinical Psychiatry at Cornell University Medical College. Interested in the relationships between Eastern and Western systems of psychology, he has investigated such topics as traditional Buddhist psychology, the physiological effects of advanced Tibetan meditation techniques, and the points of convergence of psychoanalytic theory with Buddhist philosophy of mind.

JONATHAN D. LIEFF, M.D., a graduate of Yale College and Harvard Medical School, is currently an Associate Professor of Psychiatry at Boston University Medical School; faculty member at Tufts University Medical School; Chairman of the Task Force on High Technology of the Massachusetts Psychiatric Society. He has served as the Director of Psychiatry and Chief of Geriatrics at the Lemuel Shattuck Hospital; member of the Task Force of Elderly Services of the American Psychiatric Association; and is also Geriatric Psychiatrist at Hahnemann Hospital (and recently testified before a joint session of the Special Committee on Aging, United States Senate and Select Committee on Aging, U.S. House of Representatives). Dr. Lieff is the author of numerous articles and books on psychiatry, geriatrics, computers and high technology (including *Your Parents' Keeper: A Handbook of Psychiatric Care for the Elderly; Computers and*

Other Technological Aids in Psychiatric Private Practice; and *Computer Applications in Psychiatry).*

KEN WILBER, generally regarded as the founder of spectrum psychology, is the author or editor of ten books and some hundred articles on psychology, psychiatry, sociology, philosophy, and religion. His books include *The Spectrum of Consciousness, The Atman Project, Up from Eden, Eye to Eye, No Boundary, The Holographic Paradigm and Other Paradoxes,* and *A Sociable God.*

TRANSFORMATIONS OF CONSCIOUSNESS

INTRODUCTION

Ken Wilber, Jack Engler, and Daniel P. Brown

The central theme of this volume is that the time is now ripe for what Engler and Wilber have called a "full-spectrum model" of human growth and development, a model that includes the psychodynamic, object-relational, and cognitive lines studied by conventional psychology and psychiatry, but also takes into serious account the "higher" or "subtler" lines and stages embodied in the world's great contemplative and meditative disciplines.

a "full-spectrum model" of human development

Taken together, these various approaches—conventional and contemplative—seem to point to a general, universal, and cross-cultural spectrum of human development, consisting of various developmental lines and stages that, however otherwise different their specific cultural or surface structures might appear, nevertheless share certain recognizable similarities or deep structures. Further, the different stages of this developmental spectrum are apparently vulnerable to qualitatively distinct psychopathologies, which in turn yield to qualitatively different treatment modalities (or therapies in general).

Those three topics—the various stages of development (conventional and contemplative), the corresponding levels of possible pathology or dis-ease, and the correlative or appropriate therapeutic interventions—are the central concerns of this volume. Jack Engler is speaking for all of the authors when he states: "My hope is that as Buddhist, Western, and other ethnopsychiatric systems of clinical practice confront one another in our culture, often for the

the three central concerns of this volume

first time, a more integrated, full-spectrum model of human development, its vulnerabilities and the therapeutic interventions necessary to repair them, may result."

CONVENTIONAL AND CONTEMPLATIVE SCHOOLS OF DEVELOPMENT

the "stage model" of Western psychology

The *stage model* is one of the most widely used tools in Western psychology. Although different theorists define it in slightly different ways, most would agree with the following summary by Thomas McCarthy (1978):

> [The stage model specifies] an invariant sequence of discrete and increasingly complex developmental stages, whereby no stage can be passed over and each higher stage implies or presupposes the previous stages. This does not exclude regressions, overlaps, arrested developments, and the like. Stages are constructed wholes that differ qualitatively from one another; phase-specific schematic can be ordered in an invariant and hierarchically structured sequence; no later phase can be [stably] attained before earlier ones have been passed through, and elements of earlier phases are preserved, transformed, and reintegrated in the later. In short, the developmental-logical approach requires the specification of a hierarchy of structural wholes in which the later, more complex, and more encompassing developmental stages presuppose and build upon the earlier.

This type of developmental-stage approach has been fruitfully applied to psychosexual, cognitive, ego, moral, affective, object-relational, and linguistic lines of development—in short, virtually the entire gamut of development studied by conventional psychology and psychiatry (all of which, for convenience, we will call "typical" or "conventional" development).

"quasi-universal" claims of conventional stage models of human development

Further, most of these conventional stage-models have claimed to be largely invariant, cross-cultural, and "quasi-universal" (Habermas, 1976). Thus, for example, in psychosexual development, no culture has been found where phallic development precedes oral; in cognitive development, images universally precede symbols, which precede concepts, which precede rules; and in moral development, preconventional orientations always appear to precede conventional and then postconventional modes. However much the fine points of these various models might be argued (the specific issues are far from settled), it is generally acknowledged that most of the stage-models presented by conventional psychology and psychiatry claim to be invariant and cross-cultural (in a general fashion); and, within broad limits, most of them have adduced enough evidence to make their claims plausible. As we will see below, to claim that a particular *sequence* of stages is genuinely invariant *is* to claim that it is cross-cultural: despite the vast differences in the surface structures of the stages, the deep structures are essentially similar— this is the claim of most conventional developmental-stage models.

What is not often realized, however, is that the same type of developmental-stage approach is exemplified in the world's great contemplative and meditative disciplines. As Brown and Engler carefully point out, "The major [contemplative] traditions we have studied in their original languages present an unfolding of meditation experiences in terms of a *stage model:* for example, the *Mahamudra* from the Tibetan Mahayana Buddhist tradition; the *Visuddhimagga* from the Pali Theravada Buddhist tradition; and the *Yoga Sutras* from the Sanskrit Hindu tradition. *The models are sufficiently similar to suggest an underlying common invariant sequence of stages, despite vast cultural and linguistic differences as well as styles of practice."*

the developmental-stage approach in contemplative and meditative disciplines

We seem to be faced, then, with two broad ranges or classes of development, which we have loosely called "conventional" and "contemplative"; both contain various strands or lines that are, in part, amenable to a stage conception; and both claim a general, universal, and cross-cultural validity. The question then remains, how are these two classes related, if at all? Are they different descriptions of similar developmental sequences? Do they describe parallel lines of development? Do they refer to different lines, or even levels, of development altogether? Are they related along a general continuum? If so, where does typical development stop and contemplative development begin? Indeed, can the contemplative stages be considered real in any objective-empirical sense, or are they merely idiosyn-

the relationship between "conventional" and "contemplative" stage models cratic and subjective belief-systems? In short, how are these classes related, if at all?

searching the texts of contemplative schools

One of the ways of approaching this difficult topic is to search among the texts of the contemplative schools for any that, in addition to describing the strictly contemplative stages of development, also attempt to situate these stages vis-à-vis normal or typical (or non-contemplative) development. This would give us a broad scale of reference that might indicate how the two ranges—conventional and contemplative—might be related.

Take, for example, the works of Aurobindo, perhaps India's greatest modern philosopher-sage. Aurobindo has described the overall life cycle as including the following major stages (brief explanations appear in parentheses):

developmental stages in Aurobindo's life cycle

1. Sensorimotor (physical, sensory, and locomotive aspects)
2. Vital-emotional-sexual ("prana"; roughly, libido or bioenergy)
3. Will-mind (simple representational and intentional thought)
4. Sense-mind (thought operations performed on sensory or concrete objects)
5. Reasoning mind (thought operations performed on abstract objects)
6. Higher mind (synthetic-integrative thought operations, "seeing truth as a whole")
7. Illumined mind (transcends thought and "sees truth at a glance"; psychic or inner illumination and vision)
8. Intuitive mind (transcendental-archetypal awareness; "subtle cognition and perception")
9. Overmind (unobstructed, unbounded spiritual awareness)
10. Supermind (absolute identity with and as spirit; this is not really a separate level, but the "ground" of all levels)

Notice that Aurobindo's first six stages clearly seem similar to some of the stages investigated by conventional psychology and psychiatry. In particular, if one examines Aurobindo's meticulous descriptions of these first six stages, one finds that they bear striking and detailed resemblances to aspects of the works of Piaget, Loevinger, and Kohlberg (see Chapter 3 for a brief summary of these comparisons). Almost all conventional stage-models, however, stop somewhere around Aurobindo's stage 6; none give accounts of developmental stages beyond that point (though few deny their possible existence).

On the other hand, the stages described in contemplative texts are demonstrably similar to Aurobindo's higher stages, 7 through 10. Moreover, Aurobindo's version of overall development gives a smooth account of the transitions between all the stages; there is no feeling of an abrupt rupture between the typical or normal stages (1–6) and the contemplative or transpersonal stages (7–10). Rather, one gets the impression that development, if not fixated or arrested, can proceed rather naturally into the higher or contemplative stages, each of which is marked by a refinement and enhancement of cognitive, volitional, and perceptual capacities. The point is that because Aurobindo has attempted to describe both the "lower-intermediate" stages of development (typically investigated in greater detail by conventional psychology) and the "higher" stages (of meditative development), such a scheme may be used to help tentatively situate the various developmental stages described by conventional and contemplative schools.

Aurobindo and contemplative stage models

Although this is by no means the only way to "fit together" the conventional and contemplative schools, it does seem to be one of the simplest and most appealing. As Engler and Wilber have both pointed out, the contemplative stages of development are probably not parallel (or alternative) to the normal, typical, or conventional stages of development, but rather refer to different and higher stages of development altogether (although this by no means precludes very complex interactions between the two; a rigidly linear and unidirectional model is not at all what we have in mind). This interpretation, at any rate, is corroborated by such "overview models" as Aurobindo's.

Other such general overview models can be found in Kabalah, Da Free John, Gurdjieff, Sufism, certain Christian contemplative schools, and aspects of Vajrayana and Vedanta. It should be emphasized, however, that these models give us little more than rather crude skeletal outlines. In particular, when these models describe the lower stages of development, they are almost totally lacking in a knowledge of object-relations, self-development, and psychodynamics, which so decisively define these stages and have been so intensively studied by conventional psychology and psychiatry.

lessons to be
learned by both
major schools

One of the aims of this volume is to begin to flesh out this skeleton by bringing together, for the first time, both of these major schools of development—conventional and contemplative. For if it is true that the conventional schools have much to learn from the contemplative schools (especially about possibly higher development), it is equally true—and, we believe, as urgent—that the contemplative schools surrender their isolation and apparent self-sufficiency and open themselves to the vital and important lessons of contemporary psychology and psychiatry.

THE NATURE AND MEANING OF "STAGES,"
HIGHER AND LOWER

It might be appropriate, at this point, to briefly discuss the meaning of the word "stage," as used by both conventional and contemplative schools. One of the most obvious features of the various stage-models in both traditions is that, even when they purport to describe the same developmental line, they often report different numbers of stages in that line. For example, the level of general development that Aurobindo simply calls "the intuitive mind" actually contains, according to some traditions, anywhere from three to seven discrete levels. Are these levels actually discrete? That is, do they actually exist as quasi-universal deep structures, or are they merely tradition-bound, idiosyncratic, or culturally-generated surface structures? Just how many levels of contemplative development are there?

Brown and Engler have begun to answer this question by

generating a "master template" culled from various con- *a "master*
templative traditions (Theravada, Mahayana, Hindu, *template"*
Christian, and Chinese). In Chapter 8, Brown summarizes
this template, which contains six major stages, each divided into three substages, for a total of eighteen. As of
this writing, it appears that most of these are in fact quasi-
universal deep structures, not merely idiosyncratic surface
structures. But at this point we do not have enough information to decide in *all* cases, and thus the decisions on
these types of issues (how to divide or subdivide stages)
are somewhat arbitrary, although that does not render
them the less useful: the stage-model claim is simply that,
in any developmental sequence, certain classes of behavior
stably emerge only after certain other classes; and if some
of those classes are eventually found to contain other discrete classes, then we have simply enriched our understanding of the sequence, not denied it.

Thus, for example, Jane Loevinger initially postulated four
stages of ego development. Refined research subsequently
led her to conclude that there are at least ten stages. Likewise, if someone discovered a basic cognitive stage between symbols and concepts, it still would not alter the
fact that symbols emerge before concepts, and concepts
emerge only after symbols—and it is that relative "before"
and "after" that constitutes one of the central claims of *a central*
developmental theories (i.e., if the before and after rela- *claim of*
tion of class r and class z can be demonstrated to be cross- *developmental*
culturally invariant, then we are justified in suspecting *theories*
that, at some level of analysis, there are quasi-universal
deep structures involved, regardless of how many classes
may or may not subsequently be found in between them).
Conversely, subsequent research might indicate that what
we had previously thought to be two discrete stages are
actually variations on one stage, with a broader deep structure, that alone stands up to cross-cultural scrutiny. But it
is exactly these kinds of concerns that introduce a modi-
cum of arbitrariness into any stage-model. The models
presented in this volume are no exception.

Traditionally, developmentalists have used several criteria
for establishing that a particular behavioral array has, at
its base, a quasi-universal deep structure. The most com-

mon is that "Stages may be viewed as existing in some objective sense to the extent that the behaviors associated with them emerge in an order that cannot be altered by environmental factors" (Brainerd, 1978). That various classes of phenomena emerge in an order that cannot be altered by environmental factors *is* to say that those classes possess an invariant (quasi-universal) structure, or else their sequence *could* be altered by contingent factors; that is, invariant sequence means quasi-universal class structures are involved at some level, or the sequence would not and could not be invariant. Wobble in the structure would mean wobble in the sequence (which is precisely a definition of surface structure).

quasi-universal deep structure

On the other hand, virtually all developmentalists acknowledge that "decisions about how to slice up the stream of behavioral change are based on external criteria such as economy and elegance. Hence, there might be *several different models that could be posited, all of which would be equally valid descriptions of change in the organism*" (Brainerd, 1978). (Again, the models in this volume are no exception.) However, this does not negate the possible quasi-universal nature of the different stage-models; it simply says that, if you slice the stream from this particular angle, you will always see the same basic phenomena, in the same order, wherever the stream appears. Likewise, researchers usually agree that there are no precise demarcation lines between stages. The situation appears more like a rainbow, with each color shading into the others, which nevertheless does not prevent us from recognizing that orange is different from blue.

different models and valid descriptions of change

Finally, most developmentalists acknowledge that the task of stage definition is a process whereby "We select certain instants in the course of dynamic change, take 'snapshots' of the system at those instants, and use those snapshots as descriptions of the system at a particular stage of development" (Simon, 1962). Different series of snapshots are obviously possible, and each series usually yields significant information; but if the shots effectively "catch" a deep structure, the order between the phenomena in those shots will be invariant, and vice versa: we have a "stage."

process of defining a "stage"

THE PLAN OF THIS BOOK

All of the authors of the following chapters present various stage conceptions, some of contemplative development (Brown; Brown and Engler; Chirban), some of conventional as well as contemplative development (Engler; Epstein and Lieff; Wilber). It would be useful, then, if we could introduce some very general terminology that would help situate the various authors in relation to each other. Since we have already introduced Aurobindo's simple "overview" model, we can use that, and attach our general terminology to it, as shown in Table 1. Here we have introduced three broad ranges of overall development (prepersonal, personal, and transpersonal), each divided, for convenience, into three stages. With this rough map, we can now explain the outline and basic themes of this volume. While individual authors may differ on specific points (most of which will become obvious upon reading their particular chapters), all share a general consensus.

prepersonal, personal, and transpersonal ranges of development

One of the central themes of this book is that different stages of development are vulnerable to qualitatively distinct psychopathologies. Even using Aurobindo's crude

AUROBINDO'S OVERVIEW	GENERAL TERMINOLOGY		
1. Sensorimotor			prepersonal stages
2. Vital-emotional			
3. Will-mind	typical or conventional development		
4. Sense-mind		personal stages	
5. Reasoning-mind			
6. Higher-mind			
7. Illumined-mind	contemplative development	transpersonal stages	
8. Intuitive-mind			
9. Overmind			

TABLE 1

COMPARISON OF GENERAL TERMINOLOGY OF DEVELOPMENTAL STAGES

developmental stages and their pathologies

map ("crude" because it does not take into account the different lines of development among the various stages), we might expect to find, correlative with nine general stages of development, nine general levels of possible pathology (Aurobindo himself suggested such). In Chapter 1, Jack Engler opens this discussion by keying on the three general levels of prepersonal object-relations development and their corresponding levels of psychopathology: psychotic, borderline, and psychoneurotic. These levels are all loosely referred to as "prepersonal" because this range of

prepersonal stages and their levels of pathology

development involves the stages leading up to the emergence of a rational-individuated-personal selfhood. Summarizing the relevant data from conventional psychiatric research, Engler points out that because these are developmentally distinct levels of psychopathology, they typically respond to different types of therapeutic intervention (psychotic and borderline: structure-building techniques; psychoneurotic: uncovering techniques). Engler then carefully distinguishes these psychopathologies from another qualitatively and developmentally distinct class, those we have called contemplative or transpersonal, pointing out

developmental arrest

that what conventional approaches consider normalcy (a fully differentiated-integrated ego structure) is actually, from this broader view, a case of developmental arrest (if development proceeds no further).

developmental prerequisites for transpersonal stages

Engler's central message is significant and timely: meditative disciplines effect a transcendence of the normal separate-self sense, but the developmental prerequisite for this is a strong, mature, well-differentiated psyche and a well-integrated self-structure with a sense of cohesiveness, continuity, and identity. Engler points out some of the severe psychiatric complications that can occur when individuals with significant prepersonal developmental arrests engage in transpersonal or contemplative practices. In fact, Engler notes, such individuals may actually be drawn to contemplative practices as a way to rationalize their inner sense of emptiness, poorly differentiated self and object representations, and lack of self-cohesion.

In Chapter 2, Mark Epstein and Jonathan Lieff continue this developmental line of analysis by examining the three broad stages of contemplative or transpersonal development and pointing out that each of these stages may evidence its own particular type of psychopathology. As they put it, "Meditation may be conceptualized as a developmental process that may produce side effects anywhere along the continuum. Some of these side effects may be pathological in nature while some may be temporary distractions or hindrances." The three broad classes or levels of pathology that they report involve vulnerabilities at 1) the stage of preliminary practices; 2) access stage; and 3) advanced stage (samadhi and insight). This cartography is simple and concise, and offers an immediately useful, if general, classification.

three broad classes of pathology

Wilber's presentation occupies Chapters 3–5, and serves, in a sense, as a bridge between Engler's and Epstein/Lieff's. He discusses the three general levels of prepersonal pathology noted by Engler (psychotic, borderline, and psychoneurotic), the three general levels of transpersonal pathology noted by Epstein and Lieff (which Wilber calls psychic, subtle, and causal), and then suggests three general classes of pathology intermediate between them (which he calls cognitive-script, identity, and existential). This results in nine general levels (not lines) of overall development, with nine corresponding levels of potential psychopathology. Wilber then provides a preliminary discussion of the types of therapeutic interventions that seem most appropriate for each of these levels of pathology. He prefaces all of this with a chapter summarizing his own spectrum model and the relevant research in conventional psychology and psychiatry.

prepersonal, personal, transpersonal pathologies

In the remaining chapters, contemplative development moves to the foreground. In Chapters 6 and 7, Brown and Engler present a validation study on the stages of meditation using the Rorschach. The results have significant and far-reaching implications: "In each of the criterion groups," they report, "there are unique qualitative features in the Rorschachs which are distinctly different from those of the other groups. This finding in itself suggests that there are indeed different stages of meditation practice. Even more interesting is the fact that the specific qualitative features of the Rorschachs for each group are consistent with the classical descriptions of the psychological

contemplative development and the Rorschach

changes most characteristic of that stage of practice. Such convergence of the Rorschach qualitative features on the one hand, and the classical descriptions on the other, may be an important step toward establishing the cross-cultural validation of the psychological changes at each major stage of the practice." Further, Brown and Engler point out, "These Rorschachs illustrate that the classical subjective reports of meditation stages are more than religious belief systems; they are valid accounts of the cognitive-perceptual and affective changes that occur with intensive meditation. . . ."

a cartography of contemplative development

In Chapter 8, Brown zeroes in on the meditative stages themselves, and gives perhaps the most complete, detailed, and sophisticated cartography of contemplative development yet to appear. This cartography was culled from an intensive study of Theravada, Mahayana, and Yogic texts (and later checked against other contemplative traditions, Christian, Chinese, etc.). Although Brown's contemplative cartography is essentially similar to models such as Wilber's (e.g., in *System, Self, and Structure*, Wilber, like Brown, gives six major contemplative stages, each with three substages), Brown's model has manifold advantages: it is based on the canonical languages, direct study and translation of the central texts, and extensive interviews with teachers and practitioners. As such, this cartography easily establishes itself as a standard in the field.

contemplative stages and Christian saints

With the exception of Wilber's presentation, most of the chapters in this volume deal with Eastern—and usually Buddhist—contemplative disciplines. We have every reason to believe, however, that the major contemplative stages (and their corresponding vulnerabilities) are of cross-cultural and quasi-universal applicability. Indeed, Brown and Wilber have elsewhere written extensively on this topic (see, for example, Wilber, 1981b). In Chapter 9, therefore, Harvard clinical psychologist and theologian John Chirban turns his attention to the stages of contemplative development as evidenced and described by some of the outstanding saints of Christianity. His conclusion: "Although each saint described his own experience (often in his own unique way), basic parallels emerge as one compares the stages of the saints with one another. This

sameness confirms the catholicity of their experience. . . .
Five stages can be identified which are basically consistent
amongst all ten saints." These stages are quite similar to
those of Brown and Wilber, giving added credence to the
catholicity of contemplative development. We placed this
chapter last as an invitation to *all* meditative traditions—
as well as the different psychological and psychiatric disciplines—to join us in this mutually enriching dialogue
between conventional and contemplative schools, aimed
at the creation of a more integrated, full-spectrum model
of human growth and development.

CHAPTER 1

THERAPEUTIC AIMS IN PSYCHOTHERAPY AND MEDITATION: DEVELOPMENTAL STAGES IN THE REPRESENTATION OF SELF

Jack Engler

In the Introduction, we suggested three broad ranges of development—prepersonal, personal, and transpersonal—each divided, for convenience, into three stages. In this chapter, Jack Engler focuses on the three general stages of object-relations development in the prepersonal realm, and the corresponding types of psychopathology—psychotic, borderline, and psychoneurotic—that may result due to developmental arrests or failures at a particular stage. He then carefully distinguishes this entire range of development from the contemplative or transpersonal stages. He sees two great arcs of human development: one leading up to a personal, substantially individuated self-sense, and one leading beyond it. His conclusion is simple but profound: You have to be somebody before you can be nobody.

What follows is an attempt to think through a set of clinical issues that have emerged for me in recent years regarding the development of a sense of self. Questions about the nature and status of the psychological structure we call the "self" have forced themselves on me from two sides. On the one hand, my clinical work with schizophrenic and borderline patients, all of whom suffer from pathological disturbances in their subjective sense of selfhood, has convinced me of the vital importance of developing a sense of continuity, identity and ongoingness in existence. On the other hand, my experience teaching Buddhist psychology and *Vipassana* meditation has made it equally clear that clinging to a sense of personal continuity and self-identity results in chronic discontent and psychic conflict. Every instant of our lives this clinging puts us in opposition to a

the issue of "self"

universe in which nothing lasts for more than a brief moment, in fact where there are no "things" at all in any real sense, but only events on the order of milliseconds. As we now know from psychophysics, this is true of our internal universe of images, thoughts, feelings and sensations as well. As a clinician I do everything I can to help patients develop the sense of an inner cohesiveness, unity and continuity which is so tragically lacking, with such fateful consequences. As a meditation teacher, I work just as hard to help students see through the perceptual illusion of continuity and sameness in their experience—in Zen terms, to realize there is no-self. The issue I have been wrestling with then, as a psychologist practicing in both traditions, is the importance of this sense of self and its fate. I have been particularly concerned with the sense of self individuals bring to meditation, its vicissitudes during practice, and above all the sense of self individuals bring away from meditation.

problems in terminology

The difficulty in thinking about this issue is not made any easier by the fact that key terms like "ego" and "self" are used in psychodynamic and Buddhist psychology in very different contexts and with very different values attributed to the development of an ego and the formation of a stable self-structure. (A parallel discussion of these issues, with more emphasis on psychoanalytic aspects, appears in *Psychoanalysis and Contemporary Thought*, Engler, 1983a.) The two terms are also unfortunately losing their anchorage in clearly defined conceptual and semantic traditions. Once upon a time they had a precise meaning and significance. Now they are in danger of becoming jargon, catchwords in clinical reports as well as in spiritual writing. All this makes it more and more difficult to sort out the very issues concerning the psychological structure of the self which our clinical experience and our spiritual practice both tell us in different ways are the core issues in mental illness and health. "Transcending the ego," for instance, which is often proposed to students these days as a goal in meditation, has no meaning for a psychodynamically-oriented clinician. To the clinician, the ego is a collective term designating the regulatory and integrative functions. To "transcend the ego" in this frame of reference would mean to surrender the very faculties which make us human—

the psychological structures that make it possible to think, to plan, to remember, to anticipate, to organize, to self-reflect, to distinguish reality from fantasy, to exercise voluntary control over impulses and behavior, to love. It could only refer to a condition of being a robot or a marionette, which is precisely the way very regressed, field-dependent patients with impaired ego capacities experience themselves. From this point of view it takes a fairly mature level of ego organization just to practice meditation, especially forms of meditation based on observing the moment-to-moment mind-body process, and the fears, anxieties, humiliations, rages, depression, despair, self-doubt and even ecstasies which self-discovery entails. Clinically, meditation *strengthens* the ego rather than transcends it. On the other hand, while ego psychologists might think the meditative goal of non-attachment and disidentification from all self-representations a bit odd if not impossible, they do understand the principle that all psychological growth comes about by being able to renounce outworn, infantile ties to objects and to give up or modify self-representations that have become restrictive, maladaptive or outgrown.

In wrestling with these issues, I have found for myself that a *developmental model* seems to be the most appropriate way of interpreting the clinical and meditative data. It also allows us to integrate both perspectives and see them as complimentary instead of competitive. As a starting point for this approach I turned to the *developmental spectrum concept of psychopathology* that is coming to play such a central role in current clinical thinking and practice. The heart of this concept is the notion that the pathogenesis of mental disorder follows a developmental chronology. It derives from increasing evidence in psychodynamic-psychoanalytic research (Mahler, 1975; Masterson & Rinsley, 1980) as well as in genetic-biological studies (Gottesmann & Schields, 1972; Kety *et al.*, 1968) that qualitatively different levels of personality organization and ego functioning are rooted in failures, arrests or regressions in different stages of intrapsychic development, above all the crucial line of object relations. This holds true whether the distal etiology is inborn vulnerability (Stone, 1980), developmental traumata (Masterson & Rinsley, 1980) or some com-

usefulness of a developmental model

bination of both. Its corollary is that different levels of personality organization require qualitatively different approaches to treatment.

"insight" meditation

When I refer to meditation, I will be referring to Buddhist Vipassana or "insight" meditation, so-called because its aim is insight into the nature of psychic functioning rather than the induction of an altered state of consciousness. Though Vipassana derives from the Theravada tradition of Buddhism, morphologically it is a pure form of one of the two modal types of meditation, concentration and insight (Goleman, 1977). These are differentiated by technique and by state effects. Concentration meditation is practiced by *restricting attention* to a single interoceptive or exteroceptive object and holding it fixed on the object for long periods. Insight meditation *expands attention* to as many mental and physical events as possible exactly as they occur over time. Concentration practice leads to a process of *withdrawal* from sensory input in progressive states of one-pointedness *(samādhi)* or absorption *(jhāna)* characterized by increasingly refined tranquility and bliss. Insight practice leads to a process of *observation of sensory input in progressive states of "knowledge" (ñāṇa)* of the impermanent, unsatisfactory and non-substantial nature of all phenomena. From the Buddhist point of view, concentration meditation induces transient states of happiness and conflict-free functioning by temporarily suppressing the operation of the drives and the higher perceptual-intellectual functions;[1]* but it is the insight form of practice alone which liberates from suffering by bringing about enduring intrapsychic structural change (Nyanamoli, 1976).[2]

"insight" practice

In its contemporary form, Vipassana is described as training in mindfulness, choiceless awareness or bare attention. This is the practice of a "clear and single-minded awareness of what actually happens to us and in us at the successive moments of perception" (Nyanaponika, 1973:30). Bare attention is defined by two technical paradigms: a particular form of attention deployment and a particular way of managing affect. Cognitively, attention is restricted to registering the mere occurrence of any

thought, feeling or sensation exactly as it occurs and enters awareness from moment to moment, without further
elaboration. The meditator notes only the succession of
thoughts, feelings and sensations as these arise and pass
away. In contrast to conventional psychotherapeutic work,
no attention is paid to their individual content. Affectively,
all stimuli are attended to equally without selection or censorship. Again in contrast to conventional psychotherapy,
attention is kept "bare" of any reaction to what is perceived. The meditator attempts to attend to any and all   *"bare"*
stimuli without preference, comment, judgment, reflec-   *attention*
tion or interpretation. If physical or mental reactions like
these occur, they themselves are immediately noted and
made the objects of bare attention. Even lapses in attention—distractions, fantasies, reveries, internal dialogue—
are made objects of bare attention as soon as the meditator
becomes aware of them. The aim is threefold: to come to
know one's own mental processes; in this way to begin to
have the power to shape or control them; and finally to
gain freedom from the condition where one's psychic processes are unknown and uncontrolled (Nyanaponika,
1973).

THE ISSUE OF THE SELF IN
OBJECT RELATIONS THEORY AND BUDDHISM

It may come as a surprise that though they value ego development differently, both Buddhist psychology and psychoanalytic object relations theory *define the essence of the
ego in a similar way:* as a process of synthesis and adapta-   *similar*
tion between the inner life and outer reality which pro-   *definitions of*
duces a sense of personal continuity and sameness in the   *the essence of*
felt experience of being a "self," a feeling of being and   *ego*
ongoingness in existence. Object relations theory explains
this experience of personal continuity and selfhood as the
outcome of a gradual differentiation of internalized images
of a "self" as distinct from internalized images of objects
and the eventual consolidation of these images into a com-
posit schema or self-representation (Jacobson, 1964; Mahler, 1975; Lichtenberg, 1975; Kernberg, 1976). Theravadin
Buddhist Abhidhamma explains the emergence of the
sense of "I" in a similar way as the end product of a pro-

cess of identification in which we learn to take one or more of the various components *(khandhas)* which make up our experience of objects as "me" or "myself" (Narada, 1975; Guenther, 1974; Govinda, 1974). It terms this sense of self *"sakkayā-diṭṭhi"* (lit., "personality-belief"), which is an exact equivalent of "self-representation" in object relations theory.

the constructed self

In both psychologies then, the sense of "I," of personal unity and continuity, of being the same "self" in time, in place and across stages of consciousness, is conceived as something which is not innate in personality, not inherent in our psychological or spiritual makeup, but is *evolving developmentally out of our experience of objects and the kinds of interactions we have with them.* In other words, the "self" is literally *constructed* out of our experience with the object world. This "self" which we take to be "me" and which feels so present and real to us is actually an internalized image, a composite representation, constructed by a selective and imaginative "remembering" of past encounters with significant objects in our world (Bruner, 1964). In fact, the self is viewed in both psychologies as a representation which is *actually being constructed anew from moment to moment.* Even as a representation, it is not a fixed entity or engram, but a temporal succession of discrete images, each representing a new construction, a new synthesis, in the present moment of experience.[3] But both systems also agree that the self is not ordinarily experienced this way. Our normal sense of self is characterized instead by a feeling of temporal continuity and sameness over time, by a sense of consistency in interpersonal interactions, by others' recognition of this continuity and consistency, and by our own perception of their confirming recognition that I am the same "me" (Erikson, 1959).

the central clinical issue

The fate of this self is *the* central clinical issue in both psychologies. Investigation into the doctrine of *anatta* and the nature of selfhood has been the focus of Buddhist teaching and practice from its origins in the sixth century B.C. In the history of psychoanalytic thought, the importance of the sense of self has been a rather belated discovery. As long as classical psychoanalytic thinking was dominated by a theory of development, conflict and treatment that was essentially derived from a model of neurosis, the importance of the self-structure could not come into view (Tolpin, 1980). Historically, negative therapeutic results with patients who did not suffer from a typical oedipal neurosis (Freud, 1937) eventually led to the discovery of *two distinct levels of object relations development and psychopathology:* (1) a failure in early object relations, especially in the differentiation between self and others and integration of a cohesive sense of self; and (2) a later defensive struggle of an already differentiated and integrated ego against repressed impulses and their oedipal objects (Fairbairn, 1954; Guntrip, 1961, 1969; Winnicott, 1965; Kernberg, 1975, 1976; Blanck & Blanck, 1974, 1979; Horner, 1979). Guntrip has referred to this finding as "perhaps the major discovery of research into personality problems in this century" (1971:147). In the last ten years this finding has led to the notion of a developmental diagnostic spectrum (Rinsley, 1981) according to which the various clinical syndromes are viewed as originating in specific phases of development. The new understanding of what are now called the borderline conditions and personality disorders, lying between psychotic and neurotic levels of functioning, has in fact focused current clinical attention on the separation-individuation process in preoedipal development, a stage in which the differentiation of an individuated, integrated and object-related self is the primary task, and its success or failure the main determinant of a normal or abnormal course of development.

two distinct levels

As noted in the beginning, the fate of this self is an issue on which clinical and meditative perspectives seem diametrically opposed. This is the nub of the problem. The deepest psychopathological problem from the perspective of psychoanalytic object relations theory is the *lack* of a sense of self. The most severe clinical syndromes—infantile autism, the symbiotic and functional psychoses, the borderline conditions—are precisely failures, arrests or regressions in establishing a cohesive, integrated self (Kohut, 1971, 1977) or self-concept (Kernberg, 1975, 1976). In varying degrees of severity, all represent disorders of the self (Goldberg, 1980), the inability to feel real or cohesive or "in being" at all.

the fate of the self as the nub of the problem

In contrast, the deepest psychopathological problem from the Buddhist perspective is the *presence* of a self and the feeling of selfhood. According to Buddhist diagnosis, the deepest source of suffering is the attempt to preserve a self, an attempt which is viewed as both futile and self-defeating. The severest form of psychopathology is precisely *attavadupadana*, the "clinging to personal existence" (Nyanamoli, 1976; Nyanatiloka, 1972).

"regrowing" vs. dis-identifying from a self-structure

The therapeutic issue in the clinical treatment of the severe disorders is how to "regrow" a basic sense of self (Guntrip, 1969), or how to differentiate and integrate a stable, consistent and enduring self-representation (Kernberg, 1976). The therapeutic issue in Buddhist practice is how to "see through" the illusion or construct of the self *(attā-diṭṭhi)*, how to *dis*-identify from "those essential identifications on which the experience of our personal identity is founded" (Jacobson, 1964:xii). The two great developmental achievements in the all-important line of object relations according to ego psychology—identity and object constancy—are seen by Buddhist analysis as the root of mental suffering.

self as precondition of no-self

The fate of the self in processes of transformation therefore became a kind of test case for me. Were the two therapeutic goals mutually exclusive, as they appeared to be? Or from a wider perspective might they actually be compatible? Indeed, might one be a precondition of the other? The latter is the view I eventually arrived at. Put very simply, *you have to be somebody before you can be nobody.*

I once had the good fortune to overhear a fascinating discussion between a clinical psychologist and an Asian meditation teacher concerning their respective treatments of an anorectic patient which helped to point me in this direction. The meditation teacher was visiting the U.S. for the first time and was very interested in Western psychotherapeutic approaches to mental illness. The clinical psychologist was describing a very difficult case of an anorectic woman who was proving refractory to treatment. The teacher quickly became engrossed in the case and asked many questions about the illness and the treatment. When the psychologist finished, I asked the teacher why he was so interested. He said a woman had once come to the meditation center in Burma where he was teaching with the same presenting problems. In addition she was suffering from chronic insomnia. She wanted to learn to meditate, presumably believing that might bring some relief. I asked him if he taught her. To my surprise, he said "No." For six weeks he merely let her come each day and pour out her complaints against her husband, her children, her parents *a case of* and the injustices of life in general. He mostly listened. He *anorexia* also talked with her but he did not describe precisely how. This first part of her "treatment" then was conducted in effect through the medium of a special kind of interpersonal relationship. He also encouraged her to sleep. Within a short time she began to sleep 4, 8, 12, 14, 16 and finally 18 hours a night—at which point she came to him and said, "I have slept enough. I came here to learn meditation." "Oh," he replied, "you want to learn meditation. Why didn't you say so?" I interrupted to ask if he taught her Vipassana, the type of insight meditation practiced in his Theravada lineage. "No," he said to my surprise again, "no Vipassana. Too much suffering." What she needed was to experience some happiness, some joy, some tranquility and relief from so much mental agitation first, be- *relief from* fore she would be able to tolerate the deeper insight that *mental* *all* her psycho-physical states were characterized by *agitation* change and were associated with suffering, not simply the *followed by* obvious vicissitudes in her personal life history. Since con- *meditation* centration forms of meditation lead to one-pointedness, serenity and bliss, he instructed her in a simple concentration exercise of following the breath instead. She began to sleep 16 hours a night, then 14, 12, 8, 4 and finally two hours a night again, this time because two hours was all she needed. Only at this point did he switch her over to Vipassana and have her observe the moment-to-moment flux of mental and physical events, experiencing directly their radical impermanence, unsatisfactoriness and the lack of any self or subject behind them. Within another three weeks her mind opened and she experienced the first stage of enlightenment (*sotāpatti*). The anorectic symptoms disappeared. She has not been anorectic since.

This is hardly a clinical case study. Nevertheless, it demonstrates the principle that there are different levels of psy-

ego psychologists and "developmental lines"

chopathology; that these are rooted in distortions, failures and arrests at different stages of psychological development; and that each level of pathology requires a different treatment approach or a different type of therapy. Actually ego psychologists no longer think in terms of stages of development in a global sense, but in terms of different "developmental lines" (Anna Freud, 1963) for different psychological functions with the relationship between them constituting the organization of the psyche at any given point in time. Among the diverse developmental lines, there is good reason to believe that the line of object relations is the single most important and reliable determinant of the level of development, mental health, psychopathology and therapeutic potential (Mahler, 1975; Kernberg, 1976; Blanck & Blanck, 1974; Horner, 1979; Rinsley, 1981). Object relations refers to the sequence and quality of one's experiences with interpersonal objects, especially with primary caretakers; and the internalization of these interactions in a representation of "self" and a representation of the "object" which are linked by an affect and coded in memory traces as "good" or "bad." Multiple self and object representations are gradually consolidated into composite schemas of the self and objects. It is believed that these representations in turn become the basis for the development of intrapsychic structures, above all for the development of a sense of self. I think that this developmental perspective, particularly the development of object relations, provides a clue to positioning the Buddhist and psychodynamic systems within an integrated model of therapeutic interventions. It also explains the apparent contradiction in their methods and goals.

object relations as important developmental determinant

Let me start with several observations from my teaching experience about the types of students drawn to Buddhist practice and the course their practice often seems to follow.

CLINICAL FEATURES OF MEDITATION PRACTICE

Several features stand out. First, measured in terms of the classical stages *(ñāṇas)* of insight (Nyanamoli, 1976), *progress is relatively slow.* Dr. Dan Brown and I confirmed this in a Rorschach study (see Chapter 6). After three months of continuous intensive daily Vipassana practice, fully half of the N-group of 30 showed very little change on either the post-test[4] or on teacher ratings.[5] This finding is further supported by my own research in India and Burma (Engler, 1983b) in which Asian practitioners progressed much more quickly, even though they spent considerably less time in intensive practice in retreat settings. The majority had done only one or two 2-week retreats before experiencing First Enlightenment.[6] The rest of their practice was carried on at home in the midst of daily activities.[7]

slow progress

Secondly, Western students appear to *become fixated on what may be called a psychodynamic level of experience* (Brown & Engler, 1980). Their practice continues to be dominated by primary process thinking and "unrealistic experience" (Maupin, 1965), as well as by an increase in fantasy, daydreaming, reverie, imagery, spontaneous recall of past memories, derepression of conflictual material, incessant thinking and emotional lability, including dramatic swings in mood (M. Sayadaw, 1973; Walsh, 1977, 1978; Kornfield, 1979; Kapleau, 1965).[8]

fixated practice

Thirdly, *strong transferences develop to teachers.* These often seem to be of Kohut's mirroring or idealizing types. In the first, a need for a source of accepting and confirming "mirroring" is revived in the context of the teacher-student relationship; in the second, a need for merger with a source of "idealized" strength and calmness emerges (Kohut & Wolf, 1978).[9] There is another kind of transference sometimes encountered which is more chaotic in nature, subject to rapid and extreme oscillations between omnipotence and devaluation.

transference and teachers

What to make of these observations? How might they be explained? Meditation teachers generally attribute them to several factors in the students' psychology.

The first is usually the students' *inability to develop sufficient concentration.* A specific degree of concentration, characterized by non-distractibility and one-pointed attention, is necessary before the mind-body process can be observed closely enough to attain the type of insight Vipassana med-

problems in concentration

itation aims at. The ability to keep attention fixed and steady on each mental and physical event as it presents itself to awareness, technically called "Access Concentration" *(upācara-samādhi)*, was emphasized for instance by the head of this Theravada lineage, the Ven. Mahasi Sayadaw (1973), because it is the prerequisite for entering the stages *(ñāṇas)* of insight meditation proper (Vajiranana, 1975).

Teachers also point to *the tendency to become absorbed in the content of awareness rather than continuing to attend to its process*. Students become preoccupied with individual *fascination with* thoughts, images, memories, sensations, etc., rather than *content of* keeping their attention focused on the essential character- *consciousness* istics of all psycho-physical events, whatever the content: their impermanence, their inability to satisfy even the simplest of desires, their lack of enduring substance, and their dependence on conditions which also change from moment to moment. Dwelling on content is a definite temptation in early stages of practice when the meditator is introduced, perhaps for the first time, to the vast, strange, often frightening, but also enticing and seductive world of his inner experience. In fact, it is probable that the beginning meditator's introduction to his inner world is not essentially different from that of the naive subject who begins exploration of other hypoaroused states, e.g., self-hypnosis, reverie, and free association. For example, using the Rorschach, a similar increase in primary process thinking has been reported for hypnotized subjects (Fromm, Oberlander & Gruenewald, 1970) and for patients who had undergone psychoanalysis (Rehyer, 1969). Adaptation to the internal milieu may be a common feature of any hypoaroused state of consciousness and may have little to do with the "specificity" (Tart, 1975a) of meditation per se. With the "triumph of the therapeutic" (Rieff, 1966) in West- *confusing* ern culture, there is also a tendency to confuse meditation *meditation with* with psychotherapy and to analyze mental content instead *psychotherapy* of simply observing it. This is a classical hindrance *(nīva-raṇa)* in all meditative traditions, East and West. In addition, certain cultural factors may contribute to the tendency to become absorbed in content. A longer period of adaptation to the flow of internal experience may be necessary as well as anxiety-producing in a culture that lays so much stress on external adaptation and reality-boundness at the expense of imaginative involvement (Hilgard, 1970). One possible explanation is that Western students do not necessarily meditate in a formal sense when they are "meditating." A visiting Asian teacher of Vipassana was recently asked what they were doing. He replied, "Many Western students do not meditate. They do therapy. They do not go deep with mindfulness."

Third, in being transplanted to the West, meditation has been lifted out of its larger context of a culture permeated by Buddhist perspectives and values where it is also part *lack of* of a total system of training *(bhāvanā)* and a way of life. *supportive* When this therapeutic context is eliminated, meditation is *cultural context* *practiced as an isolated technique*, with disregard for many other important behavioral, motivational, intrapsychic and interpersonal factors such as right livelihood, right action, right understanding and right intention. The Buddhist Eightfold Path of *bhāvanā* or development includes the cultivation of conceptual understanding, proper motivation, ethical behavior, appropriate livelihood and the correct type of effort in addition to the specifically meditative skills of mindfulness and concentration. This was also cited as a contributing factor by the Burmese sayadaws.

As a clinically trained teacher, however, I have been led to make a different kind of observation. In many students I see a particular vulnerability and disturbance in their *two major* sense of identity and self-esteem. At best, this appears to *problem groups* reflect stage- and age-appropriate developmental problems of identity formation (Erikson, 1950, 1956). This is particularly true of two major groups who become interested in Buddhism and appear at retreats: those in late adolescence and the period of transition to early adulthood, and those entering or passing through the mid-life transition (Levinson, 1978). Individuals in these two groups often seem attracted to Buddhist practice as a short-cut solution to the developmental tasks appropriate and necessary to their stage of the life cycle. The Buddhist teaching that I neither have nor am an enduring self is often misinterpreted to mean that I do not need to struggle with the tasks of identity formation or with finding out who I am, what my capabilities are, what my needs are, what my responsibilities are, how I am related to other selves, and what I should or could do with my life. The *anattā* (no-self) doctrine is taken to justify their premature abandonment of essential psychosocial tasks.

At their worst, these vulnerabilities and disturbances of personal identity are pathological disturbances in the subjective sense of self—what Kohut (1971, 1977) would call "self pathology" or "structural deficit pathology." Though it is necessary to be cautious in the absence of formal clinical assessment, my suspicion is that many of these students function at or close to a borderline level of ego organization. I am taking the "borderline" designation here in its psychostructural sense to refer to a *level* of personality organization and functioning rather than to a specific personality type or character disorder.[10] It represents a group of "stably unstable" (Schmiedeberg, 1947) personality trait disorders which are symptomatically and developmentally transitional along a continuum between the psychoses and the psychoneuroses. This group of disorders shares a core symptomatology, has similar internal object relations, and is believed by many researchers to have a common etiology in deviations or arrests during the separation-individuation process in early object relations development (Mahler, 1975; Masterson & Rinsley, 1980). The main feature of borderline personality organization according to one important school of thought is *identity diffusion* (Kernberg, 1976).

borderline personality organization

"identity diffusion"

Integration fails in borderline personality organization. Internalized object relations take the form of a so-called "split object relations unit" (Masterson & Rinsley, 1980). One's self, others and outside events are perceived as either "all-good" or "all-bad" in accordance with the pleasure principle: all-good if they appear to satisfy and provide; all-bad if they appear to withhold, frustrate or deprive. The result is sharply contrasting, even contradictory attitudes toward important aspects of oneself and others, which are actively dissociated from each other and held apart by the primitive defense of splitting. This produces a confusing alternation of opposite ego states and of experiences of self and the object world: now magically powerful, beneficent and good; now frustrating, devouring,

the "split object-relations unit"

threatening and bad. This all-good, all-bad perceptual dichotomy is accompanied by varying degrees of incomplete self-object differentiation. Fluid boundaries between self and world leave the borderline personality vulnerable to depersonalization and estrangement, and to regressive refusions of self and objects, or what DSM-III terms "brief reactive psychosis," under conditions of stress. Failure of repression leads to similarly fluid internal boundaries between parts of the person. Primitive drives, affects, and self and object representations have ready access to consciousness. "Inside" and "outside" are therefore dealt with by reliance on primitive defenses such as denial, projective identification, primitive idealization, and especially splitting (Rinsley, 1981).

borderline vulnerabilities

THE ATTRACTION OF BUDDHISM FOR PERSONS WITH SELF-PATHOLOGY

In my experience, Buddhism can exert a special attraction for individuals with borderline organization. In part the attraction seems to be precisely the *anattā* or no-self doctrine. It helps explain and rationalize, if not actually legitimate, their lack of self-integration, their feelings of inner emptiness, of not having a cohesive self. I recall a student in one of my courses on Buddhism at the University of California at Santa Cruz who could not understand any difference between his own state and the state of enlightenment. Meditation was superfluous—he was already enlightened. By his own description, he lived continually in a profound state of "egolessness." Our classes were as stormy as his oscillating perceptions of me. In one class I was the idealized and all-knowing teacher who alone would appreciate the depth of his passion and the originality of his mind and its pressured stream of insights; the next class I was angrily devalued for being unappreciative of his suffering, for being like all the rest in not understanding his unique contribution, and for being no help whatsoever. He either clung to me, or snubbed me with aloof superiority, bent on demonstrating his total self-sufficiency. For these personalities, there is something like Hartmann's (1958) "preadaptive fit" between the psyche and its expectable environment, in this case between the

borderline individuals and the no-self doctrine

Buddhist concept of no-self *(anattā)* and their actual self-concept. The teaching of non-attachment is also heard by these individuals as rationalizing their inability to form stable, lasting, satisfying relationships.

narcissistic personalities and meditation

Alternating omnipotence and devaluation are further derivatives of such splitting operations which affect self and object representations in the absence of a cohesive and integrated self. The character defense of omnipotence/devaluation does not necessarily indicate the presence of a narcissistic personality disorder. It is common throughout the borderline spectrum because of the characterological inability to integrate all-good and all-bad self and object representations. So once again there is a need for caution in labelling students whom we have not clinically assessed. My impression nevertheless is that narcissistic personalities represent a sizable subgroup of those individuals with borderline levels of ego organization who are drawn to meditation. Buddhism seems to have two unique attractions for this type of personality structure, as well as for individuals in the borderline range generally. The first is the enlightenment ideal itself. This is cathected as the acme of personal perfection with eradication of all mental defilements *(kilesas)* and fetters *(samyojanas)*. In other words it represents a purified state of complete and invulnerable self-sufficiency from which all badness has been expelled, the aim of all narcissistic strivings. For this kind of personality, "perfection" often unconsciously means freedom from symptoms so they can be superior to everyone else. The second attraction is the possibility of establishing a mirroring or idealizing type of narcissistic transference with spiritual teachers who are perceived as powerful, admirable beings of special worth in whose halo they can participate. The fact that those types of transference relationships appear so frequently strongly suggests that meditation often attracts personalities at this level of functioning.

a clinical view

From a clinical point of view then, I have come to believe that the explanation for some of the special difficulties some students have in meditation practice is to be found, not in the usual struggle with the classical "hindrances" *(nīvaraṇas)* or in the unique features of our cultural situation, but in the level of personality organization and ego functioning these students bring to practice. Paradoxically, it is precisely their self-pathology, the structural deficits in the formation of whole self and object representations and their consequent *lack* of a cohesive, integrated sense of self, that makes meditation practice based on self-detachment difficult, if not impossible.

It is important to recognize that self-pathology does not depend on personality or character type, and still less on symptoms or symptom clusters. Almost all the commonly recognized personality *types* can occur at any level of personality *organization:* healthy, neurotic, borderline or psychotic. Even the more pathological character types—schizoid, paranoid, infantile—can occur within a neurotic structure (Stone, 1980). Stone has suggested that it is clinically more useful to think in terms of a continuum for each character or personality type as it varies from most to least pathological. He has accordingly proposed a promising three-dimensional model of personality typology which crosses personality type, level of personality organization and degree of constitutional or genetic loading. This distinction between structure and character is only beginning to become clear in clinical psychiatry and represents a breakthrough in psychodiagnostic understanding. The classical meditation traditions have always taken personality into account when they have prescribed a specific type of practice for a specific type of individual. The classical example perhaps is the system of the Four Yogas in Hinduism—*jnan, bhakti, karma* and *raj*—for intellectual, devotional, active and experimental temperaments respectively (Vivekananda, 1953). But these typologies, like some earlier Western psychiatric diagnostic categories and classification systems, are specifications of personality type, not level of personality organization. The latter cuts across character, behavior and temperament. If Buddhism were attracting a number of students with borderline or narcissistic personality organization, its traditional ways of thinking about personality in terms of types would not allow teachers or students to recognize it.

self-pathology and personality or character type

personality type and personality organization

Given recent trends in clinical practice, this attraction is not surprising. There has been a marked shift in the prevailing psychiatric symptomatology in recent years. In contrast to the previous prevalence of neurotic and psychotic disorders, borderline and character disorders are being clinically encountered and diagnosed with increasing frequency. As more of these individuals are now presenting themselves for psychiatric treatment, so I suspect more are also attempting to use the newer so-called "innovative therapies" (Walsh, 1980a), like meditation, to get help.

recent trends in clinical practice

A PREREQUISITE LEVEL OF PERSONALITY ORGANIZATION

assumptions of Buddhist psychology

Buddhist psychology does not have much to say about this level of ego functioning and personality organization, or about this range of psychopathology. It does not take explicit account of self-pathology with structural deficits in the ego stemming from faulty early object relations development. Buddhist psychology never elaborated a developmental psychology in the Western sense. It has no theory of child development. Unlike Hinduism, it has not even elaborated a conception of the human life cycle. Nor does it have a developmental view of psychopathology. That is, it does not explicitly place different levels of mental disorder along a developmental continuum according to etiology. What Buddhist psychology and practice appear to do instead is *presuppose* a more or less normal course of development and an intact or "normal" ego. For its practices, it *assumes* a level of personality organization where object relations development, especially a cohesive and integrated sense of self, is already complete. There is an obvious danger if this assumption of normal selfhood is not understood, either by students or teachers. Students may mistake subjective feelings of emptiness for "*śūnyatā*" or voidness; and the experience of not feeling inwardly cohesive or integrated for *anattā* or selflessness. Teachers may instruct students in techniques which are designed for a different level of personality organization and these may have adverse effects in some students.

obvious danger

Like psychodynamic therapies, insight meditation is an "uncovering" technique (Blanck & Blanck, 1974). As an uncovering technique, it employs technical procedures which resemble those used in psychoanalysis and cognate systems.

1. *Technical neutrality.* Attention is kept "bare," that is, restricted to a bare registration of mental and physical events as they are observed without reaction (Nyanaponika, 1973; Kornfield, 1977; Goldstein, 1976). Any reactions or further elaborations are themselves immediately made the object of bare attention and are neither suppressed nor pursued.

four technical procedures in insight meditation

2. *Removal of censorship.* Any and all thoughts, feelings and sensations are allowed into awareness, without discrimination or selection. This of course remains to some extent a goal and outcome rather than a technique which can be practiced from the outset, much as the ability to free associate is said to be the result of a successful analysis. Like free association, it must be learned. This is also equivalent to the "basic rule" of free association in psychoanalysis: to impose no principle of censorship. Analysts have been right to point to the extraordinary uniqueness of this situation. However, it is not unique to analysis as is commonly thought. The "basic rule" has guided this and other meditative traditions for at least two and a half millennia.

3. *Abstinence.* The goal is observation rather than gratification of wishes, impulses, desires and strivings. Like psychoanalysis, Vipassana discourages mere discharge, abreaction, catharsis or acting out. Both practices depend upon a capacity for delay of gratification for the sake of eventual insight and deeper understanding.

4. *A "therapeutic split" in the ego.* The meditator is instructed to become a "witness" to his own experience. This depends upon the capacity of the ego to be subject and object of its experience at the same time (Sterba, 1934), or in nontechnical terms, the capacity to step back and observe objectively what you are experiencing while you are experiencing it.[11]

ego capacities and successful meditation

All four procedures presuppose certain ego capacities which define a normal or neurotic level of functioning and personality organization. For the borderline personality organization, these capacities which most of us take for granted either are lacking or are seriously impaired. Persons with poorly differentiated and weakly integrated representations of themselves and others cannot tolerate uncovering techniques.

when uncovering and interpretation cannot succeed Uncovering and interpretation cannot succeed with such persons because with faulty self-object differentiation the observing ego cannot take distance from what it observes. Reliance on primitive defense like projective identification, with its vicious circle of projection and reintrojection of bad self and object images, also makes it difficult to distinguish between fantasy and reality and leads to a severely diminished capacity for detached observation (Kernberg, 1972). The ability to distinguish reality from transference is easily lost and this ability is the main prerequisite for all methods of insight therapy (Zetzel, 1971). Persons with these deficits usually can't tolerate for very long the painful affects which emerge in transference reactions. Abstinence and delay also become intolerable since contradictory affects and impulses lie close to consciousness and tend to be expressed and acted on. Since love and hate, desire and fear, remain dissociated and neither polar ego state has a mitigating influence on the raw force of the other, the ego is often overwhelmed by imperious impulses and affects with which it cannot cope. In the absence of a strong integrative capacity, free association tends to become contaminated by primary process thinking which is not subject to rational review and easily leads the person to being engulfed by primitive affects and drives. Unlike the controlled regression in the service of the ego which organized personalities can endure, regression in persons with borderline personality often proves difficult to reverse (Blanck & Blanck, 1979).

significant dangers As an insight-directed therapy (Dewald, 1972) then, Vipassana presents serious risks to students with this level of functioning. All intensive and/or unstructured therapies present significant dangers to these students (Zetzel, 1971) and run the risk of further fragmenting their already fragile and vulnerable sense of self.

The "basic rule" in Vipassana to attend to all thoughts, feelings and sensations without selection or discrimination has the effect of creating just such an unstructured situation intra-psychically by plunging this kind of student into an inner world he may be ill-equipped to cope with. Fragile ego boundaries can become further blurred and self and object representations can de-differentiate. The up-surge of primitive drives and affects can then be managed only by still greater reliance on disavowal and splitting mechanisms to keep the good and the bad apart. In their practice these students will tend to oscillate between states of great rage, emptiness and depression at one extreme, and states of great euphoria, bliss or pseudomystical feel-ings of unity counterfeiting a genuine experience of self-transcendence at the other. These oscillations further weaken the ego and become an even stronger source of resistance to integrating their contradictory experiences of themselves and others. The narcissistic pathology of some of these students also induces them to form mirroring or idealizing transferences based on their primitive need for idealization and for alternatively seeing self and others as omnipotent and worthless. When the teacher refuses to meet their expectations and they no longer experience the relationship as gratifying, negative transference reactions can emerge which always threaten regression (Kernberg, 1972).

unstructured intra-psychic situations and the fragile ego

Every teacher has encountered this, and has probably been somewhat bewildered by it, not knowing its origins. When interpersonal relations have not yet reached the level of object constancy where the same object can be experienced as both bad and good, frustrating and grati-fying, every negative self or object experience is a threat to the stability and structure of the ego and further weak-ens the person's ability to maintain a relationship with ob-jects on which he depends physically and emotionally, even when they are being experienced as depriving or pu-nitive. Meditation teachers tend not to pay much attention to transference aspects of the teacher-student relationship since what carries the treatment in meditation is not a re-lationship as it is in conventional psychotherapy. How-ever, a price is often paid for this. It is a repeated obser-vation, for instance in the Psychotherapy Research Project at the Menninger Foundation (Kernberg, Burnstein, Coyne *et al.*, 1972), that when the therapist tries to avoid

negative transference relationship

"acting out" and meditation retreats

the latent negative transference relationship, the result is a chronically shallow therapeutic relationship. Patients act out their problems, keeping the treatment setting rigidly split off from the transference with the therapist. (This might partially account for a phenomenon sometimes encountered after and between meditation retreats: a prolonged orgy [the word is not too strong] of sensual gratification quite at variance with the behavior and values espoused during practice. For some this may well be a form of acting out "outside the treatment," as it were, instead of simply a resurgence of suppressed impulses and desires and their explosive discharge.) They engage in pseudosubmission to the therapist which leads to therapeutic stalemate: no change despite years of treatment. At worst then, in borderline conditions the very type of meditation designed to see through the illusion of selfhood may actually contribute to self-pathology. Fortunately, I suspect that the stringent prerequisites of the practice make it too difficult if not impossible for these students to sustain their training. To some extent a self-selective and self-protective mechanism is probably built in.

treatment goal

treatment indications

Differences in ego structure dictate differences in therapeutic goals and techniques. The goal in the treatment of borderline conditions is building structure, not uncovering repression: facilitating the integration of contradictory self-images, object-images and affects into a cohesive and stable sense of self able to maintain constant relationships with objects even in the face of disappointment, frustration and loss. Since the developmental deficits in these personalities are best understood in terms of those ego structures and functions which are established in early one-to-one relationships, the best treatment is probably through the medium of a new and different kind of dyadic relationship than they were able to achieve during earlier periods of developmental crisis (Zetzel, 1971); not through an introspective and predominantly intrapsychic activity like meditation. It is questionable whether mere observation of contradictory ego states alone will help integrate the dissociated aspects of self, objects and affects. It is questionable whether self-observation in this sense is even possible. What is required is confrontation and interpretive exposure of the split-off object relations units as they occur within a transference relationship (Rinsley, 1977). Meditation is designed for a different type of problem and a different level of ego structure.

My observation is that in order to practice an "uncovering" technique like Vipassana and to achieve the structural changes the practice aims at, it is developmentally necessary to acquire a cohesive and integrated self first, one that is differentiated from others and has a degree of autonomy. If such a self is not established, there is a clear sequence of pathological consequences. In fact, its absence forms the most severe clinical syndromes. Failures in early attachment and bonding lead to autistic and psychopathic personality structures (Bowlby, 1969) and the presymbiotic psychoses (Mahler, 1968). Failures in self-differentiation lead to schizophrenic and psychotic syndromes (Mahler, 1968). Failures in self and object integration lead to the borderline conditions and the personality disorders (Mahler, 1975; Kernberg, 1975; Horner, 1979; Masterson & Rinsley, 1980; Masterson, 1972). All are states of intense suffering for which meditation does not appear to be a viable or even possible remedy. Insight meditation, i.e., Vipassana, does not address this range of psychopathology, is not designed for it, and is probably contraindicated, though certain preliminary practices and concentrative forms of meditation may be of some incidental help in lowering chronic tension states and inducing a greater internal locus of control.

developmental necessity for integrated self

contraindications for meditation practice

A FURTHER RANGE OF PSYCHOPATHOLOGY AND OBJECT RELATIONS DEVELOPMENT

Given the developmental necessity of a cohesive and integrated sense of self, we can still ask if such a self-structure represents the culmination of object relations development or the final possible outcome of a therapeutic process. Of course in a certain sense the process of identity formation is never complete. Mahler (1975) herself describes the outcome of the separation-individuation subphases as "on-the-way-to-object-constancy." Peter Blos (1967) speaks of a "second individuation process" at adolescence. Erikson (1950) projects a life-long identity journey. Nevertheless, in most persons a consolidation of over-

review of developmental theory of object relations school

all intrapsychic structures takes place around the end of the Oedipal period when the repression barrier becomes more or less firmly established. Thereafter identification becomes increasingly selective (Kernberg, 1976). What is ego-dystonic and inconsistent with one's sense of self becomes repressed, a process essential to maintaining self-cohesion. But precisely because of such repression, a new type of psychopathology can emerge at this level of personality organization: the psychoneuroses. The core problem is no longer the lack of self-differentiation and integration but conflict between the ego and instinctual wishes which are unacceptable to the newly consolidated self and are therefore repressed or otherwise defended against. The "qualitative difference" (Blanck & Blanck, 1974) in ego structure and consequently in type of pathology requires a qualitatively different type of therapeutic approach. At this level the task is not to build intrapsychic structure but to integrate repressed aspects of the self, to "reunite with the conscious ego the contents . . . which have been withheld from consciousness by repression" (Fenichel, 1945: 570).[12]

Buddhist psychology and a third structural level of psychopathology

However, according to Buddhist psychology a still deeper level of human suffering comes into view at this level of personality organization. This kind of suffering constitutes yet another *structural level of psychopathology* which is qualitatively different from the preceding two and is not included in the developmental diagnostic spectrum of contemporary Western psychiatry. Evidently it can come into view and be addressed therapeutically only *after* identity and object constancy have been attained.

Suppose I am capable of technical neutrality or "bare" attention, non-selective awareness, abstinence and the capacity for self-observation. Suppose further that I don't become absorbed in the content of my inner world and don't pause to analyze or interpret it. Suppose instead that I continue to train my attention to merely observe the flow of psycho-physical events in their moment-to-moment manifestation without preference or reaction. Finally, suppose that I can hold my attention absolutely steady without any sort of distraction for extended periods of time.

What more will I then discover about the nature of the self and objects?

THE STAGES OF INSIGHT MEDITATION

The first thing to occur is what the classical Theravada meditation texts call "dispelling the illusion of compactness" (Vajiranana, 1975; Nyanamoli, 1976). My sense of being an independent observer disappears. The normal sense that I am a fixed, continuous point of observation from which I regard now this object, now that, is dispelled. Like the tachistoscopic flicker-fusion phenomenon which produces the illusion of an "object" when discrete and discontinuous images are flashed too quickly for normal perception to distinguish them, my sense of being a separate observer or experiencer behind my observation or experience is revealed to be the result of a perceptual illusion, of my not being normally able to perceive a more microscopic level of events. When my attention is sufficiently refined through training and kept bare of secondary reactions and elaboration of stimuli, all that is actually apparent to me from moment to moment is a mental or physical event and an awareness of that event. In each moment, there is simply a process of knowing *(nāma)* and its object *(rūpa)*. Each arises separately and simultaneously in each moment of awareness. No enduring or substantial entity or observer or experiencer or agent—no self—can be found behind or apart from these moment-to-moment events to which they could be attributed *(an-atta* = noself).

dispelling the illusion of "compactness"

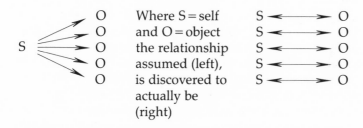

In other words, the individual "frames" appear which had previously fused in normal perception in a tachistoscopic manner to produce an apparently solid and fixed image of a "self" or an "object."[13] The only observable reality at this level is the flow of mental and physical events themselves. There is no awareness of an observer. There are just individual moments of observation.[14]

insight into the "process nature" of reality

Once attention is stabilized at this level of perception, a further refinement of this insight into the underlying nature of self and object representation becomes apparent. I observe how a self-representation is constructed in each moment as a result of an interaction with an object[15] and only as a result of such an interaction; and conversely, how an object appears not in itself (whatever that might mean) but always relative to my state of observation. I see how preceding causes operate to condition each moment of self-object representation, and how each moment conditions the next moment. In this way I begin to perceive that there are strictly speaking *no constant end-products of representation; there is only a continual process of representing.* I discover that there are actually no enduring entities or schemas at all; only momentary constructions are taking place.[16]

observing the stream of consciousness

As I become still more practiced in non-reactive and unbroken observation, I next observe the stream of consciousness literally break up into a series of discrete events which are discontinuous in space and time. Each mental and physical event is seen to have an absolute beginning, a brief duration, and an absolute end. Each arises only after the one preceding it has passed away. Representation and reality construction are therefore discovered to be *discontinuous processes.* In terms of information-processing theory, what the meditator is actually experiencing is the temporal nature of perception prior to pattern recognition, before stimuli are built up into the recognizable percepts of ordinary experience (Brown, 1977). He is experiencing the original packet of stimulus information which has been preattentively segregated into a figural unit separate from the background of other incoming stimuli and which has a real and absolute duration in time. He can distinguish the individual "psychological moments" in which those stimuli which arrive concurrently with relatively equal intensity are grouped into the same energy packet. His phenomenological experience at this stage of practice, that one event occurs only after the preceding one has totally ceased, reflects the fact that at the level of preattentive synthesis (Neisser, 1967) stimuli are processed and segregated in a temporally discrete and discontinuous fashion. From this point of view, what the meditator has actually done is *reverse—retraverse—the key stages in the representational process,* which yields individual self and object representations only as the end-products of a very long and complex reworking of stimulus information.

retraversing the stages of the making of "self"

When this total moment-to-moment "coming to be and passing away" *(udayabbaya)* is experienced, there is a profound understanding of the radical impermanence *(anicca)* of all events. Not only do I no longer perceive any durable "objects," but even the processes of thinking, feeling, perceiving and sensing themselves come to be and pass away without remainder. In this experience of perpetual and discontinuous change, such notions as a solid body, a durable perceptual object, an internal representation, or even a fixed point of observation no longer appear tenable. I come to understand the lack of any intrinsic durability anywhere; I become aware of the selflessness *(anattā)* of mind, body, external objects and internal representations. Not only does everything change all the time; there are no "things" which change.[17]

insight into radical impermanence

A DIFFERENT LEVEL OF PSYCHOPATHOLOGY

At this point, *an entirely different level of psychopathology* comes into view. First, at this level of perception, the normal affective and motivational bases of behavior are experienced as pathogenic and sources of great suffering. This becomes particularly clear in observing the painful effect of normal reactive tendencies in this state of awareness. Any affective reaction, even the simplest and seemingly innate responses of attraction and aversion, liking and disliking, preferring the pleasant and avoiding the unpleasant, wanting this and not wanting that—irrespective of their particular aims and objects—is experienced as an ex-

observing the painful effect of normal reactive tendencies

traordinarily painful and misguided effort to block the flow
of events. Such desires are now seen to be futile attempts
to deny and resist the process of change—to hold onto
this and push that away. Secondly, any attempt to constellate enduring self and object representations, or to prefer-
entially identify with some self-representations as "me"
and expel (psychotic, borderline) or repress (neurotic, normal) others as "not-me," is experienced as an equally futile
attempt to interrupt, undo or alter self and object representations as a flow of moment-to-moment constructions.

basic sources of suffering

According to classical psychoanalytic metapsychology, the
most primitive and enduring law of psychic life is the pleasure principle: the desire to maximize pleasure and mini-
mize pain. According to more recent object relations
theory, even more basic is the principle of object relatedness. Both are considered part of our constitutional endowment. In the meditative perspective however, the
striving for sense gratification and for selfhood, which
have been the basis of mental life up to and including the
stages of identity and object constancy, are seen as *the next
potential point of arrest* and source of suffering. Both striv-

thirst for life as source of suffering

ings are included in the Buddhist diagnostic category of
"*taṇhā*" or "desire." Buddhist psychology ranks them in
the same order. "*Kāma-taṇhā*," for instance, is the "thirst"
for sense gratification and includes both attraction to pleasure (*sukhakāma*) and aversion to pain (*dukkhapatikkula*).[18]
"*Bhava-taṇhā*" describes the "thirst" for existence and becoming. This refers to the desire to perpetuate life and self
and to avoid death. In one form, it is the desire for self-
preservation and self-perpetuation; in another form, the
desire for rebirth; in still another form, the desire for immortality; in yet another, the desire for continued differentiation and new experience. "*Vibhava-taṇhā*" denotes the

thirst for death as source of suffering

"thirst" for non-existence. Again, this term denotes a
range of motivations: the desire to end life and becoming;
the desire for states of inertia and homeostasis; the desire
to de-differentiate, ward off and regress. These latter two
together constitute both sides of the object-seeking pro-
pensity in Fairbairn's (1952) sense: (a) the desire for continuity of the self and its relationships to the object; and (b)
the defensive withdrawal of the self from object relations

and the object world. Precisely these strivings are now experienced as the immediate cause of psychic suffering.

But according to meditative experience, *these strivings are not innate.* The precondition of "desire" is another aspect of affect, "feeling." *(vedanā).* Buddhist psychology de-links two components of affect in a way psychoanalytic theory and contemporary theories of emotion still do not: (1) the purely spontaneous sensation of pleasure or unpleasure which accompanies every experience of an object;[19] and (2) the tendency to respond to or act on that sensation with approach or avoidance *(taṇhā).* This distinction has been confirmed by empirical findings in contemporary studies of motivation and the phenomenology of the emotions (Arnold, 1970a, 1970b; Young, 1969; Pribram, 1970; Schachter, 1970; Leeper, 1970). Normally the experience of pleasure/unpleasure leads to an "action tendency" (Arnold, 1970b) to approach the pleasant and avoid the unpleasant. Ordinarily this sequence is experienced as having drive-characteristics and is thus conceptualized in psychoanalytic theory as being innate, automatic, spontaneous, natural; as an autonomic nervous system response-sequence beyond voluntary control.[20] In contrast, trained meditative observation shows that the motivational component of affect (i.e., the tendency to act on pleasant or unpleasant experience, which is the origin of all psychic drive states; cf. Kernberg, 1976) is a *volitional* activity and in principle subject to self-regulation.[21] De-linking *vedanā* and *taṇhā,* the experience of pleasure or unpleasure *(vedanā)* and the tendency to act on these central state affect dispositions *(taṇhā),* is a fulcrum point in meditation training. It returns a previously conditioned response to voluntary control and introduces an important principle of delay.

de-linking pleasure-unpleasure and the tendency to act

What, in turn, accounts for the operation of the pleasure principle—this impulsive tendency to cling to pleasure and avoid pain—and for object-seeking behavior, especially if these are regarded as ego functions subject to self-regulation and not as instinctual drives? According to Buddhist analysis, the cause of pleasure principle dominance is faulty reality testing. Desire *(taṇhā)* is conditioned by

Buddhist analysis of pleasure principle dominance

"ignorance" *(avijjā)*. Like desire, ignorance refers to an ego function: the capacity for reality testing. Ordinary reality testing is not only faulty; it is based on a particular type of misperception which inverts *(vipallāsa)* the real order of things. We misperceive what is impermanent *(anicca)* as permanent; what is incapable of satisfying *(dukkha)* as satisfactory; and what is without substance or enduring selfhood *(anattā)* as substantial and having selfhood. In other words, owing to faulty reality testing we ordinarily perceive and experience ourselves and objects to be *just the opposite* of the way they really are *(vipallāsa* = "inverted view")*. In this sense the critical diagnostic question in Buddhist meditation practice is the same as in Western clinical practice: is reality testing intact? Clinically, this criterion differentiates normality and neurosis from psychosis (Kernberg, 1977). But in the meditative perspective, normal as well as abnormal conditions are deficient in reality testing. This is the reason why Buddhist psychology can describe the normal state of ego functioning as "deranged" *(ummattaka)* and give the term the same technical meaning it has in clinical usage: the construction of a delusional system, or a world of non-veridical percepts of self, others and the physical world. Meditation reality-tests this representational world; clinical psychiatry takes it for granted in a commonsense manner.

reality testing: clinical and meditative

THREE LEVELS OF MENTAL DISORDER

Abhidhamma's diagnostic paradigm

Though Buddhist psychology is not developmental, there is a classical diagnostic paradigm in the Abhidhamma which seems to suggest that it does in fact distinguish between three different levels of suffering which spring from different levels of object relations experience. (1) *Dukkha-dukkha* or "ordinary suffering" corresponds to neurotic conflict between impulse and prohibition within a stable self-structure and whole-object relations, as well as to "ordinary human unhappiness," which Freud once said was the exchange for resolution of neurotic suffering. (2) *Dukkha-vipariṇāma* or "suffering caused by change" corresponds to the borderline conditions and the functional psychoses where disturbance in the sense of self-continuity, fluctuating drives and affects, contradictory and dissociated ego stages, lack of a stable self-structure, and lack of constant relations with the object world are the core problem. At this level of personality organization, prior to identity formation and object constancy, change is the deepest and most pervasive threat to the fragile self. Every experience of separation and loss threatens the reality and cohesion of the self, which still depends for its felt existence on the immediate presence and benevolent regard of its objects. (3) *Samkhāra-dukkha* or "suffering as conditioned states" represents, to Western psychiatry, *an entirely new category of psychopathology* which is pervasive. At this level, object-seeking as such is experienced as pathogenic, contradictory as that may sound in terms of normal developmental theory. The very attempt to constellate a self and objects which will have some constancy and continuity in time, space and across states (Lichtenberg, 1975) emerges as the therapeutic problem. The two great achievements in the all-important line of object relations development—identity and object constancy—still represent a point of fixation or arrest. A cohesive and integrated sense of self, like the earlier paranoid and depressive part-object positions (M. Klein, 1946; Fairbairn, 1952), is seen as a developmental "position won in order to be moved beyond" (Guntrip, 1969:118f). From this perspective, *what we take as "normality" is a state of arrested development.* Moreover it can be viewed as a pathological condition insofar as it is based on faulty reality testing, inadequate neutralization of the drives, lack of impulse control, and incomplete integration of the self and the object world.

"normality" as a state of arrested development

THE THERAPEUTIC PROVINCE OF MEDITATION

This is the level of personality organization and psychopathology that insight meditation appears to be specifically designed to address. Buddhist psychopathology and diagnosis seem to acknowledge, presuppose and even partially address the first two kinds of suffering. But as a system of therapy, its major and proper concern is the third. I believe much of the confusion has arisen because this has not been clearly understood by either Buddhist or psychodynamic psychology, nor by current research paradigms. These two systems sometimes have been viewed

current confusions

as either competing at worst, or as alternative treatment modalities at best, for the same range of problems. One tendency, for example, is to contrast respective treatments and outcomes as mutually exclusive and to view them as a forced choice: psychotherapy *or* meditation, the attainment of a cohesive sense of self *or* liberation from it. Clinical psychiatry tends to view meditation as an invitation to a psychotic de-differentiation of hard-won ego boundaries. Buddhist psychology critiques the notion of "self" or "ego," points out how it leads to suffering, and sees psychotherapy as perpetuating and reinforcing the illusory self-concept and making enlightenment that much more difficult. And the two systems also have been seen as vaguely complementary but without a clear awareness of the differences in their respective methods, aims, outcomes and the problems they seek to remedy. Thus the phenomenon, which seems peculiar to traditional Buddhists, of the so-called "adjunctive" use of meditation in psychotherapy (Naranjo, 1971; Assagioli, 1971; Luthe, 1970; Carrington & Ephron, 1975). In actual fact, techniques from all the major meditative traditions have either been incorporated intact or adapted for use in both in-patient and out-patient psychiatric treatment settings with reported success (Deatherage, 1975; Glueck & Stroebel, 1975; Bloomfield, 1977; Carrington & Ephron, 1975; Candelent & Candelent, 1975; Reynolds, 1976; Shapiro, 1976, Vahia *et al.*, 1973; Kabat-Zinn, 1982; Boorstein, 1983).

difference in psychoanalytic regression and the "return" of Buddhist insight

Insight meditation, like psychoanalysis and psychoanalytic psychotherapy, is an intervention designed *to set ego and object relations development in motion again* from a point of relative arrest (Loewald, 1960, Fleming, 1972). As in psychoanalysis, the process of "separating from outgrown levels of self-object ties" (Calef, 1972) is brought about by a controlled and partial return to more elemental ways of perceiving, conceptualizing, feeling and behaving. In psychoanalysis, this is a regression which takes form in an interpersonal relationship, the transference. The "return" that occurs in the classical stages of insight meditation, however, does not take the form of transference. It is not a re-living or re-experiencing of past stages of internalized object relations. It is *a controlled retracing of the stages in the representational process itself as this occurs in each present moment.* Viewed forward, the meditator is observing the perceptual-cognitive-affective pathways by which the "self" and "object" and an entire object relational world (which is the only world we ordinarily know) are constructed and come into being as a result of object-seeking and the operation of the pleasure principle. Viewed backward, the meditator is watching the de-construction or decomposition of "self" and "object" into their elementary components, processes or events *(dharmas)*. Insight meditation "reverses the way the world appears" (Eliade, 1969).[22]

A FULL-SPECTRUM MODEL
OF OBJECT RELATIONS DEVELOPMENT

But you have to be somebody before you can be nobody. The issue in personal development as I have come to understand it is not self *or* no-self, but self *and* no-self. *not "self" or "no-self" but self and no-self* Both a sense of self and insight into the ultimate illusoriness of its apparent continuity and substantiality are necessary achievements. Sanity and complete psychological well-being *include both, but in a phase-appropriate developmental sequence* at different stages of object relations development. The attempt to bypass the developmental tasks of identity formation and object constancy through a misguided spiritual attempt to "annihilate the ego" has fateful and pathological consequences. This is what many students who are drawn to meditation practice and even some teachers seem to be attempting to do.

What I think is needed, and what has been missing from both clinical and meditative perspectives, is a *developmental psychology that includes the full developmental spectrum.* From a clinical point of view, Buddhist psychology lacks this. It has little to say about the earlier stages of personality organization and the types of suffering that result from a failure to negotiate them. There are dangers when this is not understood. As in the classical period of psychoanalysis, before the self-disorders were properly understood, the prerequisites and limitations of the treatment will not be clearly recognized. There will be similar therapeutic failures, including "interminable" treatments (Freud, 1937), which will bewilder and frustrate and sadden teacher and student alike.

Western psychology in general and psychoanalytic theory in particular do not address the other end of the developmental spectrum. Their definitions of maturity and health reach no further than psychosocial identity, object constancy, mutuality in object relations, and more adaptive, less conflicted rearrangements of impulse and defense.

Buddhist
"developmental"
practices

According to current clinical thinking, therapy does not treat a disease entity in the older Kraepelinian medical model, but reinstitutes a derailed, arrested or distorted developmental process. Vipassana addresses the developmental process which it views as arrested at the level of identity and object constancy, and sets it in motion once again to reach a more ultimate view of the self and reality. There is no term "meditation" in Buddhist psychology. The term used instead for this body of practices and their outcomes is *"bhāvanā"* or *"development"* (Vajiranana, 1975). These practices can be, and were probably meant to be, in the service of *effecting a continuation of object relations development*. For Mahler as for other object relations theorists, the separation-individuation process is "never finished; it can always become reactivated; new phases of the life cycle witness new derivatives of the earliest process still at work" (1972:333). If, however, it is seen that both "self" and "objects" are functions of a certain level or stage of object relations development, and that in a more inclusive perspective there are no objects whose loss need be mourned and no self to mourn them, if *all* self-object ties have finally been "outgrown," then perhaps not only object relations development but mental suffering itself comes to an end (Engler, 1983b).

CONCLUSION

That, at any rate, is the conclusion I have come to at this point. My hope is that as Buddhist, Western and other ethnopsychiatric systems of clinical practice confront each other in our culture, often for the first time, a more integrated, full-spectrum model of human development, its vulnerabilities and the therapeutic interventions necessary to repair them, may result. From Freud's psychosexual stage-theory to Erikson's life cycle theory to Mahlerian object relations theory, this has been the thrust and aspiration of psychodynamic thought. Part of this thrust has been implicit but not articulated in Buddhist thought. The one tradition has emphasized the importance of becoming somebody; the other, the importance of becoming nobody. As I have come to understand it as a psychologist in both traditions, both a sense of self and a sense of no-self seem to be necessary—in that order—to realize that state of optimal psychological well-being which Freud once described as an "ideal fiction" and the Buddha long before him had already described as "the end of suffering" (*Cula-Malunkya-sutta*, M.63) and the one thing he taught.

becoming somebody and becoming nobody

CHAPTER 2

PSYCHIATRIC COMPLICATIONS OF MEDITATION PRACTICE

Mark D. Epstein
Jonathan D. Lieff

In this chapter, our simple division of the transpersonal realm into three broad stages is fleshed out and refined by Mark Epstein and Jonathan Lieff. They point out that the three general stages of transpersonal or contemplative development—preliminary, intermediate, and advanced—may each be vulnerable to particular types of psychiatric complications. Their classification is simple and concise, and is of immediate help in beginning to sort out the difficult issues that are raised once one starts examining the full spectrum of human development.

One of the more widespread examples of modern adaptations of traditional consciousness training practices is the recent popularity of age-old meditation techniques among both the lay public and workers in the mental health field (Marmor 1980; Walsh, 1980b). This comes at a time of relative estrangement between psychiatric and religious ideologies (Bergin, 1980) producing a conceptual gap that threatens an understanding of the meditative experience which may be demanded of therapists by patients or clients affected by these "consciousness disciplines" (Walsh, 1980b). Research on the meditative experience has focused on psychophysiological effects, with meditation viewed as a "self-regulation strategy," while attempts to understand or measure the subjective experience of the meditator have been conceptually and methodologically more demanding (Shapiro & Giber, 1978). Meditation has been proposed as a means of establishing mental health (Goleman, 1975) and as a possible adjunct in psychotherapy (Carpenter, 1977). What has not been made clear, however, is the range of side effects of meditative practices that may present to the clinician as psychological distur- bance. Some of these complications have already been noted by Western health professionals; others are only too well known within the meditative traditions. The more obvious misuses of meditation were hinted at by early psy- choanalytic investigators, while the more subtle abuses and psychological crises of the advanced practitioner have traditionally been handled by the meditation teacher. The authors have observed hundreds of meditators over the past ten years and offer the following observations.

PSYCHIATRIC COMPLICATIONS

general psychiatric complications of meditation practice

Complications of meditation practice have not gone un- noticed by Western clinicians although they tend to be lim- ited to gross pathology in beginning students. Deperson- alization and derealization experiences are reported by many practitioners to be ego-syntonic side effects of their meditations. In some cases, the feelings may be of such intensity as to necessitate psychiatric consultation (Ken- nedy, 1977) and may, by virtue of their foreignness, precip- itate panic attacks. Anxiety, tension, agitation and restless- ness may all be paradoxically increased through the practice of Transcendental Meditation (Lazuras, 1976; Otis cited in Walsh, 1978; Carrington & Ephron, Kanellakos & Lukas, cited in Shapiro, 1978). Exacerbations of depressive affect to the point of attempted suicide may also follow Transcendental Meditation experience (Lazuras, 1976). Precipitation of extreme euphoria accompanied by power- fully compelling fantasies and MMPI evidence of "exces- sive pressure from unconscious material" followed by "unbearable" dysphoria is described in a previously well 38-year-old woman following beginning practice of medi- tation (French, Schmid & Ingalls, 1975). "Grandiose fan- tasies" evolving into "religious delusions with messianic content" are described in a 24-year-old male following pro- longed meditation in an isolated environment (Levinson, 1973). Three psychotic episodes, characterized by agita- tion, paranoia and suicide attempts, are described in indi- viduals with a history of schizophrenia participating in intensive meditation retreats associated with fasting and sleep deprivation (Walsh & Roche, 1979). Two psychotic episodes, in young psychiatric patients with previous LSD experiences, are described after TM training (Glueck, in Carpenter, 1977).

The early stages of meditation practice, then, seem to contain potentially explosive experiences for some individuals. Familiarity with the progress of meditation, to be discussed later in this chapter, will facilitate differentiation of pathological from more ordinary responses to meditation, in the early as well as the more advanced stages of practice.

THEORETICAL CONSTRUCTS

Discussions of the side effects of meditation practice depend to a significant degree on the theoretical approach of the observer. Problems of culture bias and paradigm clash tend to limit the observations of Western behavioral scientists with regard to non-Western "consciousness disciplines" (Walsh, 1980b). Psychoanalytic conceptions of states reached through meditation tend to be two-fold. The first, expounded by Freud, actually alludes to an advanced stage of meditation practice "in which the mind is emptied of all mental contents and the person experiences pure conscious awareness . . . filled with the sense of mystical oneness . . ." (Nemiah, 1980). Freud associates this "oceanic" (Freud, 1930) experience with the most primitive stage in the development of the ego, that of undifferentiation between self and mother, or primary narcissism (Kohut, 1966). In this view, meditation is seen as a "libidinal, narcissistic turning of the urge for knowing inward, a sort of artificial schizophrenia with complete withdrawal of libidinal interest from the outside world" (Alexander, 1931, p. 130). The spiritual urge, postulated Freud, seeks a "restoration of limitless narcissism" (Freud, 1930, p. 19), an evocation of the outgrown mother-child bond employed as a kind of "transitional object" designed to protect against fears of separateness (Horton, 1973, 1974; Rizzuto, 1979).

problems of culture bias and paradigm clash

Other psychoanalytically oriented observers of meditation experiences, noting that primitive thoughts, feelings and fantasies of all kinds arise during meditation, including but not limited to "oceanic" ones, emphasize the concept of "regression in service of the ego" first proposed by Kris (1936; Shafii, 1973; Maupin, 1965; Allison, 1968). According to this view, the meditation experience offers the op-

regression in service of the ego portunity to ego-syntonically reexperience and reexamine unresolved conflicts and drives embodied in material which unfolds through the practice of meditation (Fingarette, 1958). These "adaptive" regressive states have been differentiated from pathological regressive states by virtue of their transitory, quickly reversible nature and their ability to increase self-esteem (Allison, 1968). In this view, meditation can be seen as an arena in which to uncover primitive material, with side effects resulting when ego strength is not sufficient to withstand the force of such material.

With this emphasis on the regressive nature of an experience seen as "intermediate between normality and frank psychosis" (GAP, 1976, p. 731), however, it becomes easy to ignore the possibility of transformation of ego structure so often alluded to in the traditional literature (Fingarette, 1958; Deikman, 1977; Podvoll, 1979; Walsh, 1980b). To do this means committing "the fallacy of assuming that the mystical state is 'nothing but' a pathological manifestation" (Runions, 1979, p. 149). Conversely, practitioners of

"pre/trans fallacy" meditation, often swimming in the rhetoric of transformation, may fail to recognize the regressive nature of much of their experiences. These two mutually exclusive world views have been labelled the "pre/trans fallacy" (Wilber, 1980b). Succumbing to this fallacy often brings about "a mixture and confusion of pre-egoic fantasy with trans-egoic vision, of pre-conceptual feelings with trans-conceptual insight, of prepersonal desires with transpersonal growth, of pre-egoic whoopee with trans-egoic liberation . . ." (Wilber, 1980b, p. 58).

meditation as a developmental process In fact, meditation experiences may embody all of the above. Confusion arises when meditation is analyzed as one discrete state, rather than as a developmental process. Just as in psychoanalysis, beginning stages involve regression, but higher stages are progressive and only accessible when the practitioner's ego is sufficiently intact to withstand the regressive upsurge (Fingarette, 1958). Similarly, some intermediate stages of meditation do indeed have a narcissistic flavor, but not all practitioners have the ego needs to interpret these experiences solely in narcissistic terms, and are able to move beyond these experiences.

Indeed, Kohut alludes to the potential metamorphosis of primitive narcissistic feelings into one of "cosmic narcissism" whose "bounds transcend the individual" (Kohut, 1966), a possibility criticized by some (Hanley & Masson, 1976). "A genuine decathexis of the self can only be achieved slowly by an intact, well-functioning ego; and it is accompanied by sadness as the cathexis is transferred from the cherished self upon the supraindividual ideals and upon the world with which one identifies" (Kohut, 1966, p. 267).

"cosmic narcissism"

Thus, an understanding of the developmental nature of the meditative experience, coupled with traditional descriptions of side effects, will enable a comprehensive view of both the limitations and applicability of the analytic models of meditation-induced psychiatric disorders.

DEVELOPMENTAL MODELS

Two different developmental models are helpful in understanding the range of meditation-induced side effects. The first, from traditional Buddhist sources (Nyanamoli, 1976; Mahasi Sayadaw, 1965; Goleman & Epstein, 1980; Goleman, 1977; Brown, 1977; Brown & Engler, 1980), indicates the range of meditation experiences possible and puts these experiences in a developmental framework. The second, from the schools of ego psychology (Vaillant, 1971, 1977; Loevinger, 1976; Wilber, 1981a), indicates stages in the development of the self and the mechanisms of defense or adaptation utilized at each stage. Thus, any meditation experience is prone to interpretation by the individual according to where he rests along the continuum of ego development.

two developmental models

attentional
restructuring

Meditation may be conceptualized as a process of attentional restructuring wherein the mind can be trained both in concentration, the ability to rest undisturbed on a single object, and in mindfulness, the ability to observe its own moment-to-moment nature, to pay attention undistractedly to a series of changing objects. This perceptual retraining allows a finely honed investigation of the rapidly changing self-concepts that perpetuate the sense of self.

Traditional models recognize a series of stages of meditation practice, summarized as follows:

stages of
meditation
practice

Preliminary practices. This stage involves the first confrontations of the naive meditator with his or her own psychic contents. In the process of trying to train the mind in rudimentary concentration, cognitive, affective and somatic disturbances arise which tend to distract and hinder the establishment of firm concentration.

Access concentration. This stage marks the first experience of fixity in the object of meditation, the first direct understanding of what is possible through meditation. Although the achievement is precarious, at this level sufficient concentration is present to allow either the moment-to-moment observation of changing mental objects or the transiently undistributed contemplation of a single object. From the point of view of the beginning student, this stage is often experienced as a great relief, allowing a sense of achievement.

Samadhi. With the single-minded cultivation of the factor of concentration, stages may be reached which are characterized by absorption in the object of meditation. Absorption may be of varying depths and qualities, but it is uniformly associated with a trance-like inattention to the outside world and subjective feelings of contentment, joy and equanimity.

Insight. Sustained observation of the moment-to-moment nature of the mind, which involves noticing of thoughts and feelings from the very instant of their inception to their dissolution, allows the acquisition of new "knowledge" about the nature of self, according to most meditative traditions. This knowledge, or insight, cannot be obtained without adequate perceptual training.

Rorschach studies of American meditation students and American and Asian meditation teachers tend to validate the stage model of meditation practice [see Chapter 6], emphasizing the point that the experience of one group, *i.e.*, Insight, should not be confused with that of another, *i.e.*, Preliminary practices.

I. Preliminary Practice

Preliminary practices of meditation are characterized by confrontation with, and a hypersensitivity to, emotional and cognitive material, often flavored with primary process character (Walsh, 1977; 1978). The experience of this stage is one of "adaptation to the flow of internal experience" (Brown & Engler, 1980, p. 170), including "fantasies, daydreaming, preconscious mental processes and body perception" (Shafii, 1973, p. 441) which "will occasionally express the drive-dominated content of organization of primary process cognition" (Maupin, 1965). Subjects uniformly report "unusual experiences, visual or auditory aberrations, 'hallucinations,' unusual somatic experiences and so on" (Kornfield, 1979). Indeed, meditators who are tolerant of these experiences, who have the capacity for regression and who are able to remain comfortable with these experiences, respond more successfully to the process of meditation than those without that capacity (Maupin, 1965).

characterization of preliminary practices

There is obviously a range of responses to such experiences. On the more primitive end of the continuum of ego development there are some whose precarious defense mechanisms cannot withstand the onslaught of this internal experience. Thus, the "psychotic defense mechanisms" (Vaillant, 1971, 1977) of denial, delusional projection and distortion may manifest (*e.g.*, *Walsh & Roche, 1979; Levinson, 1973; French et al. 1975;* Lazuras, 1976). Early meditation experiences may also fuel "immature" defense mechanisms of schizoid fantasy and hypochondriasis in that issues of interpersonal relationships are directed back into the internal meditative experience.

Others may uncover unresolved psychic conflicts or unexplored drives and have no means of working toward a resolution or greater understanding of such material. Traditional disciplines do not incorporate analysis of the psychological content of this material—meditators are instructed to focus on "process" rather than content in the effort to develop attentional capacities. Thus, some will

uncovering uncover psychological issues and not have a framework in
psychological which to work out this material. This lack of appropriate
issues outlet for the resolution of such issues leads to what the meditative traditions recognize as the major side effect of this stage of practice: an excessive fascination with and rumination over such internal experience. Thus, Western students of meditation seem to dwell in the preliminary stage much longer than their Eastern counterparts (Walsh, 1981; Brown & Engler, 1980).

Others use the approach of "detached observer" of
the "detached thoughts and feelings taught in most meditative traditions
observer" and to intellectualize and dissociate themselves from their li-
neurotic bidinal drives, or to engage in reaction formation whereby
defenses the opposites of such drives are embraced as natural products of new-found "spirituality." These neurotic defenses (Vaillant, 1971, 1977) are common methods of ego adaptation, and both therapists and meditation teachers need to be observant of their use by beginning meditation students. Still others may use more mature adaptive mechanisms of suppression, humor and sublimation with regard to uncovered material and utilize their discoveries in more traditional therapeutic contexts while not letting fascination with such material hinder their progress in meditation.

II. Access Concentration

When the stage of access concentration is reached, a dif-
meditative ferent perspective is gained with regard to the meditative
ambition experience. Relief from incessant immersion in the mind's

flow is momentarily obtained, with the perceptual power of concentration strengthened to allow the relaxing experience of "no-thought" or of the ground out of which mental events emerge. By nature a transitory experience, this first strengthening of concentration may become the object of meditative ambition.

From the point of view of the meditative traditions, straining too tightly to achieve this state can cause a paradoxical increase in anxiety and mental agitation, associated with such physical symptoms as upper back and neck pain. In Tibetan medical theory, this disorder, specifically defined as an obsessive-compulsive-like complication of meditation, is known as a disorder of *sok-rlung* (pron.: so-loong) or of the "life-bearing wind that supports the mind" (Epstein & Topgay). "Contemplating . . . too strenuously" (Leggett, 1964, p. 145) is seen as a precipitating factor in "Zen illness" and has also been linked to "counterproductive reactions" such as agitation (Walsh, 1978, p. 20) in other forms of meditation. The paradoxical anxiety reported in TM practitioners (Lazuras, 1976; Shapiro, 1978) may also be a symptom of this phenomenon. From the point of view of ego psychology, the temporary interruption of instinctual drives may fuel escapist tendencies of narcissistic tranquility (Ostow, 1967) or of dissociation from inner anxiety-provoking stimuli (Vaillant, 1977, p. 179).

"straining to achieve" and the increase of anxiety

The most appropriate use of access concentration, however, is as a stepping stone in the development of further concentration and insight. There are two major areas of meditative complications at these higher stages, one involving attachment to unusual tranquil states of luminous clarity and one involving the process of disidentification from traditional ego structures.

III. Samadhi and Insight

Higher stages of meditation contain numerous experiences, well catalogued in the traditional literature (Nyanamoli, 1976) and variously involving visions of bright lights, joyous and rapturous feelings of body and mind, tranquil-

attachment to higher stages of meditation

lity, lucid perceptions, and feelings of love and devotion. Termed the "ultraconscious" (Dean, 1973), "transcendental experience" (Walsh, 1980b), "mystic experience" (Runions, 1979) or "awakening of the kundalini" (Sannella, 1976), these states exert seductive influences which can become quite serious according to the meditative traditions. Termed "pseudo-nirvana" (Goleman, 1977; Goleman & Epstein, 1980) in the southern Buddhist tradition and "Makyo" or "diabolical enticements" in the Zen tradition (Kapleau, 1965), attachment to these states marks a major abuse of the meditative process. It is not until the pride and attachment, themselves, are made objects of meditation that the individual can pass beyond this stage.

inspection in search of the ego

At higher stages, when the perceptual capacity to discriminate very fine changes in moments of consciousness is developed, regression in service of the ego has become transmuted to inspection in search of the ego. A period characterized by the subjective experience of dissolution is entered where traditionally solid aspects of the personality begin to break up, leaving the meditator no solid ground to stand on. This is traditionally the time of spiritual crisis, characterized by "a great terror" (Nyanamoli, 1976, p. 753), the "Great Doubt" (Leggett, 1964) in Zen, and the struggle to allow a transformation or "decathexis" of the self.

CONCLUSION

Meditation may be conceptualized as a developmental process that may produce side effects anywhere along the continuum. Some of these side effects may be pathological in nature while some may be temporary distractions or hindrances. Psychiatric complications of the early stages of meditation have been noted in the Western literature, but Western commentary on the "spiritual crises" of the higher levels is noticeably absent. Most reported cases of pathological responses to meditation are in Western practitioners; no attempts to locate this phenomenon in traditional settings have been reported. Thus, there are many gaps in our understanding. How can innocuous side effects of meditation be differentiated from debilitating

gaps in our understanding

ones? Can the transformative crises of the higher levels of meditation practice be explained using the traditional psychodynamic framework? Are the pathological responses to meditation purely a Western phenomenon, or do such reports exist within the monasteries and ashrams of the East?

Practitioners and therapists alike need to recognize that meditation experiences may be used in both adaptive and defensive ways. It could be helpful for some therapists to develop the capacity to differentiate maladaptive responses to meditation from potentially adaptive ones. In this manner both psychological impediments to meditation development and meditation-inspired hindrances to personal development may be avoided.

differentiating adaptive and maladaptive responses

CHAPTER 3

THE SPECTRUM OF DEVELOPMENT

Ken Wilber

In the following three chapters, Ken Wilber presents a summary of his particular version of a full-spectrum model of human growth and development. This model has been developed in over a half-dozen books on the topic, and represents one of the more ambitious if speculative attempts to bridge conventional and contemplative schools of thought.

Wilber's model contains, in addition to the various lines of human development (affective, cognitive, moral, ego, object-relations, etc.), several dozen levels or stages of development, through which each of the various lines may progress. Consonant with the "overview" model presented in the Introduction, Wilber has limited his presentation to nine of the most basic and central levels (three each in the prepersonal, personal, and transpersonal realms).

In this chapter, Wilber briefly discusses each of these nine levels or stages, along with the self (or self-system) that is developing through these stages. In the next chapter, he discusses the particular pathologies that may arise at any of these levels; and in the following chapter, he suggests the types of treatment modalities or therapeutic interventions that seem most appropriate for each of these classes of pathology.

In a sense, Wilber's presentation serves as a bridge between Engler's and Epstein/Lieff's. Wilber discusses the three levels of "prepersonal" pathology noted by Engler (psychotic, borderline, and neurotic), the three levels of "transpersonal" pathology noted by Epstein and Lieff (beginning, access, and advanced), and then, based on recent research in cognitive and existential psychology, suggests three classes of pathology in the intermediate or "personal" realm.

This chapter is divided into two parts. In Part I, Wilber offers a brief overview of his spectrum model. In Part II, he presents a concise summary of the recent developments in psychoanalytic developmental psychology (including the work of Mahler, Kernberg, Blanck and Blanck, and Kohut). In the closing section, he attempts to point out just how closely these two models can be integrated, to mutual advantage, and this integration serves as the platform for the central discussions of Chapter 4 and Chapter 5.

I have, in a series of publications (Wilber, 1977; 1979; 1980a; 1981a; 1981b; 1983), attempted to develop an overall or spectrum model of psychology, one that is developmental, structural, hierarchical, and systems-oriented, and that draws equally on Eastern and Western schools. Vis-à-vis psychopathology the conclusion I reached was that the spectrum of consciousness is also a spectrum of (possible) pathology. If consciousness develops through a series of stages, then a developmental "lesion" at a particular stage would manifest itself as a particular type of psychopathology, and an understanding of the developmental nature of consciousness—its structures, stages, and dynamics— would prove indispensable to both diagnosis and treatment.

an outline summary of author's prior and present work

This presentation, therefore, offers an *outline summary* of both my prior work in this area and a present work-in-progress *(System, Self, and Structure)*. This is a somewhat hazardous undertaking because large amounts of material must be condensed into rather generalized and occasionally overly-simplified statements. Within these limitations, however, the following is a brief overview of this research and theory. Readers interested in more detailed presentations may wish to consult my other works.

This presentation reflects my growing conviction that developmental theory can benefit from the contribution of both conventional psychodynamic concepts and transpersonal approaches. Connections between such apparently divergent orientations may now be productive, given recent work in both areas. In fact, an adequate grasp of the full range of human capacities, from lowest to highest, may require a combined and integrated conception—one not less comprehensive than the model outlined here.

PART I: THE SPECTRUM OF CONSCIOUSNESS

In the model of psychological development that I have proposed, the structures or formations of the psyche are divided into two general types: the basic structures and the transition structures (each of which contains numerous different developmental lines). The *basic structures* are those structures that, once they emerge in development, tend to remain in existence as relatively autonomous units or sub-units in the course of subsequent development (similar to Koestler's "holons"). *Transition structures,* on the other hand, are phase-specific and phase-temporary structures that tend to be more or less entirely replaced by subsequent phases of development. That is, where particular basic structures tend to be subsumed, included, or subordinated in subsequent development, particular transition structures tend to be negated, dissolved, or replaced by subsequent development (I will give several examples below). Negotiating these structural developments is the self (or self-system), which is the locus of identification, volition, defense, organization, and "metabolism" ("digestion" of experience at each level of structural growth and development).

the "basic structures" and the "transition structures"

These three components—1) the basic structures, 2) the transition stages, and 3) the self-system—are central to the spectrum model of development and pathology, and so I will present a brief discussion of each.

The Basic Structures

The most notable feature about a basic structure or level of consciousness is that, once it emerges in human development, it tends to *remain in existence* in the life of the individual during subsequent development. Even though it is eventually transcended, subsumed, and subordinated by the self's movement to higher basic structures, it nevertheless retains a relative autonomy and functional independence.

basic structures as Great Chain of Being

The basic structures of consciousness are, in effect, what is known as the Great Chain of Being (Smith, 1976). Some versions of the Great Chain give only two levels (matter and spirit); others give three (matter, mind, and spirit); still others give four or five (matter, body, mind, soul, and spirit). Some are very sophisticated, giving literally dozens of the basic structures of the overall spectrum.

the construction of a master template

In *System, Self, and Structure* (and to a less precise degree in *Atman Project* and *Eye to Eye*), I present several dozen basic structures that seem, at this time, to be genuinely cross-cultural and universal. These were arrived at by a careful comparison and analysis of most of the major schools of psychology and religion, both East and West. The *structural* models of Freud, Jung, Piaget, Arieti, Werner, etc. were compared and contrasted with the structural models presented in the psychological systems of the world's contemplative traditions (Mahayana, Vedanta, Sufi, Kabalah, Christian mysticism, Platonism, Aurobindo, Free John, etc.). From these structural comparisons, a master template was constructed, with each tradition (East and West) filling in any "gaps" apparently left by the others.

This master template contains, as I said, several dozen basic structures, which span both conventional and contemplative development. For this presentation, I have selected what seem to be the nine most central and functionally dominant structures. These are depicted in Fig. 1. In Table 2, I have presented a few correlations (with Aurobindo, Yoga psychology, Mahayana, and Kabalah) to give a rough idea of the apparent universality of these major basic structures (*Atman Project* gives similar correlations among more than two dozen systems, East and West, and these are greatly refined in *System, Self, and Structure*).

The basic structures of consciousness development shown in Fig. 1 may be very briefly (and somewhat simplistically) outlined as follows (proceeding up the hierarchy):

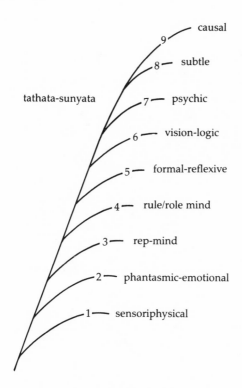

FIGURE 1
THE BASIC STRUCTURES OF CONSCIOUSNESS

1. *Sensoriphysical*—the realms of matter, sensation, and perception (the first three Buddhist *skandhas*); Piaget's sensorimotor level, Aurobindo's physical-sensory, etc.

2. *Phantasmic-emotional*—the emotional-sexual level (the sheath of bioenergy, *élan vital*, libido, or *prana*; the fourth Buddhist *skandha*, the *pranamayakosa* in Vedanta, etc.) and the phantasmic level (Arieti's [1967] term for the lower or *image* mind, the simplest form of mental "picturing" using only images). *— nine central functionally dominant basic structures*

3. *Rep-mind*—an abbreviation for "representational mind," or Piaget's preoperational thinking ("preop"). The rep-mind develops in two stages—that of *symbols* (2–4 yrs), and that of *concepts* (4–7 yrs) [Arieti, 1967; Piaget, 1977]. A symbol goes beyond a simple image (the phantasmic *— two-stage development of rep-mind structure*

TABLE 2
CORRELATION OF BASIC STRUCTURES OF CONSCIOUSNESS IN FOUR SYSTEMS

BASIC STRUCTURES	AUROBINDO	MAHAYANA	YOGIC CHAKRAS	KABALAH
Sensoriphysical	Physical subconscient		1. Physical world and instincts; hunger/thirst	Malkuth
Phantasmic-emotional	Vital-emotional	5 vijnanas (the 5 senses)	2. Emotional-sexual level	Yesod
Rep-mind	Will-mind (lower concepts; cf "preop")		3. Intentional mind; power	
Rule/role mind	Sense-mind (a concrete-based mind; cf "conop")	Manovijnana (the gross or concrete reflecting mind; coordinates senses)	4. Community-mind; love	Hod/Netzach
Formal-reflexive	Reasoning mind (not concrete-based; cf "formop")			
Vision-logic	Higher-mind (Mass-network Ideation/vision)	Manas (the higher mind; conveyor between individual mind and alaya-vijnana or collective mind)	5. Rational-verbal mind; communication	Tipareth
Psychic	Illumined mind		6. Ajna; "third eye"; psychic cognitions	
Subtle	Intuitive mind	Tainted-alayavijnana (collective-archetypal mind; vasanas-seeds)	7. Sahasrara; crown; beginning of higher "chakras" beyond and within the sahasrara	Geburah/Chesed Binah/Chokmah
Causal	Overmind	Pure Alaya	Shiva/Paramatman	Kether
Ultimate	Supermind			

mind) in this essential respect: an image represents an object pictorially, while a symbol can represent it nonpictorially or verbally. Thus, for example, the mental image of a tree looks more or less like a real tree, whereas the word-symbol "t-r-e-e" does not look like a tree at all; symbolic representation is a higher, more difficult, and more sophisticated cognitive operation. A *concept* is a symbol that represents, not just one object or act, but a *class* of objects or acts—an even more difficult cognitive task. A symbol denotes; a concept connotes. But no matter how advanced the rep-mind is over its phantasmic predecessor, one of its most striking features is that it *cannot easily take the role of other*. It is, as Piaget would say, still very egocentric. This is very similar to Aurobindo's "will-mind," the third chakra in Yoga psychology, etc.

4. *Rule/role mind*—This is, for example, Piaget's concrete operational thinking ("conop"). Conop, unlike its rep-mind predecessor, can begin to take the *role* of others. It is also the first structure that can clearly perform *rule* operations, such as multiplication, division, class inclusion, hierarchization, etc. (Flavell, 1970; Piaget, 1977). Aurobindo describes this structure as the mind that operates on sensory or concrete objects—very similar to Piaget.

5. *Formal-reflexive mind*—This is essentially Piaget's formal operational thinking ("formop"). It is the first structure that can not only think about the world but think about thinking; hence, it is the first structure that is clearly self-reflexive and introspective (although this begins in rudimentary form with the rule/role mind). It is also the first structure capable of hypothetico-deductive or propositional reasoning ("if a, then b"), which, among other things, allows it to take genuinely pluralistic and more universal views (Flavell, 1970; Piaget, 1977; Wilber, 1982). Aurobindo calls this level the "reasoning mind," a mind that is not bound to sensory or concrete objects, but instead apprehends and operates on *relationships* (which are not "things").

first structure to think about thinking

6. *Vision-logic*—Numerous psychologists (e.g., Bruner, Flavell, Arieti) have pointed out that there is much evidence for a cognitive structure beyond or higher than Pi-

highest integrative structure in the personal realm aget's "formal operational." It has been called "dialectical," "integrative," "creative synthetic," and so forth. I prefer the term "vision-logic." In any case, it appears that whereas the formal mind establishes relationships, vision-logic establishes *networks* of those relationships (i.e., just as formop "operates on" conop, so vision-logic "operates on" formop). Such vision or panoramic logic apprehends a mass network of ideas, how they influence each other and interrelate. It is thus the beginning of truly higher-order synthesizing capacity, of making connections, relating truths, coordinating ideas, integrating concepts. Interestingly, this is almost exactly what Aurobindo called "the higher mind," which "can freely express itself in single ideas, but its most characteristic movement is a mass ideation, a system or totality of truth-seeing at a single view; the relations of idea with idea, of truth with truth, self-seen in the integral whole." This, obviously, is a highly *integrative* structure; indeed, in my opinion it is the highest integrative structure in the *personal* realm; beyond it lie transpersonal developments.

lowest of the transcendental realms 7. *Psychic*—The psychic level may be thought of as the culmination of vision-logic and visionary insight; it is perhaps best epitomized by the sixth chakra, the "third eye," which is said to mark the beginning or opening of transcendental, transpersonal, or contemplative developments: the individual's cognitive and perceptual capacities apparently become so pluralistic and universal that they begin to "reach beyond" any narrowly personal or individual perspectives and concerns. According to most contemplative traditions, at this level an individual *begins* to learn to very subtly inspect the mind's cognitive and perceptual capacities, and thus to that extent begins to *transcend* them. This is Aurobindo's "illumined mind," the "preliminary stages" of meditation in Hinduism and Buddhism, etc. According to Aurobindo,

> The perceptual power of the inner [psychic] sight is greater and more direct than the perceptual power of thought. As the higher mind [i.e., vision-logic] brings a greater consciousness into the being than the idea and its power of truth [formop], so the illumined mind [psychic level] brings a still greater consciousness through a Truth sight and Truth Light and its seeing and seizing power; it illumines the thought-mind with

a direct inner vision and inspiration; it can embody a finer and bolder revealing outline and a larger comprehension and power of totality than thought-conception can manage.

8. *Subtle*—The subtle level is said to be the seat of actual archetypes, of Platonic Forms, of subtle sounds and audible illuminations *(nada, shabd)*, of transcendent insight and absorption (Aurobindo; Da Free John, 1977; Evans-Wentz, 1971; Guénon, 1945; Rieker, 1971). Some traditions, such as Hinduism and Gnosticism, claim that, according to direct phenomenological apprehension, this level is the home of personal deity-form *(ishtadeva* in Hinduism, *yidam* in Mahayana, *demiurge* in Gnosticism, etc.), cognized in a state known as *savikalpa samadhi* in Hinduism (Blofeld, 1970; Hixon, 1978; Jonas, 1958). In Theravadin Buddhism, this is the realm of the four *"jhanas* with form," or the four stages of concentrative meditation into archetypal "planes of illumination" or "Brahma realms." In *vipassana* meditation, this is the stage-realm of pseudonirvana, the realm of illumination and rapture and initial transcendental insight (Goleman, 1977; Nyanamoli, 1976). It is Aurobindo's "intuitive mind"; *geburah* and *chesed* in Kabalah, and so on. (My reasons for concluding that all of these phenomena share the same *deep structure* of subtle-level consciousness are given in *Eye to Eye* [Wilber, 1983].) *the subtle level in various traditions*

9. *Causal*—The causal level is said to be the unmanifest source or transcendental ground of all the lesser structures; the Abyss (Gnosticism), the Void (Mahayana), the Formless (Vedanta) (Chang, 1974; Deutsche, 1969; Jonas, 1958; Luk, 1962). It is realized in a state of consciousness known variously as *nirvikalpa samadhi* (Hinduism), *jnana samadhi* (Vedanta), the eighth of the ten ox-herding pictures (Zen); the seventh and eighth *jhanas;* the stage of effortless insight culminating in *nirvana (vipassana);* Aurobindo's "Overmind" (Da Free John, 1977; Goleman, 1977; Guénon, 1945; Kapleau, 1965; Taimni, 1975). Alternatively, this stage is described as a universal and formless Self (Atman), common in and to all beings (Hume, 1974; Schuon, 1975). Aurobindo: "When the Overmind [causal] descends, the predominance of the centralizing ego-sense is entirely subordinated, lost in largeness of being and finally abolished; a wide cosmic perception and feeling of bound- *the causal level in various traditions*

less universal self replaces it . . . an unlimited consciousness of unity which pervades everywhere . . . a being who is in essence one with the Supreme Self."

the ultimate as fundamental ground

10. *Ultimate*—Passing fully through the state of cessation or unmanifest causal absorption, consciousness is said finally to re-awaken to its prior and eternal abode as absolute Spirit, radiant and all-pervading, one and many, only and all—the complete integration and identity of manifest Form with the unmanifest Formless. This is classical *sahaj* and *bhava samadhi;* the state of *turiya* (and *turiyatita)*, absolute and unqualifiable Consciousness as Such, Aurobindo's "Supermind," Zen's "One Mind," Brahman-Atman, the *Svabhavikakaya* (Chang, 1974; Da Free John, 1978; Hixon, 1978; Kapleau, 1965; Mukerjee, 1971). Strictly speaking, the ultimate is not one level among others, but the reality, condition, or suchness of all levels. By analogy, the paper on which Fig. 1 is drawn represents this fundamental ground of empty-suchness.

additional remarks on basic "levels"

Allow me to make a few additional remarks on those levels, particularly the higher or transpersonal stages (7 through 10). In *System, Self, and Structure,* I present seven transpersonal stages (low and high psychic, low and high subtle, low and high causal, and ultimate), each divided into three substages (beginning or preliminary, access or practicing, and culmination or mastery), for a total of twenty-one contemplative stages (similarly, there are several dozen lower and intermediate stages and substages, which have been condensed here into six major levels). I do believe, however, that the nine major levels presented in Fig. 1 are *functionally dominant in development,* and that an adequate and fairly accurate account of development can be presented with just these nine general levels—their selection, in other words, is not entirely arbitrary (there is considerable support in the *philosophia perennis* for such "functional condensation"; Vedanta, for instance, maintains that the literally dozens of stages of overall development are functionally and structurally dominated by only five major levels, and these in turn are condensed and manifested in only three major states—gross, subtle, and causal. It is a slightly expanded version of this view that I am here representing).

More arbitrary, however, is my particular wording and description of the major stages themselves, particularly the higher or transpersonal ones. More precise descriptions and explanations of these stages can be found in *System, Self, and Structure*. The reader may also consult Chapter 8, where Daniel Brown gives a detailed explanation of some eighteen stages in transpersonal development. I should only like to point out that my contemplative cartography and Brown's are in broad and substantial agreement, reflecting the growing research and conclusion that "upon close inspection of the classical texts, the sequence of experiences reported within the concentration meditation traditions and the changes reported within the mindfulness approaches do *not* vary greatly from one meditation system to the next. Although there were noticeable differences in the progression of meditation experiences, the phenomenological reports themselves exhibited a highly similar underlying psychological organization when analyzed longitudinally (i.e., along the progression of experiences taking place from the beginning through the end of a meditative path)" (Maliszewski *et al.*, 1981). These similarities—what I call "deep structures" as opposed to "surface structures"—are here condensed and represented as four major transpersonal stages—psychic, subtle, causal, and ultimate.

condensing major higher "basic stages" into four

The Transition Stages (or Self-Stages)

The transition structures are ones that are not included and subsumed in subsequent development but tend instead to be negated, dissolved, or *replaced* by subsequent development. Take, for example, the works of Piaget and Kohlberg. Piaget's cognitive structures are, for the most part, *basic* structures (sensorimotor is level 1–2, preoperational is 3, concrete operational is 4, and formal operational is 5). Once these levels come into existence, they remain in existence during subsequent development; in fact, each level becomes, in Piaget's system, the operand or "object" of the next higher level. Thus a person at, say, basic level 5 has *simultaneous* access to, and use of, levels 1 through 4; they are all still present, and all still performing their necessary and appropriate tasks and functions.

transition structures as self-stages

Kohlberg's moral stages, however, are phase-specific *transition* structures: someone at, say, moral stage 3 does not simultaneously act equally from stage 1. Stage 3 *replaced* stage 2, which replaced stage 1, and so on. Although the moral transition structures depend on or "rest on" the basic cognitive structures (as both Piaget and Kohlberg have pointed out), the two otherwise refer to different types of structures (i.e., basic and transitional).

the metaphor of the ladder A simple metaphor may be useful to explain this distinction. The basic structures themselves are like a ladder, each rung of which is a level in the Great Chain of Being. The self (or the self-system) is the climber of the ladder. At each rung of that climb, the self has a different view or perspective on reality, a different sense of identity, a different type of morality, a different set of self-needs, and so on. These changes in the sense of self and its reality, which shift from level to level, are referred to as transition structures, or, more often, as the *self-stages* (since these transitions intimately involve the self and its sense of reality).

Thus, as the self climbs from say, rung 4 to rung 5, its limited perspective at rung 4 is *replaced* by a new perspective at rung 5. Rung 4 itself *remains in existence*, but the limitations of its perspective do not. That is why the basic structures of consciousness are more or less *enduring* structures, but the self-stages are transitional, temporary, or phase-specific.

support function of basic structures Each basic structure, then, *supports* various phase-specific transitional structures or self-stages, such as different self-needs (investigated by Maslow), different self-identities (investigated by Loevinger), and different sets of moral responses (investigated by Kohlberg). In Table 3, I have for convenience included the basic structures of consciousness with some of their correlative (and transitional) self-needs, self-identities, and self-moralities, based on the work of Maslow, Loevinger, and Kohlberg. Thus, for example, when the self is *identified* with the rule/role level, its self-need is for belongingness, its self-sense is conformist, and its moral sense is conventional; when (and if) it subsequently *identifies* with the formal-reflexive level, its need is for self-esteem, its self-sense is individualistic, its

TABLE 3

CORRELATION OF BASIC STRUCTURES OF CONSCIOUSNESS WITH THREE ASPECTS OF THE SELF-STAGES

BASIC STRUCTURE	MASLOW (SELF-NEEDS)	LOEVINGER (SELF-SENSE)	KOHLBERG (MORAL SENSE)
Sensoriphysical	(Physiological)	Autistic	(Premoral)
		Symbiotic	0. Magic wish
Phantasmic-emotional		Beginning impulsive	1. Punishment/obedience
Rep-mind	Safety	Impulsive	I. Preconventional
		Self-protective	2. Naive hedonism
Rule/role mind	Belongingness	Conformist	3. Approval of others
		Conscientious-conformist	II. Conventional
Formal-reflexive	Self-esteem	Conscientious	4. Law and order
		Individualistic	III. Postconventional
Vision-logic	Self-actualization	Autonomous	5. Individual rights
		Integrated	6. Individual principles of conscience
Psychic	Self-transcendence		
			Kohlberg has recently suggested a higher, seventh stage:
Subtle	Self-transcendence		7. Universal-spiritual
Causal	Self-transcendence		

moral sense is postconventional, and so on. *(System, Self, and Structure* presents similar correlations with the works of Fowler; Erikson; Broughton; Selman; Graves; Peck; and others. For this presentation I have selected Maslow, Loevinger, and Kohlberg as examples, simply because their work is probably best known. [For the possible relation of these different aspects of the self-stages to each other, see Loevinger, 1976.] Notice that the scales of Kohlberg and Loevinger "run out" around level 5 or 6, reflecting the neglect of most conventional researchers for the transpersonal stages of self-development).

The Self-System

the "climber" of the ladder as the self-system

So far, we have briefly examined the basic rungs or levels in the overall ladder of development, and the transition stages (or self-stages) that occur as the self "climbs" or progresses through those rungs in the course of its own growth. We turn now to the climber itself: the self (or self-system or self-structure). Drawing on the research of numerous and varied theorists and clinicians, I have postulated that the self-system possesses the following basic characteristics:

1. *Identification*—The self is the locus of identification, the locus of what the self will call the "I/me" versus the "not-I/me." I sometimes divide the overall or total self-system (what Freud called the "Gesamt-Ich") into the *central* or *proximate self* (which is experienced as "I") and the *distal self* (which is experienced as "me"); the former is the subjective self, the latter, the objective self, though both are phenomenologically felt as the Gesamt-Ich.

2. *Organization*—As in scholastic philosophy, the self is that which gives (or attempts to give) unity to the mind; this is almost identical to the modern psychoanalytic concept of the self as "the process of organizing": "The self is not merely a synthesis of the underlying psychic parts or substructures, but an *independent organizing* principle, a 'frame of reference' against which to measure the activities or states of these substructures" (Brandt, 1980).

3. *Will*—The self is the locus of free choice, but free only within the limits set by the basic structures of its present level of adaptation (e.g., the self at rung 3, or preop, is not free to form hypotheses, which occur at rung 5 or formop).

4. *Defense*—The self is the locus of the defense mechanisms (which develop and change hierarchically from level to level of the basic structures); defense mechanisms in general are considered normal, necessary, and phase-appropriate functions; however, if over- or under-employed, they become morbid or pathological.

characteristics of the self-system

5. *Metabolism*—One of the central tasks of the self is to "digest" or "metabolize" the experiences presented to it at each rung of development. "The basic assumption of developmental theory is that experience must become 'metabolized' to form structure." Object relations theorists, such as Guntrip (1971), speak of pathology as "failed metabolism"—the self fails to digest and assimilate significant past experiences, and these remain lodged, like a bit of undigested meat, in the self-system, generating psychological indigestion (pathology). The basic structures of consciousness, in fact, can be conceived as *levels of food*—physical food, emotional food, mental food, spiritual food. These levels of food, as we will see, are really levels of object relations, and how the self handles these "food-objects" ("self-objects") is a central factor in psychopathology.

6. *Navigation*—At any rung on the developmental ladder (except the two end points), the self is faced with several different "directional pulls." On the one hand, it can (within limits) choose to remain on its present level of development, or it can choose to release its present level in favor of another. If it releases its present level, it can move up the hierarchy of basic structures or it can move down. *On* a given level, then, the self is faced with preservation vs. negation, holding on vs. letting go, living that level vs. dying to that level, identifying with it vs. dis-identifying with it. *Between* levels the self is faced with ascent vs. descent, progression vs. regression, moving up the hierarchy to levels of increasing structuralization, increasing differ-

entiation-and-integration, or moving down to less organized, less differentiated and less integrated structures.
These four "drives" are represented in Fig. 2.

Summary of Overall Development

overall development summarized

We can now summarize the form of overall development
as follows: As the basic structures or rungs begin chrono-
logically to emerge and develop, the self can *identify* with
them (becoming, in turn, a physical self, an emotional-
body self, a mental self, and so on). Once centrally identified with a particular basic structure, the self, or the self's
preservation drive, will seek to consolidate, integrate, and
organize the resultant overall complex. This initial identification with a particular basic structure is normal, necessary, and phase-appropriate, and it gives rise to the particular self-stage (impulsive, conformist, individualistic, etc.)
associated with or supported by that basic structure (see
Table 3 for corrolations).

If, however, the central self is to ascend the hierarchy of
basic structural development—to grow—then eventually
it must release or negate its *exclusive* identification with its
present basic rung in order to identify with the next higher
rung in the developmental ladder. It must accept the
"death," negation, or release of the lower level—it must

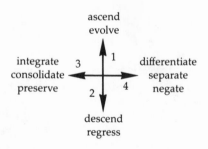

FIGURE 2
FOUR "DRIVES" AFFECTING THE SELF-STAGES

dis-identify with or detach from an exclusive involvement with that level—in order to ascend to the greater unity, differentiation, and integration of the next higher basic level.

Once identified with the new and higher basic structure, a new and phase-specific self-stage swings into existence: a new self-sense, with new self-needs, new moral sensibilities, new object relations, new forms of life, new forms of death, new forms of "food" to be metabolized, and so forth. The lower self-stage is (barring fixation) released and negated, but the lower basic structure remains in existence as a necessary rung in the ladder of consciousness, and must therefore be *integrated* in the overall newly configured individual. Once on the new and higher level, the self then seeks to consolidate, fortify, and preserve *that* level, until it is once again strong enough to die to that level, *transcend* that level (release or negate it), and so ascend to the next developmental rung. Thus, both preservation and negation (or life and death) apparently have important phase-specific tasks to accomplish.

developmental ladder and the self

It is fascinating to note that modern psychoanalytic ego psychology has come to an almost identical view. The dual-instinct theory, in fact, has evolved into a theory of *eros* as an integrating, consolidating, pulling-together, or preserving force, and aggression *(thanatos)* as a differentiating, separating, dissolving, or negating force—both of which are phase-specifically appropriate for overall development. This view began with Freud's 1940 reformulation:

similarities to modern ego psychology

> The aim of the first of these basic instincts [preservation] is to establish ever greater unities and to preserve them thus—in short, to bind together; the aim of the second [negation] is, on the contrary, to undo connections [dissolve or negate them].

Heinz Hartmann (1958) took the next step:

> Differentiation [separation-negation] must be recognized, along with synthesis [integration-preservation] as an important function of the ego. Since we somehow connect the synthetic function of the ego with the libido, it is plausible to assume an analogous relationship between differentiation and destruction, particularly since Freud's recent inferences about the role of free aggression in mental life.

Blanck & Blanck (1974) summarize the most recent view: "Libido will seek connection while aggression will seek and maintain separation and individuation." Aggression or negation, in other words, need no longer be viewed as merely or even predominantly hostile or destructive. Erikson proposed the term "aggressivity" to connote "those aspects of the aggressive drive which are growth promoting and self-assertive rather than hostile and destructive" (in Blanck & Blanck, 1974). In other words, there is "healthy aggression" as well as "morbid aggression," just as there is "healthy preservation" as well as "morbid preservation."

preservation and negation as phase-specific tasks Accordingly, it may be concluded that preservation and negation both serve important phase-specific tasks, and that *pathology seems to develop if either (or both) of these tasks is misnavigated*. "Healthy" or "normal" preservation occurs when the identifications and object relations of a particular level are being built, consolidated, and integrated ("neutralized libido builds object relations" [Blanck & Blanck, 1974]). Morbid preservation, on the other hand, occurs when the once-appropriate identifications and object relations of a particular level are not released to allow room for newer and higher ones. Morbid preservation, in other words, is nothing but *fixation*.

Healthy or normal negation serves several important functions. *Horizontally*, it helps differentiate self and object representations ("neutralized aggression powers the developmental thrust toward separation-individuation" [Blanck & Blanck, 1974]); *vertically*, it helps the disidentification, differentiation, separation, or transcendence of a lower level in favor of a higher. Morbid negation, on the other hand, is a differentiation or dis-identification from a component before it has been properly integrated, digested, and assimilated. The component is merely split off from the personality. Morbid negation, in other words, is simply *repression* (or dissociation, splitting, etc., depending upon the level of structural organization of the defense itself).

Such is a brief background summary of the spectrum model—its basic structures, the self-system, the self-stages, and repression/fixation. We can now turn our attention to a similar background summary for the recent developments in psychoanalytic ego psychology.

PART II: THE CONVENTIONAL BACKGROUND

In this section I will present a short overview of some of the newer developments in conventional psychology and psychiatry, particularly those schools known as object-relations theory, self psychology, and psychoanalytic ego psychology. For these schools, too, have increasingly adopted a *developmental* perspective, and I will briefly summarize the various stages of self-development as they conceive them. Since these schools are *particularly interested in psychopathology and its treatment,* we will also begin to focus more intently on pathology and its genesis.

overview of newer developments in conventional psychology

Towards the end of this section, I will begin to point out how these conventional stages fit in the overall spectrum of development outlined in Part I. But perhaps we can say this much in advance: These conventional schools are in general agreement that there are three broad levels or stages of self-development in the prepersonal realm (that is, leading up to and including the oedipal phase, at around age 5–7 yrs). I will try to show that these three general stages occur as the self negotiates the first three basic rungs of development (as shown in Fig. 1). Conventional psychology and psychiatry have investigated these three general stages (and their numerous substages) in great detail, and have also attempted to demonstrate that a developmental "lesion" at a particular stage tends to give rise to a particular type of psychopathology. I will attempt to summarize this research, and then fit it explicitly with the spectrum model outlined in Part I. It is this integration or synthesis that will form the platform for the discussions in Chapters 4 and 5.

The following section is necessarily technical and therefore somewhat abstruse. I have therefore included a fairly jargon-free, nontechnical summary, beginning on page 101. Those unfamiliar with psychoanalytic ego psychology may wish to skip to that summary now, and then come back and read as much of this section as desired.

The Developmental Dimensions of Psychopathology

recent explosion of theorizing and research

During the past two decades, an explosion of theorizing and research has occurred in conventional psychoanalytic psychiatry, principally surrounding three closely related schools, generally known as psychoanalytic developmental psychology (Mahler, 1975; Kernberg, 1975; Blanck & Blanck, 1979), object-relations theory (Fairbairn, 1954; Winnicott, 1965; Guntrip, 1971), and self psychology (Kohut, 1971). The excitement and interest these schools have generated are apparent in such comments as that there has recently occurred a "quantum leap in the understanding of psychopathology" (Masterson, 1981); these advances represent "perhaps the major discovery of research into personality problems in this century" (Guntrip, 1971). Some of these discoveries are indeed monumental, and may of necessity become fundamental elements in any comprehensive psychology—including transpersonal psychology. Yet, taken in and by themselves, they possess certain grave limitations and distortions, upon which it would be unwise to base a *comprehensive* developmental psychology. What follows, then, is an attempt to outline the important aspects of these recent developments as well as what seem to be their limitations and even confusions.

area of major breakthrough

The major breakthrough, so to speak, has come in the clinical investigation and treatment of the so-called borderline and narcissistic disorders. These disorders are in contrast to the classical psychoneuroses (hysteria, obsessive-compulsive neuroses, anxiety neuroses, etc.). The major difference between the psychoneuroses and the borderline-narcissistic disorders is that in the psychoneuroses, there is some sort of conflict or repression *within* the self-structure (the ego, for instance, *represses* some id impulse), whereas in the borderline and narcissistic conditions, there is too little self-structure to perform repression. On the contrary, the self-structure (or self-system) is so weak, so underdeveloped, so fluid that its self and object representations merge or fuse; the self is overwhelmed by world-engulfment or fears of annihilation; or, alternatively, it treats objects and persons as mere extensions of its own grandiose world-fusion self. The term "borderline" means, roughly, that the syndrome is borderline between neuroses and psychoses; there is thus an overall continuum of increasing severity: neurotic, borderline neurotic, borderline, borderline psychotic, psychotic (Blanck & Blanck, 1979; Gedo, 1979; Tolpin, 1971).

Traditionally it had been thought that the borderline and narcissistic syndromes could not effectively be treated by standard psychoanalytic or psychotherapeutic techniques. Part of the recent "quantum leap," however, has involved the development of treatment modalities that have proven surprisingly effective with the borderline-narcissistic conditions. These treatment modalities developed out of three closely interrelated strands of research: 1) a detailed clinical description of the "archaic transferences" of borderline-narcissistic patients (spearheaded by Kohut [1971]); 2) sophisticated theoretical reformulations of the early stages (0–3 yrs) of development, and a consequent view of pathology as developmental arrest or distortion at qualitatively different levels of structural organization (Spitz, 1965; Jacobson, 1964; Mahler, 1975; Kernberg, 1976; Masterson, 1981, Blanck & Blanck, 1974); and 3) extremely meticulous observation and description of the earliest years of infant development (here the pioneering work of Margaret Mahler is recognized).

*development of
new treatment
modalities*

Because the research of Mahler and her associates has been so pivotal—not only in furthering our understanding of the earliest stages of self-development, but also in illuminating the etiology of the borderline-narcissistic syndromes—a brief outline of her key discoveries will be useful here.

Infant Development: The Work of Margaret Mahler

In almost two decades of what can only be called brilliant clinical research, Mahler concluded that the development of the self-structure in infants (0–3 yrs) generally proceeds through three phases: autistic, symbiotic, and separation-individuation, the last of which is divided into four subphases: differentiation, practicing, rapprochement, and

*Mahler's
chronology of
development*

consolidation, giving six overall stages. In chronological order, they are (all following quotes are from Mahler, 1975):

1. *Autistic phase* (0–1 month)—"The first weeks of extra-uterine life, during which the neonate appears to be an almost purely biological organism, his instinctual responses to stimuli being reflexive and thalamic. During this phase we can speak only of primitive unintegrated ego apparatuses and purely somatic defense mechanisms, consisting of overflow and discharge reactions, the goal of which is the maintenance of homeostatic equilibrium. The libido position is a predominantly visceral one with no discrimination between inside and outside." Mahler refers to this as a "closed monadic system" or a "primal undifferentiated matrix."

neonatal phases

2. *Symbiotic phase* (1–5 months)—"From the second month on, the infant behaves and functions as though he and his mother were an omnipotent system—a dual unity within one common boundary." This is a "state of undifferentiation, of fusion with mother, in which the 'I' is not yet differentiated from the 'not-I' and in which inside and outside are only gradually coming to be sensed as different." At this stage, the infant behaves as if it cannot even clearly distinguish its sensoriphysical body from the mother's and from the environment at large. "The essential feature of symbiosis is somatopsychic omnipotent fusion with the representation of the mother and, in particular, the delusion of a common boundary between two physically separate individuals."

3. *Differentiation subphase* (5–9 months)—This stage is marked by what Mahler calls "hatching": the infant's *sensoriphysical bodyself* "hatches" or wakes up from its previous, symbiotic, fused or dual unity with the mother and the sensoriphysical surround. At this stage, "all normal infants take their first tentative steps toward breaking away, in a *bodily sense*, from their hitherto completely passive lap-babyhood. . . . There are definite signs that the baby begins to differentiate his own [body] from the mother's body."

the "hatching" subphase

Notice that this particular differentiation is basically of the sensoriphysical bodyself from its surroundings, because the infant's mind (the newly emerging phantasmic or image level) and its feelings (the emotional-sexual level) are *not* yet differentiated from their surroundings. The infant exists as a distinct sensoriphysical bodyself but not as a *distinct* phantasmic-emotional self, because its emotional self-images and emotional object-images are still fused or merged. As we will see, it is only at the rapprochement subphase that this "psychological birth" or separation-differentiation occurs.

4. *Practicing subphase* (9–15 months)—This stage is significant because it seems to mark the peak of grandiose-exhibitionistic narcissism, with the world being, as Mahler puts it, "the junior toddler's oyster." "Libidinal cathexis shifts substantially into the service of the rapidly growing autonomous ego and its functions, and the child seems intoxicated with his own faculties and with the greatness of his own world. Narcissism is at its peak! He is exhilarated by his own abilities, continually delighted with the discoveries he makes in his expanding world, and quasi-enamored with the world and his own grandeur and omnipotence." According to Blanck & Blanck (1979), at this stage "the self continues to accumulate value by magical absorption of the larger world into its image." Technically speaking, self and object representations are still a fused unit.

narcissism at its peak

5. *Rapprochement subphase* (15–24 months)—This stage, according to Mahler, is crucial to future development, for this is the stage in which there occurs the first major differentiation of self and object representations. This means that a *separate and distinct phantasmic-emotional self* has finally emerged and clearly differentiated itself from its emotional-libidinal object representations. This, in other words, is "the psychological birth of the human infant." To conceptualize it within the basic structures, there is first simple birth; then "hatching," or the birth of a distinct sensoriperceptual bodyself; and then the rapprochement crisis, or the birth of a distinct phantasmic-emotional or "psychological" self.

"the psychological birth of the human infant"

Concomitant with this birth, there is a marked loss of the grandiose-omnipotent narcissistic fused self-and-object units of the previous (practicing) stage, and a correlative vulnerability to heightened separation anxiety and abandonment depression. "The narcissistic inflation of the practicing subphase is slowly replaced by a growing realization of [phantasmic-emotional] separateness and, with *"paradise lost"* it, vulnerability. It often culminates in a more or less transient rapprochement crisis which is of great developmental significance," for the infant "must gradually and painfully give up the delusion of his own grandeur." Because there is now a separate self, there is now a separate other—the world is no longer its oyster. Researchers are fond of saying that at this stage, paradise has been lost.

But although the phantasmic-emotional body-mind of the infant is now differentiated from the "other," the infant's mind and body are themselves not yet differentiated; there is still mind-body fusion; it is only at the oedipal stage, as we will see, that the mind and body finally differentiate within the separate organism.

6. *Consolidation and emotional object constancy* (24–36 months)—This final subphase is the consolidation of the *attainment of* separation-individuation process and the attainment of *emotional object* "emotional-libidinal object constancy." It is normally *constancy* marked by 1) a clear and relatively enduring differentiation of self and object representations; 2) the integration of part-self images into a whole-self representation (which includes both "good" and "bad" aspects of the self); and 3) the integration of part-object images into whole-object representations (which include both "good" and "bad" aspects of emotional-libidinal objects).

Such, then, are the six normal stages of the psychological birth of the human infant, as presented by Mahler.

The Fulcrum of Development: The Work of Blanck & Blanck

Mahler has presented extensive clinical evidence (1975) that infantile psychoses has as its major etiological factor a developmental "lesion" in the autistic-symbiotic phases

(the infant fails to "hatch" or emerge as a separate sensoriphysical bodyself, but rather remains in the "closed monadic system" of the autistic phase or founders in the "omnipotent dual unity" of the symbiotic phase).

However, Mahler believes the borderline syndromes have
their major etiology in a rapprochement subphase lesion.
The self-structure fails to clearly differentiate-separate *borderline*
from the grandiose-omnipotent fused unit of the previous *syndromes and*
symbiotic and practicing subphases; this developmental *developmental*
arrest or lesion in self-structuralization leaves the border- *"lesion"*
line open to emotional engulfment, flooding, fusion panic,
or self-and-object grandiosity. Because there are defects in
self-structuralization at this primitive level of organization,
the borderline does not have access to higher or neurotic
defense mechanisms (repression, rationalization, displacement), but instead must rely on the primitive or less-than-
neurotic defenses (particularly splitting, denial, introjec-
tion and projection).

On the other hand, as Blanck & Blanck (1979) summarize
it, "If the symbiotic phase and the subphases of separation-individuation are experienced adequately, the child
reaches the point of true identity—that of differentiation
between self and object representations, and the capacity
to retain the representation of the object independent of
the state of need [that is the definition of 'emotional object
constancy']. Structuralization proceeds to normalcy or, at
worst, neurosis; borderline pathology is avoided." If this *the fulcrum of*
stage of separation-individuation is reached and resolved, *development*
the self-structure is then strong enough and individuated
enough *to be able* to create a neurosis; the oedipal phase
can then be engaged and either adequately resolved (normalcy) or misnavigated (psychoneuroses). On the other
hand, if this separation-individuation phase is not adequately resolved, the individual self remains "less-than-
neurotically structured," or borderline.

So central is this separation-individuation phase in general
(and the rapprochement subphase in particular), that
Blanck & Blanck (1979) call it "the fulcrum of development," and they represent it with a diagram (which they
call "self-object differentiation"), similar to Fig. 3.

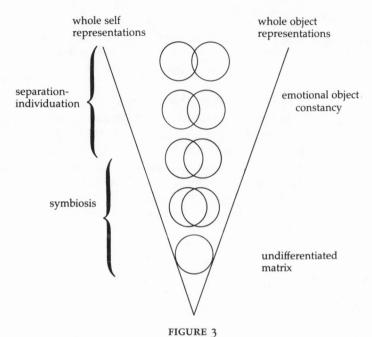

whole self
representations

whole object
representations

separation-
individuation

emotional object
constancy

symbiosis

undifferentiated
matrix

FIGURE 3
"SELF-OBJECT DIFFERENTIATION" AS PRESENTED IN BLANCK
& BLANCK, 1979

In effect, that diagram represents the major discoveries of the recent "quantum leap" in ego and object-relations theory. However, it can be further refined by including, not just the separation-individuation of the phantasmic-emotional self, but also the *previous* differentiation or "hatching" of the sensoriphysical bodyself. Blanck & Blanck (indeed, most developmental researchers) fail to adequately stress that these are two *qualitatively distinct* levels of differentiation, and thus should not be pictured as *one* continuum, as Blanck & Blanck do, but as two distinct continua as shown in Fig. 4. Where the second fulcrum leads to *emotional* object constancy, the first fulcrum leads to *physical* object constancy.

the first
fulcrum as the
"hatching
stage"

The first fulcrum (autistic, symbiotic, and differentiating subphases) is the "hatching" stage, during which the self-system must negotiate the emergence of the physical and sensoriperceptual basic structures of existence. Should this hatching fail, the self remains locked in its own autistic-

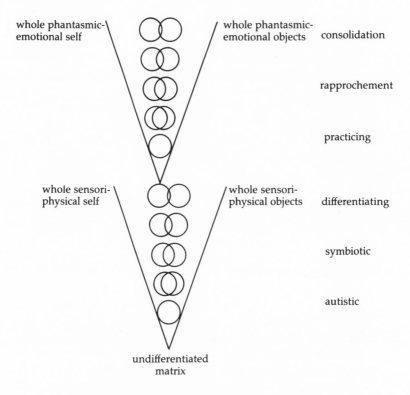

whole phantasmic-emotional self

whole phantasmic-emotional objects

consolidation

rapprochement

practicing

whole sensori-physical self

whole sensori-physical objects

differentiating

symbiotic

autistic

undifferentiated matrix

FIGURE 4

SELF-DIFFERENTIATION IN FULCRUMS 1 AND 2

symbiotic orbit, unable, in the worst cases, to even differentiate its sensoriphysical self from the sensoriphysical surround (autistic and symbiotic psychoses); consequently it cannot advance to the second major fulcrum, that of phantasmic-emotional separation-individuation.

Should it negotiate this first fulcrum adequately, however, the sensoriphysical organism is adequately differentiated from the sensoriphysical surround. At this point, the self enters the second fulcrum of development, where it must negotiate the emergence and growth of the next major basic structures of existence, the emotional and phantasmic. This involves a differentiation, not between the organism and the environment, but within the organism itself—namely, a differentiation of internalized self-images from internalized object-images. This is represented in Fig. 4 by

emergence of the phantasmic-emotional as the second fulcrum

setting the second fulcrum on the left edge of the first fulcrum, as indicated by the arrow. The arrow also indicates that at this point there is a general *emergence* of the next, new and higher basic structures of existence, in this case, the phantasmic-emotional. It is exactly this new emergence that results in a new and higher fusion state, which itself must be separated-differentiated at a new and higher level of self-structuralization (in this case, the second fulcrum).

The work of Edith Jacobson (1964) as well as Mahler (1972) and Spitz (1965) bears out this interpretation. As Abend (1983) put it, "Jacobson's work stressed that at [the earliest or autistic-symbiotic] stage there is no clear differentiation between [the infant] as a separate [bodily] entity and the outside world. He may not as yet be aware that his own tension states come from his own body or that his gratifications and easing of psychological tension are afforded him by someone other than himself [this is during the first fulcrum]. Gradually, however, there must be a building up of *mental* [phantasmic] *images* of the self and the outside world [the emergence of the second fulcrum] along with *sensory* perceptions of the self and the other [the first fulcrum]. This later stage [i.e., the second fulcrum], however, is one during which the self-representation and the object-representation are likely to be distorted [merged or fused] as a result of projective and introjective mechanisms." The second fulcrum, in other words, involves a new, higher, and qualitatively different state of fusion (phantasmic-emotional) from that of the first (sensori-perceptual), and must be negotiated by a new, higher, and qualitatively different separation-differentiation process.

difference between physical and emotional object constancy

Finally, a note on the difference between *physical* object constancy (first fulcrum) and *emotional* object constancy (second fulcrum). Mahler (1975) herself accepts this distinction, and points out that physical "object permanence in Piaget's sense is a necessary, but not a sufficient, prerequisite for the establishment of libidinal object constancy." This difference is dramatically obvious in actual chronological development: physical object constancy, as Piaget (1977) has demonstrated, is achieved by around eighteen months, whereas emotional object constancy, according to Mahler, is rarely achieved before thirty-six months. Clearly, these are two different stages of structuralization.

The Spectrum of Developmental Fulcrums

We now reach a crucial question: Are there any other major fulcrums or critical nodal points of self-structuralization and self-differentiation? At this point, most object relations theories become vague and equivocal. Some of them seem to indicate major self-development is virtually over at thirty-six months. Others give scant attention to higher developmental fulcrums: "With adequate attainment of psychological birth, at approximately three years of age, the child is 'on the way to [emotional] object constancy.' While this is another beginning, not the end . . . , the first round is decisive to how secure subsequent rounds will be. Blos [1962] thinks that a second major development takes place in adolescence. We suggest that marriage can constitute another 'round'" (Blanck & Blanck, 1979).

scant attention given to higher developmental fulcrums

This theoretical vagueness as to what exactly constitutes a "round" (or fulcrum) of self-development has dogged object-relations theory from its inception.[1] Vis-à-vis development as a whole, it is also very limiting to *define* "separation-individuation" as what occurs specifically during the rapprochement and consolidation subphases, and also say that it "continues" through "several, perhaps infinite, rounds throughout life" (Blanck & Blanck, 1979) with vague references to adolescence and marriage.

limiting effects of theoretical vagueness

The psychoanalytic object-relations theorists appear to have so focused on the *particular* form the separation-differentiation process takes in the rapprochement and consolidation subphases, that they seem to have missed the idea that the "hatching" subphase (and not the rapprochement subphase) can be described as the *first* major round of separation-differentiation. However, they seem to have implicitly recognized this, in that they actually call that first fulcrum "the differentiation subphase."

the oedipal phase as the third major fulcrum

Likewise, these theories have overlooked the fact that the oedipal phase itself can also be rather precisely defined as a fulcrum or separation-differentiation point. The oedipal phase—which can now be called the third major fulcrum of self-development—shares all of the abstract characteristics or defining marks of the first two fulcrums: it involves a process of increasing internalization, increasing structuralization and hierarchization, increasing separation-differentiation, and increasing integration. However, this process is now occurring on a new, higher, and qualitatively different level of organization, that of the *newly emerging* basic structures of the conceptual rep-mind, which bring the possibilities of a qualitatively different set of self-defenses (repression), self-needs, object relations, possible pathologies (psychoneuroses), and so on.

As we saw, at the completion of the separation-individuation subphases (the second fulcrum), the phantasmic-emotional self of the infant is differentiated from its surround, but the infant's mind (phantasmic and early symbolic) and its body (emotional-libidinal) are themselves not yet differentiated from each other. As the rep-mind (higher symbols and concepts) emerges, it initially shares this mind-body fusion. This is very clearly borne out by the works of Piaget (1977), Loevinger (1976), Broughton (1975), and others. Indeed, Freud himself announced, in *Inhibitions, Symptoms, and Anxiety* (1959), that a definitive differentiation of the ego from the id does not occur until around the time of the resolution of the oedipal stage. And that, exactly, is what is at stake in the third fulcrum: the differentiation/integration of the (rep) mind and the (emotional-libidinal) body. A developmental lesion at this fulcrum results in a *neurotic self-structure:* the central self remains fixated (morbid preservation) to certain bodily impulses, or it represses or dissociates (morbid negation) certain bodily impulses. If, however, this third fulcrum is adequately negotiated, the mind and body are clearly differentiated and integrated in the new and higher-order conceptual self-structure, with a new and higher internalization (superego), and the capacity for *conceptual object constancy*—the power to hold a *whole concept,*

negotiation of third fulcrum and conceptual object constancy

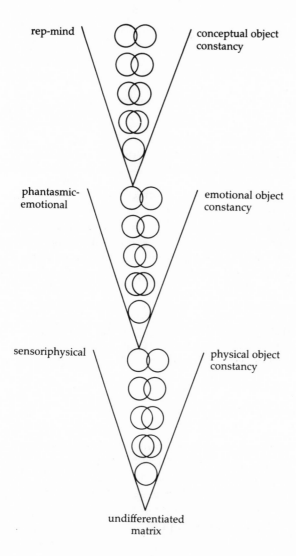

rep-mind — conceptual object constancy

phantasmic-emotional — emotional object constancy

sensoriphysical — physical object constancy

undifferentiated matrix

FIGURE 5
SELF-DIFFERENTIATION IN FULCRUMS 1–3

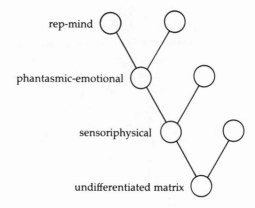

FIGURE 6

SELF-DEVELOPMENT SCHEMATIC FOR FULCRUMS 1–3

or a class of properties, without confusing or collapsing its component members due to, e.g., libidinal desires. As Piaget (1977) has demonstrated, conceptual constancy does not emerge until around the sixth year of life, with such capacities as conservation-reversibility, i.e., holding conceptual properties despite physical-emotional displacement.

This third major fulcrum can now be added to the self-development diagram, as shown in Fig. 5., and this can all be simplified and schematically represented as in Fig. 6.

The Combined Theories

implications of combining theories
The implications of combining psychoanalytic developmental psychology and object-relations theory with the basic structures or stages of consciousness may now be seen: *The first three fulcrums of self-development simply represent the self's climb up the first three rungs of the ladder of major basic structures* (depicted in Fig. 1).

At each fulcrum, the self identifies (normal preservation) with the corresponding basic structure, and thus is initially fused with, or undifferentiated from, that structure and its phenomenal objects. This is followed by a period of separation-differentiation (normal negation), wherein the self-system or self-structure learns to differentiate itself from both the *objects* of that level and the *subject* of the previous level (that is, it transcends its previous and exclusive subjective identification with the previous and lower basic structure). If at any fulcrum there is morbid preservation (fixation) or morbid negation (splitting, dissociation, repression), a characteristic pathology emerges, marked by the level of structural organization at which the lesion occurs.

separation-differentiation

pathology marked by level of organization

As I said, these first three fulcrums and their associated pathologies (psychotic, borderline, and neurotic) correspond with the first three basic structures or rungs in the ladder of overall development (depicted in Fig. 1). In the next chapter, I will suggest that the remaining basic structures or rungs (levels 4 through 9) each involve another and crucial fulcrum of self-development, and lesions at those fulcrums also generate specific and definable pathologies (which in turn respond to different treatment modalities or therapeutic interventions). In Chapter 4 I will describe these higher fulcrums—their characteristics, their typical conflicts, and their corresponding pathologies; and then, in Chapter 5, I will suggest the types of "therapies" that seem most appropriate for each.

fulcrums and rungs in the ladder of overall development

But first we must return to the previous discussion and finish our account with the first three fulcrums and their associated pathologies. And this brings us to the work of Otto Kernberg.

The Conventional Hierarchy of Pathology: The Work of Otto Kernberg

In order to discuss the specific pathologies that characterize malformations at each of the fulcrums of self-development, it will help to use a few simple symbols to refer to the subphases of each fulcrum. In Fig. 7 "a" rep-

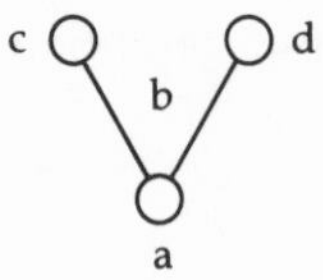

FIGURE 7
SUBPHASES AT EACH FULCRUM OF SELF-DEVELOPMENT

resents the initial fusion or undifferentiated state of each
fulcrum; "b," the process of separation-differentiation; "c,"
the stable, differentiated, integrated self that emerges at
the adequate negotiation of each fulcrum; and "d," the
correlative, differentiated-and-integrated object world of
that fulcrum. (Thus, for example, "Fulcrum 1a"—or
simply F-1a—refers to the autistic phase; F-2b refers to the
rapprochement subphase; F-2d refers to emotional object
constancy; F-3b to the oedipal phase; F-3c to the stable rep-
mind self-concept, and so on.) The developmental task of
each fulcrum can now be stated simply: it involves a horizontal differentiation between c and d, and a concomitant,
vertical differentiation of c and a. The latter is what I have
elsewhere defined as "transcendence" (Wilber, 1980a).

Previous discussion briefly outlined Mahler's view of pathology throughout the first three fulcrums. But perhaps
the most sophisticated and comprehensive map of pathology in these realms has been given by Otto Kernberg, who
has presented a very influential and widely accepted
"theory of (1) the origin of the basic "units" (self-image,
object-image, affect disposition) of internalized object relations, (2) the development of four basic stages in their
differentiation and integration, (3) the relationship between failure in these developments and the crystalliza-
tion of various types of psychopathology, and (4) the implications of this sequence of phases of general structural
developments of the psychic apparatus" (1976).

Kernberg's self-
development
stages and their
corresponding
pathologies

Kernberg's stages of self-development and corresponding
pathology are as follows (summarized by Abend, 1983):

Stage 1: Normal "Autism," or Primary Undifferentiated Stage This
phase covers the first month of life and precedes the consolidation of the "good" undifferentiated self-object constellation.

Failure or fixation of development at this stage is characteristic of autistic psychoses.

Stage 2: Normal "Symbiosis" This phase extends from the second month of life to about six or eight months of age. There is a relative incompleteness of the differentiation of self and object representations from each other and a persisting tendency for defensive refusion of "good" self and object images when severe trauma or frustration determines pathological development. Pathological fixation of, or regression to, Stage 2 is characteristic of symbiotic psychosis of childhood, most types of adult schizophrenia, and depressive psychoses.

Stage 3: Differentiation of Self from Object-Representations This stage begins around the eighth month of life and reaches completion between the eighteenth and the thirty-sixth month. It ends with the eventual integration of "good" and "bad" self-representations into an integrated self concept [that should be "self-image"; concepts do not emerge until around the fourth year of life], and the integration of "good" and "bad" representations into "total" [whole, not part] object representations. Failures in development during this stage lead to the development of the borderline personality organization. [In this general category Kernberg includes borderline syndromes, addictions, narcissistic disorders, "as if" and antisocial personality disorders; what all of them have in common, he believes, is a failure to integrate "all good" and "all bad" self and object part-images, i.e., they are all primarily characterized by splitting.] During this stage an early constellation of defenses is brought into operation, centering on splitting or primitive dissociation and fostering the other early defenses of denial, primitive idealization, projective identification, omnipotence, and devaluation.

Stage 4: Development of Higher Level Intrapsychic Object Relations-Derived Structures This stage begins in the latter part of the third year of life and lasts through the entire oedipal period. The typical psychopathology of this stage is represented by the neuroses and "higher level" character pathology. Repression becomes the main defensive operation of this stage.

Stage 5: Consolidation of Superego and Ego Integration This is a [postoedipal] stage of development with the gradual evolution of ego identity.

It is obvious that Kernberg's developmental diagnostic scheme fits the first three fulcrums precisely, as shown in

Kernberg and Fig. 8. Note that Kernberg's Stage 5 (F-3c), "the *consolida-*
the first three *tion* of superego and ego integration," is indeed a consoli-
fulcrums dation or integration, but it clearly is not to be confused
with Fulcrum 2c, the consolidation-integration of the
phantasmic-emotional self, or Fulcrum 1c, the consolidation-integration of the sensoriphysical self.

The substantial agreement between Kernberg's develop-
mental-diagnostic stages and the first three fulcrums of
self-development requires one refinement: Masterson
(1981) has suggested that the narcissistic and borderline
conditions, although very closely related, are developmentally distinct. According to Masterson, the borderline
conditions do have their primary developmental lesion in
the rapprochement subphase (F-2b), but the narcissistic
conditions must have some aspect of their developmental
lesion *before* that (i.e., in the practicing subphase, F-2a).
Masterson's The narcissistic conditions are marked by grandiose-self/
view of omnipotent-object fused units, which characterize the
narcissism practicing subphase (as Mahler put it, "Narcissism at its
peak!"). The rapprochement subphase is marked by the
breaking up or differentiation of the grandiose-omnipotent
fused self-and-object units, and thus, Masterson believes,
could not be the lesion point of the narcissistic disorders.
As he puts it, "The fixation of the narcissistic personality
disorders must occur before [the rapprochement crisis]

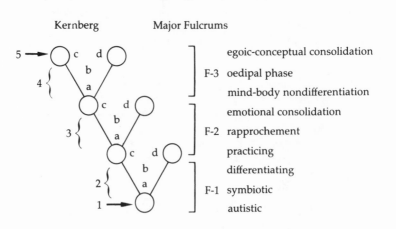

FIGURE 8
FIT OF KERNBERG STAGES AT FULCRUMS 1–3

because clinically the patient behaves as if the object-representation were an integral part of the self-representation—an omnipotent, dual unity. The possibility of the existence of a rapprochement crisis doesn't seem to dawn on this patient. The fantasy persists that the world is his oyster and revolves about him." The borderline, on the other hand, "behaves as if all life were one long, un-resolvable rapprochement crisis." Thus, according to Masterson, Fulcrum 2a: narcissistic; Fulcrum 2b: borderline.

Notice that within each fulcrum there are, generally speaking, three subphases: subphase "a," which represents the undifferentiated base of the fulcrum; subphase "b," which represents the process of *vertical and horizontal* separation-differentiation; and the subphase "c/d," which represents the ideal resolution, consolidation, and integration of the newly differentiated self and object components. This is so in each of the three fulcrums—and therefore 9 subphases—examined thus far. These three fulcrums and their 9 subphases are listed in Fig. 8 for reference.

Fig. 8, then, represents a summary of the "fit" between the conventional schools (e.g., represented by Kernberg and Mahler) and the first three rungs (and fulcrums) of the spectrum model presented in Part I. Let me repeat that these three fulcrums (and their associated pathologies) represent the three general stages in the prepersonal or prerational realms of overall development. This still leaves three general stages in the personal realms and three general stages in the transpersonal realms, as indicated in Fig. 9. In the next chapter I will go on to discuss these higher rungs and fulcrums and their associated pathologies, a discussion that will eventually take us into the contemplative and transpersonal dimensions of human growth and development.

"fit" between conventional and spectrum model

SUMMARY

This section has been somewhat technical and therefore, for the nonpsychoanalytically oriented reader, perhaps abstruse and off-putting. What I would like to do, therefore, is offer a brief, nontechnical summary of its central points.

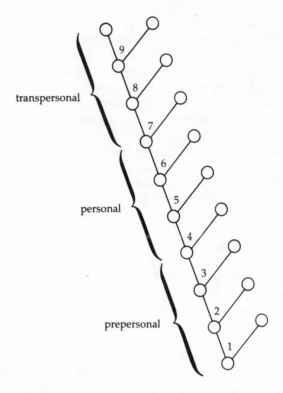

FIGURE 9
THE MAJOR FULCRUMS OF SELF-DEVELOPMENT

the three general stages in the emergence of a sense of self

In this section we have examined the emergence of a *sense of self* in the human being, and we found that it proceeds through three general stages: the emergence of a *physical self* (zero–one year), the emergence of an *emotional self* (one–three years), and the emergence of a *mental self* (three–six years). At each of these stages of growth, the individual must learn to distinguish the self from the environment, from others, and from other structures in its own psyche. If this differentiation fails, the individual remains "stuck" (fixated) at that stage, and a corresponding psychological disturbance generally results.

Thus, although the infant is born with a physical body, it does not yet possess a sense of being a distinct *physical self*, set apart from its environment and surroundings; it cannot easily distinguish inside from outside, or its own body from mother's. But sometime during the first year of life (typically five–nine months), the infant learns to distinguish (or differentiate) its physical self from the physical environment, and a genuine sense of a distinct physical self emerges (this is appropriately called "hatching"). On the other hand, if this differentiation does not occur—usually due to severe and repeated trauma or other disturbing events—then the infant remains "stuck" in its prior undifferentiated or "fusion" state: inside and outside are fused and confused, hallucinatory thought processes may predominate, and severe anxiety or depression result. This class of severe and primitive pathology is known as "psychoses." *"hatching" the physical self*

Once the physical self has emerged and been established, the infant's *emotional self* begins to emerge and develop. Again, the infant possesses emotions probably from birth, but not a distinct and separate emotional self. Even after the first year of life, when the infant has (ideally) established a firm and distinct physical self, the infant's emotions are not yet clearly differentiated from the emotions of others (and particularly the mother). The infant imagines that what it feels, others are also feeling (this is called "narcissism"); its "emotional boundaries," so to speak, are still very fluid and shifting. *emergence of the emotional self*

But sometime during the first and third year (the period 18–24 months seems most critical, and is called "rapprochement"), the infant learns to differentiate its emotional-psychological life from that of others (particularly the mother), and a stable, firm, individual emotional self emerges. A failure to achieve this "separation-individuation" leaves the individual with very weak emotional boundaries. The world then tends to "flood" the self, causing anxiety, depression, and severe thought disturbances—a class of pathology loosely referred to as "borderline" (because it is borderline between psychoses and neuroses).

Once the emotional self has emerged and been established, the child's *mental self* increasingly begins to emerge and develop, a process that is considerably aided by the acquisition of language. The mental self grows particularly *emergence of the mental self* rapidly from around the third to the sixth year, during which time the child learns not just to *feel* but to *think*—to verbalize, talk, and mentally control its behavior. But it might also learn that certain of its feelings and behaviors (particularly sexual and aggressive) are unacceptable to those around it, and it might try to "disown" or "repress" those feelings. In a sense, the mental self (and its thoughts) learns to repress the previous emotional self (and its feelings). If this repression is severe and prolonged, the repressed feelings may return in disguised and painful forms known as "neuroses" (such as phobias, compulsions, obsessions, hysterias, etc.).

Thus, during the first six or seven years of life, there are three particularly important "turning points" or "fulcrums" of self-development—the emergence of the physical self, the emotional self, and the mental self—each of which, if disturbed, may result in a particular type (or *the three* level) of pathology—psychoses, borderline, and neuroses. *turning points* As we will particularly see in Chapter 5, these pathologies are best treated by different types of therapies. In the neuroses, the individual is encouraged to "uncover" the repressed emotions and feelings and re-experience them more directly (these are called "uncovering techniques," such as classical psychoanalysis). In the borderline, on the other hand, it is not so much that the emotional self has been repressed, but that it hasn't yet fully emerged and been stabilized; the emotional boundaries are too fluid and shifting, and so the aim in therapy here is not to "uncover" anything but to *build up* a distinct and individuated sense of self (these techniques are therefore called "structure building techniques"). Finally, the very primitive pathologies (psychoses) are usually so severe that neither uncovering techniques nor structure building techniques are of much use, and the best that can usually be hoped for is some sort of stabilization using medication or, if necessary, custodial care.

We have seen the emergence of a physical self, then an *three major* emotional self, then a mental self, and these are the first *levels of mental* three major "fulcrums" of self development. In the next *development* chapter, we will see that the mental self in turn goes through three major levels or fulcrums of development (concrete, formal, and integrative, or F-4, F-5, and F-6 for short), and then the self begins to become *transmental* (transrational or transpersonal) as it enters the contemplative or spiritual realms of development. Each of these higher levels and fulcrums also has its own potential pathologies and correlative treatment modalities, which we will discuss in detail in Chapter 5.

CHAPTER 4

THE SPECTRUM OF PSYCHOPATHOLOGY

Ken Wilber

*In the previous chapter, Wilber presented a brief outline of his
spectrum model, and indicated how this model connects with the
recent developments in psychoanalytic ego psychology. In effect,
this covered the prepersonal or prerational range of development,
with its three general stages, fulcrums, and correlative pathologies (psychotic, borderline, and neurotic). In this chapter, Wilber
continues the account and discusses the intermediate or personal
range of development (with its three general stages and pathologies) and the higher or transpersonal range of development (also
with three general stages and pathologies). The result is an overall spectrum of pathology—from prepersonal to personal to transpersonal—that is comprehensive and specific.*

The following outline of the overall spectrum of psychopathology begins with a review of the first three fulcrums—which were introduced in the last chapter—and
continues to Fulcrum 9. For ease of presentation and reference, I have divided this chapter into three parts: Prepersonal, Personal, and Transpersonal, each consisting of
three major fulcrums of self-development and the corresponding pathologies. I have simply listed the fulcrums
(and their subphases) and noted the specific type(s) of pathology that are most characteristic of a developmental lesion at that phase or subphase. Needless to say, the standard cautions and qualifications about using such
hierarchical models of pathology should be kept in mind;
i.e., no pure cases, the influence of cultural differences,
genetic predispositions, genetic and traumatic arrests, and

*an outline of
pathology in
fulcrums 3
through 9*

blended cases (see Abend, 1983; Gedo, 1981; Mahler, 1975).

PART I: THE PREPERSONAL PATHOLOGIES

personality types and personality organization

The "prepersonal" or "prerational" pathologies are so named because this range of development involves the stages leading up to the emergence of a rational-individuated-personal selfhood and its differentiation from prerational structures, impulses, primary process thought, and so forth. Consonant with recent research in this field (see Chapter 3), I tend to see this range of development as consisting of *three general levels* of personality development and organization, which I have called F-1, F-2, and F-3, and whose general pathologies are psychotic, borderline, and neurotic. In the words of Jack Engler (see Chapter 1), "It is important to recognize that self-pathology does not depend on personality or character type, and still less on symptoms or symptom clusters. Almost all the commonly recognized personality *types* can occur at any level of personality *organization:* healthy, neurotic, borderline, or psychotic. Even the more pathological character types—schizoid, paranoid, infantile—can occur within a neurotic structure (Stone 1980). Stone has suggested that it is clinically more useful to think in terms of a continuum for each character or personality type as it varies from most to least pathological. He has accordingly proposed a promising three-dimensional model of personality typology which crosses personality type, level of personality organization and degree of constitutional or genetic loading. This distinction between structure and character is only beginning to become clear in clinical psychiatry and represents a breakthrough in psychodiagnostic understanding." I am in substantial agreement with Engler and Stone on this central issue.

Fulcrum 1	*1a:*	*Autistic Psychoses*
	1b/c:	*Symbiotic Infantile Psychoses*
		Most Adult Schizophrenia
		Depressive Psychoses

This follows Kernberg and Mahler specifically.

Fulcrum 2   *2a: Narcissistic Personality
                                    Disorders*

The main clinical characteristics of the narcissistic personality disorder are grandiosity, extreme self-involvement and lack of interest in and empathy for others, in spite of the pursuit of others to obtain admiration and approval. The patient manifesting a narcissistic personality disorder seems to be endlessly motivated to seek perfection in all he or she does, to pursue wealth, power and beauty and to find others who will mirror and admire his/her grandiosity. Underneath this defensive facade is a feeling state of emptiness and rage with a predominance of intense envy.

The narcissistic personality disorder must be fixated or arrested before the developmental level of the rapprochement crisis, since one of the important tasks of that crisis is not performed, i.e., the deflation of infantile grandiosity and omnipotence [i.e., the self-structure refuses to surrender "paradise"]. The intrapsychic structure of the narcissistic personality disorder preserves the infantile grandiosity and narcissistic link to the omnipotent object (Masterson, 1981).

Specifically, the self- and object-representations of the narcissistic personality structure consist of a grandiose-self-plus-omnipotent-object fused unit. Other persons are *experienced*, according to direct clinical evidence, not as separate individuals (or as separate "whole objects") with rights and wishes of their own, but as extensions or aspects of the grandiose-exhibitionistic self, serving primary need gratification (Kohut, 1971). The sole function of the world is therefore to *mirror* the self's perfection. The omnipotent fused object representation contains all power, supplies, glory, etc.; the grandiose self-representation is one of being elite, superior, exhibitionistic, special, unique, perfect. The grandiose-self/omnipotent-object fused unit forms the central self; so airtight is this fused unit that it seemingly conceals the underlying empty-rageful-envious fused unit and its affect of profound abandonment depression. Should any object or person, however, fail to give the narcissistic individual what he or she

mirroring and narcissism

is constantly seeking—namely a *mirroring* of his or her grandiose perfection—then the narcissistic individual reacts with rage, outrage, and humiliation. Typical defenses include devaluation, refusion, denial, avoidance, splitting (particularly of the grandiose-self/omnipotent-object fused unit from the empty/aggressive/depressive unit), and acting out (Kernberg, 1976; Kohut, 1971; Masterson, 1981).

2b: Borderline Personality Disorders

the
rapprochement
crisis

"The rapprochement crisis is crucial to the borderline, whose pathology can be seen as a reflection of his/her immersion in and inability to resolve it" (Masterson, 1981). Unlike the narcissistic structure, the borderline has achieved a partial or quasi-differentiation of self and object representations. A *separate* individual has started to emerge, but its structure is so tenuous or weak that it constantly fears engulfment by the other or abandonment by the other.

According to Masterson (1981) and Rinsley (1977), this splits the borderline structure into a helpless, dependent, compliant part-self with a clinging defense, and a "totally worthless," "rotten," "evil-to-the-core" part-self with a distancing or withdrawing defense. Associated with the compliant-clinging part-self is an all-good, rewarding, and protecting part-object, and associated with the "rotten-withdrawing" part-self is an all-bad, angry, attacking, and vengeful part-object.

the
unintegrated
differentiation
of the borderline

The intrapsychic structure of the borderline is thus more complex than the narcissistic, because it has accomplished more differentiation; but these differentiations are not integrated, leaving the borderline with a series of fractured structures or part-units. The borderline thus typically oscillates between an almost total or chameleon-like compliance with others, which makes him/her feel "good," "accepted," or "safe," and a withdrawn and sullen distancing from others, who—now experienced as angry, vengeful, and denouncing—make him/her feel rotten, a worm, totally worthless, despicably bad (and occasionally suicidal). The one thing the borderline will not do is assert his or her own separation-individuation (Blanck & Blanck, 1979; Kernberg, 1975, 1976).

Fulcrum 3   *3a: Borderline Neuroses*

There are several different nosological terms for this set of conditions: pathological neuroses, high level borderline, neurosis with borderline features, borderline with neurotic features, etc. The general consensus, however, is simply that these conditions are either neurotic developments burdened with separation-individuation subphase deficiencies, or a part-regression to more borderline states in the face of too difficult neurotic-oedipal developments (Blanck & Blanck, 1974, 1979; Gedo, 1981).

Thus, to give only two examples, if genital sexuality is burdened with rapprochement subphase deficiencies, the *two examples of* person's understanding of sexual responses might be *neurosis with* skewed in the direction of threats of entrapment or en-*borderline* gulfment; if burdened with an unmetabolized need for *elements* narcissistic mirroring, then in the direction of triumph, possessive extension of self-grandiosity, or rageful-sadistic domination. The person characterized by neuroses-with-borderline-elements makes careful diagnosis and well-tailored treatment especially important, because appropriate interventions for similar symptoms on the neurotic level and the borderline level are often dramatically different.

3b: Psychoneuroses

Discussion of these well-known disorders—neurotic anxiety, obsessive-compulsive syndromes, neurotic depression, phobias, hysteria, hypochondriasis—can be limited *number of* here to comments about their significance and meaning in *players on the* the overall spectrum. The lowest self-structures (autistic, *stage*

symbiotic, and narcissistic) tend to be *monadic* in nature;
the borderline structures, *dyadic;* and the psychoneurotic
structures, *triadic.* In the monadic structures, there is basically one player on the stage—the self is either oblivious
of the "other" (autistic), merged with the other (symbiotic), or part of an omnipotent dual unity with the other
(narcissistic). As the monadic structure differentiates, self
and other emerge as two distinct, if sometimes tenuous,
"Tragic Man"   units. There are now two players on the stage, self and
(m)other, with all the joy and all the tragedy that that involves (Kohut [1977] calls this stage "Tragic Man").

At the dyadic stage, the infant is still more or less pre-
genital. It only has to negotiate the differentiation of self
versus other; it does not have to negotiate the differentiation, within itself, of male versus female. Starting around
age 2 or 3, however, the self awakens to its own gender
identity, and this introduces three players on the stage:
self, female-mother, and male-father. This development
immensely enriches and complicates the situation. New
capacities, new desires, new taboos, new object relations,
a whole new set of conflicts—all come crashing onto the
stage, with far-reaching, immensely complex implications.

In the dyadic (F-2) stage, the central self is, as it was, a
more or less stable phantasmic-emotional-libidinal struc-
the dyadic stage   ture. It is not so much that the self at this stage possesses
a libido; rather, the self at this stage simply *is* a libidinal
self (Guntrip, 1971). However, by the time we move from
the F-2 dyad to the F-3 triad, the conceptual rep-mind has
emerged and (ideally) differentiated from the libidinal
body. The central self is now identified with, and exists as,
a symbolic-conceptual structure, namely, the rep-mind *ego:*
no longer a phantasmic-libidinal self, but a conceptual-
egoic self.

The egoic self, therefore, has ideally accomplished three
tasks: 1) it has horizontally differentiated from its new concept object-relations; 2) it has consolidated and integrated
its own structure, which contains new and higher inter-
nalizations (superego); and 3) it has vertically differentiated from (or transcended) its previous self-stage (i.e.,

the libidinal self)—the *exclusively* libidinal self is *negated and transcended*, but the libido itself (or the id) *remains in existence* as a fundamental, appropriate, and necessary basic structure of existence.

But this overall process results in a *tripartite* structure of the Fulcrum-3 self: ego-superego-id. Whereas, in the F-2 self, most conflict was interpersonal, in the F-3 self, most conflict is intrapersonal (or intrapsychic). Where differentiation-and-integration is not clean or complete, there is war: superego vs. id (inhibition), id vs. ego (anxiety, obsession), superego vs. ego (guilt, depression). The triadic structure of conflict in the F-3 pathologies is one of the central diagnostic aids in differentiating them from the more dyadically structured pathologies of F-2 (and the monadic pathologies of F-1). Kohut calls this "Guilty Man" in contrast to "Tragic Man." *"Guilty Man"*

The triadic structure of the F-3 self also gives a major clue to the very meaning of the psychoneuroses in the overall spectrum of development and pathology. For the self is on its climb up the basic structures of existence, matter to body to mind to soul to spirit. The psychoneuroses stand at that great branch point where consciousness starts to move from a generally bodily existence to a generally mental existence, with all the rewards, and all the conflicts, that entails. The body belongs to nature, but the mind belongs to history; the body, to impulse; the mind, to reason. The body is merely subjective; the mind, however, is intersubjective, freely taking the role of *other subjects* in communicative exchange and symbolic discourse. The body constitutes a *merely present* feeling-self; the mind, on the other hand, supports a *temporal text*-self—a historic, hermeneutic, intentional, interpretive, meaningful, caring, moral, role-playing script-self. *from a bodily existence to a mental existence*

The scripts and social roles of the F-3 or oedipal phase are, however, rather crude and simple, especially in comparison with those that are to follow. To begin with, the number and types of roles are fairly simple: child, parent, sibling. Further, the script-roles themselves are driven almost entirely (or at least predominantly) by merely libidinal *scripts and social roles of fulcrum 3* agendas. The Oedipus complex is one of the earliest and most fundamental scripts of all (and it *is* a script, as Sophocles demonstrated), but it is a script whose roles are driven almost entirely by mere bodily desires. At the next fulcrum, the roles themselves shake off their merely bodily or libidinal motives and assume their own higher function and status—and pathology.

PART II: THE PERSONAL PATHOLOGIES

"postoedipal" developmental stages and their dis-eases

Most conventional psychodynamic theorists tend to end their accounts of "serious" pathology at F-3, that is, at the oedipal phase and its resolution (or lack thereof). This is perhaps understandable; after all, the classic pathologies (from schizophrenia to hysteria) do seem to have their most disturbing etiologies in the first three fulcrums of self-development. But this by no means exhausts the spectrum of pathologies, not even the spectrum of "serious" or "profound" pathologies. Accordingly, researchers increasingly have begun to look at higher or "postoedipal" stages of development and their correlative vulnerabilities and dis-eases.

Take, for example, the whole notion of "role confusion." The very capacity for genuine role taking is a decisively postoedipal development (the capacity to take the role of other does not emerge, in any sophisticated fashion, until around age 7–8 yrs [Piaget, 1977; Loevinger, 1976], whereas the typical age of oedipal resolution is 6 yrs). Thus, one could theoretically resolve the oedipal conflict in a completely normal and healthy fashion, only to run aground on role confusion and identity confusion for reasons totally unrelated to oedipal conflicts or concerns. These seem to be entirely different levels (not just lines) of development, with entirely different conflicts and vulnerabilities. These conflicts are much more cognitive than psychodynamic in nature and origin, but can be just as debilitating and distressful. This whole range of cognitive, identity, and existential concerns, I call the "intermediate" or "personal" realm, and, based on recent research, I have divided it into three major levels (F-4, F-5, and F-6), which I call "cognitive-script," "identity," and "existential."

Fulcrum 4   *The Role Self and Cognitive-Script*
                    Pathology

Fulcrum 4 begins to emerge as the central self transcends its exclusive identification with the rep-mind (and its oedipal projects) and begins to identify with the rule/role mind. The rule/role mind (or "conop"), as Piaget (1977) demonstrated, is the first structure that not only can imitate a role, but can actually *take* the role of others. This opens up an entirely new dimension of object relations, with a new sense of self (Loevinger), a new set of self-needs (Maslow), a new moral sensibility (Kohlberg), a new mode of life and a new mode of death. In the F-3 pathologies (the psychoneuroses), the life/death (or preservation/negation) battles centered mostly on bodily concerns and impulses—desire for libidinal-body objects, fear of bodily loss (castration, mutilation, etc.). The life/death battles of the F-4 self, however, center more on its rules and roles—a desire to fit in, to belong, to find its place or role among other roles; to *understand* the *rules;* with a correlative fear of losing face, losing role, breaking the rules (Loevinger's conformist stage, Maslow's belongingness, Kohlberg's conventional, etc.).

By "script pathology" or "script neuroses" I have in mind, for example, the extensive work of Transactional Analysis on game theory and scripts and communications theorists on role-taking (Selman & Byrne, 1974; Watzlawick, 1967). Obviously conceptual games and scripts (and their forerunners) reach back into F-3 development, but it is at F-4 that they assume a central and dominant influence. The preeminent defense mechanism of this stage is the "duplicitous transaction"—the individual overtly communicates one message (e.g., "I only want what's best for you") while covertly implying another ("Don't leave me"); if the covert message is pointed out, the individual strenuously denies it. The covert messages or hidden agendas are the key pathogenic structures in the F-4 self; if extreme, they result in an interior splitting or dissociation of the text-self, analogous to repression in F-3 and splitting in F-2. Script pathology and the reasons that it cannot be reduced to psychoneurotic pathology will be discussed in more detail in Chapter 5.

"script pathology" and fulcrum 4

Fulcrum 5   *Identity Neurosis*

The emergence of the formal-reflexive basic structure opens the possibility of F-5 self-development: a highly differentiated, reflexive, and introspective self-structuralization. The F-5 self is no longer unreflexively bound to social roles and conventional morality; for the first time it *centering on* can depend on its own individual principles of reason and *reason,* conscience (Kohlberg's postconventional, Loevinger's con-*conscience, and* scientious-individualistic, etc.). For the first time, too, the *possibilities* self can conceive *possible* (or hypothetical) futures (Piaget), with entirely new goals, new possibilities, new desires (life), and new fears (death). It can conceive possible successes, and possible failures, in a way never before imagined. It can lie awake at night, riveted with worries or elated by anticipation over all the possibilities! It becomes a philosopher, a dreamer in the best and highest sense; an internally reflexive mirror, awestruck at its own existence. *Cogito, ergo sum.*

"Identity neurosis" specifically means all the things that can go wrong in the emergence of this self-reflexive struc-*"identity* ture. Is it strong enough to break free of the rule/role mind *neurosis" and* and stand on its own principles of conscience? Can it, if *fulcrum 5* necessary, summon the courage to march to the sound of a different drummer? Will it dare to think for itself? Will it be overcome with anxiety or depression at the prospect of its own emergence? These concerns—which regrettably many object-relations theorists reduce to F-2 separation-individuation dimensions—form the core of the F-5 self and its identity pathology. Erikson (1959, 1963) has written perhaps the definitive studies on F-5 self-development ("identity vs. role confusion"). All that can be added here is the observation that *philosophical problems* are an integral part of F-5 development, and philosophical education an integral and legitimate part of therapy on this level (see the relevant section in Chapter 5).

Fulcrum 6   *Existential Pathology*

I must first distinguish between "existential" as a particular level of self-development (F-6) and "existential" as a particular conflict that can and does occur on *all* levels of self-development. The latter ("existential conflict") is simply one way to look at the life/death or preservation/ negation battles that occur at each and every stage of self-development. Birth trauma, rapprochement crisis, separation-individuation, oedipal tragedies, role clashes, identity neuroses—these can all be described as "existential" in nature, simply because they involve profound and meaningful events in the course of human existence *(Dasein)*. The existential approach looks at each stage of development, not just in terms of its *content* (borderline, oedipal, etc.), but also from the *context* or categories of existence itself, or the various modes and stages of being-in-the-world. This is why the central dilemmas and drives of each stage of self-development can also be conceptualized as a life/death, preservation/negation, or existential concern, although the outward forms of this existential battle obviously vary from level to level. This is the approach of Boss (1963), Binswanger (1956), Yalom (1980), Zimmerman (1981), May (1977), and others, which I share in part.

Now the "existential level," as I use the term here, refers to a specific level of basic structure development ("vision-logic") and the correlative stage of self-development ("centaur"). It is termed "existential" for three reasons: 1) If the formal-reflexive mind is Descartes, the existential mind is Heidegger: his whole philosophy is marvelously saturated with this level of consciousness (as an actual discovery, not a merely subjective fabrication); 2) the self-structure of this level, as Broughton (1975) demonstrated, is one where "mind and body are both experiences of an integrated self." This personal mind-body integration—hence "centaur"—seems to be the goal of those therapies that explicitly call themselves "humanistic-existential." (This does not refer to many popular approaches that call themselves "humanistic" or "existential," but, in fact, are *pseudo*-humanistic/existential, and embody powerful techniques for regression to, and glorification of, the phantasmic-emotional or the narcissistic "paradise," which are mistakenly identified with "higher consciousness"); 3) this level is the *highest* level of consciousness that many authentic humanistic-existential approaches seem to acknowledge.

the "existential level" as a specific level

*fulcrum 6 or
existential self*

A review of the literature suggests that the major concerns of the F-6 or existential self are: personal autonomy and integration (Loevinger); authenticity (Kierkegaard, Heidegger); and self-actualization (Maslow, Rogers). Associated affects are: a concern for overall *meaning* in life (or being-in-the-world); a grappling with personal mortality and finitude; and finding a courage-to-be in the face of lonely and unexpected death. Where the formal-mind begins to conceive of life's *possibilities* and take flight in this new-found freedom, the existential mind (via vision-logic) *adds up* the possibilities and finds this: personal life is a brief spark in the cosmic void. How the existential self handles the new potentials of autonomy and self-actualization, and how it grapples with the problems of finitude, mortality, and apparent meaninglessness—these are the central factors in F-6 pathology.

Common syndromes include:

*existential-level
syndromes*

1. *Existential depression*—a global-diffuse depression or "life-arrest" in the face of perceived meaninglessness.
2. *Inauthenticity*—which Heidegger (1962) defined as lack of profound awareness-acceptance of one's own finititude and mortality.
3. *Existential isolation and "uncanniness"*—a strong-enough self that nevertheless feels "not at home" in the familiar world.
4. *Aborted self-actualization*—Maslow (1971): "I warn you, if you deliberately set out to be less than you are capable of becoming, you will be deeply unhappy for the rest of your life."
5. *Existential anxiety*—the threatened death of, or loss of, one's self-reflexive modes of being-in-the world (an anxiety that *cannot* occur prior to Fulcrums 5 and 6 because the very capacity for formal-reflection does not occur until then).

*existential-level
ennui*

Not all cases of, e.g., "meaninglessness" are automatically to be considered as existential (in the specific sense of existential-level origin). Borderline abandonment depression and psychoneurotic depression, for instance, also produce affective states of meaninglessness. But existential ennui has a specific and unmistakable "flavor"; a strong and highly differentiated-integrated self-structure presents the symptom; it is a thoughtful, steady, concerned, profound depression; it has none of the "whining" of the borderline or the guilt of the psychoneurotic; it looks unflinchingly at the cosmos and then, for whatever reasons, despairs of finding any personal meaning. Interpretations of this depression on the basis of lower-level structures— psychoneurotic, borderline, or whatever—intuitively sound and feel "silly" or irrelevant to the concerned therapist. A classic example of genuine ennui is from Tolstoy (1929).

Tolstoy's classic example

> The question, which in my fiftieth year had brought me to the notion of suicide, was the simplest of all questions, lying in the soul of every man: "What will come from what I am doing now, and may do tomorrow. What will come from my whole life?" Otherwise expressed—"Why should I live? Why should I wish for anything? Why should I do anything?" Again, in other words: "Is there any meaning in my life which will not be destroyed by the inevitable death awaiting me?"

PART III: THE TRANSPERSONAL PATHOLOGIES

As with the prepersonal and personal realms, the transpersonal realm is here divided into three major levels of development and corresponding pathology, which I call psychic, subtle, and causal. I should like to emphasize, however, that the following discussion is a preliminary investigation. I have, in all cases, attempted to adopt a fairly neutral and balanced stance towards the different contemplative schools, but I realize that some of them might not agree with my particular wording or description of some of these higher stages or their possible pathologies. Thus, if certain contemplative schools object to my use of the terms "psychic," "subtle," and "causal," I invite them to substitute more neutral terms, such as "beginning," "intermediate," and "advanced" stages of the practice, and then interpret the following according to their own tradition. I offer the following not as a series of dogmatic conclusions but as a way to open the discussion on a topic that has been sorely neglected by conventional and contemplative schools alike.

three levels of development and pathology in the transpersonal realm

Fulcrum 7 | *Psychic Disorders*

The emergence of the psychic basic structure brings with it the possibility of another level of self-development and associated self-pathology. By "psychic pathology" (or "F-7 pathology") I mean specifically all the "lower-level" spiritual crises and pathologies that may 1) awaken *spontaneously* in any relatively developed soul; 2) invade any of the lower levels of development during periods of severe stress (e.g., psychotic episodes); and 3) beset the *beginning* practitioner of a contemplative discipline.

1. The most dramatic psychic pathology occurs in the spontaneous and usually unsought awakening of spiritual-psychic energies or capacities. At best, these crises are annoying; at worst, they can be devastating, even to one who is securely anchored in a centauric self. The awakening of Kundalini, for instance, can be psychological dynamite. Excellent examples of these psychic pathologies can be found in Gopi Krishna (1972), John White (1979), and William James (1961).

unsought energies

2. One of the most puzzling aspects of transient schizophrenic breaks or psychotic-like episodes is that they often channel rather profound spiritual insights, but they do so through a self-structure that is neurotic, borderline, or even frankly psychotic (particularly paranoid schizophrenic). Anybody familiar with the *philosophia perennis* can almost instantly spot whether any of the elements of the particular psychotic-like episode have any universal-spiritual components, and thus fairly easily differentiate the "spiritual-channel" psychoses-neuroses from the more mundane (and often more easily treatable) pathologies that originate solely on the psychotic or borderline levels.

psychosis and "spiritual channel" psychoneuroses

3. Beginning practitioner—Psychic pathologies besetting the novitiate include:

a) Psychic inflation—The universal-transpersonal energies and insights of the psychic level are exclusively applied to the individual ego or centaur, with extremely unbalancing results (particularly if there are narcissistic subphase residues in the self-structure).

b) Structural imbalance due to faulty practice of the spiritual technique—This is particularly common in the paths of purification and purgation; in Kriya and Charya Yoga; and in the more subtle techniques, such as mantrayana. It usually manifests in mild, free-floating-anxiety, or in psychosomatic conversion symptoms (headaches, minor heart arrhythmia, intestinal discomforts, etc.).

c) The Dark Night of the Soul—Once the soul obtains a direct taste or experience of the Divine, with concomitant vision, ecstasy, or clarity, and that experience begins to fade (which it initially does), the soul may suffer a profound abandonment depression (*not* to be confused with borderline, neurotic, or existential depression; in this case, the soul *has seen* its meaning in life, its daemon or destiny, only to have it fade—that is the Dark Night).

d) Split life-goals—For example, "Do I stay in the world or retreat to meditation?" This can be extremely painful and psychologically paralyzing. It expresses one form of a profound splitting between upper and lower self-needs, analogous to text-splitting in script pathology, repression in psychoneuroses, etc.

e) "Pseudo-duhkha"—In certain paths of meditation (e.g., Vipassana), where investigation into the very nature of the phenomena of consciousness is stressed, the early phase of awareness training (particularly the "stage of reflection") brings a growing realization of the painful nature of manifest existence itself. Where this realization becomes overwhelming—more overwhelming than the training itself is supposed to invoke—we speak of "pseudo-duhkha." Pseudo-duhkha is often the result of residual existential, psychoneurotic, or, more often, residual borderline contamination of the psychic fulcrum of development. The individual does not gain an understanding of the sourness of life; he or she simply goes sour on life. This psychic depression may be one of the most difficult to treat effectively, particularly because it is often backed by the rationalization that, according to (misunderstood) Buddhism, the world is *supposed* to be suffering. In such cases, more Vipassana is exactly what is *not* needed.

insight into painful nature of existence and "pseudo-duhkha"

f) Pranic disorders—This refers to a misdirection of Kundalini energy in the early stages of its arousal. Various psychic (pranic) channels are over- or under-developed, crossed, or prematurely opened, e.g., "windhorse" *(rlung)* disorders in Tibetan Buddhism. Pranic disorders are usually caused by improper visualization and concentration. They are particularly prevalent in Raja Yoga, Siddha Yoga, Yoga Tantra, and Anu Yoga. Dramatic psychosomatic symptoms are usually prevalent, including barely controllable muscle spasms, violent headache, breathing difficulty, etc.

psychic strains on the physical-emotional body

g) "Yogic illness" (Aurobindo)—This disorder, according to Aurobindo, results when the development of the higher or psychic levels of consciousness puts an undue strain on the physical-emotional body. The great intensity of psychic and subtle energies, can, as it were, overload the "lower circuits," resulting (according to Aurobindo) in everything from allergies to intestinal problems to heart disorders. Perhaps, if he were alive today, he would have added cancer, as witness the health problems of Ramana Maharshi, Suzuki Roshi, etc.

Fulcrum 8   *Subtle Disorders*

The emergence of the subtle basic structure of consciousness brings with it the possibility of subtle-level self-development: a new and higher mode of self, with new object relations, new motivations, new forms of life, new forms of death—and new forms of possible pathology.

two vulnerable points of fulcrum 8 pathologies

The two vulnerable points of F-8 pathology concern: 1) the differentiation-separation-transcendence of the previous mental-psychic dimension, and 2) the identification-integration-consolidation of the subtle-archetypal self and its object relations. Apparently, this pathology occurs most often in intermediate-to-advanced meditators. Some of its many forms:

1. Integration-Identification Failure—The subtle basic structure—which is conceived and perceived by different

paths as a Being, a Force, an Insight, a Deity-Form, or a self-luminous Presence (all of which, for simplicity's sake, are referred to as Archetypal Presence or Awareness)—is first apprehended, to put it metaphorically, "above and behind" mental-psychic consciousness. Eventually, as contemplation deepens, the self differentiates from its psychic moorings and ascends to an intuited identification with that Ground, Insight, Archetypal Presence or Awareness. "Gradually we realize that the Divine Form or Presence is our own archetype, an image of our own essential nature" (Hixon, 1978). This Identity arises concomitantly with a stable *witnessing* of the object relations of subtle consciousness—infinite space, audible illuminations *(nada)*, Brahma realms of ascended knowledge (in Guru Yoga, this also includes an intuited identification with the Guru and Lineage as Archetypal Self). A *failure* to realize this Prior Identity-Awareness, *after* the practitioner is in fact structurally capable of it, is the central defining pathology of these syndromes, because it constitutes, at that point, a fracture between self and Archetype; in Christian terms, a pathology of the soul.

a fracture between self and archetypal awareness

This fracture arises for one basic reason: to identify with and as Archetypal Presence or Awareness demands the *death* of the mental-psychic self. Rather than suffer this humiliation, the self *contracts* on its own separate being, thus fracturing the higher and prior archetypal identity. *Fragments* of Archetypal Presence then appear as *objects* of a still dualistic awareness, instead of whole Archetypal Presence acting as prior and intuited Subject of transcendental consciousness. In other words, instead of *being* Archetypal Awareness (as a subject), the self, in meditation, merely stares at fragments of it (as objects). Consolidation (8c) is not reached.

basic reason for fracture

2. Pseudo-nirvana—This is simply the mistaking of subtle or archetypal forms, illuminations, raptures, ecstasies, insights, or absorptions for final liberation. This is not a pathology unless one is in fact pursuing causal or ultimate levels of consciousness, in which case the *entire* subtle realm and all its experiences, if clung to, are considered

pathological, "makyo," subtle illusions—Zen actually calls it the "Zen sickness."

3. Pseudo-realization—This is the subtle-level equivalent of pseudo-duhkha on the psychic. As Vipassana meditation proceeds into the subtle levels of awareness, a stage of insight called "realization" arises (beyond which lies "effortless insight," the highest of the subtle-level developments). At the realization stage, *every* content of consciousness appears terrifying, oppressive, disgusting, painful, and loathsome; there is extreme physical pain and intense mental-psychic discomfort. However, this is not the pathology of this stage, but is *normalcy* at this stage, which involves an intense insight into the ultimately unsatisfactory nature of phenomena when viewed apart from *pain and* noumenon. This intense pain and revulsion acts as the *revulsion as* motivation to transcend all conceivable manifestation in *motivation* nirvanic absorption. The pseudo-realization pathology occurs when that process fails to quicken and the soul is stranded on the shores of its own agony. Although Theravadin theorists might object to this terminology and its implications, it does seem that this pathology, in deep structure form, is identical to what was previously called a failure to engage Archetypal Awareness and its stable witnessing of all subtle-level object relations.

Fulcrum 9　　　　　*Causal Disorders*

The last major fulcrum of self-development has, for its two branches (c and d), the Formless or Unmanifest (9c), and the entire world of Form, or the Manifest Realm (9d). Normal development involves their proper differentiation (in the causal) and their final integration (in the ultimate). Pathology, on the other hand, results from miscarriages in either of these two crucial movements.

1. Failure of Differentiation—An inability to accept the final death of the archetypal self (which is simply the subtlest level of the separate-self sense) locks consciousness *attachment to* into an attachment to some aspect of the manifest realm. *liberation* The Great Death never occurs, and thus Formless Consciousness fails to differentiate from or transcend the man-

ifest realm. The fall into the Heart is blocked by the subtlest contrasting, grasping, seeking, or desiring; the final block: desire for liberation.

2. Failure to Integrate, or Arhat's Disease—Consciousness manages to differentiate itself from *all* objects of consciousness, or the entire manifest realm, to the extent that no objects even arise in awareness *(jnana samadhi, nirvikalpa samadhi, nirvana)*. Although this is the "final" goal of some paths, in fact a subtle disjuncture, dualism, or tension now exists in consciousness, namely, between the manifest and the unmanifest realms. Only as this disjuncture is penetrated does the manifest realm arise as a modification of Consciousness, not a distraction from it. This is classic *sahaj-bhava samadhi.* I have read no text, nor heard of any sage, that speaks of a level beyond this.

disjuncture of manifest and unmanifest realm

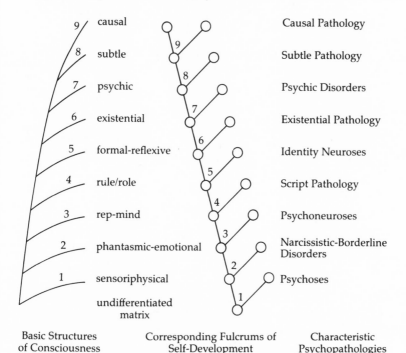

Basic Structures of Consciousness	Corresponding Fulcrums of Self-Development	Characteristic Psychopathologies
9 causal	9	Causal Pathology
8 subtle	8	Subtle Pathology
7 psychic	7	Psychic Disorders
6 existential	6	Existential Pathology
5 formal-reflexive	5	Identity Neuroses
4 rule/role	4	Script Pathology
3 rep-mind	3	Psychoneuroses
2 phantasmic-emotional	2	Narcissistic-Borderline Disorders
1 sensoriphysical	1	Psychoses
undifferentiated matrix		

FIGURE 10

CORRELATION OF STRUCTURES, FULCRUMS, PSYCHOPATHOLOGIES

Fig. 10 is a schematic summary of the discussion thus far: the basic structures of consciousness, the corresponding fulcrums of self-development, and the possible pathologies that may occur at each fulcrum.

CHAPTER 5

TREATMENT MODALITIES

Ken Wilber

In this chapter, Wilber concludes his presentation with a discussion of the various treatment modalities or therapeutic interventions that seem most appropriate for each of the major levels of psychopathology. In the closing section, he discusses the nature of narcissism, dreams, and psychotherapy/meditation, in light of the spectrum model.

We have seen that qualitatively different pathologies are associated with qualitatively different levels of self-organization and self-development. It might be expected, then, that a specific level of pathology would best respond to a specific type of psychotherapeutic intervention. In this section I would like to discuss those treatment modalities that seem best tailored to each type or level of self-pathology. Some of these treatment modalities were, in fact, specifically designed to treat a particular class of psychopathologies, and are often contraindicated for other syndromes.

Fulcrum 1 (Psychoses): Physiological Intervention

Most forms of severe or process psychoses do not respond well (or at all) to psychoanalytic therapy, psychotherapy, analytic psychology, family therapy, etc. (Greist, 1982)— despite repeated and pioneering efforts in this area (Laing, 1967). These disturbances seem to occur on such a primitive level of organization (sensoriperceptual and physiological) that only intervention at an *equally primitive level* is

primitive-level intervention

effective—namely, pharmacological or physiological (which does not rule out psychotherapy as an adjunct treatment [Arieti, 1967; Greist, 1982]).

Fulcrum 2 (Narcissistic-Borderline Disorders): Structure-Building Techniques

The central problem in the narcissistic and borderline syndromes is not that the individual is repressing certain impulses or emotions of the self, but that he or she does not yet possess a separated-individuated self in the first place (Blanck & Blanck, 1979). In a sense, there is not yet a repressed unconscious (or a "repression barrier") (Gedo, 1981). All the various thoughts and emotions are present and largely conscious, but there is considerable confusion as to *whom* these belong to—there is, in other words, a fusion, confusion, or splitting of self and object representations. The self is not yet strong enough or structured enough to "push" contents into the unconscious, and so instead simply rearranges the surface furniture. The boundaries between self and other are either blurred (narcissism) or very tenuous (borderline), and the self shuffles its feelings and thoughts indiscriminately between self and other, or groups all its good feelings on one subject (the "all-good part-object") and all its bad feelings on another (the "all-bad part-object") (Masterson, 1981).

Accordingly, the aim of therapy on this level is not so much to uncover unconscious drives or impulses, but to build structure. In fact, it is often said that the aim of therapy in these less-than-neurotically structured clients is to enable them to reach the level of neurosis, repression, and resistance (Blanck & Blanck, 1979). Therapy on the Fulcrum 2 level thus involves the so-called "structure-building techniques," as contrasted with the "uncovering techniques" used to deal with repression and the psychoneuroses (Gedo, 1979, 1981; Blanck & Blanck, 1974, 1979).

The aim of the structure-building techniques, very simply, is to help the individual re-engage and complete the separation-individuation process (Fulcrum 2) (Masterson, 1981). That involves an understanding (and undermining)

the central problem in narcissistic borderline syndromes

aim of therapy is to build structure

of the two central defenses that the individual uses to prevent separation-individuation from occurring: projective
identification (or fusion of self and object representations)
and splitting (Kernberg, 1976; Rinsley, 1977). In projective *"projective*
identification (or merger defense), the self fuses its own *identification"*
thoughts and feelings (and particularly self-representa- *defense*
tions) with those of the other. Notice that the thoughts and
feelings remain more or less conscious; they are not repressed, they simply tend to be fused or confused with
those of the other. This inability to differentiate self and
other leads to the self engulfing the world (narcissistic disorders) or the world invading and threatening to engulf
the self (borderline disorders). In splitting, the particular
thoughts and feelings also remain largely conscious, but
they are divided up or compartmentalized in a rather
primitive fashion. Splitting apparently begins in this way:
During the first 6 months or so of life, if the mothering one
soothes the infant, it forms an image of the "good *"splitting"*
mother"; if she disturbs it, an image of the "bad mother" *defense*
forms. At this early stage, however, the self does not have
the cognitive capacity to realize that the "good images"
and the "bad images" are simply two different aspects of
the *same* person (or "whole object"), namely, the real
mother. As development continues, however, the infant
must learn to integrate the "all-good part-object" and the
"all-bad part-object" into a whole image of the object,
which is *sometimes* good and *sometimes* bad. This is thought
to be a crucially important task, because if there is excessive rage at the "all-bad part-object," the infant will not
integrate it with the loving "all-good part-object" for fear
it will harm the latter. In less technical language, the infant
doesn't want to realize that the person it hates is also the
person it loves, because the murderous rage at the former
might destroy the latter. The infant therefore *continues* to
hold apart, or split, its object world into all-good pieces
and all-bad pieces (and thus over-react to situations as if
they were a dramatic life and death concern, "all-good" or
"all-bad") (Spitz, 1965; Jacobson, 1964; Kernberg, 1976).

In short, the F-2 pathologies result because there is *not
enough structure* to differentiate self and object representations, and to integrate their part-images into a whole-self
image and a whole-object world. The structure-building

techniques aim at exactly that differentiation-and-integration.

It is very difficult to describe, in a paragraph, what these techniques involve. Briefly, we may say this: the therapist, *therapists'* keeping in mind the subphases of F-2 development, gently *techniques at* rewards all thrusts towards separation-individuation, and *F-2 level* benignly confronts or explains all moves towards de-differentiating and splitting. At the same time, any distortions of reality—caused by projective identification or splitting—are pointed out and challenged wherever feasible (this is known variously as "optimal disillusionment," "confrontation," etc.). A few typical therapist comments, paraphrased from the literature, illustrate this level of therapy: "Have you noticed how sensitive you are to even the slightest remark? It's as if you want the world to perfectly mirror everything you do, and if it doesn't, you become hurt and angry" (narcissistic mirror transference). "So far you haven't said a single bad thing about your father. Was he really all that good?" (splitting). "What if your husband leaves you? Would it really kill you?" (fear of separation abandonment). "Perhaps you have avoided a really intimate sexual relationship because you're afraid you will be swallowed up or smothered?" (fear of engulfment).

A common feature of the structure-building techniques is to help clients realize that they can *activate themselves*, or *engage separation-individuation*, and it will not destroy them or the ones they love. Sources on these techniques include Blanck & Blanck (1974, 1979), Masterson (1981), Kernberg (1976), and Stone (1980).

Fulcrum 3 (Psychoneuroses): Uncovering Techniques

Once a strong-enough self-structure has formed (but not *uncovering and* before), it can repress, dissociate, or alienate aspects of its *re-integrating* own being. The uncovering techniques are designed specifically to bring these unconscious aspects back into awareness, where they can be re-integrated with the central self. Readers may be familiar enough with these techniques, which include psychoanalysis proper (Greenson,

1967), much of Gestalt therapy (Perls, 1971), and the inte-
grating-the-shadow aspect of Jungian therapy (Jung,
1971).

It is worth emphasizing here the importance of a more or
less accurate initial diagnosis of the level of pathology in- *importance of*
volved, in each case, before intensive therapy begins (cf *accurate initial*
Gedo, 1981; Masterson, 1981). It is of little use, for in- *diagnosis*
stance, to try to integrate the shadow with the ego-self if
there is insufficient ego-self to begin with. The types of
treatment modalities are characteristically different and
often functionally opposed. In F-3 pathologies, for example, resistance is usually confronted and interpreted (as
a sign of repression), but in the F-2 pathologies, it is often
encouraged and assisted (as a sign of separation-
individuation). Sources for such differential diagnosis include Kernberg (1975, 1976), Masterson (1981), Gedo
(1981), and Blanck & Blanck (1974, 1979).

Fulcrum 4 (Script Pathology): Cognitive-Script Analysis

Most conventional psychodynamic theorists tend to end
their accounts of "serious" pathology at F-3, that is, at the *"serious"*
oedipal phase and its resolution (or lack thereof) (see, for *pathology up*
example, Greenson, 1967). This is perhaps understand- *through the*
able; after all, the classic psychopathologies (from psy- *oedipal phase*
chosis to hysteria) do seem to have their most disturbing
etiologies in the first three fulcrums of self-development
(cf Abend, 1983; Kernberg, 1976). But this by no means
exhausts the spectrum of pathologies, not even the spectrum of "serious" or "profound" pathologies. Accordingly,
researchers increasingly have begun to look at higher or
postoedipal stages of development and their correlative
vulnerabilities and dis-eases.

Take, for example, the notion of "role confusion." The capacity for genuine role taking is a decisively postoedipal
development (the capacity to take the role of other does
not emerge, in any sophisticated fashion, until around age
7-8 yrs [Piaget, 1977; Loevinger, 1976], whereas the typical
age of oedipal resolution is 6 yrs). Thus, one could theo-

post-oedipal developmental conflicts

retically resolve the oedipal conflict in a completely normal and healthy fashion, only to run aground on role confusion and identity confusion, for reasons totally unrelated to oedipal conflicts or concerns. We are here dealing with different levels (not just lines) of development, with different conflicts and vulnerabilities. *These conflicts are much more cognitive than psychodynamic in nature and origin*, because at this point the self increasingly is evolving from bodily to mental levels of the spectrum.

One of Berne's (1972) contributions was the investigation of this crucial level of the self—the text self or script self—on its own terms, without reducing it to merely psychoneurotic or libidinal dimensions. He began with the tripartite ego (Parent-Adult-Child), which shows that he was starting at the F-3 level (and not F-1 or F-2), and then phenomenologically examined how this self took on more complex and intersubjective roles in an extended series of object relations. Similar but more sophisticated types of investigations have been carried out by cognitive role theorists (Selman, 1974), social learning theorists (Bandura, 1971), family therapists (Haley, 1968), and communications psychologists (Watzlawick, 1967). These closely related techniques, of whatever school, are referred to here as "cognitive-script analysis."

cognitive script pathologies

Probably the most prevalent or common pathologies are cognitive-script pathologies. These pathologies—and their treatment modalities—seem to break down into two very general classes, one involving the *roles* a person is playing, and one involving the *rules* the person is following. Though closely related, these two classes may be discussed separately:

1. *Role pathology*—This has been typically investigated by Transactional Analysis (Berne, 1972), family therapists (Nichols, 1984), and cognitive-role psychologists (Branden, 1971). The individual involved in role pathology is sending multi-level communicative messages, one level of which denies, contradicts, or circumvents another level. The individual thus possesses all sorts of hidden agendas, crossed messages, confused roles, duplicitous transac-

tions, and so on. It is the job of the script analyst to help separate, untangle, clarify, and integrate the various communicative strands involved in role-self pathology. The interior splitting of the text-self into overt vs. covert communicative engagements (or into dissociated sub-texts) is thus confronted, interpreted, and, if successful, integrated (a new and higher level of differentiation-integration).

2. *Rule pathology*—One of the central tenets of cognitive therapy is that "an individual's affect and behavior are largely determined by the way in which he structures the world," and therefore "alterations in the content of the person's underlying cognitive structures affect his or her affective state and behavioral pattern" (Beck, 1979). In other words, an individual's cognitive schemas, configurations, or rules are a major determinant of his or her feelings and actions. Confused, distorted, or self-limiting rules and beliefs can be manifest in clinical symptoms; conversely, "through psychological therapy a patient can become aware of his distortions," and "corrections of these faulty dysfunctional constructs can lead to clinical improvement" (Beck, 1979). Similar cognitive approaches can also be found in such theorists as George Kelley (1955) and Albert Ellis (1973).

I do not mean to imply that cognitive-script therapy applies solely to F-4 pathology (it appears to have significant applications in the F-4, F-5, and F-6 range). It is simply that F-4 is the first major stage in which cognitive-script concerns fully develop and begin to differentiate themselves from the more psychodynamic concerns of the previous fulcrums. As in any developmental sequence, such early stages are particularly vulnerable to pathological distortions. Just as adult sexual dysfunctions can often be traced back to early phallic/oedipal conflicts, many of the cognitive-script pathologies seem to have their genesis in the early (and possibly distorted or limited) rules and roles one learned when the mind *first* became capable of extended mental operations (i.e., during Fulcrum 4). Thus, in addition to uncovering techniques, the pathogenic cognitive-script should ideally be attacked on its own level and in its own terms.

multi-level application of cognitive script therapy

Fulcrum 5 (Identity Neurosis): Introspection

The hierarchic model of pathology and treatment presented thus far is in substantial agreement with mainstream, conventional psychiatry. To cite one example, as far back as 1973 Gedo and Goldberg presented a hierarchic model composed of, as they word it, "five subphases and five therapeutic modalities. Each modality was tailored to deal with the principal problem characterizing a different subphase: introspection [formal-reflection] for the difficulties expectable in adult life, interpretation for the intrapsychic conflicts [psychoneuroses], 'optimal disillusionment' for archaic idealizations of others or self-aggrandizement [narcissistic mirroring], 'unification' for any failure to integrate one coherent set of personal goals [borderline splitting], and 'pacification' [pharmacological/custodial] for traumatic states."

multi-level compatibility of Gedo and Goldberg model

With the exception of cognitive-script pathology and analysis, Gedo and Goldberg's model is, within general limits, totally compatible with the one I have thus far presented (i.e., F-1 to F-5). Pacification, either custodial or pharmacological, refers to F-1 pathology. "Optimal disillusionment" is a structure-building technique for the narcissistic disorders, and involves benign ways of letting the narcissistic self realize that it is not as grandiose or omnipotent as it thought or feared. "Unification" is a structure-building technique to overcome splitting, which is thought to centrally characterize F-2 pathology. "Interpretation" refers specifically to interpreting the resistances (repressions) and transferences manifested in the treatment of the F-3 pathologies (the psychoneuroses). And introspection, in this context, refers to the techniques used in dealing with the difficulties or problems that arise from F-5 development: the formal-reflexive-introspective self and its turmoils.

According to Gedo (1981), "The mode that reflects post-oedipal phases of mental organization permits the analysand to apprehend his internal life through introspection, i.e., without the interpretation of defensive operations. In such circumstances, the role of the analyst is optimally confined to lending his presence to the procedure as an empathic witness." That is, the central and defining problems of F-5 development involve neither psychoneurotic repression nor immersion in pathogenic scripts, but the *emergence* and *engagement* of the formal-reflexive mind and its correlative, introspective self-sense (with its particular vulnerabilities and distresses). No amount of uncovering techniques or script analysis will suffice to handle these problems, precisely because these problems involve structures that transcend those lower levels of organization and thus present entirely new features, functions, and pathologies of their own.

formal-reflexive mind and introspective self-sense

This is not to say, of course, that F-5 pathology has no relation to the developments (or lack of them) at the previous four fulcrums. As we will see in a subsequent discussion of COEX systems, any previous subphase deficiencies, if not enough to arrest development entirely at a lower level, can and will invade upper development in specific and disturbing ways (cf Blanck & Blanck, 1979; Mahler, 1975). In this case, for example, an individual with only partial F-2 (or separation-individuation) resolution may be very reluctant to engage the formal-reflexive mind, with its demanding call to individual principles of moral reasoning and conscience. The attempted engagement of the formal-reflexive mind might trigger abandonment-depression or separation anxiety.

Introspection may be considered simply another term for *philosophizing*, and it is philosophizing, by any other name, that seems to be the treatment modality of this level. However, I do not agree with Gedo that the therapist's job at this level is simply to be a silent empathic witness to the client's emergent philosophizing. To be merely silent at this point is to risk being absent (i.e., worthless). Gedo's psychoanalytic orientation may have instilled in him unwarranted fears of "contaminating" the client with countertransference material. But by Gedo's own definitions, *if* that occurs, it could only involve the interpretive modality, not the introspective. If the client is clearly in the introspective (not interpretive) modality, there is nothing to be lost, and much to be gained, by the therapist taking a more

introspection or philosophizing as treatment

active role, becoming, in a sense, a co-educator or co-philosopher.

a Socratic dialogue

It is exactly at this level, then, that the therapist can engage the client in a *Socratic dialogue*, which engages, simultaneously, the client's formal-reflexive mind (if, in this dialogue, lower-level residues surface, the therapist can revert to interpretation, structure-building, script analysis, etc.). As with any Socratic dialogue, the particular content is not as important as the fact that it engages, activates, draws out, and exercises the client's reflexive-introspective mind and its correlative self-sense (e.g., Loevinger's conscientious and individualistic). The therapist, then, need not overly worry about "contaminating" the client with his or her own philosophy; once engaged, the formal mind, by definition, will gravitate towards its own views, the birth of which the therapist may Socratically assist.

Fulcrum 6 (Existential Pathology): Existential Therapy

existential concerns of being-in-the-world

As introspection and philosophizing are engaged and matured, the basic, fundamental, or existential concerns of being-in-the-world come increasingly to the fore (cf Maslow, 1968; May, 1958). Existential pathology occurs if these concerns begin to overwhelm the newly formed centauric self and freeze its functioning (Wilber, 1980a). These pathologies include, as we have seen, existential depression, angst, inauthenticity, a flight from finitude and death, etc.

How these existential pathologies are handled varies considerably from system to system; for some, it is a simple continuing and qualitative deepening of the introspective mode. But a central therapeutic commonality seems to be this: the *clearer* or more transparent the self becomes (via concernful reflection), or the more it can empty itself of egocentric, power-based, or inauthentic modes, the more it comes to an *autonomous* or *authentic* stance or grounding (Zimmerman, 1981). And it is this *grounding* in authenticity and autonomy that *itself* provides existential meaning in life, that combats dread and angst, and that provides a courage to be in the face of "sickness unto death" (Tillich,

1952; May, 1977). Authentic being, in other words, carries intrinsic (not extrinsic) meaning; it is precisely the search for extrinsic or merely external meaning that constitutes inauthenticity (and thus existential despair). Analysis of, and confrontation of, one's various inauthentic modes—particularly extrinsically-oriented, non-autonomous, or death-denying—seems to be the key therapeutic technique on this level (Koestenbaum, 1976; Yalom, 1980; May, 1958; Boss, 1963).

These concepts of intrinsic meaning (or a new and higher level of interiorization) and the engagement of autonomy *two features of* (or a new and higher level of self responsibility) seem to *humanistic-* be the two central features emphasized by all genuine *existential* schools of humanistic-existential therapy. Further, their *therapy* claim that this constitutes a higher level of development has substantial clinical and empirical research support—this is, for example, Loevinger's (1976) integrated-autonomous stage (as opposed to the previous conscientious-individualistic).

I should point out that when existential therapists speak of the self becoming a clearing or opening for the "Being" of phenomena, they do not mean that the self has access to, or opens to, any genuinely transcendental or timeless and spaceless modes of being. The self is an opening to Being, but that opening is strictly finite, individual and mortal. As far as they go, I agree with the existentialists; there is nothing timeless or eternal about the centauric self, and an acceptance of that fact is part of the very definition of authenticity. But to say this is the whole picture *a preeminent* is to say the centauric self is the highest self, whereas, *defense* according to the *philosophia perennis*, there lie above it the *mechanism* entire realms of the superconscient. If this is correct, then at this point a denial of the possibility of spiritual transcendence would constitute a preeminent defense mechanism. It is my own belief that what the existentialists call autonomy is simply a higher interiorization of consciousness (see subsequent discussion); if this interiorization continues, it easily discloses psychic and subtle developments. The self is then no longer an opening to Being; it starts to identify with, and as, Being itself.

Fulcrum 7 (Psychic Pathology): The Path of Yogis

Da Free John (1977) has divided the world's great esoteric traditions into three major levels: the Path of Yogis, which predominantly aims for the psychic level; the Path of Saints, which predominantly aims for the subtle level; and the Path of Sages, which predominantly aims for the causal. That terminology will be used in the following sections, as I am in substantial agreement with his writings on these topics.

beginning, intermediate, advanced stages

However, since these terms tend to have several different connotations, many not intended by Free John or by myself, one may also refer to these levels with more neutral terms, such as beginning, intermediate, and advanced; or ground, path, and fruition. I have tried to represent the various contemplative traditions evenly, but if it appears that my own preferences and biases are coloring any of the following discussions, I invite the reader to re-interpret them according to the terms, practices, and philosophies of his or her own particular path. My central point, no matter how it might be finally worded, is that contemplative development in general possesses three broad levels or stages (beginning, intermediate, and advanced); that different tasks and capacities emerge at each level; that different distortions, pathologies, or disorders may therefore occur at each level; and that these distortions or pathologies may best be treated by different types of "spiritual" therapy (some of which may also benefit from adjunct conventional therapies).

The following discussion of psychic (F-7) pathology parallels that of Chapter 4, which outlined three general types—spontaneous, psychotic-like, and beginners.

spontaneous, unsought awakenings

1. *Spontaneous*—For pathology resulting from spontaneous and unsought awakening of spiritual-psychic energies or insights, there seem to be only two general treatment modalities: the individual must either "ride it out," sometimes under the care of a conventional psychiatrist who may interpret it as a borderline or psychotic break and prescribe medication, which often freezes the process in midcourse and prevents any further reparative developments (Grof,

1975); or the individual can *consciously* engage this process by taking up a contemplative discipline.

If the spontaneous awakening is of the kundalini itself, the Path of Yogis is most appropriate (Raja Yoga, Kriya Yoga, Charya Yoga, Kundalini Yoga, Siddha Yoga, Hatha-Ashtanga Yoga, etc.). This is so for a specific reason: the Path of Saints and the Path of Sages, which aim for the higher subtle and causal realms, contain very little explicit teachings on the stages of psychic-kundalini awakening (e.g., one will look in vain through the texts of Zen, Eckhart, St. John of the Cross, etc., for any mention or understanding of kundalini). If at all possible, the individual should be put in touch with a qualified yogic adept, who can work, if desired, in conjunction with a more conventional therapist (see, for example, Avalon, 1974; Krishna, 1972; Mookerjee, 1982; Taimni, 1975; Da Free John, 1977; White, 1979).

2. *Psychotic-like*—For genuinely psychotic or psychotic-like episodes with periodic but distorted spiritual components, Jungian therapy may be suggested (cf Grof, 1975; White, 1979). A contemplative discipline, whether yogic, saintly, or sagely, is usually contraindicated; these disciplines demand a sturdy ego or centaur-level self, which the psychotic or borderline does not possess (Engler, 1984). After a sufficient period of structure-building (which most Jungian therapists are aware of), the individual may wish to engage in the less strenuous contemplative paths (e.g., mantrayana); see section on "Meditation and Psychotherapy." *psychotic and psychotic-like episodes*

3. *Beginning Practitioner*
a) *Psychic inflation*—This confusion of higher or transpersonal realms with the individual ego or centaur can often be handled with a subtler version of "optimal disillusionment," a continual separation of psychic fact from narcissistic fantasies (cf Jung, 1971). If this repeatedly fails, it is usually because a psychic insight has reactivated a narcissistic-borderline or even psychotic residue. At that point, meditation should usually be stopped immediately and, if necessary, structure-building engaged (either psychoanalytic or Jungian). If the individual responds to these, and *psychic inflation*

eventually can understand the how and why of his psychic inflation, meditation can usually be resumed.

faulty practice

b) *Structural imbalance* (due to faulty practice of the spiritual technique)—The individual should verify this with the meditation teacher; these imbalances, which are not uncommon, point up how extremely important it is to undertake contemplative disciplines only under the guidance of a qualified master (cf Aurobindo, n.d.; Khetsun, 1982).

Dark Night agony

c) *Dark Night of the Soul*—Reading accounts of how others have weathered this phase can be very helpful (see especially St. John of the Cross, Underhill, Kapleau). In periods of profound despair, the soul may break into petitionary, as opposed to contemplative, prayer (to Jesus, Mary, Kwannon, Allah, etc.); this need not be discouraged—it is prayer to one's own higher Archetype (cf Hixon, 1978; Kapleau, 1965). It might be noted that no matter how profound the depression or agony of the Dark Night might be, the literature contains virtually no cases of its leading to suicide (in sharp contrast to existential or borderline depressions, for example). It is as if the depression of the Dark Night had a "higher" or "purgatorial" or "intelligent" purpose—and this, of course, is exactly the claim of contemplatives (see, for example, St. John of the Cross, 1959).

split-life confusion

d) *Split-life goals*—It is important (particularly in our society, and particularly at this point in evolution) that one's spiritual practice be integrated into daily life and work (as a bodhisattvic endeavor). If one's path is of exclusion and withdrawal, perhaps one ought to consider another path. In my opinion, the path of ascetic withdrawal all too often introduces a profound split between the upper and lower dimensions of existence, and, in general, confuses *suppression* of earthly life with transcendence of earthly life.

depression/ anxiety

e) *Pseudo-duhkha*—Although the details of the treatment modality for this disorder may be worked out with the meditation teacher, the teacher is sometimes the worst person to consult in these particular cases. Spiritual teachers generally have no knowledge of the dynamics of borderline or psychoneurotic disorders, and their advice may be, "Intensify your effort!," which is precisely what triggered the problem in the first place. In most cases, the meditator should cease all meditation for a few months. If moderate-to-severe depression/anxiety persists, a borderline or psychoneurotic COEX might have been reactivated (see subsequent discussion), and appropriate structure-building or uncovering therapies might be engaged. It seems inadvisable for such an individual to continue intensive meditation until the particular subphase deficiencies have received appropriate attention.

f) *Pranic disorders*—These disorders are notorious for inducing hysterical-like conversion symptoms which, if left untreated, may induce genuine psychosomatic disease (cf Da Free John, 1978; Chang, 1974; Evans-Wentz, 1971). They are best handled in conjunction with the yogic meditation teacher (and a physician if needed). Specifically suggested: Kriya Yoga, Charya Yoga, Raja Yoga and (more advanced) Anu Yoga (Khetsun, 1982; Rieker, 1971; Chang, 1974). Also, acupuncture performed by *qualified* practitioners may be very effective. *hysterical-like conversion symptoms*

g) *Yogic illness*—The best "cure" is also the best prevention: strengthening and purifying the physical-emotional body: exercise, lactovegetarian diet, restricted intake of caffeine, sugar, nicotine, and social drugs (Aurobindo, n.d.; Da Free John, 1978). *undue strain on physical-emotional body*

Fulcrum 8 (Subtle Pathology): The Path of Saints

1. *Integration-Identification Failure*—The author is not aware of any treatment modality for this pathology except to engage (or intensify) the path of subtle-level contemplation (the Path of Saints), which, at this point, usually *begins* to involve some form of *inquiry,* overt or covert, into the *contraction* that constitutes the separate-self sense (Da Free John, 1978; Ramana Maharshi, 1972; Suzuki, 1970). It is said to be an actual *seeing* of that contraction, which is blocking subtle or archetypal awareness, and *not* a direct attempt to identify with archetypal awareness itself, that constitutes the therapeutic treatment for this particular disorder (much as, in psychoanalysis, one has to deal with the resistance first, then the content). *seeing the contraction that constitutes the sense of a separate self*

stabilization of the archetypal self

According to some traditions (e.g., Aurobindo, Christian mysticism, Hinduism), if this contraction or subtle-level resistance is not relaxed to a sufficient degree (it is not totally dismantled until the causal level is reached), the consolidation and stabilization of the archetypal self will not be achieved, and the individual may then be inundated and overwhelmed by the tremendously powerful energies and dynamics released in the subtle realm—some Tantric texts speak of being "destroyed by luminosity" (e.g., Evans-Wenz, 1971); in Christian mystical terms, the soul damages itself by denying (resisting) God's love (or archetypal presence).

understanding the resistance

The common treatment modality for these disorders seems to include a *seeing* and then *understanding* of the subtle contraction or resistance to a larger archetypal awareness, a contraction that at bottom involves an inability to accept the death of the previous (or mental/psychic) self-sense and its attachments and desires—a case of morbid fixation/arrest at the psychic level (which prevents transformation to the subtle; see, for example, Aurobindo, n.d.; Da Free John, 1978: Trungpa, 1976; Khetsun, 1982).

According to Hinduism and Buddhism, it is at this point, too, that one begins to encounter and understand the "deep-seated defilements" (root *klesas* and *vasanas)* that not only obscure the next and higher stage of formless or unmanifest awareness, but ultimately give rise to all forms of human suffering and pathology, high or low (Deutsche, 1969; Feuerstein, 1975; Gard, 1962; Longchenpa, 1977).

moving from subtle to causal levels

2. *Pseudo-nirvana*—This mistaking of subtle illuminations and archetypal forms for ultimate enlightenment can only be handled by moving beyond these luminous forms to unmanifest or formless cessation; that is, by moving from subtle to causal level development. Many of the most sophisticated contemplative traditions have numerous "checking routines" that help the practitioner review the ecstatic, luminous, blissful, and "tempting" subtle experiences and thus eventually gain a distancing or nonattached stance towards this archetypal level (after, that is, it has been stably achieved in the first place) (Goleman, 1977; Da Free John, 1978; Khetsun, 1982; Trungpa, 1976).

3. *Pseudo-realization*—Unlike pseudo-duhkha, which usually demands a halting of meditation, there is usually no cure for pseudo-realization except more meditation. The only thing more painful than continuing meditation is failing to continue meditation. Zen refers to this particular type of "Zen sickness" as being like "swallowing a red-hot iron ball" (Suzuki, 1970); it is apparently one of the few *disorders* for which one can *therapeutically* say, "Intensify your efforts!"

the pain of continuing and the pain of not continuing

With most subtle-level pathologies, it apparently is not too late for adjunct psychotherapy, if, and only if, the therapist is sympathetic towards, and reasonably knowledgeable about, transcendental or spiritual concerns. The psychotherapeutic freeing of repressed emotional energies, for example, might be the crucial boost needed to negotiate subtle level integration. The structure-building techniques, while not without use, become increasingly less applicable at this stage, because most individuals with significant borderline deficiencies rarely develop to this stage.

adjunct psychotherapy

Fulcrum 9 (Causal Pathology): The Path of Sages

1. *Failure to Differentiate*—According to teachings as diverse as Zen, Free John, and Vajrayana, this final differentiation or detachment (i.e., from all manifest form) involves a subtle but momentous collaboration on the part of the student and the teacher, which may be briefly (and inadequately) described as follows: The teacher, at this point, resides within the "Heart" (or causal/unmanifest realm) of the student, and exerts a special "pull"; the student, in the final and root form of the separate-self sense (the archetypal self), is still standing in a subtly contracted form "outside" the Heart (i.e., resisting the final and total dissolution of the separate-self sense). The student and teacher "together," through an "effortless effort," release this stance, and the separate-self "falls" into the Heart. This "fall" into formless, unmanifest cessation or emptiness breaks all exclusive attachment to manifest forms and destinies, and Consciousness as Such (or Absolute Subjectivity) differentiates itself from all objects, high or low, and

the "fall" into the Heart

from all archetypal tendencies or root contractions (klesas, vasanas, etc.). Repetition of this "fall"—or repeated "movement" from manifest to unmanifest and back again—"burns" the root inclinations and desires for contracted and separated modes of self existence. This fall is the "entrance" to the stages of enlightenment (conceived by Buddhism as ground, path, and fruition enlightenment, which may be thought of as the three subphases of the enlightened or "perfectly ordinary" estate).

the re-integration of emptiness-form and wisdom

2. *Failure to Integrate*—This "ultimate pathology" (a failure to integrate the manifest and unmanifest realms) results when the root klesas and vasanas (or archetypal forms and inclinations) are seen *only* as defilements and not also as the means of *expression* or manifestation of unobstructed Wisdom (absolute Spirit or Being). The overcoming of this disjunction and the re-union or re-integration of emptiness-form and wisdom *are* the "supreme path," the path of "ordinary mind" (Maha Ati), "open eyes" (Free John), and "everyday mind" (Ch'an)—wherein all phenomena, high or low, exactly as they find themselves, are seen as already perfect expressions and seals of the naturally enlightened mind.

Fig. 11 is a schematic summary of the basic structures of consciousness, the corresponding fulcrums of self-development, their characteristic pathologies, and the correlative treatment modalities.

RELATED TOPICS

In this section I would like to comment on differential diagnosis, connections to Grof's COEX systems theory, narcissism, dreams, and meditation/psychotherapy, in light of the full spectrum of development and pathology.

Differential Diagnosis

It is important to emphasize again the great care that should ideally be given to differential diagnosis, *particularly* in light of the full spectrum of human growth and

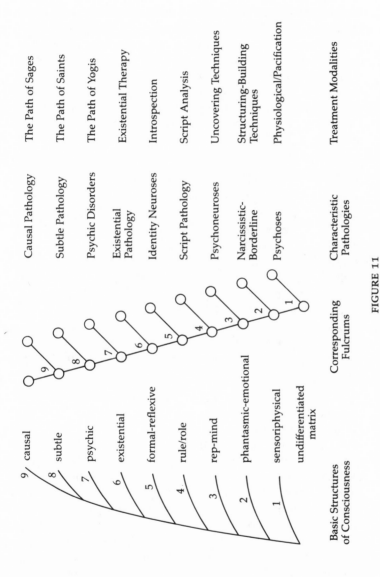

FIGURE 11

CORRELATION OF STRUCTURES, FULCRUMS, PSYCHOPATHOLO-
GIES, AND TREATMENTS

development. For example, psychic anxiety, existential anxiety, psychoneurotic anxiety, and borderline anxiety are apparently very different phenomena with very different treatment modalities, and thus any effective and appropriate therapeutic intervention depends significantly on an accurate initial diagnosis. This, in turn, rests upon a skilled understanding of the entire spectrum of consciousness—an understanding of the overall levels of self-structuralization and the particular types of needs, motivations, cognitions, object relations, defense mechanisms, and pathologies that are specific and characteristic for each stage of structural development and organization.

accurate diagnosis rests on understanding the entire spectrum

Currently, models less comprehensive than the one proposed here are being used to diagnose and treat clients, with an apparent collapse of what seem to be very different diagnostic and treatment categories. For example, Kohut's two major diagnostic categories are Tragic Man (borderline) and Guilty Man (neurotic). His theory does not address spiritual pathologies, and therefore must reduce them all to lower-level concerns. Likewise, his conceptualization apparently requires the reduction of existential pathologies to borderline "Tragic Man," as if the only existential tragedy in the cosmos is separation of child from mother.

A major therapeutic confusion among various theorists stems from what I have called the "pre/trans fallacy" (Wilber, 1980b), which is a confusing of *pre*-rational structures with *trans*-rational structures simply because both are *non*-rational. This confusion runs in both directions: pre-rational structures (phantasmic, magic, mythic) are *elevated* to trans-rational status (e.g., Jung), or trans-rational structures are *reduced* to pre-rational infantilisms (e.g., Freud). It is particularly common to reduce samadhi (subtle or causal subject-object identity) to autistic, symbiotic, or narcissistic-ocean states. Likewise, Atman, the one universal Self, is confused with the monadic-autistic F-1 self. Alexander (1931) even called Zen a training in catatonic schizophrenia. In my opinion, such theoretical (and therapeutic) confusions will continue to abound until the phenomenological validity of the full spectrum of human

the pre/trans fallacy

growth and development receives more recognition and study.

COEX Systems

Stanislav Grof (1975) has coined the term "COEX systems" to refer to "systems of condensed experience," which are developmentally layered or onion-like complexes in the psyche. This is an important concept and, although similar ideas abound in the literature, Grof has given the notion one of its clearest articulations.

Pathological COEX systems, as I see them, are simply the sum of the associated and condensed aspects of unmetabolized experiences or subphase deficiencies that result at any particular fulcrum of self-structuralization (cf Guntrip, 1971; Kernberg, 1975). Starting at Fulcrum 1, any particular subphase deficiency (provided it is not severe enough to derail development entirely at that point) is taken up—as a *dissociated pocket in the self-structure*—during the ongoing march of self-structuralization. At the next fulcrum, any subphase deficiencies or malformations likewise become split off and lodged in the self-structure, where—and this was pointed out by both Grof and Jung—they become condensed and associated with similar, previous subphase malformations. Not only do present-level malformations condense with previous ones, they tend to invade and contaminate the *subsequent* or higher-level fulcrums, skewing their development toward similar pathological malformations (quite apart from the malformations that might develop entirely due to their *own* subphase deficiencies). Like a grain of sand lodged in a pearl during its early formation, each subsequent layer tends to reproduce the defect on its own level. The result is a pathological COEX system, a multi-layered unit of associated and condensed subphase malformations, built up, fulcrum by fulcrum, and lodged, as split or dissociated subunits (or pockets of "unconscious, undigested experience") in the overall self-structure itself.

Grof's "systems of condensed experience"

A presenting symptom, therefore, may be merely the tip of a more or less extensive pathological COEX system. The particular COEX might be compounded of residues from, say, F-5, F-3, and F-2 subphase deficiencies. One of the aims of psychotherapy in general is to re-contact and re-experience the particular undigested subphase residues, layer by layer if necessary, and thus help repair structural malformations—i.e., allow those aspects of the self-system, previously lodged and stuck in various lower subphase pockets, to be released or "freed-up" to *rejoin* the ongoing march of structural organization and development.

Narcissism

a confused and confusing topic

"Narcissism" is probably the most confused and confusing topic in the technical therapeutic literature. It has been given literally dozens of different and sometimes contradictory definitions; there are vague references to *levels* of narcissism (primary, secondary, tertiary, etc.); and finally, there is said to be normal narcissism and pathological narcissism. What are we to make of all this?

Most of these confusions can be cleared up if we 1) explicitly define the levels or stages of narcissism, and 2) recognize that each stage of narcissism has both normal and pathological dimensions.

the different meanings of the term "narcissism"

To begin with, the term "narcissism," as it is used in the literature, has several major and quite different meanings. In a neutral or nonpejorative sense, "narcissism" is used to mean "self." "Narcissistic development," for instance, simply means "self-development." No negative connotations of egocentricity, grandiosity, or arrogance are implied. To say there are levels of narcissism or levels of narcissistic development means, in this usage, nothing more than that there are levels of self or levels of self-development. In this paper, for instance, we have outlined 9 major stages (each with three subphases) of "narcissism."

"Narcissism" is also used to mean "selfcentrism," or incapacity to take sufficient awareness of others. This, however, is not necessarily a pathological or morbid condition; in fact, it is usual to distinguish between "normal narcissism" and "pathological narcissism." Normal narcissism refers to the *amount of selfcentrism* that is *structurally inevitable* or normal at each stage of development. Thus, for example, primary narcissism (or incapacity to even recognize an object world) is inevitable or normal at the autistic stage. The grandiose-exhibitionistic self/object fusion is *normal* at the practicing subphase. Although this is often called "the narcissistic stage," as a matter of convention, it is universally recognized that the amount of narcissism (selfcentrism) at this stage is actually less than in the previous stage, because there is at least an awareness of objects, which the previous or primary narcissism lacked entirely.

normal narcissism

The rep-mind stage is even less narcissistic or selfcentric than the grandiose stage, but it still possesses a substantial degree of selfcentrism (or narcissism), as Piaget demonstrated, simply because it cannot yet take the role of others. This narcissism decreases with the rule/role mind, since the role of others is now recognized, and decreases even further with the emergence of the formal-mind, which can increasingly escape its own subjectivism by *reflection* on alternative viewpoints.

But at this point a certain amount of selfcentrism still remains, according to the contemplative traditions, simply because a certain amount of the separate-self sense still remains. Even into the subtle realm, according to Da Free John, Narcissus (which is his term) is still present (though highly reduced) because there is still a subtle contraction inward on self and a consequent "recoil from relationship" (Da Free John, 1977).

So here is the first point: there are nine or so major levels of narcissism, *each of which is less narcissistic (less selfcentric) than its predecessor(s)*. Narcissism (selfcentrism) starts out at its peak in the autistic stage (primary narcissism); each subsequent fulcrum of development results in a reduction of narcissism, simply because at each higher stage the self transcends its previous and more limited viewpoints and

the nine levels of narcissism

expands its horizons increasingly beyond its own subjectivisms, a process that continues until narcissism (self-centrism) finally disappears entirely in the causal realm (simply because the separate-self sense finally disappears).

Now, at each stage of this lessening-narcissistic development, there is not only the normal or healthy amount of structurally inevitable narcissism, there is the *possibility* of an abnormal, pathological, or morbid narcissism on that level. This pathological narcissism is always a *defensive* measure; the self-structure of that level is over-valued and the self-objects of that level correlatively devalued, in order to avoid a painful confrontation with those self-objects (e.g., on the mental level: "So what if they disagree with me! Who are they anyway? I know what's going on here; they're all really a bunch of clowns," etc.). The result is an amount of narcissism (or selfcentrism) quite beyond what would be structurally inevitable and expectable *at that stage*. Theorists such as Mahler maintain that pathological narcissism may occur even at the earliest stages of self-development (i.e., F-1 and F-2).

pathological narcissism as a defensive measure

In short, the "narcissistic defense" can theoretically occur at any stage of self-development (except the extreme end points), and involves an over-valuation of the self-structure of that stage and a correlative devaluation of the self-objects of that stage, as a defense against being abandoned, humiliated, hurt, or disapproved of by those objects. The narcissistic defense is not indicated merely by a very high self-esteem; if there is an equally high regard for self-objects, this is not narcissistic defense or pathology. It is the imbalance, the overestimation of self *as measured against* the devaluing of others, that marks the narcissistic defense.

the mark of narcissistic defense

It would be technically correct, then, and much less confusing, to define "narcissistic disorders" as the result of the narcissistic defense at *any level* of self-development. Thus, there is the normal narcissism of F-1, and the pathological (defensive) narcissism of F-1; there is a similar potential for normal and pathological narcissism at F-2, F-3, and so on, all the way up to and including the subtle fulcrum.

We could *also* speak of a "narcissistic disorder" if the *normal* narcissism of one stage is *not* outgrown at the *next* stage. In this case, narcissistic disorder would mean a developmental arrest/fixation at the normal narcissism of a particular lower level, and all we would have to do is specify which lower level is involved.

Unfortunately, however, the "narcissistic disorders"—and this is part of the extraordinary confusion surrounding this topic—have been solely defined as a developmental arrest at the normal narcissism of F-2. There is no way to reverse this general usage, and so I have followed it in the first part of this presentation; I will continue to use "narcissistic disorder" in the narrow sense to mean a pathological arrest/fixation at the normal narcissism of F-2.

problems with general usage

To summarize: There are nine or so levels of narcissism, each of which is less narcissistic (less selfcentric) than its predecessor(s); each of which has a normal or structurally inevitable amount of narcissism (normal or healthy narcissism), and each of which can develop, as a defensive pathology, a morbid, overblown, or pathological narcissism. The "narcissistic disorders," in the broadest sense, refer to 1) the pathological narcissism that may develop on *any* level, and 2) a pathological arrest/fixation to the normal narcissism of any *lower* level. In the narrowest sense—that of most present-day theory—a "narcissistic disorder" means an arrest/fixation at the normal narcissism of F-2.

Dreams and Psychotherapy

Dreams have long been held to be the "royal road to the unconscious," i.e., of great help in both the diagnosis and treatment of psychopathology. But given the nine or so levels of psychopathology, how might dreams best be used?

The practical theory of dream work that I have developed suggests the following: the manifest dream can be the latent carrier of pathology (or simply benign messages) from any or all levels, and perhaps the best way to work with the dream is to begin its interpretation at the lowest levels

multi-level dream interpretation

and progressively work upward. The *same* dream symbol in a single dream sequence could carry equally important material (pathological or healthy) from several different levels, and it is necessary to seek interpretations from *all* levels and see which ones elicit a responsive recognition in the individual. The therapist or analyst starts at the lowest levels—F-1 and F-2—and interprets significant dream symbols according to the meanings they might have on those levels. He/she watches for those interpretations that resonate with the client (usually by being emotionally charged), and then works through the charge surrounding each symbol. The dream is thus decathected or relieved of its emotional charge *at that level* (we "get its message"), and the interpretation then moves to the next level, reinterpreting each significant symbol according to its possible meanings on this new level (and so on up the spectrum).

"getting the message" at each level

Obviously in practice every single dream symbol cannot be interpreted from every single level—it would take hours or even days to do so. Rather, working from a general knowledge of the individual's overall self-structure and level of overall development, the therapist selects a few key symbols for each of, say, three or four most-suspected levels, and focuses on those. The more developed a person is, the higher the level of interpretation that is likely to also strike a responsive chord, although even the most highly developed individuals are by no means immune from lower-level messages (and frequently just the contrary—the lower levels are sometimes ones they have tended to ignore in their otherwise admirable ascent, a deficiency that dreams will not let them forget!).

an example of multi-level dream interpretation

The only way to indicate the apparent richness of this approach would be to present several cases with parallel interpretations across the various levels. Since that is beyond the scope of this short section, the following simple example may suffice to indicate the general thrust of this spectrum approach. A middle-aged woman presents a dream which contains a highly charged scenario composed of these central images: she is in a cave (associations: "hell," "death"); there is a silver-luminous pole leading from the cave to the sky ("heaven," "home"); she meets her son in the cave, and together they climb the pole ("release," "safety," "eternity").

What, for example, does the pole represent? From an F-1/ F-2 level, it might represent a denial of the "all-bad" mother and a fusion or "umbilicus" to the safety of the symbiotic "all-good" mother (splitting). From an F-3 level, it might represent phallic/incestuous wishes. From an F-4 level, it might symbolize the means of more closely communicating with her son. From F-6, an escape or avoidance of existential death. And from F-7, the silver-lined kundalini sushumna (which is said to be the central channel in the spine leading from the first chakra of the physical-hell realms to the seventh chakra of liberation and release in the transcendental Self).

My point is that the pole might have simultaneously represented *all* of these. The dream symbol, being plastic, is apparently invaded and informed by any pressing issue or level of insistent pathology. Thus the way one might best deal with dreams is to start at the bottom and work up, resonating with the dream at each significant level. (We start at the bottom to insure that we don't take an unrealistic or "elevationist" stance, overlooking the unpleasant lower-level messages that might be involved; we don't *stop* with the lower levels, however, because we also want to avoid the "reductionist" stance, which violates the existential and spiritual dimensions of the human condition).

multi-level nature of dream symbols

Meditation and Psychotherapy

Meditation, in my opinion, is not a means of digging back into the lower and repressed structures of the submergent-unconscious, it is a way of facilitating the emergence, growth, and development of the higher structures of consciousness. To confuse the two is to foster the reductionist notion, quite prevalent, that meditation is (at best) a regression in service of ego, whereas by design and practice it is a progression in transcendence of ego.

meditation as progression in service of the ego

However, when a person begins intensive meditation, submergent-unconscious material (e.g., the shadow) frequently begins to re-emerge or occasionally even erupt into consciousness. It is this "derepression of the shadow" that has contributed to the notion that meditation is an uncovering technique and a regression in service of ego. I believe this derepression does in fact frequently occur, but for a very different reason (possessing very different dynamics): Meditation, because it aims at developing or moving consciousness into higher levels or dimensions of structural organization, must break or disrupt the exclusive identification with the *present* level of development (usually mental-egoic). Since it is the *exclusiveness* of the identification that *constitutes* the repression barrier, its disruption, in whole or part, may release previously repressed material—hence the derepression. This happens very often in the initial stages of meditation, but it definitely seems to be a secondary by-product of the practice, not its goal, and certainly not its definition. (For a detailed discussion of this topic, see Wilber, 1983).

Can or should meditation be used in conjunction with psychoanalysis or psychotherapy? I believe that this depends largely on the type of meditation and on the level of pathology being treated by the particular therapy.

level of pathology and use of meditation
In general, meditation seems contraindicated in F-1 and F-2 pathologies. There simply isn't enough self-structure to engage the intense experiences that meditation practices occasionally involve. Not only does meditation not seem to help in these cases, it apparently can be detrimental, because it tends to dismantle what little structure the borderline or psychotic might possess. Meditation, in other words, tends to undo those intermediate-level self-structures that the borderline or psychotic is in need of creating and strengthening in the first place. Ironically, many individuals with F-2 pathologies are, according to Jack Engler (1983a), actually drawn to meditation, particularly its Buddhist forms, as a *rationalization* for their "no-ego" states. With Engler, I believe meditation is usually contraindicated in such cases.

meditation at F-2 level

meditation at F-3 level
Most forms of F-3 pathology, on the other hand, can apparently receive auxiliary benefit from meditation practice

(cf Carrington, 1975). I believe vipassana meditation, however, should be used with caution in cases of moderate-to-severe depression, due to the tendency to link psychoneurotic depression with pseudo-duhkha. The Path of Yogis can cause severe emotional-sexual upheavals, a fact that anyone undergoing F-3 therapy might consider before embarking upon that type of meditation. And in cases of psychoneurotic anxiety, Zen koan meditation—which frequently builds anxiety to an explosive peak—is probably contraindicated. But in general, most of the basic forms of meditation (following the breath, counting the breath, mantrayana, shikan-taza, ashtanga, etc.) can be an adjunct benefit to F-3 therapy. An added plus: the meditation itself will probably facilitate, as a byproduct, the re-emergence or derepression of various unconscious material, which can be worked on in therapy sessions.

Meditation may also be used with most forms of F-4 and F-5 pathologies, but there is a specific complication: someone caught in role-confusion or role-conformist pathology, *use of* or who is having a difficult time establishing formal self- *meditation at* identity, is particularly vulnerable to using meditation, *F-4 and F-5* and various meditation groups, in a cultic fashion, pledg- *levels* ing allegiance to the particular meditative "in-group" as an acting out of unresolved identity neuroses. The resulting "cultic mentality" is extremely difficult to deal with therapeutically, because allegedly "universal-spiritual truths" are being used as an otherwise airtight rationalization for simple acting out.

Most forms of F-6 or existential pathologies, in my experience, usually show a positive response to meditation. Existential anxiety, unlike psychoneurotic anxiety, does not *uses and* seem to be a contradiction for even the more strenuous *limitations of* meditation practices such as koan (cf Kapleau, 1965); with *meditation at* existential depression, however, the duhkha-intensifying *F-6 level* meditations, such as vipassana, might be used with caution. Further, individuals with existential pathologies or persistent existential dilemmas usually find the whole philosophy behind contemplative endeavors to be salutory, pointing to a genuine and transcendental meaning to life's enterprise. Notice I said existential pathology; individuals at the normal existential level itself are frequently uninterested in (and suspicious of) meditation/transcendence—they think it is a deceptive form of death denial.

In sum: meditation is not a stucture-building technique, nor an uncovering technique, nor a script-analysis technique, nor a Socratic-dialoguing technique. It cannot substitute for those techniques, nor should it be used as a way to "spiritually bypass" (Welwood, 1984) any major work needed on those levels. In *conjunction* with analysis or therapy, however, it apparently can be very useful in most forms of F-3, F-4, F-5, and F-6 pathology, both because of its own intrinsic merits and benefits, and because it tends to "loosen" the psyche and facilitate derepression on the lower levels, thus contributing in an auxiliary fashion to the therapeutic procedures on those levels.

Meditation and Interiorization

is meditation narcissistic? The charge has been circulating, for quite some time now, in both psychoanalytic and popular literature, that meditation is a narcissistic withdrawal (Alexander, 1931; Lasch, 1979; Marin, 1975). I would in this section like to challenge that claim, using the definitions and findings of psychoanalysis itself.

a psychoanalytic definition In this paper we have been discussing the *development* or *evolution* of consciousness. How, then, does psychoanalytic ego psychology define evolution? "Evolution, to [Heinz] Hartmann [the founder of psychoanalytic developmental psychology], is a process of progressive 'internalization,' for, in the development of the species, the organism achieves increased independence from its environment, the result of which is that '. . . reactions which originally occurred in relation to the external world are increasingly displaced into the interior of the organism.' The more independent the organism becomes, the greater its independence from the stimulation of the immediate environment" (Blanck & Blanck, 1974). Increasing development, for such psychoanalysts, is *defined* as increasing interiorization.

It does not follow, then, that such a theoretical orientation should applaud the increasing interiorization from body to ego-mind, but stand back aghast at the increasing interiorization from ego-mind to subtle-soul to causal-spirit (or meditation in general); but this is exactly what happens with a number of psychoanalytically oriented theorists (e.g., Alexander, 1931; Lasch, 1979) and with many popularly oriented writers who claim modern psychiatric support (e.g., Marin, 1975). This apparently occurs because, halfway up the Great Chain of increasing interiorization, these theorists begin to apply the term "narcissism." But we have seen that each higher level of development is marked by *less* narcissism. In other words, a perfectly acceptable psychoanalytic definition is: increasing development = increasing interiorization = decreasing narcissism. From which it follows that meditation, as an increasing development of interiorization, is probably the single strongest tool we have for decreasing narcissism.

increasing interiorization and narcissism

This may sound paradoxical if one does not distinguish between two very different sorts of "insideness" or "internalness." Let us call these two sorts of internalness by the names "inside" and "interior." The first point is that each higher level of consciousness is experienced as being "interior" to its lower or preceding level, but *not* as being "inside" it. To give an example: the mind is experienced as being interior to the body, but not inside the body; if I eat some food, the food feels *inside* the body; or if I have a physical ache, that also feels *inside* the body; but there is no inside physical feeling, sensation, twitch, or twinge to which I can point and say, that is my mind. My mind, in other words, is not specifically felt as inside my body (as I am using the term), but is, somehow, felt to be rather vaguely "internal" to the body—and that feeling I call "interior."

"inside" vs. "interior"

The difference is simply that each level of consciousness has its own boundaries, with an inside and an outside; but a higher level is experienced as interior to the lower, not as literally inside it. These boundaries should not be equated, because they exist on different levels entirely. For example, the boundaries of my mind and the boundaries of my body are not the same. Thoughts can *come into* and *go out of* my mind without ever crossing the physical boundaries of my body.

Notice that because my mind is interior to my body, it can go beyond or escape the insides of the body. In my mind I can identify with a country, a political party, a school of thought; in intersubjective reflection I can take the role of others, assume their views, empathize with them, and so on. I could never do this if my mind were *only* and actually *inside* my body. Being interior to it, however, it can escape it, go beyond it, transcend it. This is why *interiorization* means *less narcissism*—one level, being interior to another, can go beyond it, which it could never do if it were really and solely *inside* it.

"interiorization" means "less narcissism"

Likewise, the soul is interior to the mind; it is *not inside* the mind—the only thing inside the mind is thoughts, which is why introspecting the mind never reveals the soul. As thoughts quiet down, however, the soul emerges interiorly vis-à-vis the mind, and therefore can transcend the mind, see beyond it, escape it. And likewise, spirit is not inside the soul, it is interior to the soul, transcending its limitations and forms.

soul is interior to mind; mind is interior to spirit

Apparently, then, theorists who claim that meditation is narcissistic imagine that meditators are going *inside* the mind; but they are rather going *interior* to it, and thus beyond it: less narcissistic, less subjectivistic, less selfcentric, more universal, more encompassing, and thus ultimately more compassionate.

CONCLUSION

I would like to be very clear about what this presentation has attempted to do. It has not offered a fixed, conclusive, unalterable model. Although I have at every point attempted to ground it in the theoretical and phenomenological reports of reputable researchers and practitioners, the overall project is obviously metatheoretical and suggestive, and is offered in that spirit. But once one begins to look at the full spectrum of human growth and devel-

the full spectrum and meta-theory

opment, an extraordinarily rich array of material becomes available for metatheoretical work; a variety of connections suggest themselves which were not apparent before; and a wealth of hypotheses for future research become immediately available. Moreover, different analytical, psychological, and spiritual systems, which before seemed largely incompatible or even contradictory, appear closer to the possibility of a mutually enriching synthesis or reconciliation.

This presentation has offered one such full-spectrum approach, more to show the strong possibilities than the final conclusions; if this type of model is useful in reaching better ones, it will have served its purpose. My point, rather, is that given the state of knowledge *already* available to us, it seems ungenerous to the human condition to present any models *less* comprehensive—by which I mean, models that do not take into account both conventional *and* contemplative realms of human growth and development.

the purpose of this model

CHAPTER 6

THE STAGES OF MINDFULNESS MEDITATION: A VALIDATION STUDY

PART I: STUDY AND RESULTS

Daniel P. Brown[1]
Jack Engler[2]

The traditional accounts of the stages of meditation have often presented a problem with regard to their status as "objective" realities. Do these stages have a general cross-cultural validity, or are they merely subjective belief systems or expectation results? The task of the research reported in this chapter is, as Brown and Engler put it, "to determine just what sort of validity these textual accounts have."

In this chapter, Brown and Engler present the study itself and its results, a study that included intensive interviews with practitioners and teachers, a quantitative measure they developed and titled "A Profile of Meditative Experience" (POME), and the Rorschach. Although the Rorschach was originally used as a personality measure, Brown and Engler found that "practitioners at different levels of the practice gave records that looked very distinct. In fact, the Rorschach records seemed to correlate with particular stages of meditation. Common features were more outstanding than individual differences at each level of practice." Using the Rorschach as a measure of cognitive and perceptual change, Brown and Engler found that "the specific qualitative features of the Rorschachs for each group are consistent with the classical descriptions of the psychological changes most characteristic of that stage of practice. Such convergence of the Rorschach qualitative features on the one hand, and the classical descriptions [of the stages of meditation] on the other, may be an important step toward establishing the cross-cultural validation of the psychological changes at each major stage of the practice."

In the following chapter, Brown and Engler present a detailed discussion of the meanings of these results.

a preliminary report

This is a preliminary report of the authors' study of contemporary indigenous Buddhist meditation practitioners and the authoritative textual traditions which are the recorded source of their practices. The major traditions we have studied in their original languages present an unfolding of meditation experiences in terms of a *stage model:* for example, the *Mahamudra* from the Tibetan Mahayana Buddhist tradition (Brown, 1977); the *Visuddhimagga* from the Pali Theravadin Buddhist tradition (Nyanamoli, 1976); and the *Yoga Sutras* from the Sanskrit Hindu tradition (Mishra, 1963). The models are sufficiently similar to suggest an

stage models

underlying common invariant sequence of stages, despite vast cultural and linguistic differences as well as different styles of practice (Brown, 1980). Although such a structural convergence remains to be established on empirical grounds, the conception of meditation in terms of a stage model is intuitively appealing. Further, the traditions themselves describe the practice in terms of classical metaphors which suggest this notion, e.g., references to the "path" *(magga)* and "development" *(bhavana)*.

Vipassana stages

The current study is about one such stage model, the Theravadin Buddhist tradition of *Vipassana* or mindfulness meditation. According to this tradition there are three major divisions of the entire system of meditation: Preliminary Training, sometimes called Moral Training, Concentration Training, and Insight Training. The first is recommended for beginners; the latter two comprise meditation in its more restricted sense of formal sitting practice.

preliminary practices

Each of these divisions represents a very different set of practices and leads to a distinct goal. Each involves a very different kind of psychological transformation. The preliminary practices include the study of the teachings, following of ethical precepts, and training in basic awareness of one's daily activities as well as the flow of one's internal experience. These preliminaries may also include learning meditative postures, learning to sit quietly in order to observe and thereby calm one's thoughts, and learning to observe the flow of one's internal experience free from distraction. Concentration practice is defined in terms of one-pointed attention, the ability to hold attention steady on an object without distraction. This is said to result in a relative reduction in thinking and more complex perceptual processes. The fully concentrated meditator has learned to develop a deep concentrated state called *samadhi* in which awareness is held continuously and steadily upon very subtle activities of the mind, at a level simpler than that of thinking or perceptual pattern recognition.

concentration practice

Insight practice is the most important, and all earlier stages are regarded as preparations. The meditator has trained his awareness to observe the subtle workings of his mind and is now in a position to genuinely know how the mind works at its most refined levels. There are a number of individual stages of insight, all of which are quite technically defined in the traditional literature. The meditator is said to learn fundamental truths regarding the operations of the mind. His awareness is said to become so refined that he begins to explore the interaction of mind and reality. He explores how events come into existence and how they pass away. In so doing, he learns that there is no real boundary between the mind-inside and the universe-outside. Eventually a fundamental non-dual awareness will intuitively and experientially understand the operations of the mind/reality, leading to a radical transformation of experience called enlightenment. Moreover, there may be several transformations, more than one such enlightenment. Those readers who wish to study translations of the classical accounts of the stages of meditation in Theravadin Buddhism are referred elsewhere (Mahasi Sayadaw, 1965; Nyanamoli, 1976).

insight practice

THE PROBLEM OF VALIDATION

The traditional Buddhist accounts of the stages of meditation present a problem in regard to their status as subjective reports. These texts may contain archaic historical artifacts which have no validity in terms of describing the experience of contemporary meditators. Or the texts may represent experiences very similar to those of present-day

determining the validity of textual accounts

meditators, but both descriptions of experience may be the consequences of rigid belief systems, i.e., merely expectation effects. Then again, the texts may well be descriptions of stages of meditation experience that have external validity. The task of our current research is to determine just what sort of validity these textual accounts have.

research approach In order to approach this issue, interviews were first conducted with contemporary indigenous practitioners to see if their experiences were consistent with those in the classical texts (Kornfield, 1976; Engler, n.d.) A research questionnaire, "A Profile of Meditative Experience" (POME), was also designed to quantify these descriptions (Brown *et al.*, 1978). Secondly, an attempt was made to compare the textual accounts to constructs drawn from specific traditions of Western psychology, particularly cognitive psychology. As described elsewhere (Brown, 1977) learning meditation was likened to the acquisition of a cognitive skill, specifically, skill in attention deployment and awareness training. Those who persist in the attention and awareness training seem to undergo a set of meditation experiences which unfold in a very orderly manner, perhaps in discernible stages. These stages may be viewed according to a cognitive/developmental stage model, i.e., one in which more complex thinking and perceptual processes are deconstructed during meditation so that more subtle levels of information-processing can be observed.

independent empirical measures and the Rorschach The objective of a validation study is to establish independent empirical measures of the alleged cognitive changes described in the traditional texts and in the subjective reports and questionnaires of contemporary practitioners. The Rorschach may not seem to be a likely choice for such a validation study. In fact, the Rorschach was originally used as a personality measure. However, we began to notice that practitioners at different levels of the practice gave records that looked very distinct. In fact, the Rorschach records seemed to correlate with particular stages of meditation. Common features were more outstanding than individual differences at each level of practice. This unexpected observation raised the further question whether perhaps there were qualitative features (and quantitative variables) on the Rorschach that discriminated between the major divisions or stages of the practice. If so, this would be an initial step toward establishing the possible validity of the stage-model of meditation. In the current study, the Rorschach is used as a measure of cognitive and perceptual change, not as a personality measure. Here it serves as a *stage-sensitive* validation instrument by administering it to criterion groups defined according to their level of practice.

THE POPULATION OF MEDITATORS

A fundamental problem with contemporary meditation research is the failure to use subjects who have acquired sufficient training in the cognitive skills specific to meditation. Most experiments use naive subjects, often college students, sometimes experienced meditators of a given discipline, e.g., Zen or Transcendental Meditation. Even these experienced meditators, by traditional criteria, are beginners. For example, Maupin (1965) conducted a Rorschach study of Zen meditators. He used naive college students who were given ten 45-minute sessions in breath concentration. It is very doubtful that these Ss perfected concentrative skills in ten sessions. Nevertheless, Maupin concluded that these Ss experienced an increase in primary process thinking along with a greater capacity to tolerate it. While this may indeed be an effect of meditation, it may very well be a beginner's effect. Inexperienced Ss manifest the general effects of a hypoaroused state of consciousness (Brown, 1977). Similar reports of increased primary process thinking have been reported for another hypoaroused state, hypnotic trance (Fromm, Oberlander & Grunewald, 1970). Effects such as increased primary process may have little to do with effects of meditation in more experienced Ss as defined by the tradition.

experienced vs. inexperienced subjects

In one cross-sectional study which attempted to control for *level of meditation experience*, Davidson, Goleman & Schwartz (1976) segregated their Ss into beginning, short-term and long-term meditation groups. The criterion for the long-term group was two or more years of regular practice in either TM or Buddhist breath concentration. The problem, of course, is that *length of practice* need not

length of practice and acquisition of skill

strongly correlate with *acquisition of skill*. Such cross-sectional studies which have been attempted across criterion groups typically employ a purely temporal factor, length of time meditating, as a means to discriminate beginning, intermediate and advanced subjects. As all teachers of meditation and most students are painfully aware, however, length of time one has practiced is no index to depth of practice. This relationship is highly variable and indeterminate. This kind of global and rather artificial tripartite grouping on the basis of time has been resorted to in the absence of more appropriate criterion measures derived from the practice itself.

criterion of
subject selection

The current study does not rely on length of practice as the sole criterion of selection, although it does not abandon this. Initially, Ss were selected who had sufficient experience in intensive meditation in a well-defined tradition. Intensive practice served as the initial criterion. Moreover, teacher ratings and self reports on questionnaires were used as primary criteria to further delineate the level of experience of Ss from among this group of intensive meditators according to the textual model of stages of meditation. Presumably, the teachers are cognizant of the traditional accounts of the stages of meditation on the one hand, and are alleged to be capable of discerning through interview the type of experiences and level of skill a given Ss has achieved. Certain responses to cued items on the research questionnaire (POME) also disclose the level of skill.

a well-defined
tradition

The present study in both its Asian and American components draws upon meditators in the context of a well-defined tradition, not a college population. It utilizes meditators who attend intensive retreats of several weeks or months duration. The daily routine involves a continuous alternation between periods of sitting and periods of walking meditation, usually one hour in length to start, over a span of 18 hours. There are two meals before noon and a one hour discourse in the evening. Subjects practice 14–16 hours/day continuously for the length of the retreat. They adopt traditional Buddhist precepts such as silence and abstinence from sex and substance use. They do not interact with other meditators. There is no eye contact. They do not write or talk except for a 15-minute interview with one of the teachers on alternate days. This routine is defined as *intensive meditation* and is the basic structure for both short-term and long-term retreats. During this time practitioners have the opportunity to work uninterruptedly toward the acquisition of meditative skills and to cultivate the kind of stage-specific training and mental development *(bhavana)* toward which this tradition of meditation aims.

The instructions for formal periods of sitting and walking meditation follow the traditional mindfulness instructions of one of the major Burmese teaching lineages, that of the Venerable Mahasi Sayadaw (Mahasi Sayadaw, 1972; Goldstein, 1976). The practice begins with an initial concentration exercise. Attention is focused on the in/out movement of the breath at the tip of the nostrils or the rise and fall of the abdomen. After an initial period when some degree of concentration is developed, new classes of objects are then added in a series: bodily sensations, emotions, thoughts, images, memories, perceptions and the pleasant, unpleasant or neutral quality of each moment of experience. The meditator is instructed to become aware of any of these objects at the exact moment it occurs, for as long as it occurs, in his stream of consciousness. When no other object presents itself to awareness, attention is returned to the basic meditation object, the breath. It is mainly this extension of the range of attention to a variety of objects in their momentary arising and passing away that now converts this exercise from a concentrative to a mindfulness technique. The second core instruction in this tradition of practice is that attention should be "bare." Objects are to be attended to without reaction: without evaluation, judgment, selection, comment or any kind of cognitive or emotional elaboration. If any of these types of mental reaction occur over and above mere perception of the object, the student is instructed to make them in turn the object of "bare attention" or "choiceless awareness." The specific object chosen is not nearly as important as this quality of detached observation with which it is registered in awareness. *Bare attention,* then, denotes a non-interpretive, non-judgmental awareness of one's predominant experience, moment by moment. Emphasis is on the *process* by which

traditional mindfulness instructions

"bare attention"

a particular event occurs, *not* on the individual *content* it-self. Walking meditation is done in the same way, with the movement of the feet taken as the basic meditation object. Awareness is expanded to include all other events which occur, as they occur, during the walking. Equally impor-tant, the student is instructed to remain mindful of each and every other activity he engages in throughout the day, as he does it. In effect then, meditation is continuous and is ideally carried on without a break from rising to sleep-ing. This continuity in practice is the single most impor-tant factor in developing and maintaining that high degree of concentration which facilitates the development of in-sight.

combining data from three independent projects

The present study combines data from three independent projects: a *Three-Month Study* of intensive meditation stu-dents; data collection on *Advanced Western Students;* and a *South Asian Study* of enlightened masters. The first project used Western students. The research site was the Insight Meditation Society (IMS) center in Barre, Massachusetts. This center offers a series of two-week courses throughout the year and a three-month fall retreat annually. Data was collected at one of these three-month retreats. The second project also took place at IMS. In addition to the three-month meditators, data was also collected from the staff and teachers of the retreat center and from advanced med-itators who visited the center throughout the year. The third project took place in South Asia. The subjects of this independent study included a number of well-known meditation masters in the same teaching lineage as those represented in the Western study. Thus data is available from meditators at nearly all levels of practice, from begin-ners to enlightened masters.

THE THREE-MONTH STUDY

distinguishing between expectation and meditation effects

The design was intended to distinguish between expecta-tion effects and meditation effects. In an excellent study, Smith (1976) demonstrated that most of the enthusiastic claims about meditation outcomes were largely instances of *expectation of change* and not due to the specific medita-tion skills, e.g., concentration on a mantra. In order to distinguish between meditation and expectation effects, the staff of the IMS center served as a control. The staff live in the same setting for the same length of time as the retreat meditators. They hold the same belief system and attend each of the evening discourses. They expect the meditation to work and they devote a minimum of two hours a day to meditation along with the retreat meditators. The main difference between the staff and retreat meditators is the amount of daily practice (2 hrs. vs. 14–16 hrs.). Differences between the groups presumably are suggestive of the treatment effect (intensive meditation) and not simply of expectation, assuming that both groups expect that the meditation they are practicing will result in some positive change. The unusual Rorschach findings reported in this study were found only in the meditation group, not in the control group, thereby suggesting that the findings are not entirely attributable to expectation.

The instruments used in the study were primarily the "Profile of Meditation Experience" (POME) and the Rorschach. The POME is a 600-item questionnaire designed to discriminate different types of meditation as well as different levels within the same type of meditation. It was administered together with a Social Desirability Scale (Crowne & Marlowe, 1960) and a demographic sheet. The Rorschach was administered individually in the traditional manner by a half-dozen Rorschach clinicians, only one of whom was familiar with the hypotheses of the experiment, thus minimizing experimenter bias.

instruments used in study

The original design of the experiment called for a comparison of types of individuals, as measured by factor analytic ratings of a personality rating scale for the Rorschach, with patterns of response on the POME. The intention was to find out whether different types of individuals had different experiences with the same instructions after the course of the three-month retreat. Post-Rorschach measures were included more out of curiosity. Much to our surprise, the post-Rorschach measures looked dramatically different. The Rorschachs were collected at the beginning and end of the three-month retreat. Since the meditators had not talked for the entire period, the concluding phase of the retreat was a 5-day transition period in which they were

original design

allowed to talk and interact with other meditators and staff, but were also expected to continue their meditation. The post-Rorschachs were collected between the first and second day of the transition period, i.e., after the retreatants became used to talking again, but before the state of consciousness accumulated from three months of continuous practice had been disrupted. Only the post-Rorschachs are reported for the current study. A total of 30 Ss on the same three-month retreat from mid-September to mid-December, 1978, were tested, and one dropped out. Six Ss had attended a previous three-month retreat, but it was the first intensive retreat of this length for 24.

THE ADVANCED WESTERN MEDITATORS

The teachers at IMS nominated a small group of Western students who they felt had a "deep" practice. Whenever these Ss visited IMS, data was collected in the same manner as in the Three-Month Study.

THE SOUTH ASIAN STUDY

enlightenment as sole criterion of selection No such longitudinal pre/post-design was possible in the South Asian study, nor was it possible to employ control groups. This study was conducted on the basis of two different assumptions: First, our meditation research in the Three-Month Study had not tested subjects whose experience could be classically defined by the experience of enlightenment. Second, the experience of enlightenment (determined by consensual teacher nomination) was used as the sole criterion of selection, a criterion which superseded length of practice or even teacher ratings of practice as in the Three-Month Study. According to the tradition of mindfulness meditation, enlightenment is said to result in permanent and irreversible changes in perception and experience. The tradition distinguishes between what in Western psychology might be called state and trait changes (Davidson, Goleman & Schwartz, 1976). In the tradition, trait effects are said to be the result *only* of enlightenment and not of prior stages of practice. Meditation can produce both state and trait changes, but these are not to be confounded. The tradition itself makes this distinction and forcibly emphasizes it in warning of the dangers of self-delusion. The meditator may mistake state effects for trait effects and suffer subsequent disillusionment and discouragement to the detriment of his/her practice *(Yoga Sutras* IV.27; *Visuddhimagga,* IV, 86f. xxiii.2). Likewise, if the researcher accepts this assumption, then enlightenment must be used as a criterion independent of level of skill or stage of practice.

In this Theravadin Buddhist tradition there are four distinct stages of enlightenment. Since irreversible trait effects *four distinct* are said to occur at *each* of these four stages and only there, *stages of* experience of one or more of the subsequent stages of en- *enlightenment* lightenment became a secondary criterion. As can be appreciated, this required a rather special group of subjects. At the time this study was conceived, such a group could only be found in Asia. These were understandably individuals who had already completed a certain course of training. No pre-test measures were available for them, nor were they tested just after a period of intensive meditation as in the Three-Month Study. In fact, this was the first time any such group of yogis had agreed to be subjects for research at all, in South Asia as well as in the West.

Because a longitudinal design was not possible under the circumstances, an individual case study approach was *an individual* taken instead, based on precedents in ethnographic re- *case study* search using similar research instruments (Boyer, 1964). By *approach* using an "ideographic" case study method as it has been employed in studies of child development (Flavell, 1963; Mahler, 1975), it was hoped to discover, in the individual case, examples of nomothetic principles. Eight subjects, including two teachers, were nominated by two masters. The masters themselves also agreed to participate in the study, making a total N of 10: eight women, mostly mothers and housewives, and two men. All were middle-aged. All practiced the same type of Burmese Satipatthana-vipassana or mindfulness meditation in the lineage of the Ven. Mahasi Sayadaw of Rangoon (Kornfield, 1977) on which the subsequent Three-Month Study of Western meditators at IMS was also based. According to teacher-rating, 5 subjects had attained first enlightenment, 4 had attained second, and 1 had attained third. In interesting contrast to the Western group of meditators, most of these Asian yogis had a minimum of prior retreat experience. Most of their practice was done at home in the context of daily family and vocational activities. In all but one case, the actual experience of enlightenment did occur during a retreat, but a retreat of short duration and often the only retreat the individual had done. The length of time from first beginning practice to the experience of enlightenment ranged from six days to three years.

instruments used

The instruments used in the South Asian Study included the same instruments used in the study of American meditators at IMS with some additions. First, a case history was obtained from each practitioner. Because married women in Asia will discuss certain subjects only with another married woman, to ensure completeness of data collection the case history interviews with the female subjects were conducted by Ms. Jellemieke Stauthamer, a clinical psychologist. For the same reason, a trilingual married woman, Ms. Maitri Chatterjee, was chosen from among many interviewed as interpreter. Next a series of semi-structured interviews were conducted with each individual on his/her meditative experience. The attempt was made to obtain separate protocols of the meditative process and its experienced outcomes in the form of self-reports. The Rorschach was then administered by a colleague and Rorschach clinician from the host culture who was neither a Buddhist, nor familiar with this system of meditation and its claims, nor known to the subjects. This was followed by administration of the TAT in its Indian form (Chowdury, 1960) in a separate session. The interviewing and testing were carried out over a four-month period either in the rooms of two of the teachers or in the hall adjoining the nearby Buddhist temple. All interviews and tests were tape-recorded and translations subsequently checked for accuracy by an independent interpreter. Finally, the POME was translated into the language of the host culture, independently checked for accuracy, and administered.

THE CURRENT STUDY: CRITERION GROUPING

An attempt was made to establish clear criterion groups in order to see if the pattern of responses on the Rorschachs was different in each of the criterion groups. The five *the five groups* groups that were established followed the traditional divisions of the stages of practice: 1) beginners; 2) samadhi group; 3) insight group; 4) advanced insight group (attainment of at least first enlightenment); 5) masters (attainment of the higher stages of enlightenment as defined in Theravadin Buddhism, e.g., Nyanamoli, 1976). The criterion groups were established by two independent modes of assessment: objective ratings by four teachers for the Western group and by two masters for the Asian group; and patterns of response on the POME. The four teachers rated each of the 30 Western Ss on the three-month retreat along three different scales: a) use of the practice to work on emotional problems; b) depth of concentration (proficiency in samadhi); c) depth of insight. The scale endpoints were 1 and 10. A rating of 1 meant "little" and 10 *the scale* meant "great." Anchor points were given a specific meaning. For example, 1 meant very little concentration; very little insight; and very little evidence for working on emotional problems. A rating of 5 meant moderate concentration (Beginner's Samadhi); moderate insight ("easy" insights such as perception of the constant change of mental events); and moderate evidence of working on emotional problems. A rating of 10 meant deep concentration (Access Samadhi); deep insight (realization of the stage of Arising and Passing Away, or the stage of Equanimity); and considerable evidence of working on emotional problems. Technical terms like "Access Samadhi," "Arising and Passing Away" and "Equanimity" refer to stages recognized by tradition (Nyanamoli, 1976) and adopted by the teachers (Mahasi Sayadaw, 1965) in their assessment of the student's progress. They will be discussed in some detail later in the text. In addition, certain key questions on the POME were used as an independent means to differentiate groups. The POME contains certain questions regarding types of insight. Several of these latter questions are worded such that they are only intelligible to those who have had the direct experience of the stage, such as the experience of the state called "Access" or the state called

"Arising and Passing Away." Those students who answered these questions as "sometimes, often, usually or always" characteristic of their current practice (postretreat) were sorted into groups. A given S had to meet *both* teacher rating and questionnaire criteria in order to be placed within a given group.

number of subjects in each group

The *beginner's group* consisted of 15 Ss who received a mean rating of 6 or more by the teachers on the scale of Emotional Problems. The *samadhi group* consisted of 13 Ss who met the dual criteria of receiving a mean rating of 6 or more by the teachers and a minimum self-report of "sometimes" or more on the POME questions concerning concentration and samadhi. These 13 Ss were defined as having accomplished some level of samadhi, from Beginner's Samadhi to Access Samadhi, but no attempt was made to ascertain the exact level of the samadhi. Likewise, the *insight group* consisted of 3 Ss who met the dual criteria of a mean rating of 6 or more by the teachers and a minimum self-report of "sometimes" or more on the POME questions regarding levels of insight. There were some differences between the teacher- and self-ratings of insight. The teachers were more liberal in their ratings. They included relatively "easy" insights, such as perception of the constant change of events, in their high ratings. A total of 11 Ss were given a mean rating of 6 or more by the teachers. However, according to the POME, 8 of these Ss had only the "easier" insights. Only three had actually progressed to the more advanced Insight stages as classically defined.

concentration and mindfulness practice

Thus, in the Three-Month Study, using the very same instructions, Ss varied markedly at the end of their three months of practice. The great majority were still working through the problems of the beginning stage. About half had progressed to the next major stage of practice, the samadhi stage. These Ss had become genuine meditators by traditional standards. Some of these same Ss also began to experience pre-access levels of insight. Others, though relatively weak in their concentration, developed stronger mindfulness and insight. The reason for this variation is due at least in part to the dual set of instructions used: concentration on the breath and mindfulness of any or all categories of objects. It may also be partly due to the fact that a given meditation object like the breath can be used to develop either concentration or insight. Ss differed in their use of these instructions over the three months. Those who felt scattered tended to practice more concentration. Those who desired insight practiced mindfulness more. The reason why so many meditators achieved samadhi is explained by tradition: both concentrative skills and mindfulness can lead to the attainment of at least beginner's samadhi, although concentrative skills are necessary to deepen the samadhi state. The reason why so few reached the Insight Series of meditations is also explained. These require considerable skill to master. In addition they follow the attainment of Access Samadhi. This is supported by the strong positive correlations between concentration and insight on the POME. All 3 Ss in the Insight Group had at least five years of previous experience with the same instructions. All 3 had also received very high ratings on concentration by the teachers. Thus, it seems that those who practice mindfulness without achieving optimal concentration reach a plateau at the pre-access levels of insight, while those who practice concentration without sufficient mindfulness tend to lose their "state effects" after the retreat ends. It is difficult for each student to find the optimal balance so the variation after three months is great.

Nevertheless, it was possible to establish strict criterion groups for the traditionally defined levels of samadhi and insight. Because of the small number of Ss in the insight group, these data were pooled with data from advanced Ss collected outside the retreat yet meeting the same strict criteria. This still only brought the total N to 7, which suggests the difficulty of attaining the classical or post-access stages where the fundamental insights into the very workings of the mind are perceived during meditation in the Theravadin tradition.

establishing strict criterion groups

A fourth group was designated the *advanced insight group*. It consists of advanced Western meditators who have reached at least the first of the 4 stages of enlightenment as recognized by their Asian teachers. A fifth group was designated the *master's group*. The tradition recognizes a fundamental difference between the first two and the last two "Paths" or stages of enlightenment. This is based on qualitative differences in degree of difficulty in attainment and the extent of trait change, expressed in terms of the "fetters" or "defilements" permanently eliminated from the personality, all of which are claimed to radically differentiate the third from the second Path. In accordance with this principle, the master's group is defined in this study as those who have attained either the third or fourth Path, either the penultimate or ultimate stage of enlightenment. *"ariyas" or* This group is represented in the present study by a single *"ones worthy of* individual. Contemporary Theravadin Buddhists recog- *praise"* nize a number of such "ariyas" or "ones worthy of praise," but data is available for only one, an individual residing in South Asia and a subject in the South Asian Study. Table 4 summarizes the data:

TABLE 4

CRITERION GROUP

	Beginner's Group	Samadhi Group	Insight Group	Advanced Insight	Master's Group
Three-Month Study	15*	13	3**	—	—
Advanced IMS Study	—	—	4	4	—
South Asian Study	—	—	—	(9)***	1

*There is some overlap between the Beginner's and Samadhi Groups (5Ss).

**There is some overlap between the Samadhi and Insight Groups (3Ss). All 3 Ss in the Insight Group also met the criteria for the Samadhi Group, but are included only in the latter. This means that a total of 7 Ss did not meet the dual criteria for *any* group and are not included in this study.

***The enlightened Ss in the Advanced Insight Group are derived from the Advanced IMS and South Asian groups, pooled. A total of 9 more such Rorschachs have been collected. These have not been included, however. Only Rorschachs from Westerners are included in order to circumvent the difficulties of cross-cultural Rorschach interpretation.

DATA ANALYSIS[3]

What follows is a preliminary report based on the work
completed to date. The data reported are representative of
the outstanding features on the Rorschachs in the respective criterion groups. By "outstanding features" is meant
those *qualitative features* of Rorschachs which are characteristic of a given criterion group and relatively uncharacteristic of the remaining pool of Rorschachs. Clear-cut qualitative features are readily apparent for each group, so that
in a pilot study clinicians and experimentalists were able
to blindly sort these Rorschachs into the appropriate *a
priori* groupings. What follows is a summary of these qualitative features.

*qualitative
features of data*

RESULTS

Beginner's Group

The Beginner's Group consisted of 15 Rorschachs collected
immediately after three months of intensive meditation.
These Rorschachs were not especially different from the
respective Rorschachs collected from the same subjects
just prior to the meditation retreat. The only differences
were a slight decrease in productivity across subjects and
a noticeable increase in drive-dominated responses for
some subjects (Holt & Havell, 1960).

few differences

Samadhi Group

The most outstanding characteristic of the samadhi Rorschach is its seeming *unproductivity* and *paucity of associative
elaborations*. Recall that the test instructions are for the S to
describe what the inkblot "looks like." Meditators in deep
samadhi experience these instructions as being somewhat
incongruous with the functioning of their altered state of
consciousness. Many complained that it "took too much
energy" to produce images and associations while perceiving the inkblot. When one S was asked if he could say
what one of the inkblots "looked like" if he tried, he said

*"unproductivity"
of Samadhi
Group*

that he could produce images; and indeed, he was able to produce a record not significantly less productive than his pre-test Rorschach. He added, however, that to generate such images required "go(ing) into the various levels of perceptual layering," that is, "break(ing) down (perception) into its (perceptual) patterns and concepts." Like this S, all the Ss in the Samadhi Group showed a decrease in their overall productivity. Since the task demand was presumably contrary to the actual organization of their perceptual experience, their very accommodation to the instructions biased the results so that even this degree of productivity is probably inflated, a response to task requirements rather than to perceptual functioning.

focus on perceptual features of inkblot

What does the S experience? Subjects in the Samadhi Group distinguished between three levels of their perceptual processes: the *perceptual features* of the inkblot, *internal images* given in response to these features, i.e., the content applied to the inkblot, and *associative elaborations* of these images. During the samadhi state, Ss' focus of attention was primarily on the perceptual features of the inkblot and only secondarily on the images and associations that might follow from these features. Each Rorschach in the Samadhi Group was characterized by a mixture of responses in each of the three categories, though the overall tendency was to comment on the pure perceptual features of the inkblot. To them, the inkblot "looked like" an inkblot. The same subject says:

> . . . the meditation has wiped out all the interpretive stuff on top of the raw perception . . . like, there's this thing out here but then (when asked to make it look like something) I go into it, into the various levels of perceptual layering (IW)8.*

images and associations qualified

Those units of perception involving images and associations were often given some qualification, the kind of qualification not usually found in normal and pathological Rorschachs. For example, Ss were careful to distinguish images and associations from the raw perceptual features. Some distinguished their memory from perception with comments such as, "I remember it from last time, but I

---

*The notation following each response indicates the card number and the specific location of the response on that card (following Exner, 1974).

don't *really* see it there." Some distinguished their associative processes from perception with comments like, "My association to it is a bat, that was my first thought, and then I elaborated it." Many adopted a critical attitude toward their own image. They felt the image was non-veridical. Percepts, even those of good form-level, were often qualified with statements such as, "It doesn't *really* look like that . . . I'm just projecting." At times, Ss were unable to find words to label or describe a particular unit of an inkblot's features, even when their attention was fixed on it. Comments in such cases were similar: "I know what it is, but I can't put a name on it"; or, "It's real interesting but it's like nothing I've seen before."

Nevertheless, Ss were able to report specific images for the majority of the cards, though not for all of them. These images, however, were quite *fluidly perceived*. Ss complained, for instance, that the images "kept changing." While describing a particular image, it was not unusual for it to change into something else. Sometimes the image seemed to change so rapidly that it was difficult to specify a single image: *images fluidly perceived*

> It's becoming so many different things so quickly, they go before the words come out (IIW).

Or Ss reported simultaneous images for the same areas of the blot:

> It's a lot of things at once—could be a bat, a butterfly, a flying man (IW).

The focus of attention was less on the actual image and more on the *process* by which the image manifested itself in their stream of consciousness. For example, one S said, "It's just beginning to become something . . . (pause) . . . a bat."

The most unusual finding, yet characteristic of the entire Samadhi Group, is the high incidence of comments on the *pure perceptual features* of the inkblot. In traditional scoring language, these Ss used a lot of pure determinants: form-domination, pure color (chromatic and achromatic), pure shading, and pure inanimate movement. Form-dominated responses were those in which the Ss became fascinated *high incidence of comments on pure perceptual features* with the various shapes and configurations of a given ink-blot in their own right, without attempting to associate to them. Here is an example of a typical Rorschach response (VIII 23' 52"):

> 1. Well the color, all of it . . . colors against the white color, they're striking . . . (form?) all the different forms of the color, each shading of color has a certain form to it (what might it look like?). Nothing, nothing at all . . . last time I was struck very much with this one . . . I tried to find something, and turned it around and around . . . once somebody told me that you were real bright if you turned it around . . . I never forgot that, so I did (this time?). This time the colors were enough . . . very pleasant, pretty, doesn't look like a thing to me . . . but there is part of it that takes on a very distinct form. . . .

> 2. Rodents climbing: They look exactly like rodents (how so?) The shape . . . the feeling I get of the way they're climbing, moving their feet, tail, faces. . . .

relative paucity of associative responses

Again the main feature of this group of proctocols is the unproductivity and relative paucity of associative process which characterizes the samadhi state. The "animals" on card VIII are one of the easiest and most popular responses on the entire test because the features of the card are closely representative of an animal form. Despite the strong stimulus-pull, the immediate impact of the card is *not* the obvious pattern, but rather the pure perceptual features of color and form.

Insight Group

Insight Group's increased productivity

The Rorschachs of the Insight Group point in a direction nearly opposite to that of the Samadhi Group. They are primarily characterized by *increased productivity* and *richness of associative elaborations*. These meditators experience the test instructions as an opportunity to exercise the apparently increased availability of their associative and imaginal processes, while keeping these closely and realistically attuned to the perceptual features of the inkblot.

Whereas repeated measures of normal and clinical Rorschachs evidence many of the same responses, the post-test responses in this group showed little overlap with pre-test responses. These meditators claimed that their productivity per card was unlimited, that their mind was constantly turning over. One said:

> When I can't see anything else I hang out with it for a while . . . allow space . . . I stay with my awareness of not seeing anything . . . then, more images come . . .

This openness to the flow of internal associations and im- *openness to* ages is characteristic of the Insight Rorschach. The experi- *flow* ence may be likened to the extemporaneous music of a jazz musician.

Moreover, most of the associations are richly fabulized, with a great variability and intensity of affect. Color symbolism, or better, metaphoric use of color, abounds. The content shows great cultural diversity. One of the more unusual features of these long, elaborate associations, in light of their richness, is the relative absence of looseness. Subjects employ one of two styles of elaboration, the empathetic and the creative. In the *empathetic style,* the S puts himself fully into his percept, especially the human movement percept. This is illustrated by the slow unfolding of a single perception until the S gets a certain "feel" for it. In the *creative style,* the S also slowly unfolds his elabora- *enhanced* tion of a single percept but changes his perspective on the *reality* same image one or more times during the response. Often, *attunement* the S ascribes several very different affective states to the same image. These protocols also contain a high incidence of original responses. Thus, the Ss are able to manifest a high degree of congruency between the flow of their internal world, moment-by-moment, and the changing demands of external reality. This *enhanced reality attunement* is clearly illustrated in the following response:

> This is a wonderful one, too . . . sideways this is again, the red figure is a 4-legged animal, like a mountain lion and now he's running, leaping over a real rocky and difficult terrain . . . there's a sense of great energy and power in him, but the most wonderful thing of all is how sure-footed he is . . . a great sense of flight . . . he always lands on just the right crop of rock . . . never misses . . . always instinctively sure of his footing so he'll be able to go on like that, wonderful mastery and wonderful fit between the animal and his world, kind of perfect harmony between them, even though it's very dy-

namic, leaping, he always does it . . . here, he's in flight . . . just landed with the front paw and the back paw is still in the air and he's feeling, not very reflective, just doing it sponta- neously. He's feeling the great energy and lightness and chal- lenge. He loves the challenge because he's equal to it, but it's always keeping him out there on his limit . . . with this is another wonderful thing. It has to do with the colors again, a progression in his progress from warm wonderful colors to colder, finally very cold colors; in other words, he started from a place of warmth and security and as he started from there, he can carry it out and conquer the cold, insecure place be- cause he himself is the pink, the color of the heat, light, en- ergy, warmth . . . and so he can go out and master the cold of the world again . . . (VIII, without inquiry D1).

life-affirming insights There are also some remarkably life-affirming insights con- tained within these fabulized human movement percepts:

I see 2, I see 2 heads. It's like a large being, a tall person and a shorter person . . . a tall rather massive person and a smaller . . . could be an adult and a child . . . a father and a son or . . . probably a father and a son . . . that's what it reminds me of . . . and they're just sitting quietly together looking off into the distance . . . very at ease with each other . . . and there's a lot of real warmth between them, just a real feeling of con- nectedness . . . the feeling of knowing the limitations of the communication that can come between them . . . accepting those limits, not finding them painful, and just being real happy with what is there . . . and the limits are really the limits that are . . . not like generational, but the limits like that are there between any two people whatever their relationship might be . . . the limits of two people trying to communicate to each other . . . there's a certain place where that breaks down and you just can't get any closer, where you can't bridge the gap anymore, and yet you can come to a real deep accept- ance of that limitation (IV, without inquiry, Dd at base of D2).

conflicts Nevertheless, these insight Rorschachs are not without conflicts, such as the fusion of sexual and aggressive im- pulses in this response by the same S who gave the moun- tain lion:

. . . and this which I first saw as just the two trunks of the elephant, this I see as a circumcised penis; at first I saw it very solitary, just sort of proud of itself to be there, but now I'm beginning to see it in connection with the two red spaces above as though it's thrusting up through, between them, but they seem a little threatened as though they could damage it, could hurt it, as though they were two twin creatures with little paws, little legs outstretched wanting to pounce on it, maybe claw it . . . the feeling it seems to have, flinches a little anticipating that but it's going to keep on moving, thrusting, moving upward anyway and finally the two little creatures will withdraw their paws and snuggle against it because their shapes will fit right down in here, see the contours match here, and this will come up and it will fit snug and come together (fits red into white spaces) and it will be all right, it will be a very nice experience and a feeling of real union and sharing and closeness (II, without inquiry, D4).

Advanced Insight Group

The advanced insight group consisted of four Rorschachs collected from Western-born students of mindfulness meditation. These advanced practitioners are alleged to have achieved at least the first stage of enlightenment as defined by the tradition. Unlike the previous groups, these Rorschachs were *not* collected after a period of intensive meditation. One might think that few valid statements could be made from only four such protocols. Nevertheless, three of the four Rorschach protocols showed remarkable consistency, enough consistency to warrant a preliminary statement regarding Rorschachs from enlightened practitioners.

Rorschachs of the advanced insight group

These Rorschachs do not evidence the same outstanding qualitative features as found in the Samadhi and Insight Groups. They appear, at first glance, to be more like the Rorschachs of the Beginner's Group. The range of content is quite varied. Responses are nearly always images with brief associative elaborations. Responses are seldom dominated by the pure perceptual features of the inkblots, as was true for the Samadhi Group. Responses also lack the richness of associative elaboration so characteristic of the Insight Group.

Nevertheless, there do appear to be certain qualitative features which distinguish this group of protocols which we are calling "residual effects." We hypothesize them to be the consequences of having previously mastered both the

"residual effects"

samadhi and insight practices. Like the Rorschachs of the Samadhi Group, these Rorschachs contain occasional but less frequent references to the perceptual features of the inkblots, notably the shapes, symmetry, color, and variations in shading. Responsivity to achromatic color and shading variations is also quite high, as was true for the Samadhi Group. Such responses are, however, seldom pure shading responses. Instead, the shading is more likely to be interpreted as a certain *quality* or *state of mind* such as "pain . . . beauty," "dark and heavy," "unpleasantness," to draw examples from Rorschachs of the respective advanced practitioners. The use of inanimate movement responses, alone and in conjunction with color and shading, is also quite high, much higher in fact than in any other group. At least 10–20% of the total responses were inanimate movement responses for each of the four Ss. No S's record contained less than a raw count of 8 such responses. Compared to norms, this is extraordinarily high. Furthermore, these Rorschachs evidence residual effects akin to the effects in the Insight Group. Productivity was high for each of the Ss (total number of responses ranged from 55 to over 100). These responses, in contrast to those of the Insight Group, showed less variation in subsequent testing.

achromatic color and shading variations responses

If these Rorschachs are not so strikingly different from those of the previous criterion groups, especially the Beginner's Group, what then is distinctive about them? The most unusual feature, clearly present in a number of responses on three of the four Rorschachs, is the degree to which they perceive the inkblots as an *interaction of form and energy* or *form and space*. That is, *each* of the Ss, in several responses, perceived the inkblot primarily as *energy-in-motion* or as *empty space*. Such responses were, of course, distributed among the variety of specific images on all the cards. However, the Ss saw the specific images (content) and the energy-in-motion (process) as distinct but interrelated "levels" of perception.

the most unusual feature

A range of 5–20% of the content for each of the protocols referred specifically to various perceptions of energy. For example:

> . . . movies that I saw in science class which were talked about . . . let's see . . . talked about organism . . . um . . . atoms and molecules, and kind of a changing energy, changing energy (IX. shading in D.I.).

Most often content was given in conjunction with inanimate movement or inanimate movement/shading responses. In this respect, the S's sensitivity to inanimate movement and shading was somewhat different from comparable responses in the Samadhi Group. Whereas meditators during samadhi are likely to see the shapes themselves (or shading itself) moving on the card, these Ss seldom saw this. Instead, the movement and shading was usually "interpreted," i.e., it was given content, and usually the content referred to some manifestation of energy.

These energy responses might best be seen as representing various "levels" of energy organization. On the simplest level are responses referring to pure space from which energy unfolded. For example: *various "levels" of energy organization*

> The space between each form serves a purpose, not too compressed, and yet gives enough space for each quality to be its own and yet have enough room to exchange its own individual energy; however, it's a natural source of energy, unfolding and extending to take certain forms, um . . . almost feels more explo . . . I don't know if explosive is the right word. Let's say, such a strong source that it could come from that center core, that central orange, and go up into the blue and just push off just a little so that it could have its definite, um, shape and function . . . (VIIIDds 28).

On the next level are responses depicting the activity of the molecules of the universe or the primal elements within the body.

At still another level are responses indicating the types of energy organization within the human body, as conceptualized by any one of traditional Eastern systems of energy yoga (Avalon, 1931; Dasgupta, 1946; Eliade, 1969; Varenne, 1976). Such responses include diffuse body energies such as a "lifeforce" (X), as well as energies that have specific directions to the body (III). According to the yogic physiology, the body is said to contain both diffuse and specific energy. The latter is said to flow through invisible channels. Note that the organization of energy into specific currents represents a more complex form of energy than that of the primal elements. *All* of the Ss also made references to the main "centers" of energy within the body. Again according to yogic physiology, the body energies are said to be concentrated in specific centers called "chakras" within the body. Here we note an even further organization of energy, now into specific, quasi-stable locations.

> I see the different colors . . . going up the different energy centers of the body, starting with the whole pelvic region . . . the abdomen, chest, and head, and each color representing the different energy in that part of the body (VIIIW).

"drive energy" responses

In addition to these more common references to internal "yogic" anatomy, two of the Ss also made reference to a type of energy more akin to Western physiological processes, such as the energy of cell division (VI) or that of chromosomes dividing. Even more common were responses akin to what in Western psychology has been called "drive energy":

> I see a vagina (D12) and ovaries or some kind of organs (D11), internal organs . . . internal organs . . . I see (something) very phallic (D2) . . . a lot of thrusting energy I get from it . . . I see like an energy flow (shading D12) between like, ah, the vagina and the penis . . . it's like one continuum, the flow of energy betwen them, sexual energy . . . (VI).

Such direct references to sexual energy were found on all four protocols; one also made comparable references to aggressive energy. Finally, there were a number of responses depicting the type of energy that is bound up within inanimate objects, thereby causing them to move, e.g., spinning tops.

understanding the inter-relationship of form and energy/space

What is implicit in such responses is an understanding of the *interrelationship of form and energy/space*. The most striking feature of *all* these Ss' Rorschachs is the extent to which they view their own internal imagery, in response to the shapes on the inkblots, as merely manifestations or *emanations of energy/space*. Here is a typical but especially clear example:

I feel the energy coming from that, the whole energy of the picture . . . there's an intensity, a certain power of it, and everything else is just a dancing manifestation of that energy coming out (VIIWV).

Here we see that the advanced practitioners have a perspective that is quite unlike that of the previous groups. They see all of their percepts as merely emanations of energy, as part of the "dance of the mind." In fact, the Ss sometimes reported that such a transformation from energy/space into form actually took place before their eyes during the test. Although responses pertaining to mindstates are rare, it is important to point out that they hardly ever occur in the records of the beginner's samadhi or insight groups. They occur occasionally in the protocols of these advanced practitioners and will become even more important in records of the master's group.

While the Ss more often comment on the actual process by which forms and images come into existence, they also often comment, though less often, on the reverse process, namely, how forms and images dissolve into space. For example, one S saw a number of typical images on Card X, such as dancing insects. Then there followed a distinct shift of perception. She began to see the card as mere color and form and noticed that the colors and forms seemed to move inward, concentrating themselves at the center blue region of the card. She explained that all the forms and colors were connected by a "unifying force" by which the seemingly separate images on the card tended to "flow" back into the center region of "localized energy." Upon their return, the subject noted another perceptual shift, namely a figure-ground reversal. She ended up seeing only the white (former background) of the card, as if all the colors and forms had become absorbed into it. Such figure-ground reversals and movement toward the central unifying point were other distinctive features of these Rorschachs.

"dance of the mind"

figure-ground reversals and movement toward the center

In sum, the most distinctive feature of these Ss' Rorschachs is their unique perspective in which they actually witness energy/space in the moment-by-moment process of arising and organizing into forms and images; and conversely, witness the forms and images becoming absorbed back into energy/space. Here is one response which stands out as a particularly clear example of an advanced practitioner's perception of the momentary arising and passing away of phenomena:

> sort of like just energy forces and um like molecules . . . something like the energy of molecules . . . very much like a microscopic view . . . in some way there are more patterns of energy . . . there are different energies in the different colors . . . it looks like it's a view into the body where there's energy, there's movement, but it's steady because it's guided by a lifeforce . . . there is arising and passing away of these different elements. Inquiry: the colors seemed very alive and suggested life and they seemed very basic or elemental—both the shapes and size. They don't have heavy substance, you know; they each, um, are relatively fragile (different colors suggested different elements?) yeah . . . and then it started to seem just like a vibration, really not a swelling movement but a pulsation, just a coming and going of um kind of elemental bits (laughs because of word choice) of life (laughs) (arising and passing away of elements?) It was very far out when it happened . . . I can't um . . . some of that was because of the suggestion of the spinal column (previous response) . . . um it reminded me somewhat of those electron microscope pictures of the body and I just had this sense of movement of it all (XW).

One might expect certain consequences from seeing form as a manifestation of energy, from seeing the world as not particularly solid and durable. According to Mayman (1970), vaguely and amorphously perceived responses are interpreted as a non-committal hold on reality. These data suggest a rather different interpretation, what might be called the *relativization of perception*. No particular feature on an inkblot, or aspect of external reality, is compelling enough to suggest perception of solid and durable forms.

non-committal hold on reality vs. relativization of perception

While emphasizing the distinctive features of these Rorschachs, it is important to keep in mind that the responses discussed above constitute only a small proportion of the total Rorschach record for each advanced practitioner. The remainder of the imagery is quite varied. Examination of this imagery reveals that these allegedly enlightened advanced practitioners are not without intrapsychic conflict. Using the Holt system for scoring drive-dominated con-

intrapsychic conflict

tent, there is a consistently low but scorable number of aggression-related responses in the protocols of 3 of the 4 advanced practitioners. Overall, however, there appears to be an intensification of other drive states, e.g., sexual, relative to beginners and insight practitioners, even though the experience of aggression seems to diminish for most. Concern with the awareness and management of impulses was characteristic for all the advanced practitioners to some degree.

In addition, each of these Rorschachs evidenced idiosyncratic conflictual themes such as fear of rejection; struggles with dependency and needs for nurturance; fear and doubt regarding heterosexual relationships; fear of destructiveness. All of these issues are related to intimacy. *intimacy issues* They may reflect the peculiar role of an enlightened person in the context of modern Western culture where the struggle to uphold the ethical standards of the Buddhist teachings in a non-monastic culture makes intimate relationships more problematic. In any case, the unusual feature of these Rorschachs is *not* that these people are without conflict, but rather their *non-defensiveness in experiencing such conflicts*. Vivid drive-dominated content was often present while employing minimal or no defense against it *non-* (using Holt defense scoring criteria). This empirical finding is supported by the directness and matter-of-factness with which these advanced practitioners talked about personal problems during their follow-up interview. They tended to see their own sexual and aggressive drives, as well as their individual dynamics, as intense mind-states which could be experienced and acted on with awareness, but not necessarily invested in to any great degree.

Master's Group

The single Rorschach in this group is included because of its unusualness. It is the only data available on the final *unique single* stages of "development" *(bhavana)*, that is, from someone *Rorschach* who attained all or all but one of the 4 levels of enlightenment and has allegedly undergone a cognitive-emotional restructuring that has completely or almost completely eliminated suffering from their human experience. It should not be necessary to emphasize the extraordinary uniqueness and potential significance of data from this range of experience. This Rorschach was collected in South *problems of* Asia, and for reasons of confidentiality cannot be further *cross-cultural* identified. Analysis of this Rorschach re-opens all the com- *interpretation* plicated problems of cross-cultural Rorschach interpreta- tion. Nevertheless, several features are so striking that they are worthy of comment. First is its notable *shift in perspective.* Of the 32 total number of responses, 13 pertain to specific states of mind (41%) and 3 to states of the ordi- nary and non-ordinary world (9%). Whereas most "nor- mal" Rorschach subjects unquestioningly accept the phys- ical "reality" of an inkblot and then project their imagings onto it, this master sees an inkblot itself as a projection of the mind. All the various states of the mind and the world that might be articulated are themselves a kind of imme- diate reality. So also, the testing situation is a projection of the mind in a certain sense. The master, therefore, uses the situation as an occasion to teach about the various states of the mind and cosmos, especially those that enable others to alleviate their suffering.

The second unusual feature of the protocol is its *integrative style.* Each of the 10 cards, as it is presented, is utilized in *integrative style* the service of a systematic discourse on the Buddhist teachings pertaining to the alleviation of human suffering. Thus, Card I sets the stage with four images of humans and beasts in their everyday life of suffering. Card II de- picts a picture of the mind in its angered state, and Card III depicts the creatures of hell, the hellish state of mind produced by anger in this life, or the plane on which an angry person is believed to take birth in a future life, both in accordance with the Buddhist teachings on karmic ac- tion based on hatred. Cards IV-V depict the ignorance and craving of the mind, believed to be the two root causes of *traditional* suffering in Buddhist psychology. So far, the master has *doctrine set* set forth the traditional doctrine of the Three Poisons: an- *forth* ger, craving and ignorance. Card VI illustrates how the same mind and body can be used to gain liberation:

1. A pillar. It has taken the form of truth. This pillar reminds me of a process of getting at or discovering the human mind (D 5).

2. Inside there is envy, disease, sorrow, and hatred in the form of black shapes (W).
3. A human torso (Dd25).
4. After conquering truth, the mind has become clean and white (D 11).

Card VII gives the results of the practice:

1. I see a body (here, which reminds me of) a temple (D 6). The mind, here, like a cavern. I can also call this (with the portion identified as "mind" inside it) the physical body (term used implies a sense of lack of respect in the original language).   *results of practice set forth*
2. From it, wings have spread—the impulses (D 10).
3. Ultimately, this body has gone up to the temple (identifies a second temple, D 8). At the end of spiritual practice, the mind can travel in two temples (i.e., the first is the human body, once the source of the impulses but now the master of them; the second is the temple at the end of spiritual practice).

The remainder of the cards depict the enjoyment of the perfected practice, as well as the consequences of not perfecting practice.

Integrating all ten cards into a single associative theme is an extremely rare finding. Note that the master achieves this without any significant departure from reality testing and without ignoring the realistic features of the inkblot, though there is considerable reliance on shading responses and vague and amorphously perceived form.   *rare finding of single associative theme*

CHAPTER 7

THE STAGES OF MINDFULNESS MEDITATION: A VALIDATION STUDY

PART II: DISCUSSION

Daniel P. Brown
Jack Engler

In the previous chapter, Brown and Engler presented the results of a Rorschach validation study of the stages of mindfulness meditation. In this chapter they discuss the meanings and implications of those results. Their conclusion: "These Rorschachs illustrate that the classical subjective reports of meditation stages are more than religious belief systems; they are valid accounts of the perceptual changes that occur with intensive meditation. . . ." Brown and Engler conclude the study with some reflection on the relationship between meditation and therapeutic change.

In each of the criterion groups, there are unique qualitative features in the Rorschachs which are distinctly different from those of the other groups. This finding in itself suggests that there are indeed different stages of the practice. Even more interesting is the fact that the specific qualitative features of the Rorschachs for each group are consistent with the classical descriptions of the psychological changes most characteristic of that stage of practice. Thus, the Beginner's Rorschach is understandable in light of the classical descriptions of the preliminary stage of moral training; the Samadhi Rorschach, in terms of the classical descriptions of the stages of concentration leading to access concentration and samadhi; the Insight Rorschachs, in terms of the classical stages of insight; and the Advanced and Master's Rorschachs in terms of enduring trait changes upon attainment of the classical stages of enlightenment. The classical descriptions used in this study are those found in the *Visuddhimagga* (Nyanamoli, 1976) and

consistency with classical descriptions of psychological changes in the *Progress of Insight* (Mahasi Sayadaw, 1965). Such convergence of the Rorschach qualitative features on the one hand, and the classical descriptions on the other, may be an important step toward establishing the cross-cultural validation of the psychological changes at each major stage of the practice. What follows is a brief discussion of the convergence in each instance.

cross-cultural validation

The Beginner's Group

The qualitative features of the post-Rorschachs of the 15 Ss in the Beginner's Group were not especially different from the pre-Rorschachs, with one important exception. The Rorschachs of a significant number of these Ss manifested an increased incidence of drive-dominated content as well as significant changes in the formal aspects of their verbalizations (Holt & Havel, 1960; Watkins & Stauffacher, 1975).

These findings are consistent with those of Maupin (1965). Using the Rorschach, Maupin reported an increase in primary process thinking and tolerance for unrealistic experience for beginning Zen students practicing a cognate form of meditation. Maupin also found that such an increase in primary process thinking and tolerance predicted successful response to meditation while attentional measures did not. Maupin concludes:

> Capacity for regression and tolerance for unrealistic experience significantly predicted response to meditation, while attention measures did not. Once issues related to comfort in the face of strange inner experience are resolved, attention functions necessary to the exercise probably become available.

Thus, at the start of meditation practice, the naive S is introduced, perhaps for the first time, to the vast world of his internal experience. Maupin correctly points out that, whereas the beginning meditator's task may be to train attention, most are readily distracted from that task by the very strangeness of their internal world.

characteristic beginner's experience

There is a characteristic storminess to the beginner's experience. Subjective reports of an increased awareness of fantasy and daydreaming, of incessant thinking, and of lability of affect abound in the literature (Mahasi Sayadaw, 1965; Walsh, 1977, 1978). Objective measures such as primary process scores on the Rorschach lend some validity to these reports. Likewise, Davidson, Goleman & Schwartz (1976) have reported an increase in state-anxiety for the beginning meditator, in contrast to a decrease for the advanced meditator. Overall, the beginner's experience is largely a matter of *adaptation to the flow of internal experience*, an adaptation perhaps understandably necessary and anxiety-producing in a culture that lays so much stress on external adaptation and reality-boundness at the expense of imaginative involvement (Hilgard, 1970). What is necessary to keep in mind is that this phase of adaptation, though necessary, has very little to do directly with meditation in the formal sense.

The beginning meditator's introduction to his internal world is not essentially different from the naive S's who begins exploration of other hypoaroused states, e.g., self-hypnosis, reverie, and free association. For example, using the Rorschach, a similar increase in primary process thinking has been reported for hypnotized Ss (Fromm *et al.*, 1970) and for patients who had undergone psychoanalysis (Rehyer, 1969). Using questionnaires, an increased awareness of imagery was reported for self-hypnosis (Fromm *et al.*, 1980). According to these findings, adaptation to the internal milieu may be a common feature of *any* hypoaroused state of consciousness and may have little to do with the "specificity" of meditation per se (Tart, 1975).

beginning meditators and naive S's

The implication is that beginners, in a strict sense, are not necessarily "meditating" even when they appear to be sitting in a meditation posture for some period of time. What, then, are they doing? This question was recently put to an esteemed Asian Buddhist teacher of this practice. He was asked why only a very few of the, say, 60 students who meditate intensively for three months in this country reach the more advanced stages of concentration and insight according to classical criteria; whereas the majority of students who meditate the same way for a comparable length of time in certain meditation centers in South Asia are alleged to reach these advanced stages. He attributed the difference in part to a difference in cultural beliefs and

self-exploratory therapy and formal meditation

to the degree of conviction and understanding the students bring to the practice. In addition, he said, "Many Western students do not meditate. They do therapy . . . they do not go deep with the mindfulness." The answer is to the point. It suggests a difference between adaptation and attentional training, mindfulness in this case. Much in line with Maupin's findings, it seems that many Westerners become so fascinated with the content of their internal world, understandably perhaps since it is often their first real conscious encounter with it—fantasies, personal problems, emotional reactions, thoughts—that they become preoccupied with an exploration of this content. In effect, they fail to go beyond the content and proceed to the necessary task of training concentration, mindfulness and related processes of attention. This form of *self-exploratory therapy* often gets confounded in both practice and in the theoretical and research literature with *formal meditation*, defined in terms of the specific training of attentional skills.

the role of preliminary practices

In order to avoid such confusion, many Eastern systems have devised a more or less elaborate system of "preliminary practices" to be done before formal meditation. These practices are often referred to as the stage of Moral Training. They consist of an often elaborate set of instructions for changing attitudes about self and world, thorough exploration of internal states, and the regulation of external behavior through precepts. They demand nothing less than a radical change in one's view of oneself, an exploration of and working through of qualities of one's internal milieu, and a thorough behavioral change. Considerable time may be spent in these practices—several years is not uncommon in some traditional systems—before formal training in meditation is begun.

It is indeed remarkable that formal meditation has become so popular in this country while the preliminary moral training has been largely ignored. The psychological changes characteristic of the preliminary practices are the necessary precondition to formal meditation. What happens when they are skipped over? One can predict that the beginner is destined to "work through" these changes during meditation itself. Consequently the preliminary therapeutic change and the stages of formal meditation become confounded. In this country, meditation is indeed a form of "therapy" for many.

Unfortunately, this makes it more difficult for even the most sincere students of meditation to advance in the more formal practice. Outcome studies have shown that expectations play a significant role both in therapeutic outcomes (Frank, 1961) and in meditation outcomes (Smith, 1976). Once the cultural belief that formal meditation is a form of therapy is firmly entrenched, students are likely to engage the content of their internal milieu at the expense of attentional training, even during intensive practice. Such students are unlikely to advance in the more characteristic features of formal meditation at a very rapid rate. This is perhaps one reason why over half of the experimental Ss were still exploring emotional issues after three months of continuous 16 hr./day practice. Some, however, who become less distracted by the content and proceed to train their attention may advance. The self-reports and Rorschachs of the Samadhi Group are illustrative of such advance.

the role of expectations

The Samadhi Group

The Rorschach data of the Samadhi Group might be considered in light of the classical descriptions of the psychological changes occurring in the first set of formal meditations: the stages of concentration. These classical stages have been described in detail elsewhere, along with comparisons to constructs from Western cognitive and perceptual psychology (Brown, 1977). Briefly, according to the tradition formal meditation begins when the yogi trains his posture and learns to quiet his mind so that internal events, such as thoughts and imagery, and external events such as sights and sounds, no longer distract the meditator from an ongoing awareness of the internal milieu. The meditator begins by concentrating on some object, such as the breath. As his concentration becomes more steady, with fewer lapses in attention, the meditator slowly and systematically expands the range of his awareness to the moment-by-moment recognition of the changing events in

process of entering into samadhi

the internal milieu. As he becomes more skilled, he is able to become aware of events very quickly, so quickly that he is aware not so much of the content but of the very *process* of moment-by-moment change itself. At times he may experience a relative cessation of specific visual, auditory and other perceptual patterns during the meditation while remaining uninterruptedly aware of the process of moment-by-moment change in the flux of stimuli prior to their coalescence into particular patterns of objects. These changes mark the onset of samadhi.

Beginner's Samadhi characterized

There are different stages or refinements of samadhi. *Beginner's Samadhi* is here defined according to two criteria: the object of awareness and the quality of that awareness. With respect to the object of awareness, a Beginner's Samadhi is characterized by relative freedom from distracting thoughts. If thoughts occur, they are recognized immediately after their occurrence and subside upon being noticed. As with thoughts, the yogi is struck by the immediate awareness of all forms of sense data. Though specific gross perceptual patterns may occur, e.g., a sight or sound, emphasis is on registration of the impact, not on the pattern. For example, in glancing at a specific object like one's hand or hearing a specific sound like a bell, the yogi is more aware that he has glanced at something or that a sound has occurred than he is of the content of the sight or sound. Nevertheless, in Beginner's Samadhi there is a strong tendency to become lost in a given thought or in the interpretation of a moment of sense data and to thereby lose awareness of the immediate sensory impact. Second, with respect to the quality of awareness, Beginner's Samadhi is characterized by a relative steadiness. The yogi's awareness is relatively continuous. During each sitting period, there are fewer periods of non-awareness, that is, of becoming distracted by or lost in the content.

Access Samadhi characterized

The next stage of samadhi in this system is *Access Samadhi.* With respect to the object of awareness, Access is characterized by a distinct lack of thinking and recognizable perceptual patterns. The yogi has "stopped the mind," at least in the sense of its so-called "higher operations": thinking and pattern recognition. The yogi keeps his awareness at the more subtle level of the *actual* moment *of occurrence* or *immediate impact* of a thought or of a sensory stimulus. Thus, instead of recognizing specific thoughts, images or perceptual patterns (as still occurs in Beginner's Samadhi), the yogi is more aware of their moment of impact only. Each discrete event is experienced more as a subtle movement, vibration, at the very onset of its occurrence. Although the yogi is aware of a myriad of discrete events, happening moment-by-moment, *he no longer elaborates the cognitive or perceptual content of such events*. The meditation period is experienced as a succession of discrete events: pulses, flashes, vibrations, or movements without specific pattern or form. With respect to awareness itself, Access is characterized by completely stable and steady attention. Though mental and bodily events occur moment-by-moment in uninterrupted succession, attention remains fixed on each discrete moment. Awareness of one event is immediately followed by awareness of another without break for the duration of the sitting period, or for as long as this level of concentration remains. This succession of moments of awareness is called "momentary concentration" (Mahasi Sayadaw, 1965).

The essential distinction between these levels of Samadhi, however, is the grossness or subtleness of the object of awareness on the one hand, and the degree of uninterrupted awareness on the other. Steadiness is most important. Once stabilized, the more advanced yogi can hold his samadhi at different levels, from gross to subtle, for the purpose of insight at each level. He may, for example, purposely allow the gross content of the mind to return in full force, especially thoughts, feelings and meaningful perceptual patterns, in order to deepen insight into the nature of mental and bodily processes. However, this skilled yogi's steady awareness continues in the midst of the various content. Now, there is little problem with the distraction which was such a problem for the beginning meditator.

essential distinction between levels

The Rorschach data from the Samadhi Group are consistent with these classical descriptions of samadhi. Recall that these Rorschachs were characterized by: a) a paucity of associative elaborations; b) a significant decrease in the production of internal images; c) a concentration on the pure perceptual features of the inkblot. Despite the experimenter's demand to produce images and associations, the Ss are believed to have partially maintained their state of samadhi during the testing. This is hypothesized to account for the marked reduction in the availability of ideational and pattern recognition components of perception, concomitant with an increased awareness of the immediate impact of the inkblot. Thus, the yogis were primarily attentive to, and occasionally absorbed in, the pure perceptual features, e.g., outlines, colors, shades, and inanimate movement.

*evidence
validating
classical
description*
It is at least clear from the data that the yogis' awareness in this group is at the level of the immediate perceptual impact of the inkblot, not at the level of an elaboration or interpretation of that sensory impact. Because such pure determinant Rorschach responses are highly atypical of either normal or clinical Rorschachs, and are uncharacteristic of both the pre-test Rorschachs of the same Ss and the Rorschachs of the control group as well, these Rorschach responses may be seen as evidence validating the classical description and existence of the state of samadhi as a definite kind of perceptual event or level of perceptual experience.

The Insight Group

*the stages of
insight*
In the classical stages of meditation, Access Samadhi is merely a prerequisite for Insight Meditation. Just as a scientist may painstakingly construct a sensitive electronic instrument to measure some process, likewise the meditator has carefully prepared himself through the refinement and steadying of attention with its accompanying shifts in levels of perception in order to gain insight into the fundamental workings of the mind. The meditator is now ready to proceed to the Stages of Insight. Because the descriptions of these stages are technical, the reader is referred elsewhere (Mahasi Sayadaw, 1965; Nyanamoli, 1976). Suffice it to say that the foundation of all insight in Buddhism is understanding of the three "*laksanas*" or "marks" of existence: impermanence, suffering, and selflessness or nonsubstantiality. According to the tradition, a

genuine experiential understanding of these is possible only after having achieved Access Samadhi.

In each discrete moment of awareness the meditator concomitantly notices both the mental or bodily event and his awareness of that event. In a single meditation session he is likely to experience thousands of such discrete moments of awareness because his attention is now refined enough to perceive increasingly discrete and rapidly changing mind-moments. When this level of moment-to-moment change is actually experienced, the meditator is led to a profound and radical understanding of the impermanence (*anicca*) of all events. He may also notice a tendency to react to the events, to prefer some or to reject others. This reactive tendency disrupts the clear perception of the moment-by-moment flow and in fact has the effect of blocking the flow itself in an attempt to resist it—to hold on, or push away. The continual experience of this with clear awareness eventually leads to an understanding of the suffering (*dukkha*) inherent in the normal reactive mind and its relationship to its experience in terms of liking and disliking, attraction and aversion. Furthermore, as discrete events/moments of awareness arise and cease in rapid succession, the yogi finds it increasingly difficult to locate anything or anyone that could be either the agent of these events or the recipient of their effects. He cannot find any enduring or substantial agent behind the events to which they could be attributed. The only observable reality at this level is the flow of events themselves. From this perspective of constant change, what was once a solid body, a durable perceptual object such as a tree, a fixed idea, or even a fixed point of observation, no longer appears substantial, durable or existent in its own right. By viewing this changing process, the yogi comes to understand the lack of intrinsic durable nature or the selflessness (*anatta*) of mind, body and external perceptions. These insights into the fundamental operations of the mind and its "marks" result in a profound reorganization of the meditator's experience called, in the *Visuddhimagga*, "Purification of View."

impermanence and the suffering of the reactive mind

"Purification of View"

At first it is easier to obtain these insights by holding awareness at the level of Access, i.e., at the level of the subtle moment-by-moment pulsation of events. Eventually, the meditator is able to sustain the same insights even when allowing his awareness to return to the ordinary gross content of experience such as specific thoughts, bodily sensations, or perceptual patterns. With perfectly uninterrupted and steady awareness he observes this various content moment-by-moment and thereby deepens his insight into the three characteristics of all mental and bodily processes. This is called, again in the terminology of the *Visuddhimagga*, "Overcoming Doubt." Eventually, the very way that these events are perceived to arise undergoes a series of significant shifts, both in duration and in vividness. Regardless of the content, the events flash very quickly, like pulses of light, moment-by-moment. The beginning and ending of each event is clearly perceived. This is called "Knowledge of the Arising and Passing Away" of events and is a key stage in Insight Meditation (Nyanamoli, 1976).

"Knowledge of the Arising and Passing Away"

The moment-by-moment arising and passing away of bodily and mental events and their concomitant awareness eventually "break up." This is called the experience of "Dissolution." Only the rapid and successive passing away of discrete events and their awareness are perceived. Their arising is no longer noticeable. Events and awareness of them seem to vanish and disappear together moment-by-moment. The net effect of this level of perception is either to experience reality as a state of continual and ongoing dissolution, moment-by-moment; or to experience forms and percepts as literally void—to have no perception, for instance, of a form like one's arm or leg or even one's entire body, or of an external object like a tree in front of one, at all.

"Dissolution"

The first reaction to this experience is often one of exhilaration or ecstasy. If so, it is usually short-lived. It is soon followed in subsequent stages of practice by states of fear and terror, misery and disgust as the implications of this discovery become apparent and sink in. These are affective reactions to the experience of reality as a condition of continual dissolution or radical impermanence, but they are not affective states in the normal sense. The yogi's aware-

reaction to dissolution

ness remains steady and balanced behind these affects. They are experienced fully and observed as mind-states, but without further reaction. They in turn become objects of bare attention and continue to be observed with uninterrupted mindfulness toward further insight. They are technically described as "knowledges" (*nanas*) rather than affects and are considered separate stages in the insight series.

In subsequent meditation, events reoccur. The yogi is not only aware of each event which occurs within consciousness but is also aware of its context, i.e., he is aware that each event is located within the entire fabric of a cosmos comprised of infinite potential interactions. From this wider perspective, called "dependent origination," all potential events are again seen to break up rapidly. The yogi however has changed his attitude toward these dissolving events. He has come to realize that no event could possibly serve as an object of satisfaction or fulfillment. Precisely for this reason, he experiences a profound desire for deliverance from them, from which this stage derives its technical name, "Desire for Deliverance." He subsequently begins to re-examine these events with renewed effort and dedication: the stage of "Re-Observation for the Purpose of Deliverance." With continued practice he next realizes what is called "Equanimity About Formations": a perfectly balanced, *effortless* and *non-reactive awareness* of each rapidly changing and vanishing event moment-by-moment, with a clear perception of their impermanence, unsatisfactoriness and nonsubstantiality. Despite great individual variation at the level of gross content, there is no difference at the subtlest level of awareness or reaction to any events. Awareness proceeds spontaneously, without any referent to an individual self or personal history. A fundamental shift in time/space organization has occurred so that the yogi is now aware of the continuous occurrence of all the potential events of the mind/cosmos.

"Desire for Deliverance"

"effortless" and *"non-reactive" awareness*

These classical descriptions of the stages of insight in Theravadin Buddhism can be compared to the Rorschachs produced by the Insight Group. Recall that the insight Rorschachs were characterized by: a) increased productivity;

b) richness of associative elaboration with shifts in affect;
c) realistic attunement of the image and the blot. These
Rorschachs are strikingly different from those of the Samadhi group. In fact in some respects they are nearly opposite. In interpreting these data, we assume that a meditator skilled in insight is likely to allow a very great variety
of content to pass through his mind during a single meditation session. With uninterrupted and steady awareness
and without reaction he simply notices the great richness
of the unfolding mind states. He notices the play of mental
events from all the sensory and cognitive modes moment-
by-moment, all dependently arising according to their respective causes and conditions. In a test situation like the
Rorschach, one would predict this state of non-reactive
moment-by-moment awareness to affect Rorschach performance. According to our understanding of the insight
stages, the striking increase in productivity as well as its
richness is not at all surprising. In response to a given
inkblot one would expect a great richness of content to
arise moment-by-moment. The unfolding of such rich content would be seemingly endless with nothing experienced as especially durable or lasting. Nevertheless, just
as the Buddhist texts claim that such events arise by causes
and conditions, so also the meditators were sensitive to
and aware of the relative stimulus-pull of each Rorschach
card. In the same way, they were finely attuned to the
reality features of the blots. Moreover, during the Insight
Stages the yogi is less likely to be restricted by any form of
reaction to these subtle events, by any selection or rejection of them. Thus it is not surprising to find a distinct
acceptance and *quality of non-defensiveness* in Rorschachs of such practition-
matter-of- ers. There is a distinct acceptance and matter-of-factness
factness even of what would normally be conflictual sexual and
aggressive material. Furthermore, the experienced absence of any solid or durable self behind the flow of mental
and physical events is consistent with these yogis' flexibil-
ity in switching perspectives on the same response, a pattern atypical of normal and clinical Rorschachs. Nevertheless, despite the impersonal nature of the experience of
insights such as insubstantiality, these Rorschachs, contrary to the stereotypical and erroneous notions of insubstantiality as a void state, are deeply human and fraught

with the richness of the living process. One need only quickly scan the Rorschachs of these Ss to see that we are dealing with a very unusual quality and richness of life experience.

The Advanced Insight Group

At a specifiable point—when the mind is perfectly balanced and insight into the "three marks of existence" (impermanence, suffering, and selflessness or nonsubstantiality) is clear in each moment of perception and all forms of desire consequently cease—the most fundamental shift of all occurs. Awareness, previously tied to each momentary event, now passes beyond these events. During this moment all conceptual distinctions and ordinary understandings of the "mind" fall away. All objects of awareness and individual acts of awareness cease. There is only stillness and vastness, "the Supreme Silence" as one Asian teacher described it, without disturbance by any event whatsoever but with pure awareness. This profound shift is called the Cessation Experience *(nirodha)* and is the First or Basic Moment of Enlightenment. It is immediately followed by another shift, also a Cessation Experience, technically called Entering the Path *(magga)* or Stream (to Nirvana). When this Path-Moment (lit. *sotapatti* or "stream-entry") is experienced, certain erroneous conceptions about the nature of reality and certain emotional defilements are eradicated. This moment is followed by yet another shift, called Fruition *(phala)*, in which the "fruit" of Path-entry is experienced; mind remains silent and at peace. This is followed in quick succession by a moment of Reviewing in which awareness of the content of the meditator's individual experience returns and he becomes reflexively aware of the extraordinary thing that has happened to him. As ordinary mental events pass through awareness, the meditator simply lets his relative content run its own course while his awareness is no longer bound to it. The state immediately following Path-Fruition-Reviewing is typically one of great lightness and joy which may last several days. The important fact, however, is that *enduring trait changes* are said to occur upon enlightenment.

"the Supreme Silence" and the First Moment of Enlightenment

Several options are available to the meditator at this point. He may simply return to his daily affairs. If he does, he may or may not continue formal practice. Whether he does or not, however, the gains of this experience of First Path are thought to be permanent. If the meditator continues practice, either in the context of his daily life or in further intensive retreat settings, two courses are open to him. He may remain on the level attained at First Path and practice to develop what is technically termed the "Maturity of Fruition." This refers to the ability to enter into the state of awareness he experienced at the initial moments of both Path and Fruition. Both these moments are moments of Cessation in which all ordinary perceptual, cognitive, affective and motivational activity ceases. They each last only a brief moment before ordinary consciousness and mental activity resumes. Phenomenologically they are both experienced as a state of supreme silence. The difference between them lies in the power of the Path-moment preceding Fruition. It is at that moment that the fundamental and irreversible shift or change in the meditator takes place. This is expressed as a "change-of-lineage" (*gotrabhu*) and is traditionally defined in terms of the specific "fetters" (*samyojanas*) or perceptual-cognitive and affective modalities that are permanently eliminated at that stage of enlightenment (Nyanamoli, 1976). The experience of Path and the changes associated with it are accordingly said to occur only once at each stage of enlightenment, four times in all. The silent and peaceful mental state of Fruition, on the other hand, can be re-experienced, in principle, indefinitely. This is termed "entering the Fruition state." With practice, the mediator can learn to re-experience the Fruition state at will for extended periods of time.

First Path and "Maturity of Fruition"

The other course open to the individual who wants to continue meditation is to practice for a subsequent Path experience, which defines the advanced enlightenment experiences. There are three further Paths or stages of enlightenment in this tradition. Each is attained in the same way. If the yogi chooses to work for Second Path, for instance, he must begin by formally and deliberately renouncing the Fruition-state of the First Path. This is a consequential decision. According to tradition and confirmed by self-reports in the South Asian study, once having made

subsequent Paths and advanced enlightenment experiences

this renunciation he will never experience the Fruition of First Path again, whether or not he is successful in attaining Second Path. Attainment of a prior Path does not guarantee attainment of the succeeding Path. After making this renunciation, he returns to the stage of Arising and Passing Away. He must then pass through all the subsequent stages of insight a second time until he once more experiences a Path-moment at their conclusion. Again stage-specific changes will occur; additional and different emotional defilements permanently disappear from his psychic organization. Again this Path-moment will be followed by moments of Fruition and Reviewing and again he may discontinue practice or, choosing to continue, either cultivate Fruition or practice for the Third and finally the Fourth Path, which is said to produce a final state of perfect wisdom and compassion and freedom from any kind of suffering. Each stage of enlightenment is more difficult to attain than the previous one. The yogi passes through the same stages of practice prior to the experience of Path each time; but each time the experience is more intense, the suffering greater, as more deeply rooted fetters are extinguished and insight into the nature of reality grows. Though possible in principle, as all the advanced practitioners and masters in this study maintain, our research in the Buddhist cultures of Asia, where a higher incidence of such attainments is still to be expected, disclosed that few meditators attain all four Paths.

Second, Third, and Fourth Paths

The Rorschachs of the Advanced Insight Group can be interpreted by considering the consequences of enlightenment specified by the tradition. Enlightenment is said to be followed by a return to ordinary mental experience, though one's perspective is radically altered. One might expect such Rorschachs to reflect the idiosyncrasies of character and mental content for each of the respective practitioners. One would also expect such Rorschachs to retain some of the features of enlightenment specified by tradition. These features are: a) changes in the conception of reality, following the Cessation experience; b) eradication of certain defilements upon Path experience. The four Rorschachs, though a small sample, are consistent with the classical accounts of the trait changes said to follow the enlightenment experience.

Rorschachs of the Advanced Insight Group

issues for interpretation

Recall that these enlightenment Rorschachs did not evidence a high degree of the unusual qualitative features of the samadhi and insight Rorschachs. They are not especially distinct from the Rorschachs of the pre-test population of the Three-Month Study. Their lack of immediate distinctiveness poses some interesting issues for interpretation. One might conclude that the outcomes of long-term meditation are either psychologically insignificant or a function of unstable state changes. Or one might conclude that the Rorschach is unable to measure those psychological outcomes, whatever they may be. From another standpoint, the very mundaneness of these Rorschachs could be interpreted as a highly significant finding. Consistent with the classical descriptions of enlightenment, especially the Review following enlightenment, the practitioner is

change in reaction to content of experience

said to retain his ordinary mind. Though his perspective is radically different, nevertheless the *content of his experience is just as it was prior to meditation, though he may no longer react to it with the usual emotional attitudes* of attraction, aversion or indifference. There is a famous Zen saying which speaks directly to this point:

> Before I began meditating, mountains were mountains and rivers were rivers. After I began meditating, mountains were no longer mountains and rivers were no longer rivers. Once I finished meditating, mountains were once again mountains, and rivers were once again rivers.

In the language of the present tests from the advanced practitioners, "Rorschachs are once again Rorschachs." The advanced practitioner lives out his or her idiosyncratic life history, though in the context of a relativized perception of self and object world.

perceiving a relative reality

Though, for the most part, these are seemingly mundane Rorschachs, each contains evidence that the enlightened practitioner perceives reality differently. An enlightened person is said to *manifest awareness on different levels*. On the mundane level, such a person continues to perceive solid and enduring forms in the external world as well as habitual mind-states such as emotions and attitudes. To the extent that perception has been relativized by enlightenment, on an absolute level these external forms and mental states are no longer viewed as solid and durable. They exist only in a relative sense.

These alleged changes may be reflected in the Rorschachs. For enlightened subjects, the inkblots do indeed "look like" specific images such as butterflies, bats, etc.; and yet these images, as well as mind-states like pain and pleasure, are perceived as merely manifestations of energy/space. Such Ss perceive content, but also energy processes, in the inkblots. One possible interpretation is that the enlightened practitioner has come to understand something fundamental about the process by which this perceived world comes into existence in our ordinary awareness.

While retaining an ability to perceive external forms and ordinary mental experience on both these levels—as relatively real but ultimately mere configurations of changing energy/space—the enlightened practitioner becomes free of the constraints of non-veridical perception or attachment to external forms or internal mind-states. One alleged outcome is that the enlightened person sees that *non-attached,* man's place in the universe is not self-contained but is lo- *contextualist* cated within a fabric of many other modes of existence and *mode of* potential interactions, all of which are interrelated, and *perception* mutually conditioned. Life becomes multi-dimensional and multi-determined in its dynamism and manifestation. This mode of perception leads to a deeper acceptance of human life and death, now set within the context of an unfolding universe in which there is both form and emptiness. Here is an example of a Rorschach response which illustrates this *non-attached, contextualist* mode of perception:

> It looks like a combination caterpillar-butterfly. It seems to be in motion. It gives me the feeling of this creature, this being, walking through the meadow or through a field of grass. It has the feeling of being at home with what it's doing . . . simple and right, at one with what it's doing. It's just its movement (I, W).

The Rorschachs also contain evidence that the enlightened practitioner may experience conflict differently. One very *enlightened practitioner not without conflict*

important discovery from these Rorschachs is that the enlightened practitioners are *not* without conflict, in a clinical sense. They show evidence for the experience of drive states and conflictual themes such as fears, dependency struggles and so forth. They are, however, *less defensive* in their awareness of and presentation of such conflicts. First enlightenment does not mean that a person becomes conflict-free.

mistaken assumptions about enlightenment

According to the tradition, personal conflicts are actually likely to intensify between the second and third experience of enlightenment. This contradicts one major misconception in both Western and Eastern cultures. It is often mistakenly assumed by Western students of meditation that enlightenment solves all of one's problems. Asian teachers know this is not so. But they in turn point almost exclusively to the remaining "fetters" or "defilements" that will be eliminated only with the attainment of further degrees of enlightenment.

what does change during enlightenment

According to the tradition, only certain defilements are removed upon the experience of First Path. *What changes is not so much the amount or nature of conflict but awareness of and reactivity to it.* During enlightenment, the locus of awareness, in a manner of speaking, transcends conflict. Awareness "goes to the other shore" so that it is no longer influenced by any mental content. After enlightenment, the content, including conflictual issues, returns. In this sense, enlightenment provides sufficient distance, or better, a vastly different perspective, while one continues to play out the repetitive dynamic themes of life history. There is greater awareness of and openness to conflict but paradoxically less reaction at the same time in an impulsive, identificatory and therefore painful way. Awareness is less caught up in the relative play of conflictual content or indeed any kind of content at this stage. For example, problems concerning sexual intimacy are more likely to be seen as "states of mind." The individual may observe these clearly for what they are and thereby have more freedom in his/her possible reactions to such states. He/she may note the intense desire until it passes, like every other transient mental state; or he/she may act on it, but with full awareness.

One reported effect of first enlightenment is said to be immediate awareness of any "unwholesome" mental state. Mindfulness is said to automatically intervene between impulse or thought and action in such cases. This mechanism of delay, combined with clear and impartial observation, allows *a new freedom from drive and a new freedom for well-considered and appropriate action.* In this sense, suffering diminishes while conflictual content nevertheless recurs as long as one is alive and has not yet attained subsequent enlightenments.

If these traditional accounts of the effects of enlightenment are considered in dynamic terms, one might say that such enlightened individuals exhibit a loosening of defense with a decreased susceptibility to the usual effects of unbound drive energy or the lifting of repression because they no longer have the same power to compel reaction, i.e., to produce an affective or drive state which must be acted upon or defended against. The model of defense seems, then, not well suited to explain these processes. Likewise, the notion of insight. Enlightened practitioners do not necessarily have greater psychological insight into the specific nature of conflicts. Many may tolerate conflictual mind states and let them pass naturally. The degree to which enlightened persons achieve psychological insight varies according to the degree of psychological sophistication of the individual (cf. also Carrington & Ephron, 1975). There is apparently less need to "see through" on the level of content what can be "let go of" on the level of process.

"seeing through" vs. "letting go"

Our finding for this group then is complex. On the one hand, enlightenment at this level at least does not necessarily eliminate intrapsychic and interpersonal conflict, though the possibility of this occurring at higher levels of enlightenment is not foreclosed. On the other hand, enlightenment does enable the individual to suffer less from its effects. This suggests a rethinking of current models of the relative position of meditation and normal adult development, or meditation and psychotherapy insofar as therapy reinstitutes the normal developmental process (Blanck & Blanck, 1974). First, meditation is both different from normal development and/or psychotherapy, and something more. While meditation apparently parallels some of

rethinking current models

the processes and accomplishes some of the goals of conventional therapies in alleviating intrapsychic conflict and facilitating mature object relations, it aims at a perceptual shift and a goal-state which is not aimed at or even envisaged in most psychotherapeutic models of mental health and development. However, meditation and psychotherapy cannot be positioned on a continuum in any mutually exclusive way as though both simply pointed to a different range of human development (Rama *et al.*, 1976). Not only do post-enlightenment stages of meditation apparently affect the manifestation and management of neurotic conditions, but this type of conflict continues to be experienced after enlightenment. This suggests either that psychological maturity and the path to enlightenment are perhaps *future empirical* two complementary but not entirely unrelated lines of *research* growth; or that indeed they do represent different "levels" or ranges of health/growth along a continuum, but with much more complex relationships between them than have previously been imagined. It may be, for instance, that still higher stages of enlightenment may indirectly affect the intrapsychic structural foundations of neurotic or borderline level conflict and so resolve it, even though this is not their main intent. This will be an issue for the next group of protocols. It is also one of the most important issues for future empirical research.

The Master's Group

Masters at the third stage of enlightenment are alleged to no longer be subject to sexual or aggressive impulses and painful affects. The fully enlightened master (Fourth Path) is alleged to have perfected the mind and to be free of any kind of conflict or suffering. These two types of "ariyas" or "worthy ones" constitute a unique group according to past tradition and current practice. The single Rorschach of the *the Master's* master representing this group is certainly unusual. *Rorschach* (Though the author was not allowed to ask the question of attainment directly, data from the case history interview, corroborated by the Rorschach and the additional TAT protocols which were administered in the South Asian study, permit this classification.) The interpretive question, however, is whether this protocol can be distinguished from the dogmatic opinions of a religious fundamentalist or the fixed delusions of a paranoid character where one might also expect attempts to relate the various test cards into a single theme. There are clear differences. The decision to use the testing situation as an occasion to teach stands in direct contrast to the guardedness and constrictedness of a paranoid record. The personalized nature of a paranoid delusion contrasts with the systematic presentation of a consensual body of teaching established by a cultural tradition. These are culture-dominated, not drive-dominated, percepts. The associations are consistent and integrated across all ten cards rather than being loosely related from card to card. We know of no paranoid record that compares with its level of consistency and integration. It is a considerable feat to integrate all ten cards into a single body of teaching over and against the varied stimulus-pull of ten very different cards, and to do so without significant departure from reality testing.

One additional piece of evidence that might speak to the validity of the integrative style is its documentation in other field work. Though to our knowledge there are no other Rorschachs reported for meditation masters, Rorschachs have been reported for advanced teachers from other spiritual traditions. For example, Boyer *et al.* (1964) administered the Rorschach to Apache shamans. He also collected indigenous ratings on the authenticity of the shamans by having the Indians themselves rate whether they felt a given shaman was real or fake. The Rorschachs of the pseudoshamans looked like pathological records. The records of the shamans rated authentic were atypical. In a separate paper, Klopfer & Boyer (1961) published the protocol of a "real" shaman. It is surprisingly similar to our master's Rorschach. There also the shaman used the ten cards as an occasion to teach the examiner about his lived world-view—in that case, about his ecstatic flights through the universe. There also the shaman relied heavily upon shading and amorphously used form. Boyer was unclear as to the significance of the shading and saw it as pathological. We are not so sure, especially in light of the high use of shading by our Ss during samadhi. Shading in very high incidence for practitioners of altered states may be a valid indicator of the awareness of subtle internal and

the integrative style

possible implication of integrative style

external nuances in stimuli that is a result of disciplined exploration of these states. The integrative style is perhaps an additional feature of those individuals who have carried their skill to its completion. One possible implication of such cross-cultural similarities is that this style may be suggestive of a "master's Rorschach" regardless of the spiritual tradition. The master is not at all interested in expressing the individual content of his/her mind to an examiner. It appears that, out of compassion, the master is *test as teaching* only interested in pointing a way for others to "see" reality more clearly in such a way that it alleviates their suffering. The test situation becomes a teaching situation whereby the examiner becomes a witness to a guided exploration of the transpersonal level of the mind/universe.

A second possible inference from the master's protocol is *a second* that intrapsychic structure has undergone a radical endur- *possible* ing reorganization. The protocol shows no evidence of *inference* sexual or aggressive drive conflicts, or indeed any evidence of instinctually based drive at all. Remarkable though it may seem, there may be no endopsychic structure in the sense of permanently opposed drives and controls. We assume that "a perfectly mature person" would be "a whole unified person whose internal psychic differentiation and organization would simply represent his diversified interests and abilities, within an overall good ego development and good object-relationships" (Guntrip, 1969).

CONCLUSION

The purpose of this study has been to illustrate an ap-
purpose of proach to the empirical validation of the classical scriptural
study accounts and current reports of meditation attainments using a single instrument, the Rorschach. The Rorschachs in the respective criterion groups were so obviously different as to merit this preliminary report, even without completion of the quantitative data analysis. These Rorschachs illustrate that the classical subjective reports of meditation stages are more than religious belief systems; they are valid accounts of the perceptual and affective changes that

occur with intensive meditation toward the goal of understanding perception and alleviating suffering.

As it happens, the Rorschach, in addition to being a personality test, is an excellent measure of perception for such an investigation. Ducey (1975) has argued that the Rorschach is a measure of "self-created reality." The task requires a subject to attribute meaning to a set of ambiguous stimuli. In so doing, the experimenter learns something of how the subject constructs an inner representation of the world. This task is congruent with the meditator's own practice, namely, to analyze the process by which his mind works in creating the internal and external world. Much to our surprise, the unusual performance on these Rorschachs for most subjects seemed to give a clear indication of the most important changes in mental functioning that occur during the major stages of the meditative path.

value of Rorschach

These findings must be interpreted with some caution due to the influence of expectation effects. An attempt was made to control for such effects in the data of the Three-Month Study alone. There a staff control group was used, based on the assumption that both meditators and staff expect their meditation to work. Differences between the meditators and staff controls could not be attributed to expectation alone, but more likely to differences in the amount of daily practice. Though such differences were confirmed, they were limited to the Three-Month Study; this includes all the Ss in the Beginner's Group, the Samadhi Group, and part of the subjects in the Insight Group. It does not include Ss in the more interesting Advanced Insight group and Masters' group. Thus, because of the limits of data collection the operation of expectation effects in these latter enlightened individuals cannot be totally ruled out, unlikely though it is, since these subsequent outcomes follow so clearly and consistently upon the outcomes which *are* demonstrated practice effects.

caution in interpretation

To the extent that these findings are valid, the prospect of quick advance along the path of meditation is not realistic. Note that after three months of continuous intensive daily practice, about half the Ss showed very little change, at

realistic expectations for meditation progress

least as defined in terms of formal meditation. The other half achieved some proficiency in concentration. Only three perfected access concentration and began to have insights similar to those described in the classical accounts of the insight series of meditations. Only one of these, in turn, advanced in the insight series to the stage of Equanimity, a stage short of enlightenment. This slow rate of progress, at least for Western students, is humbling, but it is also consistent with general patterns of growth. It should also inspire confidence. Such unusual and far-reaching transformations of perceptual and intrapsychic organization could not possibly be the work of three months or a year, nor could they be attained by short-cuts without an adequate foundation being laid first. Patience, forebearance and a long-enduring mind, or what one master has called "constancy" (Suzuki Roshi, 1970), is listed among the traditional *"paramitas"* or perfections required of practitioners. On the other hand, the self-reports as well as the test data from both the South Asian and the American study seem to validate the hypothesis that meditation *is something very much more than stress-reduction or psychotherapy,* and that its apparent goal-states are commensurate with the effort and perseverance they undoubtedly require.

differences between meditation and therapy Meditation, then, is not exactly a form of therapy but a soteriology, i.e., a means of liberation. It is said to be an extensive path of development that leads to a particular end: total liberation from the experience of ordinary human suffering and attainment of the genuine wisdom that comes from true perception of the nature of mind and its construction of reality. Western therapy utilizes ideational and affective processes as its vehicle of treatment toward the end of behavioral and affective change. This is *not* so of formal meditation. As seen in the Rorschachs, ideational and affective processes do not even occur to any significant extent in the initial development of samadhi, though they re-occur much later as objects of, not vehicles for, insight. Though meditation concerns itself with a thorough analysis of all mental operations—ideational, affective and perceptual—it is primarily an analysis of perception and reality construction and how ignorance of perceptual processes contributes to human suffering. Trait transformations are indeed very difficult to achieve. Meditation may provide enduring and radical trait benefits only to a very few who attempt to practice. Yet, for those of us who have had occasion to come in contact with and study the few masters, like the one whose Rorschach is given here, they are indeed unusual and deeply compassionate individuals who stand as rare living examples of an ideal: civilization beyond discontent.

CHAPTER 8

THE STAGES OF MEDITATION IN CROSS-CULTURAL PERSPECTIVE

Daniel P. Brown

Controversy over "the stages of meditation" has usually centered on two questions: 1) whether these stages may be said to exist in any objective fashion (i.e., possess external validity); and 2), if these stages do possess external validity, to what extent are they cross-cultural or quasi-universal?

In the previous two chapters, Brown and Engler presented substantial evidence that the stages of meditation are in fact "real"— that is, they seem to represent demonstrable cognitive, perceptual, and affective changes that follow a developmental-stage model.

In this chapter, Daniel Brown addresses the second question by presenting an in-depth cartography of meditative stages drawn from three different traditions—the Tibetan Mahāmudrā, the Hindu Yogasūtras, and the Theravāda Vipassana (this cartography was subsequently cross-checked with other contemplative texts, Christian, Chinese, etc.). The results strongly suggest that the stages of meditation are in fact of cross-cultural and universal applicability (at a deep, not surface, analysis).

Not only does this cartography tend to support the more literary claims of a "transcendent unity of religions," it goes a long way towards helping to resolve some of the central conflicts between "theistic" and "nontheistic" approaches to contemplation (e.g., Hindu versus Buddhist). By cutting his analysis at a sufficiently deep level, Brown is able to demonstrate "how a Hindu and Buddhist meditator progress through the same eighteen stages of med-

itation and yet have different experiences along the stages because of the different perspectives which are taken. Since perspectivism is unavoidable in meditation, as in any other mode of inquiry, each of the descriptions of meditation experience in the respective traditions is valid, though different." The perspective, however, has an influence on the outcome of the progression of experiences: while the path of meditation stages is similar across cultures, the experience of the outcome, enlightenment, is not. In this sense, Brown's conclusion is the opposite of stereotypical notions of mystical experience that perennial philosophers have usually meant by the "transcendent unity of religions": there are many paths to the same end. Brown's in-depth analysis of meditation experiences suggests the opposite: there is one path which leads to different ends, different enlightenment experiences.

INTRODUCTION

the problem in the study of comparative mysticism

An age-old problem in the study of comparative mysticism concerns the apparent similarities and differences between contemplative traditions across vastly different cultures and periods of history. Some scholars have assumed contemplative traditions to be vastly different, that each culture creates a unique apprehension of an ultimate reality (von Hugel, 1908; Tucci, 1958). Others have assumed that all contemplative traditions describe an identical mystical experience or a common goal (Otto, 1969; Huxley, 1944; Stace, 1960). Some have tried to describe a single path to this goal (Underhill, 1955). Others believe there are numerous paths, all of which lead to the same end (Naranjo, 1972). Still others take an intermediate position and classify the mystic traditions into distinct types (Zaehner, 1957). Despite the enthusiasm, however, the debate is unfortunately far from being resolved, because most scholars of comparative mysticism, with the exception of the encyclopedic work of Eliade, lack first-hand knowledge with a variety of contemplative traditions. Most scholars are greatly familiar with one tradition, and superficially with others. As a consequence, comparisons are often reductionistic, as for example, the use of Christian mysticism as a standard by which to compare Eastern traditions (Otto, 1932). Historically, union with God and, currently, a single transpersonal dimension, unquestioningly have been taken as *the* goal of mysticism, even when such assumptions are blatantly contradictory to major non-theistic traditions like Buddhism.

This presentation is another attempt to resolve the question of such similarities and differences across contemplative traditions. It represents twelve years of study of three Eastern meditation traditions: Hindu yoga, Theravāda Buddhism, and Mahāyāna Buddhism. Every effort was made to study these traditions from the perspective of how the cultures understand themselves. This necessitated learning the canonical languages, translating classical meditation texts, interviewing contemporary practitioners and their teachers, and above all, practicing the meditations according to the traditions. In Buddhism, balance between scholarship and practice is considered necessary to avoid the extremes of intellectualism and directionless practice of meditation.[1]

twelve-year study of three traditions

As a Western psychologist learning to translate Eastern meditation texts, I first discovered that Western assumptions about the alleged ineffability of mystical experience were incorrect. These traditions, especially Tibetan Buddhism, are lineage traditions. Tibetan monastic society was organized in such a way that large numbers of monks spent most of their lives practicing, discussing practice, or studying. This approach is in sharp contrast to Western mystics, who often practiced in isolation from the spiritual community. The Tibetans had an available body of teachings with which a meditator could compare his or her experience. There were ongoing forums of debate in which to discuss meditation experience. In such traditions, where meditation practice is socially organized, a technical language for meditation experience evolved. This language was refined over generations. The technical terms do not have external referents, e.g. "house," but refer to replicable internal states which can be identified by anyone doing the same practice, e.g., "energy currents," or "seed meditations." Much like the specialized languages of math, chemistry or physics, technical meditation language is usually intelligible only to those specialized au-

first discovery

diences of yogis familiar with the experience in question. In order to understand these technical languages, specialized tools are needed, such as those drawn from philology, hermeneutics, and semiotic anthropology.

second discovery and the two types of paths The second discovery was that most meditation traditions depict a systematic progression of spiritual development, i.e., a "path." There are two types of paths—the gradual path and the quick path. The "gradual" path depicts meditation experience as unfolding in a clearly definable sequence of stages which culminate in enlightenment. The "sudden" path does not identify clear stages; enlightenment comes suddenly after becoming skilled in the practice. This presentation will be limited to a comparison of various gradual paths of meditation.

texts used This chapter is a comparison of the path of meditation in three traditions, all of which describe a stage-model for meditation-development. For purposes of illustration I have chosen to illustrate the stages using one authoritative text (and their main commentaries) for each of the three traditions. By authoritative, I mean those texts which the indigenous practitioners most often cite as representative of their tradition. These are: the Hindu yoga text, Patañjali's *Yogasūtras (Aphorisms on Yoga)* translated from the Sanskrit; the Theravāda Buddhist text, Buddhaghosa's *Visuddhimagga (Path of Purification)*, translated from the Pāli; and the Mahāyāna Buddhist text, Bkra' shis rnam rgyal's main commentary on the *Mahāmudrā, Nges don . . . zla zer (Moon-Light on the Certain Truth of Mahāmudrā)*, translated from the Tibetan. The reader who wishes to see English translations of this material can refer to respective translations by Mishra (1963), Nyanamoli (1976), and Brown (1981).

method of investigating texts The method of investigating the texts of each tradition began with identification of the main stages of meditation along the path as well as the technical terms used to express the experiences at each stage. In order to increase the reliability of the method, authoritative commentaries and related texts were also used. This helped to eliminate idiosyncratic word usage in favor of a consensual body of technical terms, and also to fill in knowledge of experiences too briefly or obscurely described at points in the texts, such as in the *Yogasūtras*, wherein an entire stage of practice may be described in a single aphorism. The result was a detailed technical description of the experiences of each stage of meditation and of the entire sequence of stages for each tradition. A detailed account of this approach is cited elsewhere (Brown, 1981).

Next, the *Yogasūtras*, *Visuddhimagga*, and *Mahāmudrā* were compared synoptically, stage by stage, to test whether there was an underlying sequence. Each tradition divided the stages of practice differently. Textual outlines of the stages proved an unreliable way to test for a common structure. However, a careful analysis of the technical language used in each text proved more useful. Using this approach it was possible to discover a clear underlying structure to meditation stages, a structure highly consistent across the traditions. The sequence of stages is assumed to be universal, despite the vastly different ways they are conceptualized and described across traditions. This sequence is believed to represent natural human development available to anyone who practices. The sequence is assumed to be invariant, i.e., the order of stages is immutable in actual experience. Furthermore, it was also possible to specify the nature of the final outcome, enlightenment, according to the ways it is similar and different across traditions.

discovering a structure highly consistent across traditions

The traditions agree there are three main divisions to the practice: preliminary exercises, concentration meditations, and insight meditations. According to the synoptic analysis used in this research, a total of six major stages of the practice were discovered: two preliminary, two concentrative, and two insight stages. These are: I. Preliminary Ethical Training; II. Preliminary Mind/Body Training; III. Concentration with Support; IV. Concentration without Support; V. Ordinary Insight Meditation; VI. Extraordinary Mind and Enlightenment. Each of these six stages can be subdivided further into three substages. There are three substages to the Preliminary Ethical Training, three to the Preliminary Mind/Body Training, etc. While each tradition may have its own way to organize the stages, the synoptic method disclosed a common underlying structure of eighteen distinct stages (6 × 3) which unfold in an

the three main divisions and six major stages

invariant sequence. The results are given in Table 5, stages I–IV.

state-bound nature of knowledge and experience

With this stage model comes the recognition that knowledge and experience in meditation are state-bound (Fischer, 1971). This means that the structure of cognition in each state, as well as in the sequence of states, is specific only to that state and discontinuous with that of other states. In this respect the approach has some affinity with Bourguignon's (1965) cross-cultural studies of glossolalia. Bourguignon was able to account for an underlying common structure to glossolalia based on the specificity of a similar hyperaroused trance experienced by many different cultures of tongue speakers. Although the differences related to cultural factors, the similarities related to the structure of the shared state of consciousness. Likewise, cross-cultural similarities in the path of meditation are due to the structure of the meditative states of consciousness, only here we are dealing with not just one state but a progression of related meditative states. Hence, the basic path with its eighteen stages is offered as something more than another conceptual model. It may represent something inherent in the structure of human experience.

biasing factor of preliminary philosophical training

While the order of the stages is fixed, the actual experience of each stage varies significantly across the three traditions. This is because each tradition introduces a biasing factor through preliminary philosophical training. Philosophical training fosters a distinct perspective in each of the respective traditions. This perspective, in turn, influences the approach to meditation, but more importantly, affects the nature of the meditation experience itself. This chapter will demonstrate how a Hindu or Buddhist, or a Theravāda or Mahāyāna Buddhist, meditator can progress through the same eighteen stages of meditation and yet have different experiences along the stages because of the different perspectives which were taken. These perspectives are more than conceptual biases because they represent something intrinsic to the acquisition of human knowledge. Since perspectivism is therefore unavoidable in meditation, as in any other mode of inquiry, except perhaps in the initial moment of enlightenment, each of the descriptions of meditation experience in the respective traditions is valid, though different.

The two most divergent perspectives are the Hindu yogic tradition on the one hand and the two Buddhist traditions on the other. The dualistic Saṃkhya philosophy with its materialist assumptions affects Hindu meditation in one way, as do the Buddhist doctrines of selflessness and dependent origination in another. The Hindus and Buddhists are well aware of the differences in experience, each believing the other's to be invalid. For example, a commentary to the *Yogasūtras* (1:32) explicitly makes reference to the Buddhist experience in order to refute it.[2] The debates are often heated in the various commentarial traditions. Without going into the complexities of the philosophical systems, suffice it to say that the different experiences can best be described by the terms *ekatattva* and *kṣanika*. *Ekatattva* characterizes the Hindu position and literally means "same stuff." *Kṣanika* characterizes the Buddhist tradition and means "momentariness." These terms refer to the way the mind's content is experienced at the various stages of meditation. For the Hindu, the vicissitudes of mental events are all manifestations of the "same stuff." For the Buddhists, each discretely observable event in the unfolding succession of mental events is "momentary." Whereas both traditions agree that mental events undergo incessant change, the nature of the change can be experienced differently: mental events unfold in a continuous manner for the Hindu yogi and in a discontinuous manner for the Buddhist meditator.

two divergent perspectives

"same stuff" and "momentariness"

This same debate is not unfamiliar to Western scientists. The paradox of continuity/discontinuity pervades the physical and social sciences—for example, field theory versus quantum theory in physics, continuous versus discontinuous models of psychiatric diagnosis in the social sciences (Strauss, 1973). Perhaps the best illustration of the continuity-discontinuity paradox comes from research on the nature of light. Presumably light is a unitary phenomenon, yet it has been described as a wave (continuous) and as a particle-like photon (discontinuous). Experiments can be constructed to support either position. This unitary

Western science and the paradox of continuity/ discontinuity

"wavelicle" appears more wave-like or particle-like depending on the point of observation.

meditation traditions and the paradox of continuity/ discontinuity

Meditators are not exempt from the relationship between point of observation and observable events. Whatever the point of observation, it affects the actual experience of meditation. Each meditation tradition offers a different theory of self, which influences the point of observation taken during meditation. As this chapter will show, the reflective point of observation in Hindu yoga biases the observable events so that they unfold as a continuous transformation of mindstuff, while the concomitant perspective in Buddhism biases the observable events so they unfold as a succession of discrete discontinuous events. Although the same eighteen stages can be identified in Hinduism and Buddhism, the vicissitudes of events unfolding in meditation can be experienced quite differently—as a continuous transformation or a discontinuous succession—in the respective traditions. What may be passed off as cultural differences in linguistic and conceptual expression of meditation experience may represent a paradox inherent in the very structure of meditative knowledge. Most of the truly important differences in actual experience are understandable in terms of the paradox of continuity/discontinuity. The remainder of the chapter will examine each of the stages and the paradox of continuity/discontinuity in some detail.

THE STAGES OF MEDITATION

Stage I. Preliminary Ethical Practices

A. The Ordinary Preliminaries: Attitude Change

ethical practices

The preliminary ethical practices affect a complete psychobehavioral transformation in order to prepare the beginner for formal meditation at some later point. The ethical practices are carried out while the beginner continues everyday life. Because most beginners doubt their own ability to reach enlightenment, the practice begins, at least in the *Mahāmudrā*, with an exercise to "awaken faith" (M, *dad pa'i 'don pa*).[3] Behavioral therapists, e.g., Bandura (1977), would similarly recognize the value in fostering a sense of "self-efficacy," i.e., a conviction that, at the onset of any anticipated behavioral change, one can successfully produce an outcome, in this case, enlightenment. In addition, the beginner must learn to change attitudes toward daily life in order to let go of mundane attachments and become increasingly motivated to practice. Such change can be affected with a set of "ordinary preliminaries" (M, *thun mong yin pa*), called the "Four Notions" (M, *blo bzhi*) in the *Mahāmudrā*. The beginner first reflects on the rare and precious opportunity to be in a situation favorable to practice, followed by a detailed visualization of one's daily behavior and its consequences, as well as a visualization on the sufferings experienced by the various beings in the world. *producing a* Taken as a unit, these exercises produce a hypermotivated *hypermotivated* state, which enables the beginner to slowly lose interest in *state* everyday activities while becoming strongly motivated to take up dharma practice. Such a hypermotivated state is analogous to what social psychologists have called "reactance" (Brehm, 1972), which occurs when an individual's freedom is threatened. The reflections on opportunity and death result in a strong positive reevaluation of spiritual affairs, relative to everyday affairs, and an intense desire to practice.

B. The Extraordinary Preliminaries: Intrapsychic Change
Having cultivated such motivation, the beginner is in a position to renounce everyday affairs and "go inside" (M, *"going inside"* *'jug sgo;* YS, *svādhyāya* 2:32).[4] Awareness is now turned to the stream of consciousness, while clearly keeping in mind the goal of the practice. The *Mahāmudrā* recommends formal repeated reflections on the goal through development of an "enlightened attitude" (M, *byang chub sems pa*). In the *Yogasūtras* the beginner is instructed to "establish a connection" to the "transcendent awareness," *puruṣa* (YS, *samprayogaḥ,* 2:44). Internal reflection on the goal is supplemented in external behavior by rigorous formal study of the philosophical foundations of the practice. In this manner the beginner slowly but thoroughly alters expectations *formal study of* and beliefs about the practice. Social psychologists have *philosophical* shown that alterations in one's outcome expectations and *foundations* belief system have a significant impact on all types of behavioral change. Frank (1961), for example, might interpret the internal reflections and the formal study as a

manipulation of one's "assumptive system" and "expectations of psychological health," so that the meditator comes more and more to believe that the practice will produce positive irreversible changes in experience through enlightenment. Smith (1976) furthermore has demonstrated the significant impact outcome expectations have on the emotional and behavioral changes experienced through meditation.

transforming the stream of consciousness and cultivating inner harmony

In order to prepare for formal meditation the beginner must effect a radical transformation of the stream of consciousness and bring harmony to the inner life. This is done in a set of exercises called the "extraordinary preliminaries" (M, *thun mong ma yin pa*) in the *Mahāmudrā* and the "observances" (YS, *niyamas*) in the *Yogasūtras* (2:40–45). The stream of consciousness is composed of various "mental factors" (M, *sems 'byung;* literally, "what occurs in the mind"). Painful affective states and their associated thoughts, images, and memories occur most frequently, all of which, as the *Yogasūtras* say, "contribute to doubt" (YS, *vitarkā,* 1:32). The beginner learns to observe and react to the events in the stream in order to alter its content. Through "confession" (M, *gshogs pa*) or "cleansing" (YS, *shaucha,* 2:40–41) the beginner identifies and then eradicates painful states. Through concurrent "offerings" (M, *mchod pa*) and the cultivation of "contentment" (YS, *saṃtoṣa* 2:42) the beginner actively cultivates pleasant states, for example, patience. Through the representation of some symbol for ultimate reality—either visually as in the *Mahāmudrā*'s "guru yoga," or subvocally, as in chanting "OM" in the *Yogasūtras'* "identification with Ishvara" (YS, *ishvarapranidhanani,* 2:45), the beginner learns to reformulate concepts regarding ultimate reality in such a way that the spontaneous "notions" (M, *blo*) which come forth in the stream of consciousness are more in harmony with the philosophical beliefs and ultimate goal of the practice.

Taken as a unit these exercises produce profound intrapsychic change. They are reminiscent of what is called "objective self-awareness theory" in social psychology (Duval & Wicklund, 1973). The Eastern practice of the observances, and the Western practice of self-focus—and for that matter, psychoanalysis—are all based on awareness of the events in the stream of consciousness. All are designed to produce intrapsychic changes in the stream of feelings and thoughts about oneself. Laboratory subjects have been studied under conditions which manipulate self-focus and require them to inwardly focus attention. The first reaction is more acute awareness of negative affect (Scheir, 1976; Scheir & Carver, 1977). Beyond these initial negative reactions, Ickes, Wicklund, & Ferris (1973) found that certain conditions can increase positive affect during self-focus. Geller & Shaver (1976) also found that self-focus can alter cognitions about oneself. Meditative self-focus on the events in the stream of consciousness can be done in such a way as to eradicate painful affective states, cultivate pleasant states, and make one's spontaneous associations more congruent with the ultimate goal.

C. The Advanced Preliminaries: Behavioral Change
The observances are supplemented by a set of behavioral practices called the "advanced preliminaries" (M, *khyad pa*), "precepts" (VM, *śīla*), and "restraints" (YS, *yamas*), respectively. These include modifications in: a) life-style and social behavior, b) sensory input, and c) degree of awareness. The beginner learns to identify harmful behavior and then "practice the opposite" behavior (M, *stobs bzhi*; YS, *prati pakṣabhāvanam*, 2:33). According to the laws of cause and effect such opponent action will manifest as positive changes in the stream of consciousness over time; behavior change contributes to intrapsychic change. *behavioral practices*

Life style and social behavior are regulated through lists of primary and secondary precepts designed to enumerate the elements of everyday living in order to bring every aspect of one's behavior under close scrutiny: daily routines and habits, work and leisure, eating and sleeping. One's ordinary activities, and also excessive sensory input, cause turmoil in the stream of consciousness. The beginner also learns to control the senses through an exercise called "binding the senses" (M, *dbang po' i sgo sdom pa*) in the *Mahāmudrā* and "heated discipline" (YS, *tapas*) in the *Yogasūtras*. The restraints are concluded with rigorous awareness-training, cultivated both during formal sitting (M, *dran pa*; VM, *sati*) and throughout one's daily activities (M, *shes bzhin*: VM, *samprajañña*). The goal is to achieve a state of uninterrupted awareness throughout the day and night.

Behavior therapists have long emphasized the importance of altering behavior, though only more recent cognitive behavioral theory has emphasized any connection between external behavior and internal processes (Bandura, 1977). Exponents of behavioral medicine and biofeedback have stressed the connection between attention/awareness and internal processes (Green *et al.*, 1970). The meditation traditions illustrate the interraction between all three—inner reality, external behavior, and attention/awareness. Eastern (Asian) behavioral theory, notably Morita therapy (Reynolds, 1976), is close to the meditation traditions in its assumption that regulation of outer behavior through simple work can greatly affect the inner life. Some Western activities therapies have likewise appreciated the value of activity for inner development (Erikson, 1976). Since the goal of meditation is to alter the stream of consciousness, it is a counterbalancing necessity to bring outer life into greater order. Once the events in the stream are more regular, it is easier to do the awareness-training, which is so vital to formal meditation.

interaction among inner reality, external behavior and attention/ awareness

Some Western researchers have begun to investigate internal processes in naive meditators. For example, beginning meditators increase absorption (Davidson, Goleman & Schwartz, 1976) and decrease in distraction (Van Nuys, 1973). While such research applies to formal meditation, Csikzentmihalyi's (1975) concept of "flow" applies to awareness during everyday activity. Flow pertains to the merging of action and awareness without distraction from the task at hand. In optimal flow the content of the stream is attuned and changes to the demands of reality without irrelevancies. Once outer behavior and inner life come into harmony the beginner is more prepared for formal meditation when awareness is added.

Stage II. Preliminary Body and Mind Training

body awareness and stream of consciousness

A. *Body Awareness Training*

Whereas the advanced preliminaries are designed to eliminate distractions to initial awareness-training, the preliminary body/mind training carries awareness-training more extensively into the internal arena, to the "stream of consciousness" (M, *rgyun;* VM, *bhavanga*). Now the meditator must learn to clearly identify "distracting activity" (M, *byas ba;* YS, *vṛtti*) in the stream and also to prevent lapses in awareness. Because the task entails careful discrimination of various types of distraction, the exercise is called the "three isolations" (M, *dben gsum*) in the *Mahāmudrā*. The meditator isolates out and specifies the nature of activity in the stream so as to make order out of chaos.

The meditator begins by training awareness of bodily processes. S/he retreats to a secluded place, curtails physical movement, and adopts a stable posture. The *Yogasūtras* recommend many postures (YS, *āsanas,* 2:46-48); *Mahāmudrā* uses a single posture, the lotus posture, but suggests being mindful of seven "points" (M, *lus gnas*) of this posture (legs, spine, chest, neck, hands, tongue and eyes). Both the *Yogasūtras* and *Mahāmudrā* supply an ideal model for the posture—the deity Ishvara, and the cosmic Buddha, Vairocana, respectively. Once perfecting the posture, the meditator carefully observes the state of the body to note any imperfections in the posture, and any restless activity. S/he quickly discovers that the body emits constant random internal activity. Constant output of controlled activity, "holding fast" (M, *sgrim ba*) the perfect posture with "effort" (M, *'bad pa*), counteracts this ordinary random activity. As a result, the gross activity of the body undergoes a shift, which the *Mahāmudrā* describes as "settlement" (M, *rang babs,* literally "falling into itself"), and the *Yogasūtras* as "steadiness" (YS, *sthira* 2:46), through which it becomes easy to maintain a stable posture for long periods without fatigue. Settlement or steadiness does not imply a cessation of bodily activity, but more accurately, a redistribution of muscle activity so that the body is restored to its "proper action" (M, *las rung*). Extensive research on meditation postures (Ikegami, 1970) has validated the claim of the meditation texts: a meditation posture is not technically relaxing, in the sense of a global reduction of random muscle activity, but stabilizing, in the sense of increased regularity in the distribution of muscle output. In addition, awareness opens up to subtle levels of bodily activity experienced as the flow of energy cur-

adopting a stable posture

redistribution of muscle activity

rents in the body. With greater experience the meditator learns to isolate discernible energy patterns which over time undergo a significant "rearrangement" (M, *sgrigs pa*) in the direction of greater regularity. Since the currents are said to correlate with mental activity, postural training also contributes to a more balanced state of mind, called "firmness" (M, *bstan pa*) in the *Mahāmudrā* and "balance" *(samapatti* 2:47) in the *Yogasūtras*.

B. Calming Breathing and Thinking

As the body settles, the random activity of the breath and the events in the stream of consciousness come more into awareness. Such disordering of the stream takes the form

calm breathing and reduced thinking

of "delusion" (YS, *indrajāla,* 2:52) of one's thinking and the incessant activity of the internal dialogue and/or daydreaming (M, *ngag*). Both irregularities in breathing and the internal dialogue are included in the Tibetan term, "speech" (M, *ngag*), hence, the exercise is called the "isolation of speech" (M, *ngag dben*) in the *Mahāmudrā* and "breath-control" (YS, *prāṇāyāma*) in the *Yogasūtras*. Starting with either the breath or the internal dialogue, the goal of the meditation is to isolate the different aspects of the breathing cycle and/or the internal dialogue so as to curtail their random activity, or as the *Yogasūtras* say, "to cut off movement" (YS, *gativicchedaḥ* 2:49). The *Mahāmudrā* starts with the internal dialogue, the *Yogasūtras* with the breath. In the former the meditator is instructed to "let go" (M, *lhod pa*) of any exertion after experiencing settlement of the body and simply notice the resultant activity of the stream until "settlement" (M, *rang babs*) of the internal dialogue occurs. Mental chatter and daydreaming then recede into the background. In the latter, the meditator actively interferes with the ordinary rhythm of the breath by manipulating its direction, duration and sequence, which produces a distinct "change" (YS, *vṛtti*) in the breathing cycle as well as in the stream (YS, 2:50).

Both approaches result in an increased regularity of the breathing cycle, a finding also validated through empirical studies of meditators (Kasamutsu & Harai, 1966; Wallace, 1970). Both also result in a reduction in ordinary thinking, called "not cognizing" (M, *mi rtog*) in the *Mahāmudrā* and "destroying the [cognitions] covering the light [of awareness]" in the *Yogasūtras* (YS, *kseeyate prakāsha/āvaranam,* 2:52). This claim of reduced thinking has been given some empirical support through a Rorschach study of intensive meditators in which a significant decrease in productivity and associative thinking was reported (see Chapters 6 and 7). The resultant increased orderliness of the stream is the first equivalent to "contemplation" (M, *bsam gtam,* literally, "steadying of reflections").

C. Rearrangement of the Stream of Consciousness;
Desconstructing Thinking
Now the meditator has created an internal milieu condu-
cive to meditation, and is in a position to bring "aware-
ness" (M, *rig pa;* YS, *sattva)* into careful scrutiny of this   *"disengaging"*
milieu. Ordinary conscious awareness, however, is fo-   *from external*
cused outwardly. This first task is to develop a "style" (M,   *reality*
lugs) of awareness called "inwardness" (M, *nang du)* in the
Mahāmudrā and "taking back into oneself" (YS, *pratyahāra,*
2:54) in the *Yogasūtras.* The meditator learns to "disengage"
(YS, *asamprayoge* 2:54) from external reality and the impact
of sense objects so as to bring awareness carefully to bear
on the stream of consciousness. Thus, the exercise is called
"sense-withdrawal" (YS, *pratyahāra)* in the *Yogasūtras.* The
meditator also learns to "isolate" its features and to see
how its events unfold. Thus the exercise is called "isolation of the mind" (M, *dben sems)* in the *Mahāmudrā.*

As a result, the meditator becomes less sensitized to external events and more to internal events. An empirical study
consistent with this claim is the report of an increased autokinetic effect during meditation (Pelletier, 1974). An increased autokinetic effect has been interpreted as increased distance from external reality (Mayman & Voth,
1969). A related result is that the remaining content of the
stream of consciousness becomes apparent—at this point,
specific memories, anticipation of future events, and cate-
gorization of current perceptual events.

The most important result, gained through extensive practice, is that awareness extends beyond content to the very   *going from*
process of how events unfold in the stream. The content   *"content" to*
of thinking drops away. Such penetrating awareness also   *"process"*
causes "rearrangement" (M, *sgrigs pa)* in the stream in the

direction of greater orderliness. It is here, however, that the two traditions diverge. The Buddhist meditator learns to discern discontinuity of the stream, the Hindu yogi, continuity. Both traditions agree, however, that the essential task of the exercise is to discern the structure of the stream of consciousness, not its content. The technical term for the Buddhist discontinuous experience is "spreading" (M, *spros ba*), i.e., a succession of one discrete event after another with a hiatus between events. The technical term for the Hindu continuous experience is "continuous change of mindstuff" (YS, *chittavṛtti*, 1:1). Ordinarily mindstuff continually modifies itself to take the shape of ever-changing sense data. Through the exercise the yogi learns "identification of mindstuff in its own form [and not in the form of sense data]" (YS, 2:54). In both traditions, however, the meditator is able to detect increasing regularity in the internal milieu, which is no longer immediately affected by changing external events.

Stage III. Concentration with Support

A.1. Concentration in Front

concentration on "external object"
The meditator begins "concentration in front" (M, *mngon du*; YS, *dhārāna*, 3:1) by selecting a place for sitting, constructing a comfortable seat and adopting a stable posture. Since the goal of concentration is to fix attention on something for sustained periods of time, any "object-of-awareness" (M, *dmigs pa*; VM, *nimitta*; YS, *alambana*) can be used so long as it is tangible and has clearly defined attributes so as to "support" (M, *rten*) concentration. The *Mahāmudrā* uses primarily visual objects, e.g., stones or pieces of wood, the *Yogasūtras*, mantras, and the *Visuddhimagga*, a variety of objects (VM, *kasiṇa*) selected according to one's temperament. The object is then set up at some optimal distance "in front" (M, *mngon du*; VM, *parikamma*; YS, *tratākam*): the distance of a yoke in the *Mahāmudrā*, or two and one half arm lengths in the *Visuddhimagga*. The traditions agree on several basic elements to the concentration practice. Controlling the gaze by looking straight ahead, as in the *Mahāmudrā*, or by half closing the eyes, as in the *Visuddhimagga*, reduces sensory input and thereby

reduces manifestations in the stream of consciousness. Firmly fixing the gaze on the perceptual "attributes" (M, *mtshan ma*), e.g., color and form, is very important (M, *sems gzung*, literally "attaching the mind"; YS, *dhāraṇa*, "holding fast"). "Effort to hold [concentration]" (M, *sgrim ba*; YS, *dhāraṇa*) is likewise important.

One result, from the perspective of the point of observation, is an ability to sustain awareness longer and longer without lapses. The *Mahāmudrā* says, "awareness partially stays [on its object]" (M, *gnas cha*). The other result, from the perspective of the observable events, is a change in the experience of the object-of-awareness. The meditator experiences only the "mere attributes" (M, *mtshan ma tsam*) of the object. "Categorizing" (M, *rtsis gdab*) and "discriminatory thinking" (M, *rtog pa*) about the object cease.

experiencing "mere attributes"

For example, if the object were a stick, only its color and form would remain without having a particular meaning as a stick. In terms of Western cognitive psychology, concentration disrupts ordinary information-processing. Microsaccadic eye movements, which are important in perceptual scanning, are suppressed by fixing the gaze (Fischer, 1971). Moreover, the categorizing function of ordinary information-processing is disrupted. According to Bruner (1973) perception is a constructive act by which perceptual information is sorted into various categories on the basis of minimally defined physical features. Through categorizing, more or less veridical models of the world are constructed which "go beyond the information given." Symbolic categories allow for rapid encoding of information even where there are minimal stimulus cues, but do so at the expense of accuracy. The world is ordinarily "seen" filtered through a vast network of abstract categories about it. Through sustained concentration, however, the meditator disrupts categorizing and returns to the actual physical features of perceptual objects, or as the texts say, to the "mere attributes."

A.2. Concentration Inside
Concentration in front is a preparatory step to the main exercise, "concentration inside" (M, *nang du*). The goal is

concentration on "internal object" to train awareness to "stay" in the face of the potential distractions of the stream of consciousness while using an internal object-of-awareness. The meditator now switches to an internal representation of the former external object. The Buddhist traditions use visual representations (M, *gzugs brnyan*, "reflected image"; VM, *uggahanimitta*, "eidetic image"); the *Yogasūtras* use a representation of the subtle energy currents in the body (YS, *dhāraṇacakra*, 3:1). Inward concentration is practiced until there is "no difference between the object-of-awareness with the eyes either open or closed" (VM, 4:30). Then, as concentration can be sustained on these internal objects, the meditator switches to even more detailed objects: the standard image of the Body of the Tathāgāta (Buddha) with its thirty-two major and eighty minor perceptual features in the *Mahāmudrā*, and likewise the image of the deity, Hari, in the *Yogasūtras* (3:1).

achieving uninterrupted concentration or "staying mind" One result, from the perspective of the point of observation, is that the meditator achieves a condition of uninterrupted concentration called the "staying mind" (M, *sems gnas*) in the *Mahāmudrā*. The other result, from the perspective of the observable events, is that the stream of consciousness undergoes a transformation. First, the internal object more and more dominates the stream so that in good sessions it may be the only event coming forth time after time in the stream. Second, the object becomes increasingly unstable. The object changes size, shape, location and luminosity. It may become, for example, as large as the ocean or as small as a mustard seed. What once seemed to be a fixed internal representation is now experienced as an image in constant change. Third, the stream "rearranges itself" (M, *rten 'brel byed pa*) so as to more and more approximate the object-of-awareness. If the image is the Buddha or Hari with their standard features, the stream of consciousness begins to approximate those features and qualities in its unfolding. In terms of cognitive *destabilizing object constancy* psychology, the meditator is destabilizing object constancy. Although there have been no empirical studies of changes in object constancy during intensive concentrative meditation, loss of object constancy has been reported during sensory deprivation (Zubek, 1969) and during conditions of sustained concentration (Hochberg, 1970).

B. Skill in Recognizing the Seed: Pattern Recognition

As concentration develops, a profound shift occurs in the object-of-awareness. It emerges in a new form called the "seed" (M, *thig le;* VM, *paṭibhāga;* YS, *bindu).* Initial encounters with the seed are striking. The field of concentration becomes reduced to a compact little seed floating in space (VM, 4:31). The seed also seems to emit its own light. The seed contains combined information from all the sense systems—all forms, sounds, fragrances, etc. Whereas information from each sense system was segregated in the previous meditations, this is not the case in the seed meditations. Sensory information is summated. The seed contains the same information from multiple sense modalities regardless of whether the original object were a visual object or a mantra. The seed also contains information about a myriad of subtle perceptual attributes (M, *mtshan ma 'phra mo)* which are not discernible in ordinary perception. It contains information about a great quantity of "particular" (M, *bye brag)* and "various" (M, *sna tshogs)* attributes. The seed undergoes constant transformation.

constant transformation of object of awareness

The exact nature of the transformation differs in the Buddhist and Hindu systems. Although both systems agree that the seed is forever changing in awareness, the change is experienced as discontinuous in Buddhism and as continuous in Hinduism. The *Mahāmudrā* describes the seed (M, *thig le)* as "emanating" (M, *'char ba' i thig le)* various and discrete perceptual events. Specific images, colored lights, vibratory patterns, fragrances, sensations, etc. pulse forth from the seed in succession. There are gaps between the emanating events. The *Yogasūtras* describe the seed (YS, *bindu)* as a "continuous transformation" (YS, *vṛtti)* of the "same continuum" (YS, *ekatānatā,* 3:2). Specific images, lights, vibratory patterns, etc., fold in and out of each other, as in the drawings of Escher, without discernible boundaries between successive events.

constant transformation in Buddhist and Hindu systems

The seed meditation requires a modification in the nature of concentration. Since effort interferes with the unfolding events from the seed, the meditator is instructed to switch to a "relaxed" (M, *glod pa)* style of concentration. This takes "skill" (M, *rtsal),* as the exercise is called in the *Ma-hāmudrā.* The switch to relaxation brings forth the unfolding events more clearly. They occur in "non-cessation" (M, *ma 'gag pa*). The meditator learns to carefully focus on the unfolding events in the stream as the seed emerges. Hence, the exercise is called "contemplation" (YS, *dhyāna*) in the *Yogasūtras* (3:2). The technical term for this quality of awareness is, "recognition" (M, *ngo shes ba*; literally, "know the stuff"; YS, *pratyaya; 3:2*). The meditator simply eases concentration and notices what the *Mahāmudrā* called "the force of the dancing emanations" (M, *sgyu ' phrul gar dbang phyug*).

As a result of such recognition a new condition of the seed establishes itself, called the "condensed seed" (M, *bsdu ba'i thig le*) in the *Mahāmudrā*. The meditator finds it increasingly difficult to recognize specific and various perceptual patterns. With increasing skill these patterns become a "mass of light" (M, *od kyi gong bu*). Similarly, the *paṭibhāga* (literally, "likeness sign") is described as a luminous disc *disappearance* like the moon or a star in the *Visuddhimagga*. It is a thou*of specific* sand times more purified than the "eidetic (*uggaha*) sign." *perceptual* The "developed seed" (VM, *saññapaṭibbhāga*) has neither *patterns and* specific colors nor shapes (VM, 4:31). In the *Yogasūtras*, *painful* likewise, emission of light along with the disappearance of *emotional states* specific patterns marks the onset of the next stage of practice, the "beginner's *samādhi*" (YS, 3:3), in which the seed appears like a precious gem (YS, 1:41). All traditions agree that specific patterns disappear. "Painful emotional states" (M, *nyon mong*; YS, *kleshas*) also disappear. The meditator no longer "particularizes" (M, *yid la byed pa*) such patterns. All that remains in awareness is a changing mass of light. Such recognition is called "great clarity" (M, *gsal bde ba*). Since the object no longer resembles the original subject it is called a "mere mode of appearance" or "likeness" in the *Visuddhimagga* (VM, 4:31).

The skill exercise describes what cognitive psychologists have called "pattern recognition," a process by which a definite pattern is constructed out of more limited information. According to constructivist theories of perception, pattern formation is a two-step process. First global perceptual synthesis is followed by specification of recognizable patterns (Hebb, 1949; Allport, 1967; Neisser, 1967).

The meditator observes these stages in reverse. In the emanating seed s/he becomes aware of a myriad of specific patterns.

C. *Stopping the Mind; Perceptual Synthesis*
It is very difficult to sustain awareness of the condensed seed. Specific patterns may easily reoccur or awareness of the seed may be entirely lost. In order to deepen concentration the seed must be "safeguarded," as the exercise is called in the *Visuddhimagga* (VM, 4:34). The meditator must "do away with" (M, *zad pa*) any remaining cognitive and perceptual content which might cause a loss of awareness of the seed. S/he must "stop the mind" (M, *sems med*) as the exercise is called in the *Mahāmudrā*. In the *Yogasūtras* it is called the "[beginner's] samādhi" wherein "the gross fluctuations of mindstuff dwindle away" (YS, *kseenavṛtti*, 1:41). One of the problems is that the object-of-awareness has become increasingly subtle. The problem of sustaining concentration has to do with the "activity" (M, *byas ba*) of the sense systems. The mind is incessantly active in registering ongoing sensory input. "The mind roams to sense objects" (M, *sems yul la phyan*). It "switches" (M, *'pho ba*) from one moment of sensory input to the next. Such activity initiates the entire sequence of processes by which the perceptual world is "constructed" (M, *bcos pa*). The meditator must learn to stop this subtle but constant activity by which sense impressions are registered and processed and deconstruct ordinary pattern perception. Therefore, the exercise is called "stopping the mind." *deepening concentration and "stopping the mind"*

The way to stop the mind is to develop simple awareness devoid of any activity. In the *Mahāmudrā*, the meditator puts her/his awareness on empty space while supressing the activity by which particular patterns are recognized. In the *Yogasūtras* the meditator develops awareness so that it "stays upon that" (YS, *tatstha*), "penetrates into that" (YS, *tananjanatā*) and "takes on identity with the object" (YS, *samāpattita*, 1:41) while "fluctuations are made to cease" (YS, *kseenavṛtti*, 1:41). If the meditator cannot develop activity-free awareness s/he can practice the "breath-holding exercise" (M, *bum ba can*; YS, *kumbhaka*). When the breath is held for longer and longer intervals, the activity of the *simple awareness as stopped mind*

mind momentarily stops. Having gotten some sense of what stopping the mind is like, the meditator proceeds to develop the exercise without the aid of the physiological manipulation.

One result from the perspective of the point of observation is that awareness becomes uninterrupted. There are no longer any lapses in awareness. Awareness "stays continuously" (M, *gnas ba' i rgyun*), or "stays upon that and penetrates into that" (YS, 1:41). Since gross mental content has ceased, nothing hinders awareness. The other result from the perspective of the observable events is that the meditator has "stopped the mind" (M, *sems med*). S/he has entered a deep concentrated state called samādhi. S/he is able to keep awareness upon the different sense doors and stop activity from building up gross mental content as it comes into awareness. Although the meditator may still notice movement at the sense doors, these do not get "constructed" (M, *bcos pa*) into gross perceptual and cognitive patterns. The meditator suppresses activity at the "[sense] doors which emanate" (M, *'char sgo*). According to the *Mahāmudrā*, "gross cognitions" (M, *rags rtog*)— thinking, percepts, emotions—cease while more "subtle" (M, *'phra rtog*) activity remains. According to the *Yogasū-tras*, the object-of-awareness loses its specific form. It is "devoid of its own form" (YS, *svarupashunyam*, 3:3). Awareness opens up to the substratum of ordinary perception, namely, an incessant flow of light in the stream of awareness. These exercises serve to deconstruct what cognitive psychologists have called "perceptual synthesis" (Hebb, 1949; Neisser, 1967), the most rudimentary stage of perceptual construction prior to pattern recognition. In so doing, the meditator learns to dismantle the gross perceptual world and stop the mind.

uninterrupted awareness as entrance to samādhi of concentration

IV. Concentration Without Support

A. Holding Fast to the Flow of Light
The next exercise concerns itself with how the yogi might develop and stabilize a new point of observation on a new dimension of observable events, namely, the substratum

object becomes more subtle

of ordinary perception experienced as a flow of light. The meditator can no longer conveniently take gross cognitions or perceptions as an object-of-awareness. The object has become increasingly "subtle" (M, '*phra rtog;* YS, *sūkṣmaviṣayā,* 1:44) and cannot support concentration in the same way as a gross object such as a thought or percept. Hence the exercises are called "Concentration without Support" in the *Mahāmudrā.* Holding awareness on this subtle flow of light requires considerable skill, hence it is called "The Ten Skills of Access" in the *Visuddhimagga.* The *Yogasūtras,* however, consider the flow of light a subtle yet tangible "support" (YS, *alambana*) for concentration and calls the exercises "seed samādhi' (*saṃprajñata*).

Stopping the mind for the duration of the meditation is no easy task because of the habitual tendency of normal gross cognitive and perceptual processes to reassert their operations. The *samādhi* must be purified of gross content. According to the *Mahāmudrā* the mind has a strong "force" (M, *mthu*) to "construct" (M, *bcos pa*) gross events. Such a habit can only be overcome by more intensive meditation, by effortfully "holding fast" (M, *sgrim ba*) so that the flow of light is "not cut off" (M, *rgyun mi chad*) by gross content. In the *Yogasūtras,* the *vitarkāsamādhi* is constantly interfered with by the "gross" (YS, *sthūla*) content of "memory" (YS, *smṛti*) which may be "recognized" (YS, *pratyaya*) over and against the "flow of light" (YS, *arthamatranirbhāsa*) "devoid of its own form" (YS, *svarupashunya iva* 1:43). This level of *samādhi* is called *nirvitarkāsamādhi.*

purifying the concentration samādhi *of gross content*

According to the *Mahāmudrā* the meditator is "subtly asleep" (M, *bying ba*) to this substratum of perception. Awareness of the subtle flow of light is simply not part of everyday consciousness; the ordinary individual does not normally see the outer world and internal events in the stream of consciousness as changing manifestations of light energy. Even upon becoming aware of this flow of light for the first time it is very dim. The key to tuning in the flow of light is the level of arousal. Since arousal level is related to effortful output, initial mastery requires immense effortful output to awaken the yogi to the light. The way to practice is to "hold fast" (M, *sgrim ba*) or "exert"

(VM, 4:51–56; 63) to keep awareness on the flow of light. Whenever thoughts or percepts occur, more exertion is needed.

In the *Mahāmudrā*, the result, in terms of the observable events, is that the flow of light becomes more clear. The frequency of the changing manifestations of light greatly increases; it becomes "faster and faster" (M, *'phral 'phral*). The intensity also gets "brighter" (M, *dwangs cha*). When the flow of light is totally clear the state is called "foreclarity" (M, *gsal ngar*) because awareness is held at the subtle level of light prior to the construction of gross mental content. Likewise the *Yogasūtras* says, "the shining forth of only light devoid of its own form" (YS, 1:43). The result, *collapse of the self* in terms of the point of observation, is the collapse of the ordinary self-representation. Ordinary awareness operates through a stable frame of reference or self-representation which serves as a central organizing principle for the interpretation of sense data. This "construction" is called the "I" (M, *nga*) in the *Mahāmudrā*, the "sense-mind" (YS, *manas*) in the *Yogasūtras*. By stopping gross mental content and holding fast to the subtle flow of light, the gross self-representation also drops away. Awareness becomes less identified with gross or subtle content of experience and more with the activity of experience. What remains is awareness of self-as-agent.

B. Letting Go So As to Observe the Flow of Light
The meditator next learns to "recognize (M, *ngo shes ba*; YS, *pratyaya*) the flow of light in a stable and clear manner. Stability implies that gross cognitive and perceptual constructions no longer occur to distract concentration. Clarity implies more careful discrimination of how the flow of *observing the* light manifests itself. It is at first difficult to recognize the *flow of light* flow of light with any degree of clarity due to the activity, or better, reactivity, associated with ordinary awareness. While having eradicated the ordinary self-representation from meditation, the meditator has not yet eradicated the ordinary sense of self-agency, called "acting" (M, *byas ba*) in the *Mahāmudrā* and "I-acting" (*ahaṃkāra*) in the *Yogasū-tras*. These terms refer to the awareness of various types of activity during *samādhi*, e.g., "directing attention" (M, *sems gtan*), "rejecting or developing" the subtle flow into gross

cognition (M, *dgasgrub*), and "exerting oneself" (M, *sgrim ba*). These very activities interfere with recognition and careful discrimination of the flow of light and disrupt the way the flow manifests itself.

The skillful yogi learns to practice by easing up on the amount of effort at just the right points in the *samādhi*. Thus, the exercise is called "letting go" (M, *lhod pa*) in the Buddhist systems. The yogi lets go of all activities that might interfere with scrutiny of the flow of light.

As a result, with respect to the point of observation, the ordinary sense of self-agency drops away. Events simply "occur by themselves" (M, *rang 'byung*) independent of any activity on the part of the meditator. As a result, with respect to the observable events, the flow of light becomes even more clear and manifests itself in a new way. It comes forth as a "succession" (M, *rgyun*, YS, *krama*) of constantly changing manifestations of light. These changing points of light come forth "slowly" (M, *cham me*) and "close to- gether" (M, *shig ge*). Any potential disruptions which might manifest as gross content become "self calm" (M, *rang zhi*). The yogi learns to focus continuously and rec- ognize the subtle flow and its vicissitudes. Because of this more "focused analysis" (M, *dpyad pa*; YS, *vicārā*), the ex- ercise is called *vicārāsamādhi* in the *Yogasūtras*.

C. Balancing the Flow of Light
The key to direct apprehension of truth rests with refining awareness of this flow of light and carefully developing one among various perspectives on it. Hence, the *Visud- dhimagga* names this exercise "access" (VM, *upacāra*). As the ordinary points of observation—self-representation and self-agency—drop away, a number of alternative points of observation become possible. Buddhism and Hindu yoga represent two very different perspectives. Each tradition refines its particular perspective so that cer- tain truths become directly accessible to the meditator. The flow of light will also appear differently from each possible perspective.

refining awareness of the flow of light

"Skillful development" of the flow of light, as the exercise is called in the *Visuddhimagga*, requires the meditator to establish just the right amount of effort while setting up the flow of light. Such effort is called "balanced" (M, *btang snyoms;* VM, *upekkā,* 4:64) as the exercise is named in *Mahāmudrā*. The meditator must also learn to give "weight" to a particular point of observation or observable event during *samādhi*.

While the meditator may be "generally aware" (M, *rtog pa;* YS, *vitarkā)* of both the point of observation and the observable event at the same time, s/he learns "specific focus" (M, *dpyad pa;* YS, *vicarā)* of either the observable event or point of observation during the *samādhi* and also to switch the weighting from one to the other. Such shifts happen very quickly prior to the time it takes to ordinarily pay attention.

"concomitant awareness" The Buddhist learns to develop a point of observation called "concomitant awareness" through which the flow of light appears discontinuous. The meditator skillfully develops the observable event, the flow of light, by scrutinizing the light until its vicissitudes become "discrete" (M, *val le),* as pulses or "movements" (M, *'gyu ba)* with gaps between them. These flashes come "close together" (M, *shig ge),* i.e., emitted in quick succession. Skillful development of the point of observation comes by switching specific focus to the awareness which "stays" (M, *gnas ba)* on each discrete event. By turning awareness back on itself, the awareness also becomes more and more discontinuous. Discontinuous experience of both the flow of light and its awareness is called "concomitance" (M, *lhan ne)* in the *Mahāmudrā* and "mentality/materiality" (VM, *nāmarūpa)* in the *Visuddhimagga.*

"reflecting awareness" The Hindu yogi learns to develop a point of observation called "reflecting awareness" through which the flow of light appears continuous. As the yogi refines the observable event, the flow of light, it begins to manifest itself more and more as a continuously vibrating energy field called *tanmātra* (literally, "coordinates of that previous gross content") which is in a state of continuous propagation. Awareness is able to particularize apparent points in the continuously transforming field. Skillful development of the point of observation comes by turning awareness

away from the apparent points in the vibrating energy field toward the eternal awareness" (YS, *puruṣa*) that transcends all states of matter. Hence, the exercise is called *nirvicarāsamādhi*, in that a specific focus of events is given up altogether in favor of the pervasive awareness of the universe. This new perspective of observation is called "reflecting awareness" (YS, *buddhi*) because it is capable of yoking the subtlest events of the mind to the eternal awareness pervading the universe. As the *Yogasūtras* say, "when there is experience in *nirvicarāsamādhi*, there is transcendence of the point of observation and settling down of the observable events" (1:47).

The meditation texts suggest a phenomenology for the earliest stages of information-processing. According to constructivist theories of perception in the West, pattern recognition occurs through discrimination of temporal fluctuations within input-stimuli (Neisser, 1967). One example of such a theory, notably, Pribram's "holonomic theory of perception," suggests that perception is constructed not in terms of the features of objects in the physical world, but through a translation of these features into temporal patterns (light and sound). Information is processed by discriminating differences in the interference patterns caused by fluctuations in the frequencies over time, and the interference effects become manifest as images of the world, much on the analogy with holography (Pribram, 1974). Pribram also points out that in holonomic perception the question of the point of observation becomes problematic, as is the case in the meditation texts.

Western theories of perception

Branch Paths: The Absorptions and Initial Psychic Powers

Certain branch paths become available at this stage largely because of the deconstruction of the ordinary point of observation and the reduction of the observable events to the very substratum of perception. First, it is possible to continue concentration so that even general awareness and specific focus drop away and the meditator enters another path called the "great seed meditation" (M, *thig le chen po*) the absorptions (VM, *appanā*), and the "recognition of states of being" (YS, *bhāvapratyaya*, 1:19), respectively.

certain branch paths available

According to the *Visuddhimagga*, there are eight absorptions, the first four being "form samādhi" *(rūpa)* and the last four being "formless *(arūpa)* samādhi.*" Second, spontaneous experiences of "psychic powers" (M, *mngon shes)* are also acknowledged by all the traditions, e.g., the Ten Signs of Skill, the two chapters on psychic powers (VM, 12–13), and mastery of physical reality (YS, 1:40), respectively. These initial experiences are unstable because the yogi has not fully eradicated the hindrances. Stable experience of psychic powers occurs again at the conclusion of Stage V because Stage V concerns itself with the eradication of the hindrances.

Stage V. Insight Meditation

A. Attaining the View

With the perception of how events unfold in the stream, as well as the new point of observation, the meditator has now arrived at a point where s/he may gain insight into how the world of ordinary experience and the self are constructed, through a new series of meditations, the Insight Meditations. Although the insights differ significantly in each of the three traditions, all systems take a detailed analysis of the flow of light as a starting point. The traditions agree that the meditator's initial perception of the way this stream comes forth is erroneous. The habitual non-veridicality of ordinary perception is based on subtle biasing factors called "propensities" (M, *bag chags)* or ."impressions" (YS, *saṃskāras)* built into the very structure of *the purpose of* perception at its most fundamental level. The purpose of *insight* insight meditation is to eradicate these biasing factors and *meditation* correct the meditator's view of the stream so that the succession of events undergoes a significant transformation, cleared of bias. This is why the initial exercise is called "attaining the view" (M, *lta ba;* VM, *diṭṭhi visuddhi)* in the Buddhist traditions. Because insight leads to *samādhi* "without the subtle seeds of bias," it is called "seedless *samādhi"* in the *Yogasūtras* (1:15).

Insight meditation is a high-speed analysis of the stream which unfolds over time as a "succession" of discontinuous or continuous movements (M. *rgyun,* VM, *bhavanga;*

YS, *krama*). Many thousands of such movements may occur in even short intervals of meditation. The meditator conducts "analysis of each and every movement" (M, *so, sor rtog pa*) occurring so rapidly as to go unnoticed in ordinary perception. The stream is constantly in the process of change. New terms are introduced to account for these subtle changes: the Buddhists look at discontinuities in change, to "whatever has arisen [discretely]" (M, *gang shar*); the Hindu yogis at continuities in the "transformation" (YS, *parināma*) of the energy field.

Each tradition makes explicit its bias as to how the stream may be viewed through preparatory philosophical training followed by *samādhi* practice. These two steps in the practice are called "examination-meditation" (M, *dpyad sgom*) and the *"samādhi* meditation" (M, *'jog sgom*) in the Mahāmudrā. The former is a review of the basic philosophical tenets of Mahāyāna Buddhism. Chapters 14–17 of the *Visuddhimagga* and chapter 1 of the *Yogasūtras* present their respective philosophical positions. Such preparatory "intellectual understanding" (M, *go ba*), though different in each tradition, serves to guide the latter *samādhi* practice. While the gross cognitive understanding of the philosophical position drops away upon entering *samādhi*, its impression nevertheless persists in the form of "single category" (M, *rtog gcig*) and has "influence" (M, *dbang*) on the *samādhi*. Each and every change in the stream of light may be compared to this category. Such an approach to *samādhi* is called a "search task" (M, *rtshol ba*) in the Mahāmudrā. Unless *samādhi* is oriented with such a category, no insight is possible. The initial category of insight used in the search task differs in each tradition: "Non-entityness" (M, *ngo bo nyid med*), "dependent origination" (VM, *pratītyasamutpāda*) and "sameness" (YS, *tulya*) or "change" (YS, *parināma*), respectively.

explicit bias of each tradition

While the view is different in each tradition, each corrects perceptual bias through a progression of insight having identical stages in each tradition. First comes a preliminary step to set up the optimal level of *samādhi* and the correct view according to the category. Next comes a serial exhaustive search of every moment to see if it matches the category insight. Finally, the meditator is able to recognize

correcting bias and the progression of insight

a profound transformation in the way events manifest in the stream. These same three stages occur for "specific focus" (M, *dpyad pa*; YS, *vicārā*, 1:17) of the observable event and the point of observation. These two perspectives are called "Emptiness of the Person and of Phenomena," and "knowledge of the body and mind" (VM, *nāma-rūpa*), and "recognition of the means [to reflecting awareness]" (YS, *upāyapratyaya*, 1:20) and "of states of matter" (YS, *bhavapratyaya*, 1:19), in the respective traditions. Table 5, Stage V summarizes the steps from each of the two perspectives in the three traditions.

In the *Mahāmudrā* the meditator begins with an examination-meditation on Emptiness of the Person. S/he studies *steps in the* the authoritative scriptures on emptiness and then applies *Mahāmudrā* this understanding to his/her own experience of self until concluding that the self is a "non-entity" (M, *ngo bo nyid med*) in that it cannot be identified in immediate experience. Then, the meditator returns to a level of *samādhi* where discrete pulses of light and its concomitant discrete moments of awareness occur. The first step is to "put-in-order [the view of] the mind" (M, *sems gtan la phebs*) by carrying non-entityness as a category of insight into the *samādhi*. The next step involves repeated comparison of each and every moment of awareness to the category in order to "bring forth insight" (M, *skabs su bab pa'i lhag mthong*). The last step occurs when s/he "reaches the limit of analysis" (M, *dpyad pa'i mthar*) and the flow of light undergoes a profound "rearrangement" (M, *gtan la phebs*). The root of perceptual bias is "cut off" (M, *rsta bcod*). This non-substantial and momentary point of observation, called "awareness itself" (M. *rang rig*), replaces any "[biased] mental representation" (M, *sems dmigs*) as the observational point. Then, the meditator repeats the same steps from the perspective of the observable events to achieve Emptiness of Phenomena.

The *Visuddhimagga* also begins with a series of philosophi-*steps in the* cal reflections (chapters 14–17) which describe the aggre-*Visuddhimagga* gates, sense systems, etc., according to Buddhist psychology. The most important is the description of dependent origination. Having understood these the meditator returns to *samādhi* and observes the discrete events from each of the two concomitant perspectives, the observed event (VM, *rūpa*) and the point of observation (VM, *nāma*), "materiality and mentality" (VM, 18:39). Taking the point of observation as the perspective, the meditator carefully searches for the "support" to the mind's momentary awareness, as if "following a snake to its house" (VM, 18:4). S/he finds no other support than the discrete event. Each discrete moment of awareness *(nāma)* is supported by only the concomitant discrete event *(rūpa)*. Taking the observable event as the perspective, the conclusion is similar: mentality and materiality are interdependent.

The *Yogasūtras* also begin with a detailed understanding of the dualist *Saṃkhya* philosophy (chapter 1). The phenomena of the physical universe (YS, *prākṛti*) as observed in the *steps in the* activity of the mindstuff in meditation appear to be in constant change, while the "transcendent self" (YS, *puruṣa*) is changeless. The yogi comes to intellectually understand the dualism between *prākṛti* and *puruṣa* and then applies it to *samādhi* experience. S/he enters a seedless *samādhi* where only impressions, no gross content, remain. S/he uses the category of "sameness" (YS, *tulya*) by which to compare the continuous changes in the energy field. At the onset of the *samādhi*, s/he is likely to observe the "seeming manifestations" (YS, *prādurbhāva*) and "non-manifestations" (YS, *abhibhāva*), i.e., patterns in a continuous field of change. Using the category of sameness during "constant practice" (YS, *abhyāspurva*, 1:18) results in a transformation of the energy field called the "transformation into cessation" (YS, *nirodhapariṇāma*, 3:9). For moments, transformation of specific wave patterns ceases and mindstuff attains an even more refined condition. Biasing impressions are eradicated. These moments of cessation leave their own impression, which subsequently affect the experience of the continuously changing energy field. The energy field is now a "calm flow" (YS, *prashāntavihīti*, 3:10) wherein wave patterns become less noticeable. This calm flow is the "means [YS, *upāya*] to realization." An important shift in emphasis has occurred. Awareness turns away from the observable events toward the transcendent, hence it is called "reflecting awareness" (YS, *buddhi*).

steps in the Yogasūtras

Western studies of high-speed information processing

The search into each and every moment during meditation is analogous to Western experimental studies of high-speed information-processing as studied extensively using a tachistoscope (T-scope). A T-scope is an instrument that can present individual visual displays to laboratory subjects at a very rapid rate, in terms of thousandths of a second, much more quickly than focused attention (Neisser, 1967). The T-scope has been used to study what humans are capable of becoming aware of at the level prior to conscious attention. There is a striking convergence of findings about the fundamental operations of perception from such diverse approaches as objective T-scope observations and yogic introspection. Most T-scope researchers agree that the basic structure of visual perception is temporal. The human mind resolves stimuli into quanta of energy, and arranges these in succession over time. Complex perceptual patterns, the images of the world, are constructed from the interaction of the energy of the quanta (Eriksen, 1967) and the different frequencies in succession (Pribram, 1974). It is perhaps no accident that T-scope authorities advance concepts such as the "temporal nature of visual perception" and the "psychological moment" (Eriksen, 1967) which are comparable to the yogic terms for the "succession" (M, *spros ba*; VM, *bhavanga*; YS, *krama*) and the "moment" (M, *'byung ba*; YS, *kṣāna*). The meditation texts provide a phenomenology for such perception.

comparable Western concepts and yogic terms

the yogi and the "high-speed search task"

The T-scope has been used to conduct high-speed search tasks (Sternberg, 1966) in which a subject is presented a stimulus far above threshold. This stimulus becomes a "memory set" because the subject encodes it in short-term memory and uses it to orient to an upcoming search task. Then a set of individual stimuli is flashed very quickly and the subject tries to "guess" whether its set contains the original stimulus encoded in memory. Thus, if the memory set is a letter "X," the set of stimuli which follow may contain different letters, "A, C, Y, T," etc. Some sets may contain the target "X," some may not. Such experiments have shown that laboratory subjects accurately perceive and process information very rapidly prior to their ability to consciously attend to it. Practice also improves information-processing. The yogi doing the insight meditations is doing what T-scope researchers have called a high-speed search task. The categories of insight—non-entityness, dependent origination, sameness in change—are kinds of memory sets. The yogi searches each and every moment of the flow of light to see if there is any match in the original category. With full awareness, the yogi searches events which pass very rapidly, unavailable to ordinary attention. S/he continues this high-speed search to learn about the structure and operations of perception and to remove the biases to ordinary perception.

B. Skill: Reverse Samādhi

Because of the rearrangement in the very substratum of temporal perception, it is no longer necessary to hold the samādhi at such a refined level where only the subtle flow of light is observable. In the Mahāmudrā the exercise is called "skill" (M, rstal) or "reverse samādhi" (M, zlog pa'i sgom pa), because the meditator attempts to keep the newly attained bias-free insights in the midst of gross mental content—thoughts, feelings, sensations, and percepts. The reverse samādhi is characterized by the return of such gross mental events. The meditator, now familiar with emptiness, may "let go" (M, lhod pa) the effort and turn awareness on "whatever happens to arise" (M, gang shar), namely "various" (M, sna thsogs) events in rapid succession. Likewise, the Visuddhimagga mentions gross *attending to* mental events, especially various painful sensations and *whatever arises* visual images common to this samādhi. The Yogasūtras require the yogi to maintain "reflecting awareness" (YS, buddhi) during the "multiplicity of things" (YS, sarvārthata, 3:11), i.e., the various events of the phenomenal world.

Once again, this is a high-speed search task, made more difficult by the new type of complex events. One problem typically encountered is the loss of insight as the meditator becomes distracted by the upsurge of gross mental con- *overcoming* tent. S/he must learn to keep the insight stable despite the *distractions to* radical shift in observable events during samādhi. Whether *stable insight* the perspective be non-entityness, dependent origination, or sameness, the meditator must learn to compare the various gross events that come forth in rapid succession to the respective category. Predictably, the same respective insights come forth. Because the same insights are disclosed in a new context, the Buddhists call this samādhi "overcoming doubt" or "skill." The *Yogasūtras* calls it "the transformation of *samādhi*" (YS, *samādhi pariṇāma)* because of the great stability of *samādhi* that is gained (YS, 3:11). While ordinary mental events recur, the same insight remains—emptiness, selflessness, and sameness-in-change, respectively. These insights become direct experiences built into the very structure of perception at both a gross and subtle level.

Continued experience with reverse *samādhi* brings forth additional skills, namely, automatic continuation of awareness and the ability to divide awareness between several types of events at the same time. Besides focusing on the content, the meditator also becomes aware of the process by which events come forth and pass away in immediate *awareness of* experience. According to the *Mahāmudrā* there are several *process of* stages of development. First, the meditator is aware of *"coming and* only the exact moment of impact of each event prior to its *going,"* elaboration as gross content—thoughts, percepts, etc. *"arising and* Further experience brings discernment of the entire dura-*passing away,"* tion of each event, i.e., awareness of the exact moment an *or "one-* event comes forth, its brief duration, and the exact mo-*pointedness"* ment it passes from awareness. This knowledge of each successive event, also reported in the *Visudddhimagga,* is called "clear comprehension" (VM, 20:1–92). Finally, the exact moment an event comes into existence and passes out of existence becomes very clear while the intermediate step, its duration, drops out of awareness. Thus, it is hard to discern the nature of the content. Each moment flashes very quickly, immersed in intense white light. This final stage is called "coming and going" in the *Mahāmudrā* and "arising and passing away" in the *Visuddhimagga* (VM, 20: 93–130) because of the flashing of light, moment by moment. The *Yogasūtras* call this stage the "transformation into one-pointedness" (YS, *ekagratāpariṇāma,* 3:12). Whereas both involve intense light, the Buddhist discontinuous experience is like the quick pulsing of a strobo-scope, and the Hindu continuous experience is like a volley of gongs so fast they blend into each other and seem to be the same continuous vibration.

The work of Schneider and Shiffrin (1977) on high-speed tachistoscopic search can be used to understand the reverse *samādhi*. Their work compares the performance of subjects during high-speed search when the sets of search stimuli are like and unlike the original memory set. For example, if the memory set were a letter "X," the search might occur when the sets of stimuli, flashed at high speeds, contained all letters or all numbers, and some of the sets also contained the target "X." Subjects learn high-speed search when the memory set and search frames are of like category (all letters). Such search requires sustained effort, and attentional capacity is limited while learning. This is called "controlled search." Ordinary subjects increase the accuracy and rate of information-processing under such conditions after thousands of trials. Then subjects manifest another mode of information-processing, called "automatic detection." Subjects are then able to conduct effortless high-speed search accurately when the memory set and search frames are of unlike category (letter, number). Moreover, the subjects become able to divide attention between one and several stimuli at once.

parallels with Western high-speed tachistoscopic search

Just as ordinary laboratory subjects are able to learn high-speed search, meditators in *samādhi* are likely to do the same. While learning insight, meditators use like categories (non-entityness, or sameness vs. gross mental content). Just as in the T-scope experiments, insight becomes automatic. Moreover, the yogi learns to divide awareness between the gross mental content and the process by which it comes forth during the search task. As a result, the perceived duration of events changes. One would expect an increase in luminosity according to Bloch's Law, which says that perceived duration and luminosity are inversely related. The white light occurring at this stage of practice is predicted according to research on perception.

learning in high-speed search and in samādhi

C. Arising/Passing Away Samādhi

Arising and passing away *samādhi* is one of the most important stages along the path of meditation because the meditator has refined awareness of the flow of light to its very limit, to the temporal structure of ordinary perception. From this now stable and bias-free vantage point, s/he is able to discern the very process by which phenomena seem to come into and go out of existence. Since the same laws governing how mental phenomena pass in and

the interface of mind and cosmos

out of existence are operable in the wider universe, the meditator has reached the interface of mind and cosmos.

While the traditions agree that observation of how events come into and go out of existence is the main feature of the exercise, the actual experience is quite different due to discontinuous and continuous perspectives taken. In Buddhism the experience is of a succession of discrete events seeming like very intense light which flashes in and out of existence rapidly like a high-frequency stroboscope. In Hinduism, the experience is of a continuous succession of changes (YS *parināma*) of the more "[observable] aspects" (YS, *dharma*) of wave patterns, which are more or less manifest at any given moment, much like the peaks and dips in an unfolding musical score.

new questions and new categories of insight

As the meditator observes the discontinuous coming/going or more or less continuous manifestations of wave phenomena, an important shift in emphasis occurs. Awareness opens up and attends to the very temporal/spatial structure of the flow of light. New questions occur. Is the seeming coming and going itself a perceptual bias? Are the seeming many manifestations reducible to a single unitary phenomenon? To resolve these questions the meditator begins to examine the very subtle causal and spatial relationships in which ordinary perception is embedded. To do so, s/he adopts a new category of insight, often paradoxical or dialectical in nature.

Theravādan category of disappearance

The *Visuddhimagga* uses the category of disappearance. With respect to observable events the yogi focuses on the disappearance of each discrete flash, moment-by-moment, while ignoring its arising (VM, 21:10). As a result, all events dissolve. This is called the "dissolution" experience (VM, *bhaṅgañyana*). With respect to the point of observation, the yogi focuses on the disappearance of each discrete moment of awareness until all such moments of awareness cease for a period. While the resulting experiences are profound, the experience still assumes a time/space matrix. The Mahāyāna has criticized the Theravāda for its failure to fully resolve the bias of time/space and therefore adopts dialectical negation as the category to do so, as in Nāgārjuna's famous instruction:

Mahāyāna dialectical negation

That which is already gone *(gatam)* is not being gone over *(gamyate)*. Moreover, that which is not yet gone *(agatam)* is not being gone over. A being gone over *(gamyamāna)* separate from that already gone *(gatam)*, and that not yet gone *(agatam)*, is not known.[5]

Such dialectics applied to arising/passing away *samādhi* result in a "non-dissolution" experience (M, *ma 'gag pa*) or "entrance to the middle path," in which the multiplicity of all potential events of the unvierse come forth simultaneously yet are co-dependent on each other for their existence. In the *Yogasūtras* the meditator completely resolves the relationship between sameness and change by applying that category not only to changing events (YS, *parināma*), but now to the very temporal organization of these events. The yogi first observes the changes (YS, *dharma*) in the patterns, properties, and states of the energy field (YS, 3:13) and then observes the underlying "unchanging aspect" (YS, *dharmin*):

change and sameness in the Yogasūtras

> The same substratum *(dharmin)* underlies observable aspects *(dharma)* which become manifest *(udīta)*, cease manifestation *(shānta)* or are potentially manifest *(avyapadeshya)* (3:14).

Having contrasted the changing *(dharma)* and unchanging *(dharmin)*, the yogi examines the causal relationship between change and sameness:

> The differences of the succession *(krama)* are the cause for the differences in the transformations *(parināma)* (3:15).

As a result, a unity experience comes forth in which all the potential events of the universe come forth simultaneously as a dimension of the same underlying substratum.

There is a common structure to the experience at least in the *Mahāmudrā* and *Yogasūtras*. Each is a variation on the theme of interconnectedness. The ordinary time/space matrix of ordinary perception is transcended and awareness opens up to another order in which all the potential events of the universe and the fabric of potential connections between these events comes forth. Within this undivided interconnectedness of the universe, interactions occur not by causal laws but by relative relationships to everything else. Positionality in space and properties also depend on relative relationship to everything.

nihilist, middle path, and externalist positions

While each tradition describes transcendence of ordinary time-space perception, the experiences are different, as described by the distinctions of nihilist, middle path, and eternalist positions. The Theravāda dissolution experience is nihilistic in that successive events and moments of awareness disappear. The Hindu unity experience is eternalist because the experienced interconnectedness is of some underlying substratum to the universe (YS, *prākṛti*) and its reflecting awareness is unchanging (YS, *puruṣa*). The *Mahāmudrā* experience is the middle path because the interconnected events and their awareness change; the specific events experienced as interconnected are dependent on their relation to all potential events for their apparent existence, and the concomitant awareness changes as the events seem to change.

Stage VI. The Extraordinary Mind and Enlightenment

A. The Relationship Between Ordinary Perception and the Extraordinary Interconnectedness of the Mind

the various traditional categories of insight

Opening up awareness to the level beyond the time/space matrix of ordinary perception constitutes a profound shift in consciousness—what the *Mahāmudrā* calls the "extraordinary mind" (M, *thun mong ma yin pa'i sems*), and the *Yogasūtras* "another class of existence" (YS 4:2). The first task is to experience *samādhi* for longer and longer intervals. The meditator must eradicate misperceptions and corrupting influences, while being careful not to lose track of the initial category of insight now applied in a totally new context. The *Visuddhimagga* reminds the meditator to focus on the instant of passing away even when seeing only the death of all formations (VM, 21:29). The *Mahāmudrā* gives another examination-mediation, "pointing out" (M, *ngo, sprod ba*), which serves to remind the yogi that the vast interconnectedness seeming to spring forth is neither substantial nor self-existent, but rather, an empty emanation of the mind, much like a dream which emanates from a dreamer. The *Yogasūtras* apply the category, sameness of change, to a new context. The meditator becomes aware of subtle acausal interactions, called *vāsanās*, between the potential events during the extraordinary *sa-*

mādhi. Initially, s/he may notice "differences in the activity" (YS, *pravṛttibhede*) stemming from these subtle interactions. If the category, sameness of change, is applied to the *vāsanās,* then "the impetus of what is not the same is the same" (YS, 4:5).

Keeping a particular category in view during the extraordinary *samādhi* influences the actual experience, summarized as the nihilist, middle, and eternalist positions. By focusing on disappearance within time, the wholeness of potential interactions is not fully reported in the *Visuddhimagga,* although "levels of formations" are alluded to in the text (VM, 21:29). By focusing on the dialectic of the Middle Path in the *Mahāmudrā,* simultaneity of events emerges according to the experience of dependent origination. Events have a relative reality but no lasting substance. Awareness, likewise, stays relative to the change in events. By focusing on sameness in change in the *Yogasūtras,* simultaneity of events emerges as an eternal substance *(āshreya),* primordial *prākṛti,* capable of reflecting the eternal unchanging transcendent awareness *(puruṣa).*

Despite such differences, the extraordinary *samādhi* has a common structure across traditions. In terms of structure, it represents an undivided wholeness (M, *kun gzhi,* literally, "basis of everything"; YS, *āshreya; vastu)* wherein parts exist only in their relationship to all other parts. One relative mind-moment contains the information of the entire universe through its interconnectedness. In terms of activity, it represents the movement of the universe in which every subtle activity moves into every other subtle activity. The Buddhist concept of dependent origination and the Hindu description of the *vāsanās* convey such acausal interactions.

truth of undivided wholeness and interconnectedness across traditions

The meditator must learn to carry forth the category of insight into the extraordinary *samādhi* and compare the new insight to that of the previous ordinary insights. The meditator establishes links between the unmanifest potential interactions and the manifest events of the mind, subtle and gross. S/he learns to "couple" (M, *zung 'jug)* or "remove the interval" (YS, *ānantara,* 4:9) between the extraordinary and ordinary mind. This is done by first entering the extraordinary *samādhi* and the observing the return of the ordinary mind in the transition back to waking consciousness (M, *rjes thob*). Through repeated practice the states beome contiguous. In the *Mahāmudrā* this coupling exercise is called "simultaneousness of the mind" (M, *lhan cig skyes sbyor pa'i sems*, wherein the simultaneous experience of all interconnected potential events is coupled with the successive subtle stream and gross content of ordinary meditation experience. The resultant state of meditation is paradoxically in and out of time. The comparable experience in the *Visuddhimagga*, called "misery" (VM, 21:29–42), still lays heavy stress on the successive breakup of events/awareness but expands the range to "all formations everywhere" (VM, 21:29) so that interactions between past, present, and future events become clear. In the *Yogasūtras* the yogi first opens up awareness to the subtle acausal interactions *(vāsanās)* and gross activity *(vṛtti)* of mental content during the transition to ordinary meditation. Using the category, sameness in change throughout, the yogi comes to realize that the extraordinary and ordinary levels "have no interval" between them *(ānantara,* YS, 4:9).

Because the experience of the extraordinary *samādhi* is so compelling, meditators tend to react to it. They must repeat the practice until "indifferent" (M, *rang lugs*), "dispassionate" (VM, 21: 43–44) or "having cut off desire" (YS, 4:10). Then, the links in the chain of karmic activity become clear. The subtle acausal interactions between relative interconnected events (M, *las;* VM, *kamma;* YS, *vāsanā)* are the "storehouse" of karmic activity (YS, 4:6). These interactions affect changes in the flow of light (M, *spros ba;* VM, *bhavanga;* YS, *parināma),* at the subtle level of ordinary experience, which in turn produce changing manifestations (M, *spros ba;* YS, *vṛtti)* in the gross mental content in the stream of consciousness. The meditator not only learns the stages by which every action becomes manifest over time according to the Doctrine of Cause and Effect, but also sees that it is possible to stop the karmic chain. Such insight is called the "dawning of wisdom" (M, *ye shes skyes ba),* the "desire of deliverance" (VM, 21: 45–46), and the "[possible] non-existence of the *vāsanās* "(YS, 4:11) in the respective traditions.

the doctrine of cause and effect and the karmic chain

Next, the yogi proceeds to more carefully observe the subtle karmic activity and its manifestations. This is called the "simultaneousness of cognition and perception" (M, *lhan skyes rtog snang*), "reobservation" (VM 21: 47–60) and seeing the "same entity [*vastu*] in diverse mindstuff" (YS, 4: 4–17) in the respective traditions. The meditator comes to recognize that all observable events—simultaneous or successive, subtle or gross—are but emanations as a consequence of this subtle karmic activity. Furthermore, through practicing session after session, subtle reactivity drops away and the meditator comes to realize events in a new way, just as they are in their primordial state. According- *events realized* ing to the *Mahāmudrā*, "reactivity" *(byas ba)* and "false cog- *in a new way* nitions" *(rtog pa)* drop away so that emanations are experienced "freshly" in their original "spontaneity" *(gnyug ma)*. This is called "ordinary knowledge" (M, *tha mal gyi shes ba*). In the *Visuddhimagga* reactivity also fades and the three marks—impermanence, selflessness, and reactivity—become clear in each arising. This is called "equanimity." For both Buddhist traditions the primordial state is one of immediacy. Events quickly settle before they become built up into constructs—time/space, self, gross percepts and thoughts. The *Yogasūtras* call the primordial state "Thatness of an entity" (YS, 4:14). It is one of substantiality. The Hindu yogi sees all the continuously changing and seemingly different manifestations and mindstuff as the same "entity" *(vatsu)*, primordial *prākṛti,* which merely appears differently due to the activity of the *vāsanās* (YS, 4:17). Despite differences in the primordial state, the tra- *a return to* ditions agree that, with respect to observable events, there *some original* is a return to some original condition. With respect to the *condition* point of observation, awareness proceeds without reactivity and with ideas about the original experience as it is presented. The paradoxes, arise/pass away, one/many, successive/simultaneous, are all resolvable through an understanding of the subtle acausal interactions of the extraordinary mind.

B. *The Relationship Between the Extraordinary Interconnected Mind and the Enlightened Mind*
Having gained insight into the nature of the karmic activity of the extraordinary mind and its relation to ordinary mental events, the meditator begins to question how

equanimous awareness of karmic activity might also relate to enlightenment. Two conditions must be met, one from the perspective of the point of observation, the other from the observable events.

awareness turned upon itself

From the point of observation, awareness changes its direction away from the emanating interconnected events toward itself. When awareness turns upon itself the shift in experience is often distinct, like space opening up amidst changing events. In the *Mahāmudrā*, this is called "recognizing the wisdom in the continuum." The Tibetans introduce the technical term, "mindfulness-awareness" (M, *dranrig*), to convey that moment-by-moment awareness itself becomes the object of mindfulness. The comparable shift in the *Visuddhimagga* is called "insight leading to emergence" (VM, 21:83–110). The three marks are clear in each moment. As a consequence, moment-by-moment awareness has nothing further to alight upon, so enlightenment *(nibbana)* is said to become the object of awareness. In the *Yogasūtras* continuous awareness shifts away from the continuous activities *(vāsanās)* of the same entity, primordial *prākṛti*, toward itself, toward transcendent awareness, *puruṣa*. The relationship between the primordial *prākṛti* and the transcendent awareness, *puruṣa*, becomes clear, (YS, 4: 18–23).

awareness itself as the object of mindfulness

From the perspective of observable events, the activity observed during equanimity more and more approximates the perfect primordial state; it must conform to the natural condition of the mind's activity so that enlightenment can occur. The key to understanding this stage of practice is the mind's activity. An important distinction is made between artificial "activity" (M, *byas ba*)—gross reactivity and subtle activities which interfere with the realization of enlightenment—and the spontaneous activity of the primordial state. The meditator must learn to negate the more common forms of reactivity—expectations, doubts, evaluatory thought, and the incessant attempt to categorize the unfolding experience. The meditator must also negate subtle activities of meditation which also interfere with the realization of enlightenment. The very tools of meditation, e.g., "mindfulness" (M, *dran pa*) and "taking-to-mind" (M, *yid la byed pa*), become obstacles to enlightenment and

tools of "mindfulness" become obstacles to enlightenment

need be negated. This is why the Tibetans entitle the set of exercises "the yoga of non-meditation" (M, *sgom med*). Likewise, the *Yogasūtras* say enlightenment cannot be an activity "achieved" (*prapya*) or "procured" (*utpadya*) (YS, 2:20). Instead of talking about activities to bring forth enlightenment, the Tibetans speak of establishing conditions which increase its probability, namely, the "means to set up" (M, *bzhag thabs*). In addition to negating artificial activity, the meditator must also recognize and "safeguard" (M, *skyongba*) the natural spontaneous activity when it occurs. In the *Visuddhimagga* the comparable instructions are called "conformity knowledge" (VM, 21: 128–136), which also contain negation instructions, "dispassion" (VM, *nibbida*), and safeguarding instructions, the "seven factors of enlightenment." The *Yogasūtras* use only safeguarding instructions given in a single aphorism:

> That (mindstuff), although diversified by innumerable *vāsanās*, is for the sake of the Other (*puruṣa*) because its function is to affect interactions (YS, 4:24).

The phrase, "for the sake of the Other" describes an important realization in which the *vāsanās'* very activity is seen to exist in support of transcendent awareness. The meditator realizes that pure awareness exists as a continuous backdrop to the innumerable activities of the *vāsanās*.

When the exact conditions are fulfilled, enlightenment comes forth. All the traditions agree that enlightenment comes forth as a series of three instantaneous shifts in awareness. These are called moments of enlightenment: basis, path, and fruition. The structure of enlightenment is identical across traditions, but the experience of the latter two moments of enlightenment is different because of the different perspectives taken throughout the entire path of meditation.

moments of enlightenment: basis, path, and fruition

The experience of the first moment, basis-enlightenment, is identical across traditions. From the perspective of observable events, all events, content and activity—everything—drops away. This is called "cessation" (VM, *nirodha*; VS, *vinivṛtti*; 4:25–26). What remains? Vast awareness. From the perspective of the point of observation, as the events recede from awareness, the locus of

basis-enlightenment and "dropping away"

awareness shifts; it "goes to the other shore" or "changes its lineage" (VM, 22: 3–9). Prior to enlightenment, awareness is inextricably bound up with mental activity and events. The point of observation and observable event occur as if inseparable. When awareness shifts its locus during basis-enlightenment, the association between event and awareness is permanently severed.

The second moment of enlightenment, path-enlightenment, is characterized by a return of observable events, now viewed from a different locus of awareness (VM, 22:10–14; YS, 4: 27–28). Since awareness is no longer associated with the observable events, nothing can interfere with the natural activity of the events, no new karma is generated. The traditions agree that the eradication of *freedom from* karmic activity occurs during path-enlightenment. The re-*reactivity and* turn of observable events, free from reactivity and activity *activity in* regarding them, is likened to entering a stream with its *regarding* natural currents (VM, *sotapanna*, literally "stream-*observable* enterer)." In the *Mahāmudrā* all potential events fill up *events* awareness and come forth paradoxically, simultaneously, and successively. In the *Visuddhimagga*, observable events empty out of awareness, so that the content of path-enlightenment is not very different from that of basis-enlightenment except for the experience of another shift and its consequence, the burning up of karma. In the *Yogasūtras*, the simultaneous activity of the *vāsanās* and the successive activity of the impressions (*saṃskāras*) return to recognition:

> In the interval [following] that, there are other Recognitions coming from the *saṃskāras* (4:27).

The main difference between the observable events in the *Mahāmudrā* and *Yogasūtras* is the interconnected insubstantial relativity of discontinuous events in Buddhism, in contrast to the interconnected continuous activity of the substantial *prākṛti* in Hinduism.

Fruition-enlightenment is the final moment in which a *fruition-* permanent transformation of consciousness occurs. The *enlightenment* nature of the transformation again varies across traditions. In the *Mahāmudrā* the meditator becomes the "three Buddha bodies," one on the plane of awareness (M, *chos sku*), one in the various potential interconnected cosmic realms (M, *longs sku*), and one on the plane of ordinary time/space existence (M, *sprul sku*). These three conditions now co-exist as part of the meditator's consciousness. In the *Visuddhimagga*, the meditator experiences deep peace and stillness without extraneous mental activity (VM, 22: 15–18). In the *Yogasūtras*, the meditator experiences the "raincloud samādhi" (YS, *dharmameghasamādhi*, 4:29), in which all possible forms of knowledge and existences pour forth as if from a full raincloud.

C. Review

Following these three moments of enlightenment, ordinary time/space experience with its gross mental content returns. Ordinary consciousness unfolds as if in the waking state, prior to any meditation experience. Yet, the meditator is reflexively aware that a profound shift has occurred. While the content of ordinary experience returns, the perspective is now vastly different. During the review, emphasis is given to the relationship between enlightened awareness and ordinary waking consciousness. The meditator learns to further eradicate misperceptions and biases through which the enlightened perspective may be lost and thereby stabilize enlightenment as a dimension of ordinary waking experience.

stabilizing enlightenment as a dimension of ordinary waking experience

SUMMARY

The Path of Meditation

Despite the apparent differences across traditions of meditation, there is strong evidence for a single underlying invariant sequence of stages. These stages represent a predictable progression of changes in psychological structure and are experienced subjectively as a systematic unfolding of distinct states of consciousness. This underlying path is best conceptualized as a systematic deconstruction of the structures of ordinary waking consciousness. As illustrated in Table 6 the paths of meditation in every tradition entail progressive deconstruction of each of these structures of ordinary waking consciousness: attitudes and behavioral schemes (stage I); thinking (stage II); gross per-

underlying invariant sequence of stages

systematic deconstruction

ception (stage III); self-system (stage IV); time-space matrix (stage V). As a result of dismantling the coordinates of ordinary perception, the meditator gains access to a non-ordinary, or extraordinary, structure of consciousness which does not operate by ordinary psychophysical laws. Deconstruction of even this deep structure results in enlightenment (stage VI). Each of these shifts manifests "state specificity" (Tart, 1971), and each is experienced as *state-bound* a discrete shift in one's state of consciousness. The nature *experience* of the experience and insight of each of these states of consciousness is specific to that state and does not transfer across states. Experience is "state-bound" (Fischer, 1971).

The progression of alterations in the structure of consciousness is triggered under certain conditions. Diminished sensory/motor interaction between organism and environment is a prerequisite.[6] The main contributor, *importance of* however, is attention deployment. Prolonged use of selec- *attention* tive attention, effort, and pure awareness, and the devel- *deployment* opment of these as attentional skills, are essential for activation of the changes along the path of meditation. Rapaport (1967) and Neisser (1976) have implicated attention for its role in affecting changes in cognitive structure. Tart (1975a) has specifically demonstrated how attention can be used to "disrupt" the stability of normal waking consciousness and produce altered states. Brown (1977) has further shown how attention can be used to produce the progression of states of consciousness in Tibetan meditation.

Western theorists, notably Tart, and the authors of the *Ma-* *the mechanisms* *hāmudrā* have set forth similar theories to explain the *of structured* mechanisms of structural change. Both emphasize the re- *change* lationship between awareness and psychological struc- *according to* ture. According to Tart, consciousness is composed of *Tart* three elements: structure (a relatively stable organization), energy (that which activates or deactivates structures), and attention/awareness (either volitional attention or pure awareness). One may disrupt a relatively stable organization like the waking state by application of effort. A discrete altered state of consciousness—a relatively stable pattern with a structure unique from the waking state—

may ensue. Such a stable state can be observed with less effort. One experience with the state may also learn to "free awareness from structures" altogether and experience pure awareness:

> Consciousness as we ordinarily know it in the West, is not pure awareness but rather awareness as it is embodied in the psychological structure of the mind or the brain. Ordinary experience is of neither pure awareness nor pure psychological structure, but awareness embedded in and modified by the structure of the mind/brain, and of the structure of the mind/brain embedded in and modified by awareness. These two components, awareness and psychological structure, constitute a gestalt, an overall interacting, dynamic system that makes up consciousness.[7]

> Techniques exist, however, that are intended to free a person's awareness from the dominance of the structure, of the machinery that has been culturally programmed into him.[8]

Similarly, the *Mahāmudrā* speaks of three "styles" (M, *lugs*) of attending: "holding fast" with exertion (M, *sgrim ba*), "letting go" of effort (M, *lhod pa*), and "pure awareness" (M, *rig pa*). The *Mahāmudrā* contributes something lacking in Tart's work, namely an illustration of how these three styles of attending apply to each of the main stages of meditation. In each stage, effort is used to dismantle the structure in question. By letting go of effort, the meditator can observe the resultant discrete stable state of consciousness. Finally a reorganization occurs, wherein the structure decomposes and awareness is temporarily freed from the structure. Substage A is where the structure is disrupted, substage B, where the resultant stage is observed, and substage C, where the reorganization occurs and awareness is freed.

"holding fast," "letting go," and "pure awareness"

The entire path of meditation unfolds like a musical score with a repeated theme. Note the profound regularity: I, A, B, C; II, A, B, C . . . VI, A, B, C. IA, disrupt; IB, observe the resultant state; and IC, deconstruct and develop pure awareness. The habitual structures drop off during substage C of each stage: attitude, thinking, gross perception, etc. Such is the music of the mind. It climaxes in Stage VI when the subtlest structure of perception drops away and

enlightenment as freedom from psychological structure

awareness becomes permanently freed from psychological structure. This is enlightenment.

meditation as intensive attention training

Since attention has been ignored in Western developmental and cognitive theories until recently (Brown, 1977), it is not surprising that the path of meditation has been a rather incomprehensible product of the East. Meditation is, simply, a form of intensive attention training and its consequences, the major consequence being the triggering of an atypical sequence of adult development. It is atypical only in the sense that the path of meditation-development is not available to all adults, only to those who rigorously train attention. Those who do, become maestros of the great masterpiece of the mind's inherent music.

different perspectives, different experiences in comparable stages

Although there is convincing evidence for a single underlying path across traditions, there are different perspectives which can be taken, which in turn result in different experiences during comparable stages along the path. These differences become apparent during the third substage (C) of each stage along the path because deconstruction occurs and awareness is released from its embeddedness in structure during this substage: deconstruction of thinking (II C); gross perception (IIIC); self (IVC); time/space (VC); and extraordinary interactions (VCI). Once awareness is released it is possible to take different perspectives, e.g., concomitance in Buddhism or reflecting awareness in Hindu yoga. Such reapplication of awareness according to different perspectives results in different experiences during the same substage. These differences are summarized in terms of discontinuity and continuity: discontinuous vs. continuous thinking (IIC); flow of light (VC); interconnectedness (VC); enlightened mind (VC). As a result, the final enlightened mind is different across traditions.

one path, several outcomes

The conclusions set forth here are nearly the opposite of that of the stereotyped notion of the perennial philosophy according to which many spiritual paths are said to lead to the same end. According to the careful comparison of the traditions we have to conclude the following: *there is only one path, but it has several outcomes.* There are several kinds of enlightenment, although all free awareness from psychological structure and alleviate suffering.

States of consciousness are patterned according to culture (Wallace, 1959). The preliminary practices serve to pattern meditative states. The beginner rigorously studies the basic philosophical tenets of the tradition until these "influence" the perspective adopted during *samādhi*. There can be no escape from such influence except in the basic moment of enlightenment, i.e., so long as awareness is not permanently freed from psychological structure. Most meditation traditions explicitly acknowledge the biasing role of philosophical perspective. Systematic encounter with a particular view will pull the discrete meditative states toward particular perspectives and experiences. It is reasonably guaranteed that the yogi will *only* experience the insights recognized by the tradition. Other experiences are certainly possible, part of the array of human potential. This is perhaps why there is so much debate across traditions, each denying the validity of the other's experience. *validity of* The Mahāyānists honestly acknowledge the validity of *different* other experiences, though they see their experiences as *experiences and* more profound. Therefore, they include "safeguarding" *enlightenments* (M, *skyon ba)* instructions after each substage of practice, wherein the yogi's experience is compared to those accepted by the tradition. The debates and biases aside, however, the conclusion must be the following: while all the experiences as well as the kinds of enlightenment are valid, each represents a different point of view.

Another difference in perspective is that between successiveness and simultaneity. As awareness becomes temporarily freed from the fundamental time/space structures of ordinary perception (stage VC), it becomes possible to view human experience from either successive (VM) or simultaneous (YS) or both (M) perspectives (stages VIA, B). In fact, from this extraordinary state it is possible to view the entire path of meditation as either successive, or simultaneous, or both. This is the distinction between *gradual and* gradual and quick paths, i.e., successive or simultaneous. *quick models* Whereas this presentation has adopted the successive perspective for heuristic purposes, both are legitimate. It is correct to say the mind can operate successively or simultaneously depending on the perspective. This position is consistent with contemporary research in cognitive psychology. Two models of information-processing exist: a serial (successive) and parallel (simultaneous) model (Hoffman, 1979). Convincing evidence has been cited for each model. The heated debates between these models can be circumvented by saying that both are correct. The mind is equipped to process information both successively and simultaneously depending on the conditions and the perspective taken. Likewise, the mind unfolds in meditation in a successive or simultaneous manner depending on perspective.

THE FINAL OUTCOME: THE EFFECTS OF ENLIGHTENMENT

two major changes produced by enlightenments

The traditions are in agreement that enlightenment produces two major changes: the view of external reality is permanently altered and the internal experience of suffering is alleviated. Both changes are derived from the shift in the association between awareness and mental events that occurs during enlightenment.

dismantling ordinary perception of reality

The meditator experiences several profound shocks to the ordinary view of reality. Some occur prior to enlightenment, some during. Long before enlightenment, during the concentrative meditations, the meditator learns to stop the mind, to dismantle ordinary perception. The meditator arrives at the conclusion that the world is not simply what is seen, heard, etc.

psychic powers as challenge to ordinary reality

The challenge to the ordinary view of reality is even greater with the discovery of psychic powers, especially since many of the psychic powers entail the mind's effect on physical reality. According to the texts, psychic powers become available at two points along the path, stage IVC and stage VC. This is not surprising. They become available after deconstruction of gross perception and the ordinary self-system (stage IVC) and after deconstruction of the time/space matrix of ordinary perception (stage VC). In other words, psychic powers are a result of perceptual experiences that are part of our human potential but become manifest only after our most habitual perceptual structures are removed. This finding is consistent with Western research on psychic abilities which has shown the greatest increase in psychic ability to come during transitional states of consciousness, e.g., the hypnagogic state (Ullman & Krippner, 1973). Many texts agree that it is difficult for the yogi to fully master the psychic powers during stage IVC. This is because the yogi has not yet mastered insight meditation. Such psychic powers as arise in stage IVC are solely a result of intense concentration. Once, however, the yogi masters the insight meditations, s/he has removed even the subtlest of biasing factors and has deconstructed the very basis of ordinary perception, its time/space matrix. By achieving such insight into perception the psychic powers become available in a stable way. This is perhaps why the *Yogasūtras* fail to mention psychic powers during their description of the concentration meditations while greatly emphasizing them during the insight series (YS, 3: 16–52).

An even greater challenge to the view of ordinary reality comes with the discovery of the extraordinary *samādhi*. Despite the important differences in perspective all the traditions agree that the extraordinary *samādhi* entails some sort of experience of interconnectedness of all potential acausal interactions of mind/universe. Through these direct experiences of the mind's subtlest structure, the meditator discovers a set of operations in the mind quite different from the ordinary psychophysical laws. The mind in its deepest operations obeys another set of laws, those of universal interconnectedness and relativity. Moreover, it is possible to specify the exact stage at which the transition from ordinary laws to extraordinary laws occurs. The key is the deconstruction of the time/space matrix of ordinary perception.

the challenge to ordinary reality of extraordinary samādhi

The greatest challenge to the view of ordinary reality comes with enlightenment. Whether the experience be from the nihilist, middle, or eternalist perspective, basis-enlightenment is identical across traditions. During basis-enlightenment the content of experience drops away and awareness shifts its locus. The relationship between awareness and structure is permanently altered. Aware-

the challenge to ordinary reality of enlightenment

ness is once-and-for-all freed from mental structure. This, in turn, alters the view of reality after enlightenment. The meditator is now "aware" that ordinary reality is but an elaborate "construction" (M, *bcos pa*), simply a model constructed from incessant acausal and causal interactions in the mind. Such models generate "erroneous ideas" (M, *rtog pa*) about the nature of reality. Once, however, awareness is freed from such constructions, the yogi realizes these models and concepts are not in themselves accurate statements about reality. According to the *Yogasūtras* they pertain to "illusion" (YS, *māyā*).

constructivist theories of perception in the West

Such descriptions are very close to the constructivist theories of perception in the West (Bruner 1973; Neisser, 1967; Pribram 1974). According to Bruner ordinary perception is "non-veridical." The organism actively translates stimuli into units of information and then makes a model for the stimuli through category operations. Although categories may resemble the physical features of the world, so that perceptual constructs approximate the features of the physical world, nevertheless, this act of construction often "goes beyond the information given." Perception, then, is always biased to some extent; it is non-veridical. Bruner's work on the non-veridicality of ordinary perception is a theory comparable to the Mahāyānist theory of emptiness and the yogic notion of *māyā*. What all these constructivist and deconstructivist theories of perception share is an understanding that the view of the ordinary world is a merely rough approximation. Better not to be so attached to it. Empirical studies of enlightened meditators have shown how they both "see" and "see through" ordinary reality (see Chapters 6 and 7).

impact on the experience of human suffering

The shift in the relationship between structure and awareness also has a profound impact on the experience of human suffering. The main claim, and therefore the reason to meditate in the first place, is that enlightenment can alleviate human suffering. During path-enlightenment particularly, the reactivity of the mind to its content ceases, so that no new karma can be generated. The content of experience that reoccurs after enlightenment is based on the ripening of past karma even though no new karma is generated. Because awareness has shifted its locus, there is no reactivity to this emerging content. All the traditions agree that reactivity stops, although the fate of emotional reactions differs in each tradition. In the nihilist Theravāda Buddhist tradition, intense emotional states may cease altogether after a number of enlightenment experiences. According to the eternalist Hindu yoga position, blissful states endure in a relative sense although there is an experience beyond even this where no emotions exists *(sagunam* versus *nirgunam puruṣa,* YS, 4:38). According to the middle path, intense emotional states occur in a relative and dependent manner, but are ultimately empty. In any case, the human experience of suffering is altered because of the change in how information about emotions is processed.

This view is very close to cognitive information-processing theories of emotions (Tompkins, 1962–1963; Singer & Antrobus, 1972). Affect is that part of the information-processing system which serves to give feedback on information-processing itself, and serves as the basis for motivation and action. For example, if there are too many novel stimuli to process, a startle response may ensue. Moderate information-processing results in interest; discrepant stimuli, in fear. It stands to reason that a major and permanent alteration in the manner of information-processing would also produce a major and permanent alteration in the experience of emotion. What the meditation texts claim is quite radical: nothing short of a life without the experience of emotional pain. Freud was more pessimistic about psychoanalysis, through which the interpretation of free associations might only replace neurotic suffering with ordinary human unhappiness. The meditation masters have picked up where Freud left off. In the words of the Buddha, "If there's one thing only I teach you, it is the end of suffering."[9] Disciplined deployment of attention, which may permanently alter human information-processing, may alleviate all traces of everyday unhappiness.

life without the experience of emotional pain

TABLE 5

STAGE I. PRELIMINARY ETHICAL PRACTICES

Underlying Structure	Mahāmudrā	Visuddhimagga	Yogasūtras	Psychology
Faith	Causing Faith to Arise (dad pa'i 'don pa) Awakening Recognition			self-efficacy
I.A. Attitude Change	ORDINARY PRELIMINARIES Opportunity Impermanence/Death Cause/Effect Sufferings of Saṃsāra			attitude change reactance perceived control
I.B. Intrapsychic Change Turning Inward	EXTRAORDINARY PRELIMINARIES Refuge Vow		OBSERVANCES (niyama) Going into Onself (svādhyāyāḥ, 2:32)	
Fostering Outcome Expectations	Enlightened Attitude which Desires		Establishing a Connection (samprayogaḥ)	expectation effects
Study/Reflection	Enlightened Attitude which Perseveres		Practice (abhyāsa)	
Transformation of the Stream of Consciousness	Mental Factors		Removing Doubt (vitarkābandhane)	objective self-awareness of:

TABLE 5

STAGE I. PRELIMINARY ETHICAL PRACTICES (cont.)

Eradication of Negative States	Confession/rDorje Sems 'pa Meditation		Cleansing (*shaucha*)	negative affective states
Cultivation of Positive States	Offerings/Maṇḍala Offering		Contentment (*saṃtoṣa*)	positive affective states
Transformation of Cognitions in Stream	Guru Yoga		Identification with Ishvara (*Ishvaraprani-dhanani*)	cognitions
I.C. Behavioral Change	ADVANCED PRELIMI-NARIES		RESTRAINTS (*yamas*)	behavioral therapy
Regulation of Life-Style & Social Behavior	Virtue-Practice	PRECEPTS (*śila*) 13 Ascetic Practices (*dhutanganiddesa*)	Five Restraints	
Restriction of Sensory Input	Binding-Senses		Subjugation of Body/Mind (*tapas*)	environmental/milieu therapy
Awareness Training	Recollection/Total Awareness			absorption/flow

TABLE 5

STAGE II. PRELIMINARY BODY AND MIND TRAINING

Underlying Structure	Mahāmudrā	Visuddhimagga	Yogasūtras	Psychology
II.A. Body Awareness Training	THREE ISOLATIONS ISOLATION OF THE BODY (lus dben)		POSTURES (āsana, 2:46–53)	regulation of muscle output
II.B. Calming the Breath and Thinking	ISOLATION OF SPEECH (ngag dben)		BREATH-CONTROL (prāṇāyāma, 2:49–53)	voluntary control of breathing rhythm; reduction of thinking
II.C. Rearrangement of the Stream of Consciousness	ISOLATION OF THE MIND (sems dben)		SENSE-WITHDRAWAL (pratyahāra, 2:54–55)	increased reality-distance
Deconstruction of Thinking				deautomatization of thinking

TABLE 5

STAGE III. CONCENTRATION WITH SUPPORT

Underlying Structure	Mahāmudrā	Visuddhimagga	Yogasūtras	Psychology
III.A.1. Effortful Concentration on external object	CONCENTRATION IN FRONT (mngon du)	BEGINNER'S SIGN (parikammanimitta 4:22)	CONCENTRATION (external) (dhāraṇā traṭākam) (3:1)	categorizing
III.A.2. Maintaining Effortless Concentration on internal object	CONCENTRATION INSIDE (nang du) visualization of the Body of the Tathāgatā	EIDETIC SIGN (uggahanimitta 4:30)	CONCENTRATION (internal) (dhāraṇā cakra) (3:1) visualization of the deity, Hari	object constancy
III.B. Relaxed Recognition of changing internal events of the seed	SKILL (rtsal) Recognition (ngo shes) of the various (sna tshogs) discontinuous events of the emanating seed ('char ba'i thig le)	LIKENESS SIGN (paṭibhāganimitta 4:31)	CONTEMPLATION (dhyāna) (3:2) Recognition (pratyāya) of continuous transformation (vṛtti) of same continuum (ekātanatā) of seed (bindu)	pattern recognition
III.C. Stopping Gross Perception	BEING DONE WITH (zad pa) Breath-Holding (bum ba can) Space Yoga	SAFEGUARDING THE SIGN (4:34)	DWINDLING FLUCTUATIONS [OF MIND-STUFF] (kseenavrtti, 1:41) Breath-Holding (kumbhaka)	preattentive perceptual synthesis
Awareness of the Flow of Light	STOPPING THE MIND (sems med)		SEED SAMĀDHI, GROSS OBJECTS (sthūla) (3:3)	

TABLE 5

STAGE IV. CONCENTRATION WITHOUT SUPPORT

Underlying Structure	Mahāmudrā	Visuddhimagga	Yogasūtras	Psychology
IV.A. Tuning in Subtle Perception	HOLDING FAST (*sgrim ba*)	TEN SKILLS OF ACCESS (*upacāra*) exertion (4:51–56)	SEED SAMĀDHI, SUBTLE OBJECT (*sūkṣma*) (1:44) *nirvitarkāsamādhi*	change in self-system
loss of self-representation	loss of "I" (*nga*)		loss of sense-interpreter (*manas*)	loss of self-representation
discovering flow of light without gross constructions	subtle cognition (*phra rtog*)		shining forth only of light (*arthamatranirbhāsa*) devoid of its own form (*svarupashūnya*, 1:43)	
IV.B. Recognizing the Subtle Flow	LETTING GO (*lhod pa*)	relaxing (4:57–62)	*savicārasamādhi*	
loss of self-agency	loss of "acting" (*byas ba*)		loss of "I-acting" (*aham-kara*)	loss of self-agency
flow of light as a stream	recognition (*ngo shes*) of flow of light		Recognition (*pratyaya*) of flow of light	

TABLE 5

STAGE IV. CONCENTRATION WITHOUT SUPPORT (cont.)

IV.C. Collapse of Ordinary Observer; Re-structuring Perspective	BALANCING (*btang snyoms*)	SKILLFUL DEVELOPMENT (4:50)	*nirvicārasamādhi*	
new perspective of awareness	concomitant awareness (*lhan ne; sgo nas*)	mentality/materiality (*nāmarūpa*)	reflecting awareness (*buddhi*)	freeing awareness from self-structures
discontinuous/continuous stream	discrete discontinuous flashes (*val le*)		continuously vibrating energy field (*tanmātra*) (1:47)	temporal information-processing holonomic perception
Branch Paths	GREAT SEED (simultaneous) PSYCHIC POWERS	ABSORPTIONS (successive)	[PSYCHIC POWERS]	

TABLE 5
STAGE V. INSIGHT MEDITATION

Underlying Structure	Mahāmudrā	Visuddhimagga	Yogasūtras	Psychology
V.A. High-Speed Search of Subtle Flow	THE VIEW	PURIFICATION OF VIEW (18:1-36)	SAMĀDHI WITHOUT SUPPORT	high-speed controlled search
Arising factors / Nature of flow	propensities (bag chags) discontinuous (so sor rtog pa)		impressions (saṃskāras) continuous (pariṇāma)	
Establishing the Category of Insight / Category of insight	Examination-Meditation (dpyad sgom) non-entityness (ngo bo nyid med)	Chapters 14–17 on the aggregate, etc. dependent origination	Chapter I. sameness (tulya) in change (pariṇāma)	
Underlying category in meditation on Flow	Samādhi-Meditation (jog sgom)	KNOWLEDGE OF BODY AND MIND	TRANSFORMATION INTO CESSATION (nirodhapariṇāma, 3:9)	
	Emptiness of Person — Emptiness of Phenomena	Nāma — Rūpa	Recognition of Means — Recognition of Matter	
Setting Up / Serial Exhaustive Search / Recognition of Flow	Putting-in-Order / Bringing Forth Insight / Rearrangement		nirodhapariṇāma (3:9) calm flow (prashāntavahita, 3:10)	
B. High-Speed Search of Gross Mental Contents	SKILL; REVERSE SAMĀDHI	OVERCOMING DOUBT (19:1-27) REVERSE ORDER	TRANSFORMATION INTO SAMĀDHI (samādhipariṇāma)	high-speed automatic search

TABLE 5

STAGE V. INSIGHT MEDITATION (cont.)

Search of Gross Events	whatever arises (gangshar)	CONDITIONALITY	multiplicity of things (*sarvārthata*, 3:11)	high-speed search of temporal interactions
Divided Attention	immediately arising arise, stay, cease (the unit) arise/pass away	PATH/NOT PATH (20:1–130) CLEAR COMPREHENSION (20:13→92)	TRANSFORMATION INTO ONE-POINTEDNESS (*ekagratāpari-nāma*, 3:12); "that rising up and ceased as similar"	
V.C. High-Speed Search of Temporal Interactions	YOGA OF UNSPREADING	ARISING/PASSING AWAY SAMĀDHI (20:93–104; 21:3–9)		
Category	arising/passing away of discontinuous flashes	arising/passing away of discontinuous flashes	sameness of change of one/many manifestations of continuous field	
Analysis	Nāgārjuna's dialectic	focus on passing away	change of dharma vs. unchanging substrate (*dharmin*) (3:14)	
Result: interconnectedness	Non-Dissolution (*ma'gag pa*)	Dissolution (21:10–28)	Unity (3:53–55); "Wisdom is That which pertains to the entire universe, everything outside of time"	
Branch Path	Ten Corruptions	Ten Corruptions	Psychic Powers	

TABLE 5

STAGE VI. EXTRAORDINARY MIND AND ENLIGHTENMENT

Underlying Structure	Mahāmudrā	Visuddhimagga	Yogasūtras	Psychology
VI.A. Relationship of Interconnected and Ordinary Time/Space Minds	YOGA OF ONE TASTE	KNOWLEDGE & VISION	ANALYSIS OF VASANAS	
Keeping the View Category Coupling	Pointing Out non-entityness SIMULTANEOUSNESS OF MIND (*zung 'jug*)	cessation MISERY (21:29–42)	sameness in change remove interval (*ānantarya*, 4:9) eternal desire (4:10)	
Non-Reactivity	self-occurring (*rang' byung*) dawning wisdom	DISPASSION (21:43–44)	possible non-existence of *vāsanās* (4:11)	
Chain of Karmic Activity across Levels of Mind		DESIRE FOR DELIVERANCE (21:45–46)	diverse mindstuff/same entity (*vastu*, 4:14–17)	
Recognition of Subtle Karmic Interactions	SIMULTANEOUSNESS OF COGNITION & PERCEPTION	REOBSERVATION (21:47–60)		
Resultant Spontaneous Interactions of Extraordinary Mind	KNOWLEDGE OF THE ORDINARY	EQUANIMITY (21:61–78)	Thatness of an Entity (4:14)	

TABLE 5

STAGE VI. EXTRAORDINARY MIND AND ENLIGHTENMENT (cont.)

VI.B. Relationship of Interconnected and Enlightened Minds	YOGA OF NON-MEDITATION	INSIGHT LEADING TO EMERGENCE (21:83–110)	relation of *prākṛti* & *puruṣa* (4:18–23)	
awareness turned on itself	RECOGNIZING WISDOM IN THE CONTINUUM	"	"	
establishing the primordial state of mental interactions	MEANS TO SET UP	CONFORMITY (21:128–136)	[mind] for the sake of Other (*parārtham*, 4:24)	
ENLIGHTENMENT	Basis	Change-of-Lineage (22:3–9)	Cessation (*vinivṛtti*, 4:25–26)	quantum shifts
	Path	Path	Other Recognitions (*pratyayātaraṇi*, 4:27)	
	Fruition (Three Buddha Bodies)	Fruition (Supreme-Silence, 22:15–18)	Raincloud Samādhi (*dharmameghasamādhi*, 4:29)	
VI.C. Relationship of Enlightened and Ordinary Minds	REVIEW	REVIEW (22:19)	review (4:33–38)	
		Second, Third & Fourth Enlightenment (22:22–30)		

TABLE 6

	THE STAGES OF MEDITATION	PERSPECTIVE Buddhism	Yoga
Attitude, Affect Behavior	I. PRELIMINARY ETHICAL PRACTICES A. Generation of Faith; Attitude Change B. Formal Study; Intrapsychic Transformation C. Sensory/Behavioral Regulation Uninterrupted Awareness Training	(photon-like)	mind-as-light (wave-like)
Thinking	II. PRELIMINARY MIND/BODY TRAINING A. Body Awareness Training B. Calming Breathing and Thinking C. Re-arrangement of the Stream of Consciousness	discontinuous momentariness	continuous transformation of same thing
Perception	III. CONCENTRATION WITH SUPPORT A.1. Concentration Training; Decategorizing A.2. Internalization; Rearrangement of Image B. Recognition of Various Patterns of all Sense Modalities from the Seed C. Stopping the Mind, i.e., Gross Perception	discontinuously emanating seed	continuously transforming seed
Self	IV. CONCENTRATION WITHOUT SUPPORT A. Tuning in Subtle Perception B. Recognizing the Subtle Flow C. Collapse of Ordinary Observer; Restructuring of Perspective	discontinuous immediate events Concomitant Perspective (Access)	continuous vibration of *tanmātras* Reflection of *puruṣa (buddhi)*

TABLE 6 (cont.)

	V. INSIGHT PRACTICE		
	A. High-Speed Search of Subtle Flow; Eradication of Self; Derealization	emptiness non-entityness (*ngo bo nyid med*)	cessation of sense-impressions
	B. High-Speed Search of Gross Mental Events; Shifts in Perceived Duration & Frequency of Events of Subtle Flow: Arising Only; Full Event in Slow Motion; Quick Flashing Psychic Powers; Raptures; White Light		sameness (*tulya*)
Time/Space	C. Analysis of Mind-Moments and Their Succession; The Problem of Perceived Time-Space	discrete flashes	transformation of one substratum (*dharmin*)
	Interconnectedness of all potential events	Non-dissolution Co-dependent Origination of All Realms and Times	Unity Unity of Manifest Cosmos (*prākṛti*)
	VI. ADVANCED INSIGHT		
	A. Equanimity of Interrelated Events; Interaction of Specific Events		
Cosmos	B. Stopping all Mental Activity/Reactivity Enlightenment Moments: Basis: Cessation of Mental Content; Vast Awareness Path: Return of Mental Content from Changed Locus of Awareness	Non-dissolution	All Interactions of Manifest Cosmos Raincloud Samādhi

CHAPTER 9

DEVELOPMENTAL STAGES IN EASTERN ORTHODOX CHRISTIANITY

John T. Chirban

In previous chapters, both Wilber and Brown have argued for the cross-cultural or quasi-universal nature of the deep structures of the stages of contemplation (although, in Wilber's opinion, different contemplative traditions reach different heights of that development). In this chapter, John Chirban examines the lives of some of the great saints of the Eastern Orthodox Church, a church that, within the Christian tradition, has particularly kept alive the contemplative path. "Although each saint described his own experience (often in his own unique way)," reports Chirban, "basic parallels emerge as one compares the stages of the saints with one another. This sameness confirms the catholicity of their experience. . . ." Chirban concludes that "five stages can be identified which are basically consistent amongst all ten saints and theologians." These stages are: 1) Image, 2) Metanoia (conversion), 3) Apatheia (purification or transformation), 4) Light (illumination), and 5) Theosis (union).

For comparison, we may note the similarities with Wilber's model. The stage of Image is the "natural state of the person," i.e., the state before contemplative development begins (the personal realm). Metanoia is a conscious decision to begin the life of contemplation; this is similar to the "preliminary practices" described by Wilber, Brown, Epstein, etc. Apatheia is the stage of "purification" and the beginning transcendence of exclusively worldly pursuits, i.e., the psychic stage of initial contemplative immersion. Light is the stage of illumination, i.e., the subtle realm of audible illumination and archetypal luminosity. Theosis is the stage of God-union, which, when described by the saints as "unknowing," "invisible," "darkness," "mystery," "glorious nothingness," clearly refers to the unmanifest or causal realm. Similar correlations can be drawn with Brown's model, providing added evidence for the "catholicity of contemplative development."

Christian
traditional
doctrine

The Christian doctrine concerning the nature of the human being has been based traditionally upon the interpretation of the expression κατ' εἰκόνα καί καθ' ὁμοίωσιν, wherein God is said to have created man in His image and according to His likeness.* Christian writers have been indebted to St. Basil for the distinction between the two

distinction
between
"image" and
"likeness"

words "image" and "likeness." The word "image" refers to the innate, natural quality of the person; the word "likeness," to that dimension of the person which yearns to become God-like. Therefore the human being is created with the potential to become God-like.

spiritual
growth from
"image" to
"likeness"

What is the *process* of spiritual growth from "image" to "likeness"? Although there exists no single, systematic discussion or prescriptive plan by the Church concerning development or stages in Eastern Orthodox spirituality, the concern for growth is basic and essential to the faith. This chapter, first, identifies the elements that inform one of the attitudes concerning growth and development in Eastern Orthodoxy and, second, identifies stages that emerge as consistent, whole and hierarchical experiences in the Tradition of Saints in Orthodoxy. Heretofore, there has not been an effort to parallel the stages of spiritual growth in individual lives and to identify discrete patterns that emerge from the individual experiences.

---

*It is virtually impossible, when dealing with many early Christian writings, to remove what would be identified today as sexist language without doing violence to the texts themselves, for the simple reason that many of these texts arose in cultures that were in fact sexist by modern standards. Neither the editors nor Dr. Chirban wish to support sexist (as opposed to gender) differentiation. Nevertheless, translating the above passage as "God created man/woman in His/Her Image and according to His/Her likeness" is virtually unintelligible. While we have attempted to remove the sexist language in many places, we have occasionally been forced to follow a literal translation of gender terms.—K.W.

PART I. GROWTH AND DEVELOPMENT

Anthropology

The meanings of the terms "image" and "likeness" influenced the thought of many Christian Fathers. They have served the purpose of expressing the basic Orthodox teaching that men and women were not initially created as perfect, but that they were endowed with all the gifts that were necessary for communion with their Creator (St. Basil, N.D., St. Gregory of Nyssa, N.D., Cyril of Jerusalem, N.D.).[1]

Therefore, the human being is endowed with *intrinsic gifts*. According to Irenaeus, "man was created as a child," νήπιον, who emerged from a state of *innocence*, destined and *empowered to grow* to maturity (Irenaeus, N.D.).

endowment with "intrinsic gifts"

In the writings of the Church Fathers, the term "image" includes the qualities of one's *rational faculties* (Clement of Alexandria, N.D., Origen, N.D., St. Athanasios, N.D., St. Basil, N.D., St. Gregory of Nyssa, N.D., St. John Chrysostom, N.D.). The Church Fathers have emphasized reason because they believed that by proper use of reason one is able to learn of his or her Creator and to enjoy communion with that Creator. By stressing the rational nature of the human being, the Fathers have tried to emphasize the faculty that gives humanity superiority over other creatures.

gift of rational faculties

Many Church Fathers relate the Image of God of the person to humanity's original state of sinlessness and innocence, as well as to the individual's capacity for *moral perfection*. This capacity was given to humans potentially (δυνάμει) and it was required of them to develop from the stage of innocence and childhood to mature holiness, and to approximate the Holiness of God in accordance with the divine commandment: "Εσεσθε οὖν ὑμεῖς τέλειοι ὡς ὁ Πατήρ ὑμῶν ἐν οὐρανοῖς τέλειος ἔστιν" (Matthew 5:48).

moral perfection

St. John of Damascus points out that, although having this gift, men and women are in need of the sustaining power of God's grace in order to be able to achieve any degree of similarity to the Holiness of God (John of Damascus, N.D.). In this way it is suggested that there is a natural *relational "dependency"* in human beings upon love shared with God and neighbor.

creativity

Further, the human person is presented by the Patristic sources as a *"creative being"* (δημιουργικόν ζῶον) (John Chrysostom, N.D., Theodoret of Cyrus, N.D., St. John of Damascus, N.D.). One is able to create civilizations and cultures and to realize the ideas that he or she conceives, reflecting the example of the First Creator: "And God said, 'Let us make man in our image, after our likeness; and let them have dominion over the fish of the sea, and over every creeping thing that creepeth upon earth'" (Genesis 1:26). Theodoret of Cyrus explains the manner in which a person differs from God in the exercise of this power *to create* (Theodoret of Cyrus, N.D.). He notes that God alone is able to create (ex nihilo) without effort and pain. But the human being is in need of pre-existing matter in order to build, and his or her creativity requires time and effort.

free will

One of the most important characteristics of the human person according to the Church Fathers is one's choice to act, or *free will* (αὐτεξούσιον). Inextricably related to God's unconditional love, the individual has the freedom to choose between good and evil. According to the way in which one exercises his or her free will he or she is able to know self and God (St. Basil, N.D. Cyril of Jerusalem, N.D., St. Gregory of Nyssa, N.D., St. John Chrysostom, N.D., St. John of Damascus).

ability to rise above impulses

Another important element of the Image, which sheds light upon the human being as a *spiritual* being, is the fact that one is able *to rise above his or her impulses* (Basil, N.D.) and to direct his or her spiritual powers toward realities other than those which are naturalistic (Tatian, N.D.). This human power to transcend the material being is called "innate" by the Fathers (Basil, N.D., Caesarios, N.D., Cyril of Alexandria, N.D.).

love

Also, we note that the image of God in men and women is discussed by the Church Fathers in terms of one's capacity *to love*, a capacity that St. Basil also feels is innate for humanity (Basil, N.D.). St. Gregory of Nyssa is emphatic concerning the importance of love as a quality of the image. He is of the opinion that if this love is lacking, then the whole character of the image is altered (Gregory of Nyssa, N.D.).

Theology and Life

The spirituality of Eastern Orthodoxy is characterized by a quality of sobriety and contemplation. This is not by chance but a direct result of how theology affects life, specifically, how the Eastern Orthodox search for likeness to God necessarily requires inner peacefulness and attentiveness to the "movement of the soul." In order for one to experience the meaning of "image" as it has been presented here, contemplation is essential. Through such contemplation, I would suggest, we may speak of Orthodoxy's "theology of silence." The fundamental purpose of "silence" is to provide a setting, an opportunity for the re-identification of one's person with his or her true, genuine, original identity—the image of God:

a "theology of silence"

> If you gaze upon yourself attentively, that will adequately lead you to the knowledge of God. If you reflect upon yourself, you will not have need of the structure of the universe to look for the Demiurge, but in yourself, as in a microcosm, you will clearly see the great wisdom of your Creator (Basil, pp. 213D–316A).

And St. Isaac the Syrian admonishes:

> Enter eagerly into the treasure-house that lies within you, and so you will see the treasure-house of heaven; for the two are the same, and there is but one single entry to them both. The ladder that leads to the Kingdom is hidden within you, and is found in your own soul. Dive into yourself and in your soul you will discover the rungs by which to ascend (Chariton, p. 164).

It is precisely this type of self-evaluation and internalizing that cultivates one's intrinsic faith and move toward "likeness." This is not to suggest that this quality of silence in Eastern Orthodox spirituality is characterized alone by a physical posture or that it is a spiritualist sect. The fact is

internalizing and cultivating intrinsic faith

quite the contrary. Although there is a tone of sobriety in Orthodox spiritual growth and development, the work in this process is quite rigorous and active.

In the New Testament there are numerous references to methods which clarify this silent spirit for cultivating one's "image": γρηγορεῖτε (Romans 7:5–25)(keep awake); ἀγρυπνεῖτε (Matthew 26:38–43, Mark 14:34–40)(keep sleepless); ἔγειρε (Mark 13: 33–37, Luke 21:24:36)(awake); Βλέπετε (Ephesians 5:14–15)(look). These directives took on even greater definition by the Desert Fathers, who expand upon the notion of active contemplation from their experiences. They advise προσοχή (attention); νήψις (wakefulness); αντίρρησις (opposition); ἔρευνα (observation); φύλαξις νοός (guarding of the mind); and νοερά ἡσυχία (mental quietness)(φιλοκαλία, 1893).[2]

understanding spiritual development through the lives of the saints

In summary, the nature of the human person in the Christian tradition emphasizes that there is a godliness in the human being—"the image"—and a potential for growth to self-perfection—"the likeness." Often, however, religious literature speaks of the goal, perfection, in a vacuum, in the sense that one is left with the impression that there are missing links or there is a lack of clarity concerning the process between the present and future (perfected) states. A better understanding of spiritual development is provided through focusing upon the lives of Orthodox saints' processes for change as well as their goal. The autobiographies of saints or their other writings reveal their human struggles and document the valuable processes for change that biographies often mistakenly omit. When the saints speak of themselves, one can easily relate to their humanity and thereby understand their growth in development. It is precisely their activity of being in touch with the self and engaging in movement towards a spiritual goal which makes them what they are.

St. Gregory of Nazianzos writes after the death of St. Basil:

> You ask how I am. . . . Well, I am very bad. Basil I have no longer; Caesarios I have no longer; the intellectual and the physical brothers are both dead. "My father and mother have left me," I can say with David. Physically I am ill, age is descending on my head. Cares are choking me; affairs oppress

me; there is no reliance on friends and the church is without shepherds. The good is vanishing; evil shows itself in all its nakedness. We are travelling in the dark; there is no light-house and Christ is asleep. What can one do? I know only one salvation from these troubles, and that is death. But even the world to come seems terrible to judge by the present world (Campenhausen, 1955, pp. 101–102).

In spite of this full-fledged depression, however, St. Gregory has not given up. For the goal of his life, *theosis*, glimmers ahead and he pursues his spiritual path. The dynamic between individual struggle and spiritual forces is a very essential point for understanding Eastern Christian development. The saints are not static and perfect, but they work to develop themselves and ultimately they grow.

Theosis, deification, or the acquisition of the Holy Spirit, constitutes the aim of the Orthodox Christian life. The life of Jesus Christ serves as the model for *theosis*. St. Athanasios says, like St. Irenaeus before him, "God became man so that man might become God." It is said that Christ inaugurates the Kingdom of God on earth which is yet to be fulfilled, fully realized. *Theosis*, however, is not an eschatological potentiality or mere promise but, rather, it is the intense ascent of one who struggles and who is graced to find the Kingdom *in this present life*. *Theosis* is a *par excellence* example of theological and spiritual doctrine that is demonstrated in the alert, arduous spiritual *askesis* (exercise) or development of the Christian as he or she yearns to achieve union with God.

the aim of Orthodox Christian life

the Kingdom "in this present life"

From the very earliest Christian times, Orthodox spirituality has been characterized by the *theosis* goal. One may observe that Western Christianity oftentimes treats "mysticism" as a subjective and emotional religious state. In the final analysis, this understanding evokes a feeling that mysticism is both unstable and undemonstrable. As Orthodoxy interprets mysticism, or the development to *theosis*, it is neither a static ideal nor an abstraction, nor an idealistic potentiality for the human being. Orthodox mysticism is an objective, historical reality achieved first and fully by Jesus Christ who redeemed humanity by His incarnation, death and resurrection. Likewise the Orthodox understanding of "mystical" participation in the Body of Christ does not suggest a symbolic or metaphysical meaning but an "invisible participation in Christ's nature" (Monk, 1968). The spiritual process towards *theosis* is demonstrated in the life-long struggle and life-style of numerous church saints, some of whom will be presented in this chapter. The saints' lives, therefore, serve as testimonies of the objective reality that they describe and that this author regards as Orthodox spiritual development.

saints' lives as testimony

Knowledge and Experience

Those who have defined knowledge and faith in the Orthodox tradition have done so on the basis of their lives. Although they express consensus in their doctrinal beliefs, their experiences in "knowing" and "faithing" (the activity that results from their beliefs), if you will, bear unique descriptions. The thrust of the Orthodox approach to knowing (since understanding God's essence is impossible) is not by way of concept or formula but through union which transcends human intellectual category and expression. By underscoring the necessity of life in a "holistic" (body, mind, soul) harmony with Christ's transfiguring Message, one sets upon an eternally continuous path of knowing. The path of knowing which is more fully participatory leads one to discover that there is always more to be comprehended (Turner, 1975).

"knowing" and "faithing"

In the fourteenth century, St. Gregory Palamas developed an *experiential* concept of knowledge, emphasizing that by being in communion with God one may enjoy a direct knowledge of God which is differentiated from a purely intellectual process. This knowledge is based upon the theology of the Image of God in the human person which emphasizes that one naturally possesses the property of transcending oneself and reaching the Divine (Meyendorff, 1975).[3]

In Patristic thought, the understanding of "knowledge" follows, in part, the tradition of Greek philosophy which emphasizes that knowledge is a spiritual activity of a fruit of inner illumination. Theology therefore denotes the *pure*

understanding "knowledge"

science of in-depth knowledge (ἐπιστήμη) as used in Greek philosophy. It is this usage of knowledge that points out that there is no dichotomy between reason and spiritual reality. (For example, St. Gregory of Nyssa, in spite of the "mystery" surrounding Trinitarian theology, without any hesitancy, states that the Trinitarian dogma is in accord with "the exact standard of rational knowledge.") And at the same time, Orthodox epistemology is diametrically opposed to both idealism and empiricism—because they suffer the limitations of locking one into the realms of ideas or matter, respectively. In the final analysis, Orthodox epistemology affirms that reason (in full operation) is the guide to truth according to the degree in which it maintains communion with the Holy Spirit (Stephanou, 1976). This approach to knowing explains why Orthodoxy cannot limit itself to scholarly research and writing alone, but *requires* the experience of faith in life, i.e., a place for solitude, prayer, quiet. *opposition to both idealism and empiricism*

St. Basil very clearly explains that one may have both *eo ipso* and *a priori* knowledge. He explained that this knowing is influenced by evil and good powers and a third (ἀπαθῆ or ἀδιάφορα)—where one discerns things within himself (which leads to confusion). He notes, however, that the purpose of the mind is apprehension of truth and that God is truth. Therefore, the Cappadocians emphasized the positive value of reason, stating that it may lead one to "true knowing." St. Gregory Palamas says that true reason leads one to follow the Commandments of God (understood to include not only form but content experience of prayer, fasting, sacraments, almsgiving and actions as results of knowing—all of which lead to the two love commandments) and to approach knowledge which is accessible to God (Krivoshine, 1955). *purpose of mind*

Natural knowing can be understood within a framework which strives to accentuate "true knowing." When it is seen as an end in itself, however, it is considered to be self-deluding and empty: *natural knowing and true knowing*

> . . . those who possess not only powers of sensation and intellection but have also attained spiritual and supernatural grace are not limited by being in their knowledge but know also spiritually about sense and intelligence, that God is Spirit.

For their entirety they become God and know God in God (Meyendorff, 1964, p. 127).

Therefore, natural knowing has always been valued in Orthodoxy but it has been considered to be only a partial and sometimes digressed approach to true knowing. Clearly, no denial of intellectual knowing is suggested. True knowledge includes both *intellectual* and *existential* dimensions: the former provides some insight and (if one is sensitive) leads towards the latter or towards salvation and communion with God. It is the spiritual dimension, however, that is considered to be the higher type of knowing.

The knowledge about which the Fathers speak is more than intellectual; it is moral, affective, experiential, ontological, and in agreement with connaturality. Intellectual knowledge alone is viewed as placing limitations upon the subject and object. So, even a superior degree of knowledge (as conceptual and intellectual) remains partial without the moral, affective and experiential. True understanding comes from the dynamics of all these dimensions.

two aspects of knowing

St. Basil delineates basically two aspects of knowing: 1) sensorial-intellectual knowledge, which is philosophical, and 2) extra-sensorial knowledge, which is ethical and experiential. He believes that the former leads to the latter—or to knowledge of faith (Basil, 1955, Letter 235).

Basil observes that intellectual knowledge is not able to pass beyond its bordered conditions. True knowing, therefore, surpasses the cognitive abilities of the mind. Hence, faith-knowing requires that one go through the second category of knowing, beyond intelligence. Basil explains that intellectual knowledge leads to knowledge by faith. Faith is not simply belief, as emotional and moral elements are present. It is that "whole experience" which is faithfulness (Basil, 1955, Letter 234).

knowledge through prayer

According to St. Gregory Palamas, knowledge comes through prayer. He states that there are those who know nothing about knowledge except through experimental sciences. Again, it would be inaccurate to infer that Palamas or other Orthodox writers, in general, ignore the values of natural science or scholarship,[4] but they insist that when one permits this more basic approach to knowledge to dominate his or her work, "neglecting the knowledge of true reason," then, according to St. Gregory, "They recognize nothing on account of the ignorance of their science."

St. Gregory further emphasizes that natural knowing will not help one apprehend God because "God knowing" cannot be described. It is, rather, knowing out of *participation* in God that gives one clarity in the True vision of the world.

"God knowing" and "participation" in God

In his treatise, "On the Three Degrees of Knowledge," St. Isaac the Syrian clarifies the point further:

1. The first form of knowledge is paralleled to the body. This knowledge gathers provisions in riches, vainglory, honors and elegant things, bodily comfort, means to guard the body . . . zeal for rational wisdom . . . and to be the originator in wisdom for crafts and learning. . . . Dependent upon human knowledge, this works in darkness.

2. The second form of knowledge turns toward meditation and psychic love. Although this knowledge is still of a bodily nature it is occupied with excellence of person. As an outward stage, it accomplishes its activity by deeds perceptible to the senses of the body.

three degrees of knowing

3. Called God-presence ($\vartheta\epsilon\omega\varrho\iota\alpha$), this stage is raised above the cares of the world. When knowledge elevates itself above earthly things . . . faith swallows knowledge, gives a new birth to it. It is now able to examine spiritual mysteries which are attained by simple and subtle intellect. This light is perceived by spiritual eyes (concealed by eyes of fleshly men) according to Christ's words: "I shall send you the Spirit, the Comforter, whom the world cannot receive and He will guide you in all truth" (John 16:13).

St. Isaac explains that the first stage of knowledge "cools the soul" and actually forbids the work of God; the second stage "warms the soul and leads to faith" and the third stage "brings rest and faith." One should note that this direction of knowledge does not aim at being dead to the world (actually it is quite the contrary) but it is being dead to the motivations of the "worldly" (Isaac, N.D.).

Finally, what becomes apparent is that the Eastern Orthodox attitude and approach to knowledge and experience are directly related to growth of the image of God of the person. St. Basil states that in the image "a particle" of God's grace orients one to God. For St. Basil, the image is the starting point in the journey to knowledge; thus, the mind is naturally directed to knowing God.

> The mind is a wonderful thing (καλόν μέν ὁ νοῦς) and therein we possess that which is after the image of the Creator (. . . καί ἐν τούτῳ ἔχωμεν τό κατ 'εἰκόνα τοῦ κτίσματος . . .) and the operation of the mind is wonderful; in that in its perceptual motion it is frequently carried to the truth (Basil, Letter 233).

PART II. STAGES

Although many individuals seek to grow in their faith, they are not always clear about how this is to occur, i.e., the process by which one achieves his or her goal. For Orthodox Christians, the process is not so opaque since the saints of the Church "light the way."

the saints and stages of growth   In Orthodox Christian literature, one notes that distinctions are made by saints which reflect their sensitivities to the different needs one may have as he or she develops in faith. The saints may even differentiate between "stages of growth" from their own experiences. St. Paul, for example, distinguishes that some are (spiritually) to be fed milk and others meat. In this way, St. Paul is attentive to individual abilities or capacities. St. Maximos the Confessor writes about three levels in development: 1) εἶναι (being), 2) εὐ εἶναι (well-being), and 3) ἀεί εἶναι (eternal being). In this way, St. Maximos is attentive to actual stages in spiritual development (Lossky, 1963).[5]

Although one frequently comes across references to spiritual "development" in Church literature, no statement or systematic explanation is to be found regarding *the process* of spiritual development in the Orthodox Christian Church. In attempting to answer the question, "What is the model for Orthodox Christian development?," it seems that we could learn the answer through approaching the

question and the search for an answer with an appreciation of "true knowledge" (as it has been discussed in this
chapter), i.e., with an appreciation of both the intellectual
and existential dimensions of growth in the lives of saints.

After reading the lives of Church saints, it was found that
no single pattern outlines *the* path in the spiritual development of all, but, rather, that there is a similar foundation   *similar*
in the experiences of the saints which emphasizes that one   *foundation in*
is: 1) to be grounded in "the right faith," the Holy Scrip-   *experiences of*
tures, Holy Tradition, all of which St. Irenaeus includes as   *the saints*
"the arsenal of faith," and 2) to encounter first-hand experience of the Holy.

In reading the lives of ten saints and two Early Church
theologians with particular attention to their spiritual
growth patterns, we find that although each saint or theologian uses different language to discuss his spiritual development, they do, nevertheless, witness or encounter
similar experiences or stages of growth. The "different language" for the saints and theologians may be accounted
for by the fact that their discussion of growth is a product
of *personal* experiences, rather than of formula, in development. What is particularly interesting, however, is that
although each saint describes his own experience (often in
his unique way), basic parallels emerge as one compares
the stages of the saints with one another. This sameness
confirms the catholicity of their experience, affirming their
"right faith." It appears that five stages can be identified
which are basically consistent among the ten saints and
two theologians.[6]

On the basis of this study of the spiritual development of   *five stages in*
these twelve Church leaders, I have defined the five stages   *Orthodox*
in Orthodox spiritual development as: 1) Image, 2) *Meta-*   *spiritual*
noia (conversion), 3) *Apatheia* (participation or transforma- *development*
tion), 4) Light (illumination) and 5) *Theosis* (union).

Stage One: Image

"Image" refers to the natural state of the person—what
has already been discussed in this chapter as the "nature

image of man," that is, the potential of the individual to develop (to love, to reason, to create). By beginning the model of development in this way, all human beings are, by birth, in the process of spiritual growth.

Stage Two: Metanoia (Conversion)

conversion *Metanoia* is a stage of conversion where the individual makes a conscious commitment, a choice, to direct his or her life "in Christ."

Stage Three: Apatheia (Purification or Transformation)

purification *Apatheia* (purification or transformation) occurs when one is loosened from worldly passions and is free in his or her spirit from things which distract the individual from his or her goal. The saints say that in this stage one is "purified." Often this term is translated as "passionlessness" which connotes that the person at this level is without emotion. This is an inaccurate rendering of the meaning of the term, as the stage of *apatheia* does not exclude emotion but reflects the stage at which one's emotions are consonant with one's goals.

Stage Four: Light (Illumination)

illumination Light is the stage of illumination, an experience of God's Light. The Church Fathers use the image of fire and iron to describe how a person as a product of creation (iron) is illumined as he or she approaches the Light of God (fire).

Theosis (Union)

union *Theosis* (union) is not an end state but a goal into which one enters, as St. Gregory of Nyssa says, "from glory to glory." It is a state of being "in communion, participation" with the Holy Spirit in life. Fig. 12 illustrates the findings of this inquiry concerning the stages of spiritual development with a five-stage model. Brief summaries of development in the saints' and theologians' lives are given in the following section.

PART III: EXAMPLES

The following excerpts of saints and theologians focus upon the stages in spiritual development as they discuss them. It may be helpful to compare the content of these sections with the schematic drawings of spiritual development in Figure 12.[7]

Origen and Evagrios and the intellectual cataphatic approaches

Both Origen and Evagrios are presented for background rather than as examples of Eastern Orthodox Fathers. They typify the intellectual, cataphatic approaches.

Origen: Systematized Spirituality

The theme of prayer recurs continuously in the Fathers; the priority of prayer, time and again, for the Fathers indicates that these learned men were first pastors. Although he is not considered a Father, a discussion of spiritual development would be incomplete without noting the contributions of Origen—"A mystical writer in the highest sense of the word" (Cayre, 1969). Origen outlined the contemplative life by "observing" that Christians are divided into camps, types of life: the active and the contemplative. The former, he said, "stand in the outer courtyard of the temple" (like Martha), while the latter "enter into the house of God" (like Mary). He explains that Christians must climb to three levels: πραϰτιϰή, struggle for *apatheia* and love; φυσιϰή θεωρία, knowledge of the mysteries of God; and θεολογία, the knowledge of the mysteries of creation. Origen emphasizes that perfection consists in being assimilated to God, noting St. Paul, who says if the human mind is made "one mind with God" it is because in the totality of consciousness the mind comprehends God. Contemplation, according to these steps, enables one to be deified. In his twenty-seventh homily on Numbers, Origen explains that the Israelite "stations" in the desert are stages on the road to the vision of God. Calling the journey "the exodus of the soul," Origen artic-

Origen's outline of the contemplative life

FIGURE 12
SCHEMATIC DRAWING OF SPIRITUAL DEVELOPMENT

APOPHATIC APPROACHES

STAGES	St. Isaac the Syrian	St. Seraphim of Sarov	St. Gregory Palamas	St. John Climacos	St. Maximos	St. Dionysios
V THEOSIS	(3) Perfection	Acquisition of the Holy Spirit	(3) Theosis	Step 30 Likening	(3) Ἀεὶ Εἶναι Eternal Being	(3) Unification Prayer of Union
		Kingdom Righteousness Peace		29		(Prayer of Quiet)
IV LIGHT		Illumination	(2) Divine Light Pure Hesychasm	Steps { 28, 27 Hesychasm		(2) Illumination
						(Prayer of Recollection)
III APATHEIA	(2) Purification					(1) Purification
				Spiritual Development		(Prayer of Mind)
II METANOIA	(1) Repentance		(1) Prayer Labor	(1) Steps 1–26	(2) Εὖ Εἶναι (Well-Being)	
		Prayer Fasting Almsgiving				(Prayer of Simplicity)
I IMAGE					(1) Εἶναι (being)	

APOPHATIC APPROACHES   CATAPHATIC APPROACHES

	St. Gregory of Nyssa	St. Basil	St. Macarios	Evagrios	Origen
V	(3) Knowledge of God	(3) θέωσις	Ἀποκάλυψις		Ὁμοίωσις
IV	(2) Cloud (Darkness)	Luminous			(3) Πνευματικός Γάμος Θεολογία
	(Light)	(Illumination)	φωτισμός	(3) Προσευχή	(2) Φυσική θεωρία
III	Ἀπάθεια Παρρησία (God Confidence)	(2) Καθαρότης Καρδίας		(2) θεωρία (Γνῶσις)	Πρακτικός
				(1) Πρᾶξις (Πνευματική)	
II	Ἐπίκτασις (Tension)	(1) Σοφία	(Baptism)		
	(Darkness of Sin)	(Intellectual Knowledge)			
		(Journey of Knowledge)	Γλυκήτις		
I	(Image of God)	(Image of God)			(Εἰκών) INTELLECTUAL STATES

ulates the growth in terms of progressive disattachment from corporeal things.

Lossky explains Origen's notion about spiritual growth in this way:

Origen's notions about spiritual growth

> The Word comforts the soul by visions or visitations which undoubtedly correspond to the perception of the divine by the spiritual senses—the first contacts of the soul with God. But at more elevated levels the visions cease, making room for gnosis, for illumination of the purely intellectual order which tends to become and is already a contemplation—θεωρία. However, the intellectual elements in gnosis appear only at first; they are obliterated more and more, to the extent that the soul is united with Christ and the spiritual marriage (πνευματικός γάμος) with the Logos is accomplished (Lossky, 1963, pp. 48–52).

Origen comments that in the Logos the soul is an image (εἰκών), and that by vision of God it recovers likeness (ὁμοίωσις), being deified.

Evagrios—Pure Prayer

"intellectual" or perpetual prayer

Although in the company of the Great Cappadocian Fathers, Evagrios of Ponticos tried to realize the ideal of contemplation outlined through the intellectual system of Origen. Evagrios' stages follow Origen's pattern; however, he tried to adopt the life of the Egyptian desert anchorites in his system of spiritual ascent. Evagrios distinguishes between πρᾶξις or πρακτική μέθοδος and θεωρία or γνῶσις; the former being a fight against the passions and essentially a prerequisite to entering the latter, "intellectual" or perpetual prayer; the latter is the crown of ascetic practice—St. Paul's "pray without ceasing" (I Thes. 5:17). Προσευχή, true prayer, is Evagrios' comparison to Origen's last stage, θεολογία. Only after passing *apatheia* (which he analyzes as overcoming gluttony, lewdness, avarice, sadness, anger, vainglory, pride, etc.) can one enter this "supreme love" which carries one off to the "summit of intellect." Here, the light of the "Trinity shines in the spirit of purified man." This state of "intellect" is the summit through which prayer is compared to vision, being more divine than all virtues (Meyendorff, 1969).

Evagrios' doctrine of θεωρία is used in the spirituality of St. Gregory of Nyssa (who will be presented shortly). Evagrios understands the vision of the light of God in the deified νοῦς as the summit, "the end which admits no transcendence." Evagrios vigorously rejects all visible theophanies. He claims that this doctrine belongs to the stoics, who imagined that God, having no physical nature, assumes appearance according to His Will in order to appear to men. He considers this demonic illusion (Lossky, 1963).

vision of the light of God as summit

St. Macarios: Mysticism of the Heart

St. Macarios represents a major shift between Eastern Orthodox spirituality and the intellectual systems of mysticism from such thinkers as Origen and Evagrios. "Experience" is the proof of truth rather than formulae. St. Macarios says, "ἐγεύσαμεν καί πείραν ἔσχυμεν . . . ," "We have tasted of God, we have experienced Him." St. Macarios emphasizes that one develops spiritually through all the senses rather than the "limited intellect." He does not see life as activity proper to the intellect but as actively generated towards a deeper fulfillment of Baptism by way of the Holy Spirit (*ibid.*). So, as Christ was clothed in human flesh, our response is to be clothed in the Holy Spirit: being "kindled by the Holy Spirit . . . making them burn like candles before the Son of God. This divine fire flows the fluctuations in the human will; now it is shining brilliantly as it embraces the entire being; now it diminishes and no longer sheds its radiance in hearts that are darkened by passions . . ." (Meyendorff, 1974, pp. 26–29). For St. Macarios the unceasing prayer of the monk does not yearn to free the spirit from the flesh but, rather, allows man to enter the eschatological reality of the Kingdom of God. So, he emphasizes, "The whole man, body and soul, was created in the image of God and the whole man is called to divine glory." He explains: "Christians live in a different world: they have a table that belongs to them alone, a delight, a communion, a way of thinking uniquely theirs." And elsewhere, "The sons of light, ministers of the New Covenant in the Holy Spirit, have nothing to learn from men; they are taught by God. Grace itself en-

major shift to the heart

graves the laws of the spirit on their hearts . . . for it is in the heart that intelligence dwells. . . ." St. Macarios explains that God is the food and drink, the sweetness (γλυκήτις) of grace we taste within. He says, "He who enjoys illumination (φωτισμός) is greater than he who only tastes, for he has within himself the assurance of vision (τίνα ὁράσεων)." But beyond even this, he explains, is revelation (ἀποκάλυψις); here the mysteries of distinction are revealed to the soul (Lossky, 1963).

St. Basil the Great: Journey of Knowledge

St. Basil discusses a person's spiritual development as a "spiritual journey" from the image of God which is in all persons to the "Archetype." It is a journey which enables one to "know" God. St. Basil explains that as individuals "advance" in knowledge they realize their own weaknesses; such is the case with Abraham and Moses: "When they had seen God as much as it is possible for a man to see Him, each humiliated himself; the former called himself 'clay and dust,' the latter described himself as 'being of few words and stammering.'" About the state of knowledge in this journey, St. Basil says:

"spiritual journey" to "true knowledge"

> The word wise (σοφός) applies equally to whoever desires wisdom, and to whoever already finds himself in progress in the contemplation of wisdom, and to whoever is already perfected (ὁ τετελειωμένος) in this contemplation by habituation (ἕξις). Now, all of them, the lover (ἐραστής) of wisdom, or the one who has already advanced in wisdom, will become wiser always progressing in the knowledge of "divine dogmas" (Θείων δογμάτων) *(ibid.)*.

St. Basil notes that the knowledge of God through observing the Commandments of God, for example, is "intellectual" knowledge in the restricted sense, which is to know God "half-way" (εξ ἡμισείας). He insists, "knowing" God occurs by participation in "the true life . . . returning to the original good." In this participation God offers "intimacy," a result of our "affective" and "moral" knowledge of God. Further, St. Basil elaborates that advancement in the journey comes by "casting off the old man who goes corrupting himself in the thread of delusive desire and clothing (oneself) in the new man who plods toward true knowledge." The continuous renewal and progress that are recommended presuppose purification and ascesis, spiritual training. St. Basil notes, "The words of God are not written for all but for those who have ears according to the interior man." This is developed by preparation through two steps: first, "destruction of sophisms and all haughty power (ὕψωμα) which rise up against the knowledge of God (κατά τῆς γνώσεως)," and, second, "making all thought captive to lead it to obey Christ." Later he presents "elements" which comprise the "advancement." In terms of the negative step, one must leave "the anxiety of life" (τήν βιωτικήν) and slavery to the senses and to the passions (πάθη) of the body.

two-step preparation for spiritual training

In the positive step, one must be concerned with "purification of the heart" (καθαρότης καρδίας) so that the Spirit is permitted to illumine. St. Basil's Trinitarian formulations are thereby possible. "The indwelling (ἐνοίκησις) of the Spirit entails that the Son (παρενοικήσαντες . . . δια . . . 'τόν Χριστόν) leads us to the Father (ἐπάνοδος εἰς οἰκείωσιν Θεοῦ)." In the last analysis, St. Basil explains the last stage is the "journey from the conscience to God." This, he says, comes to those who are worthy (according to the outlined preparation) of God. Finally, it is noted that one does not meritoriously achieve but "the Lord grants it by Himself to those who have believed in Him" (Aghiorgoussis, 1964).

"journey from conscience to God"

St. Gregory of Nyssa: Developing from Glory to Glory

St. Gregory points out three levels of spiritual development. These, however, advance beyond Origen's understanding. What is the apex of most spiritual systems, the way of light, is only the beginning for St. Gregory. He says, "Moses' vision of God began with light; afterwards God spoke to him in a cloud. But when Moses rose higher and became more perfect, he saw God in the darkness" (Gregory of Nyssa, 1969). This "darkness" is not anything like the "darkness of sin," for, quite obviously, "the darkness of sin" precedes the first stage, where one struggles against the passions. Now at one level of *apatheia*, St. Greg-

three levels of spiritual development

ory explains, the parrhesia (παρρησία), or a child-like confidence in God, develops which comes when "fear and shame" are banished. Then the second stage, which St. Gregory compares to a cloud, comes in view. St. Gregory raises the rhetorical question and then responds,

unknowability
of God

> What is the significance of Moses into the cloud and his vision of God? . . . Leaving behind all appearances . . . it turns always more to the interior world, until by the effort of mind it penetrates even to the Invisible and the Unknowable and then it sees God. For in fact true knowledge and true vision of the One it seeks consists in seeing that He is invisible, wrapped all around by His Unknowability as by a cloud (Meyendorff, 1974, pp. 42–43).

It is the knowledge of God "within the mirror of the soul," which overshadows all appearances and slowly guides "the soul to look towards what is hidden." This rather obscure-sounding stage is the "awareness of grace," an experience of God's presence.

The more the soul discovers that God infinitely transcends all that it can know of Him, the nearer it comes to the third stage—knowledge of God in what St. Gregory explains in his life of Moses:

true vision and
true knowledge
seen as
contained in
"not seeing"

> . . . as the soul makes progress, and by a greater and more perfect concentration comes to appreciate what knowledge of truth is, the more it approaches this vision, and so much the more does it see that the divine nature is invisible. It thus leaves all surface appearances, not only those that can be grasped by the senses but also those which the mind itself seems to see, and it keeps on going deeper until by the operation of the spirit, it penetrates the invisible and incomprehensible, and it is there that it sees God. The true vision and the true knowledge of what we seek consists precisely in not seeing . . . thus that profound evangelist John, who penetrated into the luminous darkness, tells us that no man hath seen God at any time, teaching us by this rejection that no man—indeed, no created intellect—can attain a knowledge of God (Gregory of Nyssa, 1969, p. 29).

The darkness is not negative but a "luminous darkness"; as our awareness of God always falls short, it is still enticed to a more and more perfect knowledge, that knowledge always being mixed with ignorance. St. Gregory, thus, emphasized a doctrine of continuous progress, perpetual growth, what he called ἐπέκτασις (tension, expansion). This word captures the double aspect of the soul's progress: ἐπί, at, towards, in the sense being at participation, divinization; at the same time God is constantly beyond, ἐκ, out of, as one must continuously move out to go beyond the stage one has reached. In the last analysis, St. Gregory explains that all the stages are good, and for the one who participates in the growth each stage is always being obscured by the new "glory" that constantly exists beyond (Boyer, 1961).

Dionysios the Areopagite: Apophatism and the Ladder of Prayer

Dionysios, in turn, distinguishes three levels of spiritual development: first, a purification stage; second, an illumination stage; third, a unification stage. Dionysios, like St. Gregory of Nyssa, speaks of mystical theology through divine darkness. He uses "apophatic" (negative) theology. With ἀγνωσία (unknowing, darkness), the realization that no finite knowledge of God can reveal Him, one may know Him better. Dionysios explains that as excess of light yields darkness invisible, likewise excess of knowledge destroys ignorance, which leads to God. Dionysios delineates five ascending stages of degrees in prayer and contemplation that constitute a ladder which leads the aspiring soul from finitude into infinitude: 1) The prayer of simplicity (vocal); 2) The prayer of mind (voiceless); 3) The prayer of recollection (the perfume or answer prayer); 4) The prayer of quiet (beyond thoughts); 5) The prayer of union, degrees of rapture, ecstasy, "glorious nothingness" (Dionysios, 1965).

three levels of spiritual development

five ascending stages and "glorious nothingness"

St. Maximos: Wills of Man and God

St. Maximos the Confessor discusses deification by offering a striking application of Christological dogma to spiritual life. This he does by identifying human will with divine will. He explains that our experiences of Christ's 1) incarnation, 2) death, and 3) resurrection "contain the meaning of all the symbols and enigmas of scripture, as well as the meaning concealed in the whole of sensible and intelligible creation." By employing the tripartite schema, again, Maximos discusses three successive levels of perfec-

three levels of
perfection with
"darkness" in
the last stage

tion: εἶναι, attainment of being, through the Incarnation; εὖ εἶναι, attainment of well-being, through conforming to divine will leading to the Cross; ἀεί εἶναι, attainment of eternal being, through the Resurrection. In this system St. Maximos recreates the Evagrian program with the Dionysian "darkness" in the last stage. Rather than seeing intellectual participation in terms of perfection as focal (Evagrios), Maximos emphasizes "total participation" in Jesus Christ:

> The admirable Paul denied his own existence and did not know whether he possessed a life of his own: "I live no more, for Christ lives in me . . ." (Gal. 2:20). . . . [Man], the image of God, becomes God by deification; he rejoices to the full in abandoning all that is his nature . . . because the grace of the Spirit triumphs in Him and because manifestly God alone is acting in him. . . .(Meyendorff, 1974, pp. 44–45).

Importantly, St. Maximos observes that ἀγάπη, love, is the instrument of growth:

love as the
instrument of
growth

> . . . . knowledge of God is not the goal of charity in the sense that would make charity purely a means to an end. We would speak more accurately if we said that knowledge is the effect, the sign of the union which God brought about by love, but an effect which reacts in turn from the cause, intensifying the love. (Lossky, 1963, pp. 105–109).

St. Isaac the Syrian: Spirituality of Balance

fusion of
intellectual and
experiential
approaches to
spirituality

As a product of a tradition which placed value on the intellectual approach to spirituality, reflected in works by Origen and Evagrios, and an approach which was highly experiential, as reflected in works by St. Maximos the Confessor and St. Dionysios the Areopagite, St. Isaac's spiritual development is a fusion of both of these streams of spirituality. His writings are written by a "solitary" to "solitaries"—focusing on the person of Jesus Christ. The process of growth unfolds through one's continuous experience of *metanoia,* a radical "change of behavior" and attitude. He recommends that this awareness of change must be kept alive "at every moment of the twenty-four hours of the day." It is a continuous awareness of God's presence, "remembrance of God."

In the process of this *metanoia*, St. Isaac emphasizes that one must be totally trusting in God and know that there are "no fortuitous events," nothing occurs by mere chance—but as an opportunity for growth. The posture for one's spiritual growth necessitates that one "approach God with a childlike mind." In this spiritual experience, St. Isaac discusses a state of ecstasy or "spiritual drunkenness." The spiritual journey, St. Isaac notes, however, is one which most do not follow. He points out that "only one in 10,000 is found worthy of" it (Brock, 1975). St. Isaac's spirituality breathes a personal spirit. And through the personal, mystical, spiritual ascent he notes that one moves from 1) repentance to 2) purification to 3) perfection (Wensink, 1969).

three-stage spiritual ascent

St. John Climacos: Steps to Paradise

St. John Climacos prepared one of the most remarkable manuals of spiritual attainment, entitled *The Ladder of Divine Ascent*. St. John describes the way of spiritual attainment through thirty steps. Each step addresses spiritual virtues or sins, and as illustrated in the icon of the ladder, angels or demons work upon the faithful to assist them or thwart them, respectively. The ladder, having thirty rungs whose base is fixed on earth and whose top reaches heaven, indicates (when illustrated) the first steps at an angle (enabling one to climb more easily) and the later steps going up vertically (indicating the greater difficulty involved in attaining the higher spiritual levels). The thirty steps must be mastered if spiritual progress is to be attained. In general, the steps are not ordered or developmental but are often thematic, e.g., steps 17–30 address virtues of positive achievement, i.e., solitude, prayer, love.

the thirty-step ladder to spiritual attainment

The choice of the word "ladder" in the title (probably inspired by the vision of Jacob's Ladder) symbolizes the author's conception of the whole purpose and progress of spiritual life. Therefore, it does not offer a systematic pro-

dynamic, holistic process

gram for growth, i.e., it does not purport that Step 14 necessarily *precedes* Step 20. The process is dynamic and holistic. St. John approaches each step analytically, using anecdotes by way of illustration, e.g., step one Obedience—one of the longest on the ladder. The method presupposes and insists on direction by a spiritual father. In summary of his work, the author writes:

> . . . Let us hasten until we attain to the unity of faith and of the knowledge of God, to mature manhood, to the measure of the stature of the fullness of Christ, who, when he was baptized in the thirtieth year of his visible age (note the correlation in St. John's ladder), attained the thirtieth step in the spiritual ladder (concerning the linking together of the supreme trinity among the virtues); since God is indeed love, to whom be praise, dominion, power in whom is and was and will be the cause of all goodness throughout infinite ages. Amen (John Climacos, 1959, p. 226).

St. Symeon the New Theologian:
Spiritual Experience and Realism

intense realism

More so than any of the "guides" of Orthodox spiritual development cited, St. Symeon emphasizes the freshness and authority of experience of the divine, and the importance of the intense realism in Christocentric mysticism. St. Symeon prayerfully writes:

> . . . by Your Grace, I was granted to contemplate a still more awesome mystery. I saw You take me with Yourself, and rise to heaven; I know not whether I was still in my body or not— You alone know, You who alone created me. . . . For the first time You allowed me, a vile sinner, to hear the sweetness of Your voice. You spoke so tenderly that I tumbled and was amazed, wondering how and why I had been granted Your gifts. You said to me: "I am the God who became man for love of you. You have desired me and sought me with your whole soul, therefore, henceforth you shall by my brother, my friend, the co-heir of my glory . . ." (Meyendorff, 1974, pp. 49–51).

Understandably, St. Symeon's approach and emphasis for genuine form created ecclesiastical provocation and raised the conflict of prophet vs. priest and experience vs. insti-

tution. Although he opposed any suggestion of mechani- *conflicts of*
zation in worship, prayer or sacraments, these methods *prophet vs.*
were an integral part of his "spiritual universe." (Because *priest and*
St. Symeon does not offer a developmental approach he is *experience vs.*
not presented on the schematic drawing). *institution*

St. Gregory Palamas: Experience of Theoptia

Often associated with hesychasm,[8] St. Gregory Palamas
was actually the inheritor of the rich spiritual tradition and
hesychasm, which actually has its roots in the Early Desert
Fathers. St. Gregory, however, defended hesychasm as a
viable method for attaining the vision of God, Θεοπτία,
thereby *theosis.* Questions had been posed by hesychasts,
accusing them of an illogical system of prayer. Barlaam the
Calabrian condemned them on two points, particularly: 1)
the Aristotelian postulate that all knowledge, including
knowledge of God, is derived through perception of experience; 2) a Neoplatonic postulate that explains God as
being beyond sense experience and therefore as unknowable. St. Palamas responded by saying, "God is indeed
unknowable but does he not reveal himself?"

For one to attain contemplation he or she must pass *intellectual*
through the negative stage of intellectual perfection. He *perfection*
writes:

> Illumination appears to be pure intelligence to the extent that
> it is liberated from all concepts and becomes formless. . . . All
> visions having a form to the intelligence, that is to say to the
> act on the passionate part which is the imagination . . . come
> from a ruse of the enemy (Meyendorff, 1964, p. 141).

Then, St. Gregory explains, by "monological prayer" (προσευχή μονολόγιστος ἀδιάλειπτος) one enters the positive
realm of spirituality. This is St. Paul's "pray[er] without
ceasing." He says, "We supplicate with this continuous
supplication, not to convince God . . . but to lift ourselves
to him." This prayer cannot be mechanical but is conscious
and active. Palamas explains that fulfillment in spiritual
life comes through progression inwards (συνεξέλιξις). The
neophyte hesychast perceives this stage by specific tech-

the unceasing
Jesus Prayer

niques but the mature hesychast realizes this through his strong will and the unceasing Jesus Prayer.* The total individual (body, mind and soul) participates and experiences the eternal warmth, the fire which Elias mentions as he sees God, a part of the experience of the Divine Light. Hesychasm places great emphasis on the immediate vision of God, but this is not to be confused with pantheism. St. Gregory says, "We partake of the divine nature, and yet at the same time we do not partake of it at all." St. Palamas argues that the existence of God cannot be proved, by answering that the proof of God's existence (the genuineness of the vision of God) is founded upon other than Aristotelian logic. Gregory maintains that the spiritual purposes of the ascetic are fulfilled through συνεξέλιξις of the mind,

turning within
and
experiencing
"uncreated
light"

that is, through the continuous self-concentration and looking or turning within (ἐσωτρεφόμενον). In reaching this state one encounters the Divine Light, achieving mystical union with God (Christou, 1966). He clarifies that the difference between the vision of light the Apostles witnessed on Mount Tabor and that of the hesychasts is that Peter, James and John saw the light "exteriorly," while Christians contemplate the light "interiorly." But, further, the hesychasts can develop potentialities with God's grace to the point that they find God, thereby experiencing "uncreated" light.

Knowledge, according to St. Gregory, comes through

knowledge
through prayer

prayer. He states there are those who know nothing else about knowledge except through the experimental sciences. He sees those persons as adoring and protecting the Hellenistic studies and neglecting the Gospel. In the end, he points out, they recognize nothing on account of the ignorance of their sciences:

> If we ask how the mind is attached to the body, where is the seat of imagination and opinion, where is memory fixed, what part of the body is most vulnerable and so to say directs the others, what is the origin of the blood . . . it is the same . . . with all questions of this sort about which the spirit has given us no plain Revelation; for the spirit only teaches us to know the truth which penetrates everything (Meyendorff, 1964).

*"Lord Jesus Christ, Son of God, have mercy upon me, a sinner."

St. Seraphim of Sarov: Acquisition of the Holy Spirit

Just a century ago, the ascetic St. Seraphim of Sarov responded to the question of the "purpose of Christian life," in his famous "Conversation Concerning the Aim of Christian Life." Although, at first, his response of "acquiring the Holy Spirit" may sound vague and nebulous, a closer examination of his response and its background and implications adequately captures the plethora of teaching about Orthodox spiritual growth. He explains that while such means, "prayer, fasting, watching, almsgiving, and all Christian acts," are not the ends, they are the only means of acquiring the "Spirit of God." St. Seraphim notes that "prayer is always possible for everyone" but that the "method" which must be grounded is a "right faith in our Lord": "Thus, if prayer and watching give you more of God's grace, pray and watch; if fasting gives much of God's Spirit, fast; if almsgiving gives more, give alms. . . ."

Here, he expresses the doctrine of unity and diversity: Christians, though unified in the same truth, diversify as they express it. In response to the questions, "Is the Holy Spirit then to be seen? How am I going to know whether He is with me or not?" Seraphim answers that there is nothing incomprehensible about true visual encounters with God. He explains, "This fortune to understand comes about when we have wandered from the spacious vision of the early Christians. Under the pretext of education we have reached such a darkness of ignorance that now to us seems inconceivable what the ancients saw clearly." He continues by explaining that because of our inattentiveness to the work of salvation "we do not seek the grace of God, because in the pride of our minds we do not allow it to enter our souls . . . we have no true enlightenment. . . ." Seraphim's life was a testimony of his words rather the inverse. It is out of experience that he concludes, "For the Kingdom of God is the human heart . . . the Kingdom of God is not meat and drink, but righteousness and peace in the Holy Spirit. Our faith consists not in persuasive words of human wisdom, but in the demonstration of the Spirit and of power" (Seraphim, 1973).

the doctrine of unity and diversity

the human heart as the Kingdom of God

CONCLUSION

This presentation seeks to clarify the notion of, and approach to, growth in Eastern Orthodoxy. What is learned from this study is that although the spiritual journeys of the saints are very personal and experientially based, they nonetheless reveal discrete patterns of development. Somewhat paradoxically, although the stages of growth may be discussed *rationally*, they are necessarily encountered *experientially*. Balancing the rational and experiential aspects of life is necessary for those who seek to respond to the needs of the whole person. Attention to the lives of those who described the experiences of growth may illumine us as we seek effectively to attain the important goal to be whole.

NOTES

CHAPTER 1

[1] All the meditative and yogic traditions are extremely sophisticated in differentiating genuine extinction of the causes of suffering from its counterfeit forms, suppression and repression, and designate each psychic process by a different technical term. They recognize that functioning can be experienced *subjectively* as conflict-free in states of intense concentration, for instance, though the latent sources of conflict will become reactivated when concentration falls below a specified level.

[2] In Theravadin Buddhist psychology (Abhidhamma), intrapsychic changes have been catalogued with great care in traditional lists of reported outcomes following the different stages of enlightenment. These changes are classified differently in different lists, but the lists are remarkably specific and internally consistent. They have also remained stable and uniform over the long course of Abhidhamma development. They can be consulted in Narada (1975) and Nyanamoli (1976).

[3] This issue has been obscured by the structuralist language of object relations theory and traditional psychoanalytic metapsychology with its tendency to reify functions and treat self and object representations as fixed, discrete entities with powers of their own (Schafer, 1976). Representations are actually memorial *processes* of representing which only occur in the present (Rizzuto, 1978).

[4] The only differences were a slight decrease in productivity across subjects and a noticeable increase in drive-dominated responses for some subjects.

[5] The remaining half achieved some proficiency in concentration but only three mastered "access level" concentration *(upacāra-samādhi)* and progressed through some of the formal stages of insight. Only one of these advanced to the stage of Equanimity *(Saṅkhārupekkha-ñāṇa),* the stage prior to enlightenment (Nyanamoli, 1976; M. Sayadaw, 1973).

[6] There are four distinct stages of enlightenment in insight meditation practice. Each is entered on through a momentary cessation experience *(magga-phala)* as the culmination of a preceding series of discrete and

invariant stages of practice. In each of these four moments, specific sets of pathogenic mental factors and behaviors are said to be sequentially and irreversibly "extinguished" *(nirodha)*, until by the fourth stage *(Arahatta)* all the possible sources of mental conflict *(kilesas)* are said to be entirely removed (see Nyanamoli, 1976; M. Sayadaw, 1973).

[7] Interviews with the head of this teaching lineage, the Ven. Mahasi Sayadaw, and with his associate sayadaws (teachers) at the Thathana Yeiktha center in Rangoon, also revealed a rather remarkable difference in rate of progress between students there and students in this culture. Though there is reason to believe that Thathana Yeiktha may be a somewhat exceptional case even among Asian Buddhist centers (Jack Kornfield, personal communication), a more rapid rate of progress in Asian centers generally seems to be a widespread finding based on interviews with their resident teachers and with Western students who have studied in them.

[8] This was reflected in the increased evidence of drive-dominated content as well as significant changes in the formal aspects of Ss' verbalizations in our Rorschach study (Brown & Engler, 1980). Likewise, Davidson, Goleman & Schwartz (1976) report an increase in state-anxiety for the beginning meditator, in contrast to a decrease for the advanced meditator. These results are consistent with Maupin's (1965) finding that an increase in primary process thinking and tolerance for unrealistic experience predicted successful response to meditation, while attentional measures did not. Maupin apparently was not aware, however, that this finding is specific to the early stages of practice only.

[9] The development of the transference relationship would have to be observed over time before concluding that these narcissistic transference manifestations indicated the presence of a narcissistic personality disorder. I have not yet been in a position to do this myself; nor have other teachers systematically monitored transference manifestations in practice since Vipassana as a technique does not work through the medium of a transference relationship. This is an important area for future research.

[10] That is, as it is understood for instance in DSM-III, and by psychiatric researchers such as Klein (1975) and Akiskal (1978) who are not psychoanalytically oriented. The concept is used by Kohut (1971) and his school of psychoanalysis (Goldberg, 1980) in still a third sense as a designation for non-analyzable patients who are nevertheless not delusional.

[11] In a strict sense, a therapeutic split between observing and experiencing in the way that is usually meant occurs only in the preliminary but not in the final stages of meditation practice. Beginning with the formal stages of insight (the *"ñāṇas"* or "knowledges") which constitute insight meditation proper, the illusion of the observer or witness is seen through and observation is experienced now as merely a mental process or function instead of an activity of an agent "self." The observer is no longer separate from the thing observed, but in quantum mechanical terms experiences "himself" as part of the observation as well as the object observed.

[12] Because of its similarities to psychoanalysis as a technique, repression will be lifted to varying degrees in the earlier stage of Vipassana practice. To what extent psychodynamic insight and conflict resolution occur in insight meditation depends on a number of factors, some of them cultural. Classically, however, this stage of the meditative process is consid-

ered preliminary and transitional. It is hardly attended to as the practice is cultivated in the traditional centers of South and Southeast Asia because the lifting of repression and psychodynamic insight is not specific to meditation and is not the level of insight aimed at. The far greater attention given to this phenomenon in Western practice is attributable in part to our greater psychological-mindedness and cultural predisposition to attend to psychodynamics, but perhaps especially to our confusion about the proper goals of meditation, since our currently dominant spiritual and therapeutic systems do not include this range of experience and psychological functioning in their models of health and development.

[13] Tachistoscopic research on advanced Vipassana practitioners is currently being undertaken by Dr. Daniel P. Brown of Cambridge Hospital, Harvard Medical School, to empirically test this very point. Preliminary findings confirm a perceptual discrimination capacity well beyond hitherto reported norms, and tend to support the hypothesis that meditators are actually discriminating temporal stages in high-speed processing *prior* to the build-up of stimuli into durable percepts (D.P. Brown, personal communication).

[14] The technical term for this is *"nāma-rūpa-paricceda-ñāṇa,"* or "analytical knowledge of the distinction between form *(rūpa)* and mind *(nāma)."* The term "mind-and-form" *(nāma-rūpa)* is meant to exclude any ontological assumption of matter existing as a substance behind perceptible forms. Aristotelian and Newtonian physics contrast matter, form and mind: mind gives form to pre-existing matter. Buddhist physics, like twentieth century quantum physics, eliminates the notion of "matter" or substance altogether, except as a non-veridical percept on a macro-level of observation. Instead it contrasts mind *(nāma)* and form *(rūpa)* only, where "form" denotes the percept constructed out of sense data, not hypothesized "matter" existing independently of perception and its constructive activity. "Form" *(rūpa)* designates appearance only, without postulating any principle of substance behind appearances.

[15] This tends to confirm Kernberg's controversial assumption, which is otherwise difficult to substantiate on the level of clinical observation, that internalization is an ongoing process. The present moment of experience is always being internalized in the form of linked self and object representation, not merely significant events or the cumulative impact of events as most other object relations theorists imply.

[16] The technical term for this stage of practice is *"paccaya-pariggaha-ñāṇa,"* or "knowledge of conditionality." The central Buddhist doctrine of Co-Dependent Origination has its origin at this level of practice.

[17] The technical term for this stage of practice is *"sammasana-ñāṇa,"* or "knowledge by comprehension." This perception that each individual form is ultimately void of substance and, further, that the uniqueness of each form arises from the fact that it exists, and only exists, in relation to every other form is systematically formulated in the most central of all Buddhist teachings in both Theravada and Mahayana, the doctrine of Co-Dependent Origination. This is the quantum mechanical vision of the universe which underlies modern physics (see also Whitehead's ontological notion of "actual occasion").

[18] *Kāma-taṇhā* corresponds to libido and aggression and the dynamics of the Pleasure Principle in the older metapsychology based on dual instinct

theory. In object relational terms, it corresponds to the wish to possess the exciting (Fairbairn), gratifying (Kernberg) or good (Jacobson) object; and the desire to expel the rejecting (Fairbairn), frustrating (Kernberg) or bad (Jacobson) object.

[19] Neurophysiological and experimental psychological research supports a conception of affects as primarily "central state" phenomena; that is, primarily subjective states of pleasure/unpleasure which are crucially involved in psychic motivational systems rather than "peripheral" discharge phenomena. Kernberg (1976) has recently made the most ambitious attempt yet to integrate this view of affect into psychoanalytic theory.

[20] This has misled psychoanalytic metapsychology in general and object relations theory in particular—as well as common sense psychology—into conceptualizing these behaviors as innate "drives."

[21] Though this is a novel idea in terms of traditional psychoanalytic thinking, Kernberg's (1976) recent integration of a central state theory of affect and biological systems thinking with psychoanalytic dual instinct theory allows of this possibility in principle. It explains the drives not as blind, innate forces pressing for discharge but as psychic motivational systems which are actually built up and organized developmentally on the basis of central state affects of pleasure and unpleasure in response to experience. By accepting the distinction between hedonic appraisal and hedonic impulse as the two components of affect, it also admits of the possibility, at least in principle, of de-conditioning the automaticity of the usual stimulus-response relationship between them. Neither psychoanalysis nor other contemporary therapies train for that, so Kernberg, like experimental researchers, does not consider the possibility. The meditation traditions do, because they have developed appropriate techniques to decondition this response sequence.

[22] Analysts would not disagree with this as a description of the course of psychoanalytic therapy. An analogous "reversal of appearances" at the level of whole object relations results from interpreting and resolving the transference, which is precisely not *"yathābhutam"* or *"*in accordance with reality," i.e., with the way the therapist really is.

CHAPTER 3

[1] Object-relations theory is a general name for several schools of psychoanalytic theory that began to put emphasis not solely on the subject of development but on its relations with its object world. Classical libido psychology thus gave rise to two somewhat different schools of analytic theory: psychoanalytic ego psychology (Anna Freud, Heinz Hartmann) and object-relations theory (Fairbairn, Winnicott, Guntrip), the former stressing the subject of development, the latter, its objects (i.e., the former tends to emphasize nature, the latter, nurture [Gedo, 1981; Blanck & Blanck, 1974]). Most modern psychoanalytic schools use a combination of both theories, but, as Gedo points out, the two theories as generally presented are actually incompatible in fine point, and no one apparently has yet succeeded in satisfactorily uniting them in a coherent framework.

The central reason, I believe, is that both schools contain certain confusions or reductionisms—holdovers from the "bad aspects" of libido psychology. Ego psychology, for instance, still tends to be bogged down in drive psychology; it has few theories of motivation that don't implicitly rely on libido (e.g., see Blanck & Blanck's [1979] attempt to reformulate motivation by reformulating the libido). In my opinion, these approaches tend to overlook the fact that *each* basic structure might have its own intrinsic motivations, forces, or need-drives (for physical food, emotional food, conceptual food, spiritual food, etc.); that the self-system has its *own* drives (preserve, negate, ascend, descend); and that none of these should be confused with, derived from, or reduced to the others. Drive psychology tends to take the dynamics of *one* basic structure of existence (phantasmic-emotional) and make them the primary drives for all other basic structures *and* the self-system!

Object-relations theory, on the other hand, has attempted to present an adequate theory of motivation by making the templates of early object-relations the motivators of subsequent development. However, as Gedo has pointed out, not only is this a subtle form of reductionism, it *implicitly* amounts to a predominant reliance on environmental conditioning.

In my opinion, object-relations theory has also failed to clearly distinguish between two different types of "objects"—objects of the basic structures ("basic objects") and objects of the self-system ("self-objects"). *Basic objects* include physical objects, emotional objects, image objects, conceptual objects, rule objects, psychic objects, and subtle objects (there are no causal objects; the causal is the state of consciousness-without-an-object). These basic objects are the "levels of food" that correspond with the *basic structural needs* of each rung in the ladder of existence—the need for physical food, the need for communicative exchange, the need for formal reflection, the need for spiritual engagement, and so on—real and genuine need-drives that reflect the *structural* demands or needs of each basic level of existence (Wilber, 1981b).

Self-objects, on the other hand, are basic objects that are appropriated by the self-system, at each stage of its development, as being most centrally important for (and sometimes constitutive of) its own sense of identity and selfhood. Self-objects, in other words, are basic objects that also serve as objects of the *self* at each stage of its growth. If, for instance, I am thinking of a mathematical theorem, that theorem is a *formal basic object* of my mind; if I *invented* the theorem, however, and think of it as *mine*, or am very attached to it, then it is not just a basic object in my mind but a self-object in my ego. For an infant at the breast, the mother is not only a physical basic object providing food, but a self-object providing primary care and early identity information. The mother does not just feed the body, she feeds the self.

The self-objects, in other words, are basic objects that not only satisfy the basic structural needs, but also the correlated *self-needs* (see Table 3). Using Maslow's hierarchy as an example, the basic structural need of, say, rung 5 is for formal-reflexive "food for thought," a real *need-drive* to think and to communicate and to exchange ideas; the corresponding self-need, however, is for reflexive self-esteem, and thus any basic objects of the formal-mind that also become important in one's own self-esteem needs become *self-objects*. Basic objects become self-objects when they are in any way associated with the "I," the "me," or the "mine."

Thus, there are basic structures and basic objects, and self-structures and self-objects. In my opinion, a failure to differentiate these objects lies at the heart of some of the confusions now plaguing object-relations theory. These confusions have recently been exacerbated by Kohut's introduction of what he calls "selfobjects" (without a hyphen), which I would define as self-objects that are experienced not as objects of the self-system but as *part* of the self-system, in which case they can indeed be called "selfobjects." Kohut's description of these selfobjects is an extremely important contribution to the field, but it has tended to add to the confusion as to what exactly constitutes an object, a self-object, and a selfobject.

Kohut has also suggested that self-development ("narcissistic development") proceeds independently of libidinal object development, which object-relations theorists usually claim is impossible, because self and object relations, they believe, must develop correlatively. Here, however, they are again overlooking the difference between basic objects and self-objects. Basic structures and basic objects develop correlatively, and self-structures and self-objects develop correlatively, but basic structures/objects and self-structures/objects do not necessarily develop correlatively. Libidinal development *as* libidinal is a basic structure development, and so of course it is largely independent of self-structure development, although, as we saw, at F-2 development they are *virtually* identical simply because the self-system, at F-2, is *identified* with the libidinal basic structure. For the same reason, we differentiate the oedipal stage, which is a phase of self-development, from the phallic stage, which is a libidinal basic structure development.

Although I cannot indicate in this short note how a spectrum approach might handle these and other related problems, perhaps enough has been said to indicate how a *nonreductionistic* approach to motivation, coupled with a distinction between basic structures/objects and self-structures/objects, might not only allow a reconciliation of ego and object psychology, but also allow room for the acceptance of the phenomenologically higher subjects *and* objects that appear in higher and contemplative development.

CHAPTER 6

[1] Rorschach data on the American meditators was collected under a Postdoctoral Training Grant in Social-Behavioral Sciences (NIMH-#T32MH14246-04) through Harvard Medical School under the supervision of Elliot Mishler, Ph.D. The author wishes to acknowledge the inspiration of Dr. Charles Ducey, then Director of Psychological Services, The Cambridge Hospital, who supervised the data collection, as well as contributing greatly to an understanding of Rorschach scoring and interpretation. The author also wishes to thank the staff of the Insight Meditation Society, especially Michael Grady and James Roy, for not only allowing these data to be collected at IMS but dedicating themselves to organizing and ensuring the data collection. The author would also like to thank all of the teachers at IMS for their cooperation in this study, especially Dr. Jack Kornfield, whose training as both a meditation teacher and a psychologist allowed him to be a model for the integration of Eastern and Western psychologies, thereby making the project of collecting research data in a quasi-monastic setting credible to the meditation students. He would also like to thank Joseph Goldstein, resident teacher at IMS, who was kind and patient enough to read a draft of this paper and offer corrections so that the final draft presented an understanding of Buddhist practice that was free of serious distortions and misunderstandings. The

author would also like to thank the Ven. Mahasi Sayadaw, U. Javana Sayadaw, U. Agga Dhamma for the opportunity to study the stages of meditation under expert guidance at Thathana Yeiktha, Rangoon, Burma. The author would also like to thank the following people for their careful reading of the paper and their offering of helpful suggestions: Drs. Roger Walsh & Dean Shapiro; Charles Ducey, Ph.D., Bennett Simon, M.D., Gerald Epstein, M.D., Paul Fulton, M.A., Erika Fromm, Ph.D.

²Interview and test data on the South Asian meditators was collected under a Fulbright Research Fellowship to India in 1976-77, through the University of Chicago. The author wishes to thank first of all Prof. Don Browning and Prof. Frank Reynolds of the Divinity School, The University of Chicago, who supervised the planning of this research and have kept faith through its many vicissitudes; also Ven. Dr. U Jagara Bhivamsa, Prof. of Pali at the Nalanda Pali Institute of Post-Graduate Buddhist Studies, Nalanda, who supervised the actual execution of the project in the field. The author would also like to acknowledge Ven. Nyanaponika Mahathera of Sri Lanka, who first introduced him to this tradition and suggested the site for research; and Dr. Jack Kornfield and Mr. Joseph Goldstein, resident teachers at IMS, who ensured that the proper foundation for the research was laid before leaving and who suggested the only approach by which the author was able to gain access to this group of subjects. The many friends and colleagues in Asia to whom the author is indebted are too numerous to mention. He would like to thank two in particular who contributed directly to the data collection as test consultants: Dr. Manas Raychaudhari, Prof. of Clinical Psychology at Rabindra Bharati University, Calcutta, for the Rorschach; and Dr. Uma Chowdhury, Prof. of Clinical Psychology at the All-India Institute for Public Hygiene, Calcutta, for the TAT. Dr. Chowdhury is herself the author of the Indian adaptation of the TAT used in this study. The author also wants to acknowledge the Ven. Mahasi Sayadaw, the head of this teaching lineage, for his invitation to study at Thathana Yeiktha and for his active support of this research. Most of all, the author wants to thank the subjects of this study, who volunteered several months of their time during the hottest months of the hot season, under conditions which are difficult to imagine at this distance and under the press of family and professional lives, without complaint. Two especially deserve his thanks: the teacher who represents the Master's Group in this paper and who made her home available for the bulk of the interviewing and testing; and her teacher, who was the author's own mentor and main "informant" throughout his stay in Asia and who first identified the Ss for this study and then solicited their cooperation on the author's behalf. Lastly, he would like to acknowledge and thank Ms. Jellemieke Stauthamer of The Wright Institute in Berkeley, who collaborated in every phase of this study, especially the data collection. In the interviewing and testing, she opened the study in a unique way to the lives of women which are not shared with men, especially in Asia.

³A number of traditional and non-traditional procedures were used for scoring the Rorschach. These included scoring of: *determinants* (a version of the Exner system [Exner, 1974], modified in that it uses the Mayman system [Mayman, 1970] for scoring form-level and the Binder system [Binder, 1932] for shading); *formal variables* (Holt and Havel, 1960; Watkins & Stauffacher, 1975); and the *fabulization scale* (Mayman, 1960). Because of the unusualness of the post-Rorschachs, a non-traditional scoring manual was developed by the senior author, the Manual of Feature-Dominated Responses.

CHAPTER 8

[1] *Paṇḍita* and *kuśali*. The intellectuals *(paṇḍita)* and the experiential yogis *(kuśali)* often were at odds. Meditation involves a balance between these two extreme positions.

[2] See Patañjali, *Yogasūtras*, translated by James Houghton Woods. Delhi, India: 1927. The volume includes a translation of Vyasa's *Yogabhāshya*. This commentary on *Yogasūtras* 1:32 takes the position of *ekatattva* in contrast to the Buddhist position of *kṣaṇika*, e.g. Dharmakīrti.

[3] These preliminary instructions are abbreviated in Bkra shis rnam rgyal's work on the *Mahāmudrā*. For an expanded text on the faith exercises see: Kung dga' bstan dzin (Khams sprul III). *Phyag rGya Chen Po Lhan Cig sKyes sByor gyi sNgon 'Gro'i Khrid Yig Zab rGyas Chos kyi rGya mTso Chen Po nas sNyin po Ye Shes kyi Nor bu 'Dren par Byed pa'i Gru Chen*. Palampur, India: blockprint from Byar Skyid phug blockprint of the Tibetan Craft Community, 1974.

[4] The notation system used for scriptural references is as follows: M = *Mahāmudrā*; VM = *Visuddhimagga*; YS = *Yogasūtras*. The abbreviation is followed by the foreign technical word, for example, M, *'jug sgo* implies the Tibetan term from the *Mahāmudrā* text of Bkra shis Rnam Rgyal, and YS, *svādhyāya*, the Sanskrit term from Patañjali's *Yogasūtras*. VM would imply a Pali term.

[5] Nāgārjuna, *Mūlamādhyamakakārikās* (Fundamentals of the Middle Way), 2:1.

[6] Fischer (1971) sees diminished interaction with the environment and an alteration of perceptual scanning of external stimuli as necessary for the induction of an altered state.

[7] Charles T. Tart, *States of Consciousness*. New York: E.P. Dutton, 1975, pp. 258–59.

[8] Ibid., 278.

[9] *Culamalunkyasutta*, M. 63.

CHAPTER 9

[1] See Zachary C. Xintaras, "Man—The Image of God According to the Greek Fathers," *The Greek Orthodox Theological Review* (Volume 1, Number 1), August, 1954, pp. 48–62; this is a helpful guide although some references that Xintaras reports are not accurately interpreted, e.g., Xintaras credits St. Irenaeus rather than St. Basil for the theological distinction of "image" and "likeness."

[2] The precept to watch, not allow oneself to be weighed down by sleep, is strongly emphasized by Eastern Fathers. It demands the full consciousness of the human person in all degrees of its ascent towards perfect union. See Vladimir Lossky, *The Mystical Theology of the Eastern Church* (London, England: James Clarke & Co., Ltd., 1968), p. 202.

[3]Meyendorff explains that St. Gregory's position differs from Western Christianity since Western Scholasticism has assumed that knowledge is based upon revealed premises—Scripture or church magisterium—which serve as a foundation for development by the human mind, in conformity with the principles of Aristotelian Logic.

[4]St. Gregory does not deny that scientific research is important, but he warns that its conclusions are relative and incomplete and need to be complemented by true knowledge—participation in the Divine Light.

[5]The first stage, εἶναι, refers to the natural state of every human being, who is created in the image of God—i.e., blessed with the potential to love, to create, to reason, to choose. St. Maximos correlates this stage with human participation in the stage of Christ's Incarnation. The second stage, εὖ εἶναι, is the point of decision, where one makes a conscious commitment to follow Christ. It is the human response to change one's ways and to embrace the life in Christ's Kingdom: μετάνοια, a radical change of mind. St. Maximos relates this stage to one's "picking up his cross and following Christ" or to the stage of Christ's Crucifixion. Finally, ἀεί εἶναι is the eternally ongoing experience of illumination or θεοπτία, a stage at which one enjoys God-presence. This goal parallels the stage of Christ's Resurrection.

[6]Origen and Evagrios are Early Church theologians whose spiritual "formulations" compared to the lives of the saints. The two theologians are representative of the cataphatic approach to theology (frequently the form of Western Christian spirituality), in distinction from the saints, who are representative of the apophatic approach to theology (which typifies Eastern Orthodox spiritual development). For a discussion of the two different approaches in spiritual development, see John T. Chirban, *Human Growth and Faith: Intrinsic and Extrinsic Motivation in Human Development* (Washington, D.C.: University Press of America, 1981).

[7]The schematic diagram is read from right to left. The first two theologians are representative of cataphatic theological approaches; the saints are representative of apophatic theological approaches. The five stages that are described begin from the bottom of the page (left column) and progress upward. Note that terms which are shared by the Church leaders who are presented in the schematic are not repeated in the diagram.

[8]Hesychasm, ἡσυχασμός, "the way of stillness and repose," was a psycho-physical method of prayer which leads to "vision of God" (See S.I. Hausherr, "A Propos de la Spiritualité Hesychaste." *Orientalia Christiana Periodica*, Volume 3 (Rome: Pontificum Institutum Orientalium Studiorum, 1939), p. 261.

REFERENCES

ABEND, S., PORDER, M., & WILLICK, M. *Borderline patients: Psychoanalytic perspective.* New York: International Univ. Press, 1983.

ADLER, G. *Dynamics of the self.* London: Coventure, 1979.

AGHIORGOUSSIS, M. *La dialectique de l'image de Dieu chez Saint Basil Le Grand.* Unpublished doctoral dissertation. University of Louvain, France; School of Theology, 1964.

AKISKAL, H.S., DJENDEREDIJIAN, A.H., BOLINGER, J.M., BITAR, A.H., KHANI, M.D., & HAYKAL, R.F. The joint use of clinical and biological criteria for psychiatric diagnosis, II: Their application in identifying subaffective forms of bipolar illness. In H.S. Akiskal & W.L. Webb (Eds.), *Psychiatric diagnosis: Exploration of biological predictors.* New York: Spectrum Publications, 1978, 133–45.

ALEXANDER, F. Buddhist training as an artificial catatonia. *Psychoanalytic Review,* 1931, *18,* 129–45.

ALEXANDRIA, CYRIL OF. MIGNE. *Patrologia Græcæ,* 276.

ALLISON, J. Adaptive regression and intense religious experiences, *J. Nervous Mental Disease,* 1968, *145,* 452–63.

ALLPORT, F.H. *Theories of perception and the concept of structure.* New York: Wiley, 1967 (1955).

ALLPORT, G. *Becoming.* New Haven: Yale Univ. Press, 1955.

AMERICAN PSYCHIATRIC ASSOCIATION. *Diagnostic and statistical manual of mental disorder.* 3rd Ed. Washington, D.C.: American Psychiatric Association, 1980.

AQUINAS, T. *Summa theologiae.* 2 vols. New York: Doubleday/Anchor, 1969.

ARIETI, S. *Interpretation of schizophrenia.* New York: Brunner, 1955.

ARIETI, S. *The intrapsychic self.* New York: Basic Books, 1967.

ARNOLD, M.B. Brain function in emotion: A phenomenological analysis. In P. Black (Ed.), *Physiological correlates of emotion.* New York: Academic Press, 1970a, 261–85.

ARNOLD, M.B. Perennial problems in the field of emotion. In M.B. Arnold (Ed.), *Feelings and emotions*. New York: Academic Press, 1970b, 1969–85.

ASSAGIOLI, R. *Psychosynthesis: A manual of principles and techniques*. New York: Hobbs, Dorman, 1971.

ATHANASIOS, ST. MIGNE. *Patrologia Græcæ*, 101B.

AUROBINDO. *The life divine* and *The synthesis of yoga*. Pondicherry: Centenary Library, XVIII-XXI, n.d.

AVALON, A. *The serpent power*. New York: Dover, 1974 (1931).

BALDWIN, J. *Thought and things*. New York: Arno Press, 1975 (1906–15).

BANDURA, A. *Social learning theory*. New York: General Learning Press, 1971.

BANDURA, A. Self-efficacy: Toward a unifying theory of behavioral change. *Psychological Review*, 1977, 34, 191–215.

BASIL, ST. MIGNE. *Patrologia Græcæ*, 20B, 29C, 30, 31, 32, 32B, 32C, 37A, 213D–216A, 864C, 908, 909, 909B,C.

BASIL, ST. (Phillip Shaff & Henry Wase, Trans.) Letters. *The Nicene and Post-Nicene fathers*. Vol. VIII. Grand Rapids, MI: 1955.

BECK, A., RUSH, A., SHAW, B., & EMERY, G. *Cognitive therapy of depression*. New York: Guilford Press, 1979.

BECKER, E. *The denial of death*. New York: Free Press, 1973.

BERGIN, A.E. Psychotherapy and religious values. *J. Consulting Clinical Psychology*, 1980, 48, 95–105.

BERNE, E. *What do you say after you say hello?* New York: Bantam, 1972.

BINDER, H. *Die Helldunkeldeutungen im Psychodiagnostischem Experiment von Rorschach*. Zurich: Urell Fussli, 1932.

BINSWANGER, L. Existential analysis and psychotherapy. In F. Fromm-Reichmann & J. Moreno (Eds.), *Progress in psychotherapy*. New York: Grune & Stratton, 1956.

BLANCK, G. & BLANCK, R. *Ego psychology: Theory and practice*. New York: Columbia Univ. Press, 1974.

BLANCK, G. & BLANCK, R. *Ego psychology II: Psychoanalytic developmental psychology*. New York: Columbia Univ. Press, 1979.

BLOFELD, J. *The tantric mysticism of Tibet*. New York: Dutton, 1970.

BLOOMFIELD, H.H. Some observations on the uses of the Transcendental Meditation program in psychiatry. In D.W. Orme-Johnson & J.T. Farrow (Eds.), *Scientific research on transcendental meditation, Vol. I*. Weggis: M.E.R.U. Press, 1977.

BLOS, P. *On adolescence: A psychoanalytic interpretation*. New York: Free Press, 1962.

BLOS, P. The second individuation process of adolescence. *The Psychoanalytic Study of the Child*, 1967, 22, 162–86.

BOHM, D. Quantum theory as an indication of a new order in physics: Part B. Implicate and explicate order in physical law. *Foundations of Physics*, 1973, 2, 139–68.

BOORSTEIN, S. The use of bibliotherapy and mindfulness meditation in a psychiatric setting. *J. Transpersonal Psychology*, 1983, *15*, 2, 173–9.

BOSS, M. *Psychoanalysis and daseinsanalysis*. New York: Basic Books, 1963.

BOURGUIGNON, E. The self, the behavioral environment, and the theory of spirit-possession. In Melford E. Spiro (Ed.), *Context and meaning in cultural anthropology*. New York: Free Press, 1965.

BOUYER, L. In Markey Perkins Ryan (Trans.), *Introduction to spirituality*. Collegeville, MN: Liturgical Press, 1961.

BOWLBY, J. *Attachment and loss, Vol. I: Attachment*. New York: Basic Books, 1969.

BOWLBY, J. *Attachment and loss*. 2 vols. New York: Basic Books, 1973.

BOYER, L. & GIOVACCHINI, P. *Psychoanalytic treatment of characterological and schizophrenic disorders*. New York: Aronson, 1967.

BOYER, L.B., KLOPFER, B., BRAWER, F.B. & KAWAI, H. Comparison of the shamans and pseudoshamans of the Apache of the Mescalero Indian Reservation: A Rorschach Study. *J. Projective Techniques & Personnel Assessment*, 1964, *28*, 173–80.

BRAINERD, C.J. The stage question in cognitive-developmental theory. *The Behavioral and Brain Sciences*, 1978, *2*, 173–213.

BRANDEN, N. *The psychology of self-esteem*. New York: Bantam, 1971.

BRANDT, A. Self-confrontations. *Psychology Today*, Oct. 1980.

BREHM, J.W. *Responses to loss of freedom: A theory of psychological reactance*. Morristown, N.J.: General Learning Press, 1972.

BROCK, S. St. Isaac of Ninevah and Syrian spirituality. *Sobornost*, 1975, *7*, 2.

BROUGHTON, J. The development of natural epistemology in adolescence and early adulthood. Doctoral dissertation, Harvard, 1975.

BROWN, D.P. A model for the levels of concentrative meditation. *International J. Clinical and Experimental Hypnosis*, 1977, *25*, 236–73.

BROWN, D.P. Mahāmudrā meditation: Stages and contemporary cognitive psychology. Doctoral dissertation, University of Chicago, 1981.

BROWN, D.P. & ENGLER, J. The stages of mindfulness meditation: A validation study. *J. Transpersonal Psychology*, 1980, *12*, 2, 143–92.

BROWN, D.P., TWEMLOW, S., ENGLER, J., MALISZEWSKI, M. & STAUTHAMER, J. The profile of meditation experience (POME), Form II, Psychological Test Copyright, Washington, D.C., 1978.

BRUNER, J. The course of cognitive growth. *American Psychologist*, 1964, *19*, 1–15.

BRUNER, J.S. Beyond the information given. Jeremy M. Anglin (Ed.). New York: Norton, 1973.

CAESARIOS. MIGNE. *Patrologia Græcæ*, 38, 1125.

CALEF, V. A theoretical note on the ego in the therapeutic process. In S.C. Post (Ed.), *Moral values and the superego concept in psychoanalysis*. New York: International Univ. Press, 1972.

CAMPENHAUSEN, HANS VON. *The fathers of the Greek church*. New York: Pantheon, 1955.

CANDELENT, T., & CANDELENT, G. Teaching transcendental meditation in a psychiatric setting. *Hospital & Community Psychiatry*, 1975, 26, 3, 156–59.

CARPENTER, J.T. Meditation, esoteric traditions: Contributions to psychotherapy. *American J. Psychotherapy*, 1977, 31, 394–404.

CARRINGTON, P. & EPHRON, H. Meditation as an adjunct to psychotherapy. In S. Arieti & G. Chrzanowski (Eds.), *The world biennial of psychotherapy and psychiatry*, 1975, 262–91.

CAYRE, F. In W. Webster Wilson (Trans.), *Spiritual writers of the early church*. New York: Hawthorne, 1969.

CHANG, G. *Teachings of Tibetan yoga*. Secaucus, N.J.: Citadel, 1974.

CHARITON, IGUMEN OF VALAMO (Ed.). In E. Kadloubovsky and G.E.H. Palmer (Trans.), *Philokalia: The early church fathers*. London: Faber and Faber, 1967.

CHIRBAN, J.T. *Human growth and faith: Intrinsic and extrinsic motivation in human development*. Washington, D.C.: University Press of America, 1981.

CHOWDHURY, U. *An Indian modification of the thematic apperception test*. Calcutta: Sree Saraswaty Press Ltd., 1960.

CHRISTOU, PANAGIOTIS "Γρηγόριος ὁ Παλαμάς." Θρησκευτική καί 'Ηθική 'Εγκυκλοπαίδεια. Athens, Greece: Martios, 1966.

CHRYSOSTOM, ST. JOHN. MIGNE. *Patrologia Græcæ*, 53, 56, 158D, 443, 443C.

CLEMENT OF ALEXANDRIA. MIGNE. *Patrologia Græcæ*, 9, 74, 140A, 277D.

CLIFFORD, T. *Tibetan Buddhist medicine and psychiatry*. York Beach, ME: Samuel Weiser, 1984.

CROWNE, D.P. & MARLOWE, D.A. A new scale of social desirability independent of psychopathology. *J. Consulting Psychology*, 1960,24,349–54.

CSIKZENTMIHALYI, M. Play and intrinsic rewards. *J. Humanistic Psychology*, 1975, 15, 3, 41–63.

CYRIL OF ALEXANDRIA. MIGNE. 74, 76, 276D, 277D, 1087.

CYRIL OF JERUSALEM. MIGNE. *Patrologia Græcæ*, 33, 477, 836B.

DA FREE JOHN. *The paradox of instruction*. San Francisco: Dawn Horse, 1977.

DA FREE JOHN. *The enlightenment of the whole body*. San Francisco: Dawn Horse, 1978.

DARGYAY, E. *The rise of esoteric Buddhism in Tibet.* New York: Weiser, 1978.

DASGUPTA, S. *Obscure religious cults.* Calcutta: F. Klmukhopadhyay, 1946.

DAVIDSON, R.J., GOLEMAN, D.J., SCHWARTZ, G.E. Attentional and affective concomitants of meditation: A cross-sectional study. *J. Abnormal Psychology,* 1976, *85,* 235–38.

DEAN, S.R. Metapsychiatry: The interface between psychiatry and mysticism. *American J. Psychiatry,* 1973, *130,* 1036–38.

DEATHERAGE, O.G. The clinical use of "mindfulness" meditation techniques in short-term psychotherapy. *J. Transpersonal Psychology,* 1975, *7,* 2, 133–43.

DEIKMAN, A.J. Comments on the GAP report on mysticism. *J. Nervous Mental Disease,* 1977, *165,* 213–17.

DEUTSCHE, E. *Advaita Vedanta.* Honolulu: East-West Center, 1969.

DIONYSIOS THE AREOPAGITE. Translated by the Editors of the Shrine of Wisdom, *The mystical theology and celestial hierarchy.* Surrey, England: The Shrine of Wisdom, 1965.

DUCEY, C. Rorschach experiential and representational dimensions of object relations: A longitudinal study. Unpublished doctoral dissertation, Harvard University, 1975.

DUVAL, S. & WICKLUND, R.A. Effects of objective self-awareness on attribution of causality. *J. Experimental Social Psychology,* 1973, *9,* 17–31.

ELIADE, M. *Yoga: Immortality and freedom.* Princeton: Princeton Univ. Press, 1969.

ELLIS, A. *Humanistic psychotherapy: The rational-emotive approach.* New York: McGraw-Hill, 1973.

ENGLER, J. Vicissitudes of the self according to psychoanalysis and Buddhism: A spectrum model of object relations development. *Psychoanalysis and Contemporary Thought,* 1983a, *6,* 1, 29–72.

ENGLER, J. Buddhist Satipatthana-Vipassana meditation and an object relations model of therapeutic developmental change: A clinical case study. Unpublished dissertation, University of Chicago, 1983b.

ENGLER, J. Therapeutic aims in psychotherapy and meditation: Developmental stages in the representation of self. *J. Transpersonal Psychology,* 1984, *16,* 1, 25–61.

ENGLER, J. "The undivided self: Clinical case studies of object relations in Buddhist mindfulness meditation." In preparation (n.d.).

EPSTEIN, M. & TOPGAY, S. Mind and mental disorders in Tibetan medicine. Unpublished manuscript.

ERIKSEN, C.W. Some temporal characteristics of visual pattern perception. *J. Experimental Psychology,* 1967, *74,* 476–84.

ERIKSON, E.H. *Childhood and society.* New York: Norton, 1950, 1963.

ERIKSON, E.H. Ego identity and the psychosocial moratorium. In H.L. Witmar & R. Kosinski (Eds.), *New perspectives for research in juvenile delinquency.* U.S. Children's Bureau, Publication #356, 1956, pp. 1–23.

ERIKSON, E. *Identity and the life cycle.* New York: International Univ. Press, 1959.

ERIKSON, J.M. *Activity, recovery, growth: The communal role of planned activities.* New York: Norton, 1976.

EVANS-WENTZ, W. *Tibetan yoga and secret doctrines.* London: Oxford Univ. Press, 1971.

EXNER, J.E. *The Rorschach: A comprehensive system.* New York: Wiley, 1974.

FAIRBAIRN, W. *An object relations theory of the personality.* New York: Basic Books, 1954.

FAIRBAIRN, W.R.R. *Psychoanalytic studies of the personality.* New York, Basic Books, 1952.

FENICHEL, O. *The psychoanalytic theory of neurosis.* New York: Norton, 1945.

FEUERSTEIN, G. *Textbook of yoga.* London: Rider, 1975.

FINGARETTE, H. The ego and mystic selflessness. *Psychoanalytic Review,* 1958, 45, 5–40.

FISCHER, R.A. A cartography of the ecstatic and meditative states: The experimental and experiential features of a perception-hallucination continuum are considered. *Science,* 1971, 174, 897–904.

FLAVELL, J. *The developmental psychology of Jean Piaget.* Princeton, N.J.: Van Nostrand, 1963.

FLAVELL, J. Concept development. In P. Mussen (Ed.), *Carmichael's manual of child psychology.* Vol.1. New York: Wiley, 1970.

FLEMING, J. Early object deprivation and transference phenomena: The working alliance. *Psychoanalytic Quarterly,* 1972, 10, 439–51.

FOWLER, J.W. *Stages of faith: The psychology of human development and the quest for meaning.* San Francisco: Harper & Row, 1981.

FRANK, J.D. *Persuasion and healing: A comparative study of psychotherapy.* Baltimore: Johns Hopkins, 1961.

FRANKL, V. *Man's search for meaning.* Boston: Beacon, 1963.

FRANKL, V. *The will to meaning.* Cleveland: New American Library, 1969.

FRENCH, A.P., SCHMID, A.C., & INGALLS, E. Transcendental meditation, altered reality testing and behavioral change: A case report. *J. Nervous Mental Disease,* 1975, 161, 1, 55–8.

FREUD, A. *The ego and the mechanisms of defense.* New York: International Univ. Press, 1946.

FREUD, A. The concept of developmental lines. In *The psychoana-*

lytic study of the child. New York: International Univ. Press. 1963, *8*, 245–65.

FREUD, A. *Normality and pathology in childhood.* New York: International Univ. Press, 1965.

FREUD, S. *Civilization and its discontents.* New York: W.W. Norton, 1930, 1961.

FREUD, S. *Analysis terminable and interminable.* SE. London: Hogarth Press, 1937, vol. 23, pp. 209–53.

FREUD, S. *Inhibitions, symptoms and anxiety.* SE. vol. 20. London: Hogarth Press, 1959 (1926).

FREUD, S. *The ego and the id.* SE. vol. 19. London: Hogarth Press, 1961 (1923).

FREUD, S. *An outline of psychoanalysis.* SE. vol. 23, London: Hogarth Press, 1964 (1940).

FREUD, S. *A general introduction to psychoanalysis.* New York: Pocket Books, 1971.

FREY-ROHN, L. *From Freud to Jung.* New York: Delta, 1974.

FROMM, E., BROWN, D., HURT, S., OBERLANDER, J., PFEIFFER, G., & BOXER, A. The phenomena of self-hypnosis. *International J. Clinical Experimental Hypnosis,* 1980.

FROMM, E., OBERLANDER, M.I., & GRUNEWALD, D. Perception and cognitive processes in different states of consciousness: The waking state and hypnosis. *J. Projective Techniques & Personnel Assessment,* 1970. 34: 375–87.

GARD, R. *Buddhism.* New York: Braziller, 1962.

GEDO, J. *Beyond interpretation: Toward a revised theory for psychoanalysis.* New York: International Univ. Press, 1979.

GEDO, J. *Advances in clinical psychoanalysis.* New York: International Univ. Press, 1981.

GEDO, J. & GOLDBERG, A. *Models of the mind: A psychoanalytic theory.* Chicago: Univ. of Chicago Press, 1973.

GELLER, V. & SHAVER, P. Cognitive consequences of self-awareness. *J. Experimental Social Psychology,* 1976, *12*, 99–108.

GILLIGAN, C. *In a different voice.* Cambridge: Harvard Univ. Press, 1982.

GLUECK, B.C., & STROEBEL, C.F. Biofeedback and meditation in the treatment of psychiatric illnesses. *Comprehensive Psychiatry,* 1975, *16*, 303–21.

GOLDBERG, A. (Ed.). *Advances in self psychology.* New York: International Univ. Press, 1980.

GOLDSTEIN, J. *The experience of insight: A natural unfolding.* Santa Cruz: Unity Press, 1976.

GOLEMAN, D. Meditation and consciousness: An Asian approach to mental health. *American J. Psychotherapy,* 1975, *30*, 41–54.

GOLEMAN, D. *The varieties of meditative experience.* New York: Dutton, 1977.

GOLEMAN, D. & EPSTEIN, M. Meditation and well-being: An Eastern model of psychological health. *ReVision*, 1980, 3, 73–85.

GOTTESMAN, I.I. & SCHIELDS, M. *Schizophrenia and genetics: A twin study vantage point.* New York: Academic Press, 1972.

GOVINDA, L. *The psychological attitude of early Buddhist philosophy.* New York: Samuel Weiser, 1974.

GRAVES, C.W. Levels of existence: An open system theory of values. *J. Humanistic Psychology*, 1970, 10, 131–55.

GREEN, E., GREEN, A. & WALTERS, D.E. Voluntary control of internal states: Psychological and physiological. *J. Transpersonal Psychology*, 1970, 2, 1–26.

GREENSON, R. *The technique and practice of psychoanalysis.* New York: International Univ. Press, 1967.

GREGORY OF NYSSA, ST. In Jean Danielou and Herbert Musurillo (Eds.), *From glory to glory.* New York: Scribners, 1969.

GREGORY OF NYSSA, ST. MIGNE. *Patrologia Græcæ*, 44, 137, 184, 273A, 273B.

GREGORY THE THEOLOGIAN, ST. MIGNE. *Patrologia Græcæ*, 37, 77A.

GREIST, J., JEFFERSON, J., & SPITZER, R. (EDS). *Treatment of mental disorders.* New York: Oxford Univ. Press, 1982.

GROF, S. *Realms of the human unconscious.* New York: Viking, 1975.

GROUP FOR THE ADVANCEMENT OF PSYCHIATRY (GAP). *Mysticism: Spiritual quest or psychic disorder?* New York: GAP (Publication 97), 1976.

GUENON, R. *Man and his becoming according to Vedanta.* London: Luzac, 1945.

GUENTHER, H. *Philosophy and psychology in the Abhidhamma.* Boulder: Shambhala, 1974.

GUNTRIP, H. *Personality structure and human interaction.* New York: International Univ. Press, 1961.

GUNTRIP, H. *Schizoid phenomena, object relations and the self.* New York: International Univ. Press, 1969.

GUNTRIP, H. *Psychoanalytic theory, therapy and the self.* New York, Basic Books, 1971.

HALEY, J. *Strategies of psychotherapy.* New York: Grune & Stratton, 1963.

HALEY, J. & HOFFMAN, L. (EDS.). *Techniques of family therapy.* New York: Basic Books, 1968.

HANLY, C. & MASSON, J. A critical examination of the new narcissism. *International J. Psychoanalysis*, 1976, 57, 49–65.

HARTMAN, H. *Ego psychology and the problem of adaptation.* New York: International Univ. Press, 1958.

HEBB, D.O. *The organization of behavior: A neuropsychological theory.* New York: Wiley & Sons, 1949.

HEIDEGGER, M. *Being and time.* New York: Harper & Row, 1962.

HILGARD, E.R. Issues bearing on recommendations from the behavioral and social sciences study committee. *American Psychologist*, 1970, 25, 5, 456–63.

HIXON, L. *Coming home*. New York: Anchor, 1978.

HOCHBERG, J. Attention, organization and consciousness. In D. Mostofsky (Ed.), *Attention: Contemporary theory and analysis*. New York: Appleton-Century, 1970.

HOFFMAN, J.E. A two-stage model of visual search. *Perception and Psychophysics*, 1979, *25*, 319–27.

HOLT, R. & HAVEL, J. A method for assessing primary and secondary process in the Rorschach. In M.A. Rickers-Ovsiankina (Ed.), *Rorschach psychology*. New York: Wiley, 1960.

HORNER, A.J. *Object relations and the developing ego in therapy*. New York: Jason Aronson, 1979.

HORNEY, K. *Neurosis and human growth*. New York: Norton, 1950.

HORTON, P.C. The mystical experience as a suicide preventative. *American J. Psychiatry*, 1973, *130*, 294–96.

HORTON, P.C. The mystical experience: Substance of an illusion. *J. American Psychoanalytic Association*, 1974, *22*, 364–80.

HUGEL, F. VON *The mystical element in religion*. London: Dent, 1908.

HUME, R. (TRANS.). *The thirteen principle Upanishads*. London: Oxford Univ. Press, 1974.

HUXLEY, A. *The perennial philosophy*. New York: Harper & Row, 1944.

ICKES, W.J., WICKLUND, R.A., & FERRIS, C.B. Objective self-awareness and self-esteem. *J. Experimental and Social Psychology*, 1973, *9*, 202–19.

IKEGAMI, R. Psychological study of Zen posture. In Yoshiharu Akishige (Ed.), *Psychological studies on Zen*. Tokyo: Zen Institute of Kamazawa University, 1970, 105–33.

IRENAEOS, ST. MIGNE. *Patrologia Græcæ*, 1105A, C.

ISAAC THE SYRIAN. Οἱ Ἀσκητικοί τοῦ Ἰσάχ. Athens, Greece.

JACOBI, J. *The psychology of C.G. Jung*. London: Routledge & Kegan Paul, 1942.

JACOBSON, E. *The self and the object world*. New York: International Univ. Press, 1964.

JAMES, W. *Principles of psychology*, 2 vols. New York: Dover, 1950 (1890).

JAMES, W. *The varieties of religious experience*. New York: Colliers, 1961 (1901).

JOHN CLIMACOS, ST. In Archmandite Lazarus Moore (Trans.), *The ladder of divine ascent*. Willets, CA: Eastern Orthodox Press, 1959.

JOHN OF DAMASCUS, ST. MIGNE. *Patrologia Græcæ*, 94, 95, 97A, 924A, 1037C.

JOHN OF THE CROSS. *The dark night of the soul*. Garden City, NY: Anchor, 1959.

JONAS, H. *The gnostic religion*. Boston: Beacon, 1958.

JUNG, C.G. *The undiscovered self*. New York: Mentor, 1957.

JUNG, C.G. *Analytical psychology: Its theory and practice.* New York: Vintage, 1961.

JUNG, C.G. *Man and his symbols.* New York: Dell, 1964.

JUNG, C.G. *The portable Jung.* J. Campbell (Ed.). New York: Viking, 1971.

KABAT-ZINN, J. An outpatient program in behavioral medicine for chronic pain patients based on the practice of mindfulness meditation. *General Hospital Psychiatry,* 1982, *4,* 33–47.

KAHN, H. *The soul: whence and whither.* New York: Sufi Order, 1977.

KALFF, M. The negation of ego in Tibetan Buddhism and Jungian psychology. *J. Transpersonal Psychology,* 1983, *15,* 2, 103–24.

KAPLEAU, P. *The three pillars of Zen.* Boston: Beacon, 1965.

KASAMATSU, A. & HARAI, T. An electroencephalographic study on the Zen meditation (Zazen). *Folia Psychiatry Neurologica Japonica,* 1966, *20,* 315–36.

KASTENBAUM, R. & AISENBERG, R. *Psychology of death.* New York: Springer, 1972.

KELLEY, G. *The psychology of personal constructs,* vols. 1 & 2. New York: Norton, 1955.

KENNEDY, R.B. Self-induced depersonalization syndrome. *American J. Psychiatry,* 1976, *133,* 1326–28.

KERNBERG, O. Borderline personality organization. *J. American Psychoanalytic Association,* 1967, *15.*

KERNBERG, O. The treatment of patients with borderline personality organization. *International J. Psychoanalysis,* 1968, *49,* 600–19.

KERNBERG, O. Prognostic considerations regarding borderline personality organization. *J. American Psychoanalytic Association,* 1971, *19.*

KERNBERG, O. Treatment of borderline patients. In P. Giovacchini (Ed.), *Tactics and techniques in psychoanalytic therapy.* New York: Science House, 1972.

KERNBERG, O. *Borderline conditions and pathological narcissism.* New York: Jason Aronson, 1975.

KERNBERG, O. *Object relations theory and clinical psychoanalysis.* New York: Jason Aronson, 1976.

KERNBERG, O. The structural diagnosis of borderline personality organization. In P. Hartocollis (Ed.), *Borderline personality disorders.* New York: International Univ. Press, 1977, 87–122.

KERNBERG, O., et al. Psychotherapy and psychoanalysis: Final report of the Menninger Foundation's psychotherapy research project. *Bulletin Menninger Clinic,* 1972, *36* (1/2).

KETY, S., ROSENTHAL, D., WENDER, P.H., et al. Mental illness in the biological and adoptive families of adopted schizophrenics. In D. Rosenthal & S. Kety (Eds.), *The transmission of schizophrenia.* Oxford: Pergamon Press, 1968, 345–62.

KEHTSUN SANGPO RINBOCHAY. *Tantric practice in Nying-Ma.* Ithaca, NY: Gabriel/Snow Lion, 1982.

KIERKEGAARD, S. *Fear and trembling* and *The sickness unto death.* New York: Doubleday/Anchor, 1953.

KIERKEGAARD, S. *The concept of dread.* Princeton: Princeton Univ. Press, 1957.

KLEIN, D.F. Psychopharmacology and the borderline patient. In J.E. Mack (Ed.), *Borderline states in psychiatry.* New York: Grune and Stratton, 1975, 75–92.

KLEIN, M. *The psychoanalysis of children.* London: Hogarth Press, 1932.

KLEIN, M. Notes on some schizoid mechanisms. In M. Klein, *Envy and gratitude and other works, 1946–1963.* New York: Delacorte Press/Seymour Lawrence, 1946, 1–24.

KLOPFER, B. & BOYER, L.B. Notes on the personality structure of a North American Indian shaman: Rorschach interpretation. *J. Projective Techniques & Personnel Assessment,* 1961, *25,* 170–78.

KOESTENBAUM, P. *Is there an answer to death?* New York: Prentice-Hall, 1976.

KOHLBERG, L. *Essays on moral development,* vol 1. San Francisco: Harper & Row, 1981.

KOHUT, H. Forms and transformations of narcissism. *J. American Psychoanalytic Association,* 1966, *5,* 389–407.

KOHUT, H. *The analysis of the self.* New York: International Univ. Press, 1971.

KOHUT, H. *The restoration of the self.* New York: International Univ. Press, 1977.

KOHUT, W. & WOLF, E.S. The disorders of the self and their treatment. *International J. of Psychoanalysis,* 1978, *59,* 4, 413–425.

KORNFIELD, J.M. The psychology of mindfulness meditation. Unpublished doctoral dissertation, The Humanistic Psychology Institute, 1976.

KORNFIELD, J. *Living Buddhist masters.* Santa Cruz: Unity Press, 1977.

KORNFIELD, J. Intensive insight meditation: A phenomenological study. *J. Transpersonal Psychology,* 1979, *11,* 1, 41–58.

KRIS, E. The psychology of caricature. *International J. Psychoanalysis,* 1936, *17:* 285–303.

KRISHNA, G. *The secret of yoga.* London: Turnstone Books, 1972.

KRIVOSHINE, BASIL. The ascetic and theological teaching of Gregory Palamas. *Eastern Churches Quarterly,* 1955.

LACAN, J. *Language of the self.* Baltimore: Johns Hopkins Univ. Press, 1968.

LAING, R.D. *The politics of experience.* New York: Ballantine, 1967.

LASCH, C. *The culture of narcissism.* New York: Norton, 1979.

LAZARUS, A.A. Psychiatric problems precipitated by transcendental meditation. *Psychological Reports,* 1976, *39,* 601–02.

LEEPER, R.W. The motivational and perceptual properties of emotions as indicating their fundamental character and role. In M. B. Arnold (Ed.), *Feelings and emotions*. New York: Academic Press, 1970, 151–85.

LEGGETT, T. *The tiger's cave*. London: Routledge and Kegan Paul, 1964.

LEVINSON, D.J. et al. *The seasons of a man's life*. New York: Knopf, 1978.

LEVINSON, P. Religious delusions in counter-culture patients. *American J. Psychiatry*, 1973, *130*, 1265–69.

LICHTENBERG, J. The development of the sense of self. *J. American Psychoanalytic Association*, 1975, *23*.

LOEVINGER, J. *Ego development*. San Francisco: Jossey-Bass, 1976.

LOEWALD, H.W. On the therapeutic action of psychoanalysis. *International J. Psychoanalysis.*, 1960, *41*, 16–33.

LOEWALD, H. *Psychoanalysis and the history of the individual*. New Haven: Yale Univ. Press, 1978.

LONGCHENPA. *Kindly bent to ease us*. 3 vols. H. Guenther (Trans.). Emeryville, CA: Dharma Press, 1977.

LOSSKY, V. In Asheleigh Moorhouse (Trans.), *The vision of God*. Clayton, WI: Faith Press, 1963.

LOWEN, A. *The betrayal of the body*. New York: Macmillan, 1967.

LUK, C. *Ch'an and Zen teaching*. 3 vols. London: Rider, 1962.

LUTHE, W. *Autogenic training: Research and theory*. New York: Grune & Stratton, 1970.

McCARTHY, T. *The critical theory of Jürgen Habermas*. Cambridge, Mass.: MIT Press, 1978.

MADDI, S. The existential neurosis. *J. Abnormal Psychology*, 1967, *72*.

MAHASI SAYADAW. *Progress of insight*. Kandy: Buddhist Publ. Society, 1965, 1973.

MAHASI SAYADAW. *Practical insight meditation*. Santa Cruz: Unity Press, 1972.

MAHLER, M. *On human symbiosis and the vicissitues of individuation*. New York: International Univ. Press, 1968.

MAHLER, M. On the first three subphases of the separation-individuation process. *International J. Psychoanalysis*, 1972, *53*, 333–38.

MAHLER, M., PINE, F., & BERGMAN, A. *The psychological birth of the human infant*. New York: Basic Books, 1975.

MALISZEWSKI, M., TWEMLOW, S., BROWN, D., & ENGLER, J. A phenomenological typology of intensive meditation: A suggested methodology using the questionnaire approach. *Re-Vision*, 1981, *4*.

MARIN, P. The new narcissism. *Harper's*, Oct. 1975.

MARMOR, J. Recent trends in psychotherapy. *American J. Psychiatry*, 1980, *137*, 409–16.

MASLOW, A. *Motivation and personality.* New York: Harper & Row, 1954.

MASLOW, A. *Toward a psychology of being.* New York: Van Nostrand Reinhold, 1968.

MASLOW, A. *The further reaches of human nature.* New York: Viking, 1971.

MASTERSON, J.F. *Treatment of the borderline adolescent: A developmental approach.* New York: Wiley, 1972.

MASTERSON, J. (Ed.). *New perspectives on psychotherapy of the borderline adult.* New York: Brunner/Mazel, 1978.

MASTERSON, J. *The narcissistic and borderline disorders.* New York: Brunner/Mazel, 1981.

MASTERSON, J.F., & RINSLEY, D.B. The borderline syndrome: The role of the mother in the genesis and psychic structure of the borderline personality. *International J. Psychoanalysis,* 1975, *56,* 163–77.

MASTERSON, J.F., & RINSLEY, D.B. The borderline syndrome: The role of the mother in the genesis and psychic structure of the borderline personality. Revised and reprinted in R.F. Lax, S. Bach, & J.A. Burland (Eds.), *Rapprochement: The critical subphase of separation-individuation.* New York: Jason Aronson, 1980, 299–329.

MAUPIN, E. Individual differences in response to a Zen meditation exercise. *J. Consulting Psychology, 1965, 29: 139–45.*

MAY, R. *Love and will.* New York: Norton, 1969.

MAY, R. *The meaning of anxiety* (rev.ed.). New York: Norton, 1977.

MAY, R., ANGEL, E., & ELLENBERGER, H. (Eds.). *Existence.* New York: Basic Books, 1958.

MAYMAN, M. Measuring introversiveness on the Rorschach Test: The fabulization scale. Unpublished manuscript, Aug., 1960.

MAYMAN, M. Reality contact, defense effectiveness and psychopathology in Rorschach form-level scores. In Klopfer, B., Meyer, M. & Brawer, F. (Eds.), *Developments in the Rorschach technique III: Aspects of personality structure.* New York: Harcourt Brace Jovanovich, 1970, 11–46.

MAYMAN, M. & VOTH, H.M. Reality closeness, phantasy, and autokineses. *J. Abnormal Psychology,* 1969, *74,* 635–41.

MEAD, G. *Mind, self, and society.* Chicago: Univ. Chicago Press, 1934.

MEYENDORFF, J. *A study of Gregory Palamas.* London: Faith Press, 1964.

MEYENDORFF, J. *Eastern Christian thought.* Washington, D.C. and Cleveland, OH: Corpus Books, 1969.

MEYENDORFF, J. *St. Gregory Palamas and Orthodox spirituality.* Crestwood, NY: St. Vladimir's Press, 1974.

MEYENDORFF, J. *Byzantine theology.* New York: Fordham University, 1975.

MEYER, J. *Death and neurosis.* New York: International Univ. Press, 1975.

MISHRA, R. (Trans.). *Yoga sutras (The textbook of Yoga psychology),* by Patañjali. Garden City, NY: Anchor Press, 1973.

MONK OF THE EASTERN CHURCH. *Orthodox spirituality—An outline of the Orthodox ascetical and mystical tradition.* London: SPCK, 1968.

MOOKERJEE, A. *Kundalini.* New York: Destiny Books, 1982.

MUKERJEE, R. (Trans.). *The song of the self supreme (Astavakra Gita).* San Francisco: Dawn Horse, 1971.

MURPHY, G. *Human potentialities.* New York: Basic Books, 1958.

NAGERA, H. *Early childhood disturbances, the infantile neuroses, and the adult disturbances.* New York: International Univ. Press, 1966.

NARADA. *A manual of Abhidhamma.* Kandy: Buddhist Publication Society, 1975.

NARANJO, C., & ORNSTEIN, R.E. *On the psychology of meditation.* New York: Viking, 1971.

NARANJO, C. *The one quest.* New York: Viking, 1972.

NEISSER, U. *Cognitive psychology.* Englewood Cliffs, N.J: Prentice-Hall, 1967.

NEISSER, U. *Cognition and reality.* Ithaca: Cornell Univ. Press, 1976.

NEMIAH, J. Dissociative disorders. In A. Freedman, H. Kaplan & B. Sadock (Eds.), *Comprehensive textbook of psychiatry* (3rd ed.). Baltimore: Williams and Wilkins Co., 1980.

NEUMANN, E. *The origins and history of consciousness.* Princeton: Princeton University Press, 1954.

NICHOLS, M. *Family therapy.* New York: Gardner Press, 1984.

NYANAMOLI, B. (Trans.). *Visuddhimagga: The path of purification by Buddhaghosha.* 2 vols. Boulder, CO: Shambhala, 1976.

NYANAPONIKA. *The heart of Buddhist meditation.* New York: Samuel Weiser, 1973.

NYANATILOKA. *A Buddhist dictionary.* Colombo: Frewin & Co., Ltd., 1972.

ORIGEN. *Φιλοκαλία τῶν Ἱερῶν Νηπτιχων* Volume II. Athens, Greece: 1893.

OSTOW, M. The syndrome of narcissistic tranquillity. *International J. of Psychoanalysis,* 1967, *45,* 573–83.

OTTO, R. *Mysticism East and West.* New York: Macmillan, 1932.

OTTO, R. *The idea of the holy.* New York: Oxford, 1969.

PECK, R. & HAVIGHURST, R. *The psychology of character development.* New York: Wiley, 1960.

PELLETIER, K.R. Influence of transcendental meditation upon autokinetic perception. *Perceptual and Motor Skills,* 1974, *39,* 1031–34.

PERLS, F. *Gestalt therapy verbatim.* New York: Bantam, 1971.

PIAGET, J. *The essential Piaget.* Gruber & Voneche (Eds.). New York: Basic Books, 1977.

PODVOLL, E.M. Psychosis and the mystic path. *Psychoanalytic Review,* 1979, *66,* 571–90.

Pratyabhijnahrdayam. J. Singh (Trans.). Delhi: Motilal Banarsidass, 1980.

PRIBRAM, K. Feelings as monitors. In M.B. Arnold (Ed.), *Feelings and emotions.* New York: Academic Press, 1970, 41–53.

PRIBRAM, K.H. Toward a holonomic theory of perception. In S. Ertel & L. Kemmler (Eds.), *Gestalt-theorie in der Modern Psychologie (Gestalt theory in modern psychology).* Cologne: Erich Wergenroth, 1974.

RAMA, S., BALLENTINE, R. & AJAYA, S. *Yoga and psychotherapy.* Glenview, Ill.: Himalayan Institute, 1976.

RAMANA MAHARSHI. *The collected works.* London: Rider, 1972.

RAPAPORT, D. The theory of attention cathexis: An economic and structural attempt at the explanation of cognitive processes. In Merton M. Gill (Ed.), *The collected papers of David Rapaport.* New York: Basic Books, 1967, 778–94.

REHYER, J. Electroencephalogram and rapid eye movements during free imagery and dream recall. *J. Abnormal Psychology,* 1969, *74,* 574–82.

REYNOLDS, D. *Morita therapy.* Berkeley: Univ. California Press, 1976.

RIEFF, P. *The triumph of the therapeutic.* New York: Harper & Row, 1966.

RIEKER, H. *The yoga of light.* San Francisco: Dawn Horse, 1971.

RINSLEY, D. An object relations view of borderline personality. In Hartocollis, P. (Ed.), *Borderline personality disorders.* New York: International Univ. Press, 1977, 47–70.

RINSLEY, D.B. Dynamic and developmental issues in borderline and related "spectrum" disorders. *Psychiatric Clinics of North America,* 1981, *4,* 1: 117–31.

RIZZUTO, A.M. *The birth of the idea of God.* Chicago: Univ. Chicago Press, 1978.

RIZZUTO, A. *The birth of the living God.* Chicago: Univ. Chicago Press, 1979.

ROGERS, C. *On becoming a person.* Boston: Houghton Mifflin, 1961.

RUNIONS, J.E. The mystic experience: A psychiatric reflection. *Canadian J. Psychiatry,* 1979, *24,* 147–51.

SANNELLA, L. *Kundalini—psychosis or transcendence?* San Francisco: H.S. Dakin, 1976.

SCHACHTER, S. The assumption of identity and peripheralist-centralist controversies in motivation and emotion. In M.B. Arnold (Ed.), *Feelings and emotions.* New York: Academic Press, 1970, 111–21.

SCHAFER, R. *A new language for psychoanalysis.* New York: International Univ. Press, 1976.

SCHAYA, L. *The universal meaning of the Kabbalah.* Baltimore: Penguin, 1973.

SCHEIR, M.F. Self-awareness, self-consciousness, and angry aggression, *Journal of Personality,* 1976, *44,* 627–44.

SCHEIR, M.F. & CARVER, C.S. Self-focused attention and the experience of emotional attraction, repulsion, elation, and depression. *J. Personality and Social Psychology,* 1977, *35,* 625–36.

SCHNEIDER, W. & SHIFFRIN, R.M. Controlled and automatic information processing: I. Detection, search, and attention. *Psychological Review,* 1977, *84,* 1–66.

SCHUON, F. *Logic and transcendence.* New York, Harper & Row, 1975.

SEGAL, H. *Introduction to the work of Melanie Klein.* New York: Basic Books, 1974.

SELMAN, R., & BYRNE, D. A structural analysis of levels of role-taking in middle childhood. *Child Development,* 1974, *45.*

SERAPHIM OF SAROV, ST. In Franklin Jones (Ed.), *Saint Seraphim of Sarov.* Los Angeles: Dawn Horse Press, 1973.

SHAFII, M. Silence in the service of the ego: Psychoanalytic study of meditation. *International J. of Psychoanalysis,* 1973, *54,* 431–43.

SHAPIRO, D. Zen meditation and behavioral self-control strategies applied to a case of generalized anxiety. *Psychologia,* 1976, *19,* 134–38.

SHAPIRO, D.H. & GIBER, D. Meditation and psychotherapeutic effects: Self-regulation strategy and altered state of consciousness. *Archives General Psychiatry,* 1978, *35,* 294–302.

SIMON, H.A. An information processing theory of intellectual development. In W. Kessen and C. Kuhlman (eds.), *Thought in the young child. Monographs of the Society for Research in Child Development,* 1962, *27,* no. 2 (whole no. 83).

SINGER, J.L. & ANTROBUS, J.S. Daydreaming, imaginal processes, and personality: A normative study. In Peter Sheehan (Ed.), *The function and nature of imagery.* New York: Academic Press, 1972.

SINGH, K. *Naam or word.* Tilton, NH: Sant Boni Press, 1974.

SINGH, K. *Surat Shabd yoga.* Berkeley: Images Press, 1975.

SMITH, H. *Forgotten truth.* New York: Harper & Row, 1976.

SMITH, J.C. Psychotherapeutic effects of TM with controls for expectation of relief and daily sitting. *J. Consulting Clinical Psychology,* 1976, *44,* 630–37.

SPECK, R. & ATTNEAVE, C. *Family networks.* New York: Pantheon, 1973.

SPITZ, R. *A genetic field theory of ego formation.* New York: International Univ. Press, 1959.

SPITZ, R. *The first year of life.* New York: International Univ. Press, 1965.

STACE, W.T. *Mysticism and philosophy.* New York: Lippincott, 1960.

STEPHANOU, EUSEBIUS A. *Charisma and gnosis in Orthodox thought.* Fort Wayne, IN: Logos Ministry for Orthodox Renewal, 1976.

STERBA, R.F. The fate of the ego in analytic therapy. *International J. Psychoanalysis,* 1934, *15,* 117–26.

STERNBERG, S. High-speed scanning in human memory. *Science,* 1966, *153,* 652–54.

STONE, M.H. *The borderline syndromes: Constitution, personality and adaptation.* New York: McGraw-Hill, 1980.

STRAUS, J. Diagnostic models and the nature of psychiatric disorder. *Archives General Psychiatry,* 1973, *29,* 444–49.

SULLIVAN, H. *The interpersonal theory of psychiatry.* New York: Norton, 1953.

SUZUKI, D.T. *Studies in the Lankavatara Sutra.* London: Routledge & Kegan Paul, 1968.

SUZUKI, D.T. *Essays in Zen Buddhism.* 3 vols. London: Rider, 1970.

SUZUKI ROSHI. *Zen mind, beginner's mind.* New York: Weatherhill, 1970.

TAIMNI, I. *The science of yoga.* Wheaton: Quest, 1975.

TAKAKUSU, J. *The essentials of Buddhist philosophy.* Honolulu: Univ. Hawaii Press, 1956.

TART, C.T. Scientific foundations for the study of altered states of consciousness. *J. Transpersonal Psychology,* 1971, *3,* 93–124.

TART, C. *States of consciousness.* New York: Dutton, 1975a.

TART, C. *Transpersonal psychologies.* New York: Harper & Row, 1975b.

TATIAN, MIGNE. *Patrologia Græcæ,* 6, 837B.

THEODORET OF CYRUS, MIGNE. *Patrologia Græcæ,* 80, 104B, 105B, C.

THONDRUP TULKU. *Buddhist civilization in Tibet.* Santa Cruz, CA: Maha Siddha Nyingmapa Center, 1982.

TILLICH, P. *The courage to be.* New Haven: Yale Univ. Press, 1952.

TOLPIN, M. On the beginnings of a cohesive self. *The psychoanalytic study of the child,* 1971, *26* (New York: Quadrangle Books).

TOLPIN, M. Discussion of "Psychoanalytic developmental theories of the self: An integration" by Morton Shane and Estelle Shane. In A. Goldberg (Ed.), *Advances in self psychology.* New York: International Univ. Press, 1980, 47–68.

TOLSTOY, L. *My confession, my religion, the gospel in brief.* New York: Scribners, 1929.

TOMPKINS, S. *Affect, imagery and consciousness.* Vols. 1–2. New York: Springer, 1962–63.

TRUNGPA, C. *The myth of freedom.* Berkeley: Shambhala, 1976.

TUCCI, G. *Minor Buddhist texts, Part II: First Bhavāna krama of Ka-*

malaśila. Rome: Instituto Italian Perg, 1958.

TURNER, H.J.M. St. Gregory of Nyssa as a spiritual guide for today. *Eastern Churches Review*, 1975, *7*, 1.

ULLMAN, M. & KRIPPNER, S., with Alan Vaughan & Gardner Murphy. *Dream telepathy*. New York: Macmillan, 1973.

UNDERHILL, E. *Mysticism*. New York: Meridian, 1955.

VAHIA, H.S , DOENGAJI, D.R., JESTE, D.V. *et al. Psychophysiologic therapy based on the concepts of Patanjali. American J. Psychotherapy*, 1973, *27*, 557–65.

VAILLANT, G.E. Theoretical hierarchy of adaptive ego mechanisms. *Archives General Psychiatry*, 1971, *24*, 107–18.

VAILLANT, G.E. *Adaptation to life*. Boston: Little, Brown and Co., 1977.

VAJIRANANA, P. *Buddhist meditation in theory and practice*. Kuala Lumpur: Buddhist Missionary Society, 1975.

VAN NUYS, D. Meditation, attention, and hypnotic susceptibility: A correlational study. *International J. Clinical and Experimental Hypnosis*, 1973, *21*, 59–69.

VARENNE, J. *Yoga and the Hindu tradition*. Chicago: Univ. Chicago Press, 1976.

VENKATESANANDA (Trans.). *The supreme yoga*. Australia: Chiltern, 1981.

VIVEKANANDA. *The Yogas and other works*. S. Nikhilananda (Ed.). New York: Ramakrishna-Vivekananda Center, 1953.

WALLACE, A.F.C. Cultural determinants of response to hallucinatory experience. *Archives General Psychiatry*, 1970, *1*, 58–69.

WALSH, R. Initial meditative experiences: I. *J. Transpersonal Psychology*, 1977, *9*, 2, 151–92.

WALSH, R. Initial meditative experiences: II. *J. Transpersonal Psychology*, 1978, *10*, 1, 1–28.

WALSH, R. Meditation. In R. Corsini (Ed.), *A handbook of innovative psychotherapies*. New York: Wiley, 1980a.

WALSH, R. The consciousness disciplines and the behavioral sciences: Questions of comparisons and assessment. *American J. Psychiatry*, 1980b, *137*, 663–73.

WALSH, R. Speedy Western minds slow slowly. *ReVision*, 1981, *4*, 75–7.

WALSH, R., & ROCHE, L. Precipitation of acute psychotic episodes by intensive meditation in individuals with a history of schizophrenia. *American J. Psychiatry*, 1979, *136*, 1085–86.

WATKINS, J.G. & STAUFFACHER, J.C. An index of pathological thinking in the Rorschach. In P.M. Lerner (Ed.), *Handbook of Rorschach scales*. New York: Internat. Univ. Press, 1975.

WATZLAWICK, P., BEAVIN, J., & JACKSON, D. *Pragmatics of human communication*. New York: Norton, 1967.

WENSINK, A.J. *Mystical treatises by Isaac of Nineveh*. Wiesbaden, Germany: 1969.

WERNER, H. *Comparative psychology of mental development.* New York: International Univ. Press, 1964 (1940).

WHITE, J. *Kundalini, evolution and enlightenment.* New York: Anchor, 1979.

WILBER, K. *The spectrum of consciousness.* Wheaton: Quest, 1977.

WILBER, K. A developmental view of consciousness. *J. Transpersonal Psychology,* 1979, 11.

WILBER, K. *The Atman project.* Wheaton: Quest, 1980a.

WILBER, K. The pre/trans fallacy. *ReVision,* 1980b, 3, 51–73.

WILBER, K. Ontogenetic development: Two fundamental patterns. *J. Transpersonal Psychology,* 1981a, 13, 33–59.

WILBER, K. *Up from Eden.* New York: Doubleday/Anchor, 1981b.

WILBER, K. *A sociable god.* New York: McGraw-Hill, 1982.

WILBER, K. *Eye to eye.* New York: Doubleday/Anchor, 1983.

WILBER, K. The developmental spectrum and psychopathology; Part I, stages and types of pathology. *J. Transpersonal Psychology,* 1984, 16, 1, 75–118.

WILBER, K. *System, self, and structure.* In preparation.

WILDE, J. & KIMMEL, W. (Eds.). *The search for being.* New York: Noonday, 1962.

WINNICOTT, D. *Collected papers.* New York: Basic Books, 1958.

WINNICOTT, D. *The maturational process and the facilitating environment.* New York: International Univ. Press, 1965.

YALOM, I. *Existential psychotherapy.* New York: Basic Books, 1980.

YOGESHWARAND SARASWATI. *Science of soul.* India: Yoga Niketan, 1972.

YOUNG, P.T. Affective processes. In M.B. Arnold (Ed.), *The nature of emotion.* New York: Penguin Books, 1969, 222–37.

ZAEHNER, R.L. *Mysticism, sacred and profane.* New York: Oxford, 1957.

ZETZEL, E. A developmental approach to the borderline patient. *American J. Psychiatry,* 1971, 127, 7, 43–47.

ZIMMERMAN, M. *Eclipse of the self.* Athens, OH: Ohio Univ. Press. 1981.

ZUBEK, J.P. (Ed.), *Sensory deprivation: Fifteen years of research.* New York: Appleton–Century–Crofts, 1969.

INDEX